Writing Against Expulsion in the Post-War World

OXFORD MID-CENTURY STUDIES

The Oxford Mid-Century Studies series publishes monographs in several disciplinary and creative areas in order to create a thick description of culture in the thirty-year period around the Second World War. With a focus on the 1930s through the 1960s, the series concentrates on fiction, poetry, film, photography, theatre, as well as art, architecture, design, and other media. The mid-century is an age of shifting groups and movements, from existentialism through abstract expressionism to confessional, serial, electronic, and pop art styles. The series charts such intellectual movements, even as it aids and abets the very best scholarly thinking about the power of art in a world under new techno-political compulsions, whether nuclear-apocalyptic, Cold War-propagandized, transnational, neo-imperial, super-powered, or postcolonial.

Series Editors

Allan Hepburn, McGill University
Adam Piette, University of Sheffield
Lyndsey Stonebridge, University of Birmingham

Writing Against Expulsion in the Post-War World

Making Space for the Human

DAVID HERD

OXFORD
UNIVERSITY PRESS

Great Clarendon Street, Oxford, OX2 6DP,
United Kingdom

Oxford University Press is a department of the University of Oxford.
It furthers the University's objective of excellence in research, scholarship,
and education by publishing worldwide. Oxford is a registered trade mark of
Oxford University Press in the UK and in certain other countries

© David Herd 2023

The moral rights of the author have been asserted

All rights reserved. No part of this publication may be reproduced, stored in
a retrieval system, or transmitted, in any form or by any means, without the
prior permission in writing of Oxford University Press, or as expressly permitted
by law, by licence or under terms agreed with the appropriate reprographics
rights organization. Enquiries concerning reproduction outside the scope of the
above should be sent to the Rights Department, Oxford University Press, at the
address above

You must not circulate this work in any other form
and you must impose this same condition on any acquirer

Published in the United States of America by Oxford University Press
198 Madison Avenue, New York, NY 10016, United States of America

British Library Cataloguing in Publication Data
Data available

Library of Congress Control Number: 2023935105

ISBN 9780192872258

DOI: 10.1093/oso/9780192872258.001.0001

Printed and bound in the UK by
Clays Ltd, Elcograf S.p.A.

Cover image: Reena Saini Kallat, Woven Chronicle, 2011/2016, Circuit boards, speakers, electric
wires and fittings; single channel audio (10 min.); 127 x 570 x 12 in. (332 x 1447 x 30 cm.).
Installation view, Museum of Modern Art, New York. Photo: Reena Kallat Studio.

Links to third party websites are provided by Oxford in good faith and
for information only. Oxford disclaims any responsibility for the materials
contained in any third party website referenced in this work.

Endorsements

Writing Against Expulsion in the Post-War World is a lucid and compelling report on the individual at the mercy of the bureaucracy of immigration control, 'the geopolitical non-person', and how the condition of this figure relates to the aftermath of the 1939–45 War and the subsequent moment of decolonization. It takes us through the political, philosophical, and literary contexts with fluency, passion, and rigour. Its engagement with the texts through which the argument progresses is extensive and thoroughly persuasive, allowing the reader to witness the personal journey Herd himself travelled in understanding the issues that are the subject of this wonderful and important book.

    Abdulrazak Gurnah, Winner of the Nobel Prize in Literature 2021

Writing Against Expulsion is one of those books that arrives in the world and immediately feels necessary. David Herd asks—and brilliantly answers—two questions about the condition of unwelcome migrants and the UK government: 'How did we get here?' and 'How do we move away from where we are?' Drawing on and building from the works of writers such as Hannah Arendt, Frantz Fanon, and the poet Charles Olson, as well as his own work with Refugee Tales, Herd re-casts conversations around 'political non-persons' to allow space for imagination, humanity, and truth. A profound and inspiring book.

    Kamila Shamsie, author of *Home Fire*

*For Mum and Dad
and Lily and Eli*

Contents

Introduction: Making Space for the Human	1
1. The Non-Place	43
2. Writing Against Expulsion	84
3. Moving	126
4. Making	172
5. Speaking	209
Conclusion	256
Acknowledgements	268
Bibliography	270
Index	283

Introduction

Making Space for the Human

At the Threshold

The figure at the heart of this book is the individual we might call the geopolitical non-person. Such an individual might be assigned various categories, where the categories themselves quickly become part of the issue. They might be termed a refugee, a stateless person, a displaced person, a person seeking asylum. They are a person whose relation to the political formations we call nation states has become unclear. They will have been compelled to move and so might be termed a migrant, and they will probably lack the kind of documentation that confirms their identity, '*sans papiers*'. They will have found themselves occupying a kind of space that, as it relates to national settings and in a way that is borderline impossible, is somehow outside or between.

I first came into contact with such a borderline impossible space, and with people who were compelled to inhabit it, in 2009, at the tail end of the New Labour government. The space in question was the Dover Immigration Removal Centre, at the time, one of eleven such centres in which, under UK immigration rules, people could be indefinitely detained. The United Kingdom was then, as it still is, the only country in western Europe that detains people indefinitely under immigration rules, though it has this practice in common with certain other anglophone states, notably Canada and Australia. To visit the Removal Centre at Dover was to gain an unusually graphic sense of what such spaces signify. Although it was not offshore, like the US Detention Camp at Guantanamo Bay or the Australian Regional Processing Centre on Manus Island (the 'prison' where Behrouz Boochani both pictured and set out to reimagine the geopolitical non-person's space), the Dover Immigration Removal Centre was at the edge.[1] Housed in the buildings of a Napoleonic-era fort and situated on top of Dover's white cliffs, the Removal Centre looked out across the Channel towards Calais. As it related to the nation, it was situated at the limit; it was where the nation ended; it was outwith.

Although the Dover Immigration Removal Centre was closed down in 2015 (shortly after the addition to the detention estate of The Verne, a former Category C Prison, on the Isle of Portland off the coast of Dorset), the political practice of which it was strikingly symbolic is still very much with us. The increased numbers tell the story. In 1973, ninety-five people were indefinitely detained in the UK under immigration rules, rules introduced by the Immigration Act of 1971. By 1987, that number stood at 2,166.[2] In the year ending June 2021, according to Home Office Statistics, over 24,497 people were detained across a detention estate that currently includes ten immigration removal centres and has recourse to various prisons.[3] Shocking as this number is, it nonetheless represents a partial decrease since the historic high of 2015, when 32,053 people were indefinitely detained in the UK. At the same time, since detention is arbitrary and re-detention is common, tens of thousands of people in the UK are currently, which is to say at any one moment, vulnerable to detention and re-detention.

Such growth in the UK detention population is mirrored elsewhere in the anglophone world. In the United States, as the Global Detention Project reports, 'The number of people placed in detention annually increased from some 85,000 people in 1995 to a record 477,523 during fiscal year 2012.'[4] As in the UK, the US figure has fallen somewhat from that historic high, standing at 323,591 in 2017. One explanation for that decrease, as the Global Detention Project reports US officials as claiming, is the reduction in 'unauthorized arrivals', a measure in itself of an increasingly aggressive border regime. At the same time, the number of unaccompanied children detained has risen 'from just over 10,000 in the early 2010s to nearly 70,000 by 2019.'[5] A similar graph can be drawn in the case of Australia, which, as has been well reported, externalizes the process by the practice of offshoring detention and where (unlike in the US and the UK) detention is mandatory for all non-citizens without a valid visa.

Such rates of increase should be alarming to us. Really to grasp their significance, however, we have to hear them not piecemeal, as the result of the practices of individual regimes and governments, but as elements in a trend. Consider how frequently in the present moment news reporting turns to the question of detention, frequently in outrage that these practices are occurring somewhere else. Consider, for instance, the detention of Uyghurs and other Muslims in Xinjiang Province. Consider the use of cages as forms of detention at the US–Mexican border, where children and adults were separated out. Or consider, the UK government's plan, as announced at the time of writing, to transport people who have sought asylum in the United Kingdom to an asylum processing centre in Rwanda.[6] And then start scaling up. Start to think about the numbers of people for whom some form of detention, though not their immediate reality, exists as a constant structural threat. This number will include people whose documents are not in order and who might therefore either be working illegally or waiting, endlessly, forbidden to work. It will therefore include, for instance, undocumented migrants in the United States who, though integral to their local economy, know that they can be detained at any moment subject to, for instance, a driver's licence check by Immigration and Customs Enforcement (ICE). Or the number will include all those in the United Kingdom who are prohibited from working while seeking asylum (a process that can take many years) and whose form of government relief, a kind of top-up card that sets them outside the cash economy, cannot be spent on public transport. It is difficult to gain a perspective on the scale of this kind of existence, an existence in which precarity arising from a fraught relation to national setting is framed and underwritten by the fact or prospect of some form of protracted incarceration, whether in detention centres, removal facilities, or various forms of camp, but recent United Nations High Commissioner for Refugees (UNHCR) figures start to help. In the year ending 2020, the UNHCR reported, 82.4 million people were displaced, which is to say one person in every 100 people on the planet.[7] Not all of those displaced are forced to seek an existence in another country, and not all those who are displaced to another country meet with structural prohibition. In Uganda, for example, currently host to the largest refugee operation in Africa, refugees have 'the right to work and establish businesses and access to services such as health care and education'.[8] Even so, the UNHCR statistics for the year ending 2020 indicate the scale of the issue in hand. To speak about the geopolitical non-person and the impossible spaces they are compelled to inhabit is to speak, in the present moment, of a global condition.

The reason for framing geopolitical non-personhood in relation to the specific of detention, when there are many other ways such precarious personhood could be framed, is that it focuses our thinking on what is at stake. Or rather, it brings into focus the need for a different kind of thought. Writing about the establishment of the US Detention Camp at Guantanamo Bay, the philosopher Giorgio Agamben issued a warning:

> Faced with the unstoppable progression of what has been called a 'global civil war', the state of exception tends increasingly to appear as the dominant paradigm of government in contemporary politics.

This transformation of a provisional and exceptional measure into a technique of government threatens radically to alter—in fact, has already palpably altered—the structure and meaning of the traditional distinction between constitutional forms. Indeed, from this perspective, the state of exception appears as a threshold of indeterminacy between democracy and absolutism.[9]

In using the term 'state of exception', drawn from the work of the German political theorist Carl Schmitt, what Agamben points to is a setting in which people are subject to the force of the law but where they cannot apply to the law's protections. The camp at Guantanamo was a paradigm case, where the US authorities detained indefinitely and without trial 'aliens' allegedly suspected of activities that endangered national security.[10] To detain in this way was to commit an absolutist action in the name of, or at least in the seeming context of, democracy. It was to stand at the threshold of indeterminacy between those two kinds of regime, to alter the traditional distinction between the constitutional forms.

Since Agamben's book was published in 2005, the scope of the state of exception has been dramatically extended. As the escalating use of detention as a means of controlling human movement shows, regimes of all kinds now deem it acceptable to detain 'aliens' *en masse* on the grounds not only that they are suspected of endangering national security but also simply of their 'alien' status. Or rather, to fold the logic tighter, it is deemed acceptable to detain 'aliens' on the grounds that it is by their presence, as 'aliens', that the security of the nation is endangered. There seems no question, if Agamben's logic and metaphor are right, that in the years since the publication of *State of Exception*, we have crossed the threshold, that for regimes which would publicly identify otherwise, certain absolutist practices have become the norm. To which a reader might respond, yes, but, think of the numbers. Alarming as it is, a reader might say, that the border has become a site and trigger for the production of geopolitical non-personhood, where the state of exception is routinely applied, think of the number of people, as the UNHCR reports, who are being displaced. To which it must be replied that it is precisely the scale of the condition of geopolitical non-personhood that calls present paradigms into question. In a moment in which one in every 100 humans finds themselves displaced, it is of the utmost urgency that we arrive at ways of thinking that do not default to absolutist practices; ways of thinking that do not produce geopolitical non-personhood on an industrial scale, that do not position people impossibly outside.

The argument of this book is that one way to help undertake this necessary, urgent, and, of course, difficult thinking—difficult because the logic Agamben warns about is now deeply established—is to go back to a moment when comparable questions and issues were at stake. The moment in question is the period immediately following the Second World War. There are clear prima facie reasons, when considering the current crisis of forced displacement, for revisiting the period following the war, principal among which is that, as the UNHCR Global Trends report of 2015 stated, 'the current number of [people] displaced globally is . . . the highest since the aftermath of World War II'.[11] It is instructive, in other words, if we are to understand the contemporary moment of forced displacement, to revisit a comparable period of mass migration, as Peter Gatrell has done authoritatively, most recently in *The Unsettling of Europe: How Migration Reshaped a Continent*.[12] It is instructive also, in considering that moment, to observe the structures that were rapidly evolved and imposed in response to the fact of mass human movement. Seventy-seven years on from the end of the Second World War, international considerations of forced migration continue to be largely shaped by the conventions and frameworks that emerged in the period immediately following the end of the conflict. The headline statement, in this respect, was the 1951 Convention Relating to the Status of Refugees, a document to which this book will return, and we learn a great deal by observing, as Gerard Daniel Cohen has in *In War's Wake*, how the categories and practices that continue to structure thinking about the status of refugees were formed in situ in post-war displaced persons camps.[13]

It follows from the fact that, in these broad terms, the period immediately following the war prefigures the present moment of forced movement (both in terms of scale and in the vestigial categories through which contemporary thinking operates), that post-war commentators on the consequences of displacement continue to have much to teach. When Agamben set out to explain what he took to be emerging at Camp X-Ray, one of the writers to whom he turned was Hannah Arendt. Much will be said about Arendt in the course of this book, but it is worth observing immediately that however one addresses and critiques the larger structures of Arendt's thought (and Arendt's thinking requires continued and constant critique), her accounts of the lived experience of geopolitical non-personhood remain crucial to an understanding of the suspensions and cruelties the state of exception inflicts. As she observes, in 'The Decline of the Nation-State and the End of the Rights of Man', the chapter that ends the second part of *The Origins of Totalitarianism*,

The nation-state, incapable of providing a law for those who have lost the protection of a national government, transferred the whole matter to the police. This was the first time the police in Western Europe had received authority to act on its own, to rule directly over people; in one sphere of public life it was no longer an instrument to carry out and enforce the law, but had become a ruling authority independent of government and ministries.[14]

The fact that Arendt speaks so pressingly to the interplay of authority and vulnerability that constitutes the lived reality of contemporary geopolitical non-personhood—the reality of those, for instance, in the UK who might, at any moment, without warning or process, find themselves detained—is an indicator of the degree to which current structures of citizenship relate to mid-century categories and practices.

Agamben's concern, in excavating post-war commentary, was to grasp the relation of the individual to the sovereign state. Geopolitical non-personhood, as this tradition of thinking proposes, concerns the person's status before the law; whether or not, in being captured by the law's force, they are also granted its protections. Such juridical-political thinking is crucial to a full expression of geopolitical non-personhood, and this book will draw repeatedly on its terms. As Arendt understood, however, writing in the moment of decolonization (and as Agamben overlooks), relations to the law, however real in their impact on lived experience, can obscure other political realities. Recent commentators on the UK's Hostile Environment regime have drawn on a different aspect of the post-war moment to explain the institutionalized racism that drives the production of non-personhood through immigration and asylum law. In *Hostile Environment: How Immigrants Became Scapegoats*, Maya Goodfellow traces such policies to the 1948 British Nationality Act and to the simultaneous attempts by politicians of all affiliations to redirect the *Empire Windrush* when it docked at Tilbury, Essex.[15] The history of juridical non-personhood, a history recently dramatized by the scandal of the detention and deportation of members of the Windrush generation, is also, as Goodfellow and David Olusoga have demonstrated, the history of institutionalized racism and must be framed by the moment of decolonization.[16] As Goodfellow observes, with reference to the 1948 Nationality Act, preparatory as it was for hostile legislation to come, 'Empire might have been caving in on itself, but its organizing principles—race and its hierarchy of humanity—stubbornly persisted.'[17]

INTRODUCTION: MAKING SPACE FOR THE HUMAN   7

To observe how these commentators from their different disciplinary traditions (migration studies, refugee studies, juridico-political theory, postcolonial race studies) direct their inquiries to the period in question is to register a significant convergence. To pull at the threads of contemporary geopolitical non-personhood is to be drawn back to the post-war moment. What one finds when one goes there, and when one looks from the vantage of the present, are analogues and causes of contemporary concerns. In a proper genealogical way, one can trace contemporary structures of expulsion to the thinking and decision-making that formed the post-war world, and one can find accounts of the lived reality of geopolitical non-personhood that speak painfully and pertinently to the present time. This book has benefited hugely, as will be abundantly clear, from these and many other such accounts. The aim here, however, is to make a different move.

The premise of *Writing Against Expulsion in the Post-War World: Making Space for the Human* is that the figure of the geopolitical non-person, the person situated outside, was so *present,* however paradoxically, in the post-war moment as to constitute a condition of thought. To think seriously in that moment—the moment immediately following the Holocaust, which is to say the mass production and liquidation of people rendered non-persons in the Second World War, the moment of unprecedented forced migration that followed, and the moment of the de-colonial struggle that was the war's aftermath—was to register the fact that the legal production of non-personhood, of personhood situated impossibly in spaces outside the law, was a global question. It was a global question because, as Arendt observed, the world had organized itself to make it such. As she put it,

> What is unprecedented is not the loss of a home but the impossibility of finding a new one. Suddenly, there was no place on earth where migrants could go without the severest restrictions, no country where they would be assimilated, no territory where they could found a new community of their own. This, moreover, had next to nothing to do with any material problem of overpopulation; it was a problem not of space but of political organization. Nobody had been aware that mankind, for so long considered under the image of a family of nations, had reached the stage where whoever was thrown out of one of these tightly organized closed communities found himself thrown out of the family of nations altogether.[18]

How this form of radical expulsion related to other forms of expulsion, how such modes of expulsion twisted and intertwined with one another, is a key question for this book. What principally the book wants to document, however, is that where, as Arendt articulates, the world had come to construct itself spatially such that to be forced out of one organized space was to be forced out of all such spaces, so there were contemporary authors seriously committed to undertaking the task of reimagining the organization of space.

To go back to the period immediately following the war, conditioned as it was by the paradoxical presence of the non-person and where such non-personhood was variously understood to be a function of the organization of geopolitical space, is to find a series of texts whose aim was to recast spatio-political relations, to arrive at new political imaginaries whereby persons would not be thrown out. What we learn, in considering those interlocking inquiries, as this introduction will begin to detail, is not only the real and profound cost of geopolitical non-personhood but also how mid-century authors considered such a political condition might begin to be countered; how we might begin to work towards a language in which a space for the human is to be made. Before indicating how the writers in question began to articulate such a space, however, we need to understand how the geopolitical non-person was produced, how, in all its contradictions, their presence came to be felt.

A Short History of the Production of Non-Personhood

The argument of this book is not that the post-war decade in question, the period 1948–1958, saw the invention of the geopolitical non-person. As the discussion unfolds and is framed by the history of European self-definition through settler colonialism, so (as the introduction outlines below) the argument necessarily draws on the long history of non-personhood ascribed to enslaved Africans and colonized indigenous peoples. The object of the book is not to document the entirety of those histories, necessary as it is to engage them throughout. The argument, rather, is that there was a particular form of non-personhood, whose outline we now recognize as shaping and determining contemporary politics, which first became politically and culturally visible in the period immediately following the war.

What is meant, in this context, by the term 'non-person' is an individual whose personhood has been suspended, where personhood is registered as a juridical category and where it entails a certain level of recognition by the law. The individual compelled to occupy this category is both present and absent. They are present in the obvious sense that they are physically in situ. They are absent in that the law and related discourses do all they can to deny them the recognition that would permit their presence to be felt. From the outset, this is a barely sustainable position and so entails the production of various deeply contradictory, barely conceivable kinds of space. The geopolitical non-person must occupy spaces which, while necessarily falling within a given territory, are constructed so as to render the individual outside. The history of such spaces, and of the non-personhood they produce, is, by definition, not easy to tell, but one place to start is the border.

As we recognize it today, with its brutally enforced regime of barbed wire and categorization, the border is a relatively recent invention. There has always been a border, of course, as the border theorist Thomas Nail eloquently lays out, but as a setting for the brutal suspension of an individual's personhood, the border is a late-nineteenth-century or early-twentieth-century configuration. There were many kinds of check, as Nail's history of passport documentation records, but the border, broadly speaking, retained a permeability until that point.[19] This is to present an historical reality, or rather multiple historical realities, in sweeping and highly abstract terms. What justifies such abstraction is the fact that, with the turn of the twentieth century, the reality of the border was definitively altered. What resulted, at that moment, was a conceptual shift.

Where that shift occurred was in a series of acts of legislation, notably in the United States and the United Kingdom. In the US context, the pivotal document was the Immigration Act of 1891, legislation that introduced a provision known as the 'entry fiction'. According to the terms of that provision, an individual at the point of entry could be removed to shore for examination (subject as migrants were to rigorous health checks) but that this would not be '"considered a landing during the pendency of examination"'.[20] We should pause to underline this: the person designated by this legislation would be present but not present. It is a refrain that will continue to haunt the arguments of this book.

Coupled with the emergence of that impossible space, and to underpin its execution, the 1891 Act was the first legislation in the US juridical tradition to mention 'detention', with the first 'large-scale exclusion and detention' being directed at Chinese immigrants on the West Coast and including 'many longstanding lawful Chinese residents'.[21] The first comparable UK legislation was the 1905 Immigration Act which, following the recommendations of the 1903 Royal Commission on Immigration, enacted the power to inspect and exclude immigrants, authorizing also that, pending a hearing, '"the Immigrant may be placed under suitable charge"'.[22] As Daniel Wilsher records, this was 'the first official mention of a system of administrative detention for immigrants in UK law'.[23] In neither context were the numbers of detentions high and, given the relatively low initial impact of the change, an historian might choose to record these acts of legislation as simply formalizing administrative convenience. It is there, though, in the impossible formulations of early-twentieth-century legislation, that a principal question of the modern border opens up.

As contemporary commentators were quick to register, such legislative authorization of detention constituted a breach of principle. As the constitutional theorist A.V. Dicey observed, it represented an 'indifference to that respect for the personal freedom, even of the alien, which may be called the natural individualism of the common law'.[24] For Sibley and Elias, on the other hand, writing in *The Aliens Act and the Right of Asylum* (1906), the introduction of immigration detention infringed '"the principles of the common law and Magna Carta [since] a person should be liable to be sent to prison without being charged with committing a crime"'.[25] What is at issue, then, historically, is not a matter of administrative convenience but a fundamental question of personhood.[26] To authorize detention in the name of immigration legislation was not simply and uncontroversially to adjust policy to changing reality; it was to alter the conception of the border such that an individual might no longer be entitled to fundamental legal recognition. The implications of this were grave, as critics realized. The most immediate consequence, however, was the construction of an impossible space. The person held in immigration detention was 'deemed not to have been landed, even if conditionally disembarked'.[27] The phrasing must be underlined: disembarked but *not* landed; compelled at the point of appearance to disappear.

The turn-of-the-century legislative developments that saw both the United States and the United Kingdom contradict the principles of *Magna Carta* are critical moments in the history of the concept of geopolitical nonpersonhood. Such conceptual histories do not develop in a straightforward way or in an even fashion and nor, therefore, can they be easily plotted. One kind of marker, however, is the moment the concept is formally named. Such a naming occurred in the work of Carl Schmitt, and in particular in his 1922 work *Political Theology*.

To link the emergence of detention in UK and US juridical traditions with Schmitt's political theory is to draw on a larger conceptual history. What the turn-of-the-century decision about the border (about what can be decided at the border) clearly signifies is a hardening of a commitment to the idea of sovereignty. The value of Schmitt in this context is that, with full understanding of the implications of its excesses, he articulates a modern theory of sovereign power. In other words, he lays it bare. As he observes, famously, in the single sentence paragraph with which he opens *Political Theology*: 'Sovereign is he who decides on the exception.'[28] Sovereignty, this is to assert, is defined by both 'decision' and 'exception', and so it should be no surprise that where a newly hardened form of sovereignty displayed itself was in the decision to exempt certain people from the rule of law. Sovereignty, as Schmitt put it, is 'a borderline concept' one 'pertaining to the outermost sphere'.[29]

The abiding interest of Schmitt's theory lies in the way it came to align with history, anticipating as it did the Nazi party's use of Article 48 of the German Constitution in 1933 to suspend such rights as habeas corpus and the right to assembly. Implicit in his theory of sovereignty, in other words, with its concept of the border and of arbitrary decision-making, is the production, in actual historical circumstances, of the juridical non-person. What Schmitt argued, and what the history that followed his theory showed, is that for the sovereign to exist, there had to be non-persons, and where both became visible was in the suspension of habeas corpus, which is to say the moment when individuals were arbitrarily detained.

To link the appearance of detention in turn-of-the century immigration legislation with the description of sovereignty in Schmitt's work is to register two moments in the history of the production of geopolitical non-personhood: the first juridical and the second theoretical. A third moment is represented by the publication of Arendt's *The Origins of Totalitarianism*, providing as it does a history of the production of non-personhood. Completed in 1949 and first published in 1951, Arendt's monumental study offers a history of European politics from the end of the nineteenth century to the post-war moment, the central thread of which was an account of the processes through which the juridical non-person was produced. It was a history from which Arendt herself could not easily escape. Having fled Germany for France in 1933, precisely at the moment the Nazi party enacted its suspension, expelled as a Jew by the German anti-semitic regime, Arendt was then detained as a German, an enemy alien, in 1940, interned along with 7,000 other women at the Gurs transit camp prior to the fall of Paris.[30] It was a history also, as she knew, from which the post-war world would not easily disentangle, and so with each new edition of her major work she would revise the text, the second edition (published in 1958) incorporating passages that updated Arendt's analysis from the vantage of twelve years after the war. *The Origins of Totalitarianism* is thus singularly positioned as an attempt to describe both the historical processes that led to totalitarianism as a form of political organization and also the legacies of such politics for the post-war world. The object of the work was to 'comprehend' the processes, structures, and movements that enabled or gave rise to totalitarian practices, a principal character in the narrative, albeit in their juridical absence, being the geopolitical non-person.

'Comprehend', or rather 'comprehension', is Arendt's term. As she puts it,

> Comprehension [...] does not mean denying the outrageous, deducing the unprecedented from precedents, or explaining phenomena by such analogies and generalities that the impact of reality and the shock of experience are no longer felt. It means, rather, examining and bearing consciously the burden that events have placed upon us—neither denying their existence and submitting meekly to their weight as though everything that in fact happened could not have happened otherwise. Comprehension, in short, means the unpremeditated, attentive, facing up to, and resisting of, reality—whatever it may be or might have been.[31]

What 'comprehension' entailed for Arendt was a narrative tightrope, the aim being both to trace the sequence of events that had led to the systematic production of non-personhood and to observe that the sequence, and therefore the outcome, might possibly have been otherwise. The latter was, and remains, crucial because in key respects, as she patiently observed, the underlying political structures that had resulted in non-personhood still obtained. In practice, what this act of historical comprehension amounted to was a wide-ranging story of the geopolitical settings in which non-personhood was produced, the defining setting being the European nation state. Dating the full emergence of the concept of the nation state to the French Revolution, Arendt's project was to chart its decline, where that decline was discernible as a developing contradiction between the idea of nation and the rule of law. Whereas law, in its claim to universality, had underwritten an implicit equality of recognition, however mis-observed in practice, two developments in the period in question (the late nineteenth-century to the post-war moment) came to oppose that fundamental principle: the first was empire, the second, the political settlement that followed the end of the First World War.

The key consequence of imperial economic expansion for the history of the juridical non-person, as Arendt described it, was that the idea of law and the idea of nation came into opposition, the basis of that opposition being the racist differentiation between domestic legal principle and colonial practice. The juridical non-person, in this context, was the colonized subject, and whereas the idea of the rule of law was maintained at home, the colonized environment was governed as a police state and by decree. As she put it, describing government by decree, 'There are no general principles which simple reason can understand behind the decree, but ever-changing circumstances which only an expert can know in detail.'[32] Word for word, what Arendt might be describing here are the processes that sustain a contemporary hostile immigration environment, those 'ever-changing circumstances' that make the person seeking asylum always vulnerable to the law. Ask a UK immigration lawyer how they keep up. They will tell you they can't; or, at best, that they barely can. Imagine how their clients feel. Imagine how the person seeking asylum who, because of cuts to legal aid has no representation, feels. What they experience is rule by decree, a process that functions by the speed with which it changes; a process which, Arendt's description reminds us, resembles nothing quite so much as the colonial regime.

How the political settlement following the First World War contributed to the production of the geopolitical non-person was in the production of two intimately related groups: the so-called 'minorities', determined by the Minority Treaties, and those rendered 'stateless' by the redrawing of the European political map. The failure of those treaties is the subject of extended discussion in *The Origins of Totalitarianism*. What matters here, in tracing the production of geopolitical non-personhood, is how Arendt reads the effects of the principal designation of the treaties themselves. As she explained it, the logic was such that, 'only nationals could be citizens, only people of the same national origin could enjoy the full protection of legal institutions, that persons of different nationality needed some law of exception until or unless they were completely assimilated and divorced from their origin.'[33] From which it followed, as she argued, that, 'the transformation of the state from an instrument of the law into an instrument of the nation had been completed.'[34]

The effect of the Minority Treaties, as Arendt saw it, was to designate the geopolitical non-person historically, just as Schmitt named them theoretically, and as US and UK immigration legislation had named them in law. What followed from that designation was the adoption of 'denationalization' as 'a powerful weapon of totalitarian politics', where expulsion from one national context all but entailed expulsion from all such contexts:

> Those whom the persecutor had singled out as scum of the earth [. . .] actually were received as scum of the earth everywhere; those whom persecution had called undesirable became the indésirables of Europe [...] when unidentifiable beggars, without nationality, without money, and without passports, crossed their frontiers.[35]

Arendt's contribution in *The Origins of Totalitarianism* was to make such individuals the subject of history, which is to say both the focus of an account of recent historical processes and a defining figure in the political and cultural consciousness of the post-war world. Which is to observe that while the category of the geopolitical non-person was produced by a series of decisions taken in the period up to, and during, the Second World War, it was in the immediate aftermath of the war that such a figure became the subject of concerted inquiry and thought.

Such an historical development presents a contradiction. In the moment immediately following the war, the end of which revealed, in the extermination camps, the unspeakable horror of a politics grounded in the anti-Semitic production of non-personhood, a category of individual rendered systematically invisible came to occupy the central intersection of certain kinds of writing and thought. This did not mean, of course, that the phenomenon of geopolitical non-personhood was therefore eliminated from history; quite the reverse. The end of the war issued in the largest forced movement of people in human history until, as the UNHCR recorded, 2015.[36] What did follow was that the geopolitical non-person, a defining hollow at the centre of the historical process, became the subject of extensive consideration and thought, where what that consideration entailed, as Arendt herself articulated, was a radical reimagining of the category of space. As she put it, in 'Ideology and Terror',

> By pressing men against each other, total terror destroys the space between them: compared to the condition within its iron band, even the desert of tyranny, insofar as it is still some kind of space, appears like a guarantee of freedom. Totalitarian government does not just curtail civil liberties or abolish essential freedoms; not does it, at least to our limited knowledge, succeed in eradicating the love for freedom from the hearts of man. It destroys the one essential prerequisite of all freedom which is simply the capacity of motion which cannot exist without space.[37]

Whereas totalitarianism is to be understood as the production of negative space, so what is called for is a way of thinking, a discourse, in which the space of personhood was newly imagined. Two things, broadly speaking, had to be articulated by such a discourse: first, what it meant to inhabit the spaces in which non-personhood was produced and then, second, with that reckoning properly undertaken, how one might arrive at an understanding of geopolitical space such that persons should not subsequently be forced out. It is for the light it throws on these issues that the post-war discourse in question needs to be recovered, in a moment when, once again, the production of non-personhood has become global and intense.

Towards a Mid-Century Discourse of Space

It was Arendt who first gave concerted expression to the spatiality of mid-century geopolitical non-personhood from an historical perspective. As she observed in 'The Decline of the Nation-State and the End of the Rights of Man', 'The Second World War and the DP camps were not necessary to show that the only practical substitute for a non-existent homeland was an internment camp. Indeed, as early as the thirties this was the only "country" the world had to offer the stateless.'[38] Arendt exactly catches the brutal spatial dynamic at issue. Precisely because the geopolitical non-person had become such, because they had been forced outside any existing homeland, so the situation set aside for them had to be the physical equivalent of a non-, or barely existing, space. It is partly for her accounts of such impossible spaces, and what it meant to inhabit them, that Arendt speaks to our own moment. Once again, it is too often the case that the only country the world has to offer those displaced is the internment camp. And if not the internment camp, some barely tenable spatial existence behind which detention is always the threat. It is to literature, however, that we might look for expressions of the shape of non-personhood itself, for an outline of the non-person as historical figure. In his poem 'La Préface', written in 1946, the scholar, political administrator, and emerging poet, Charles Olson presented a radically negated speaker:

> "I will die about April 1st..." going off
> "I weigh, I think, 80lbs..." scratch
> "My name is NO RACE" address

> Buchenwald   new Altamira cave
> With a nail they drew the object of the hunt.
>
> Put war away with time, come into space
> It was May, precise date, 1940. I had air my lungs could breathe.
> He talked, via stones   a stick   sea rock   a hand of earth.
> It is now, precise, repeat. I talk of Bigmans organs
> he, look, the lines! are polytopes.
> And among the DPs—deathhead
>   at the apex
>   of the pyramid.[39]

Olson's poem throws two kinds of light onto the immediate post-war situation. In the first place, it brings the historical figure of the geopolitical non-person into view, showing them in outline through the administrative procedures by which their condition was recorded. In the second place, just as it names this new individual, so the poem gestures towards the complex and overlapping historical circumstances that gave rise to such a condition. One marker of those historical circumstances is the reference to 'DPs', or 'displaced persons', a term that described the condition of many millions of people across the world following the Second World War but which, by official convention, referred principally to those who found themselves dislocated within Europe, held within Europe's displaced persons camps.

In Olson's poem, it is the displaced person who speaks, giving an account of their essential details: anticipated life span, weight, ethnicity, current location. The details themselves are profoundly negative, affording an image of a person rendered almost invisible: emaciated, of uncertain origin, speaking from the confines of a camp. The details are given in the form of answers, as if the speaker is responding to an interview or questionnaire; the kind of questionnaire used by Allied administrators to sift the camps in which displaced persons were held, and in which many of the categories which continue to grip asylum regimes were first formed.[40] This is the voice, in other words, as far as Olson could interpret it, of the individual at the border of personhood, speaking through the format by which their status may or may not be confirmed.

'La Préface' is a subtly inaugurating statement. On the one hand, it introduces the geopolitical non-person as an historical figure who must now be heard and addressed, definitive as they are of the post-war moment in which

Olson found himself. On the other hand, the poem gestures towards the complex of historical circumstances—the displaced persons camps and concentration camps—that had resulted in such an individual's emergence. 'La Préface' was thus an initiating move in a searching, shifting, sometimes desperate, sometimes consciously admonitory discourse, whose overarching object was to respond to the historical emergence of the geopolitical nonperson. The principal term in this context is 'space'. 'Put away war with time', says Olson, 'come into space.' In saying so, Olson is not advocating a crude opposition. He is not arguing—because why would he—that mid-century writers should not concern themselves with time. His own major poetic project, *The Maximus Poems*, rooted as it was in archival research, and modelled in part after his Modernist forbears, would have far-reaching temporal concerns. What Olson is urging, rather, is that in a world which has permitted the brutal foreclosures first of Buchenwald and then of the displaced persons camp, the need to reimagine and recalibrate space is profound and urgent.

The forms that spatial reimagining took, the way the foreclosures of mid-century geopolitics were pressed at and reopened, constitute the subject of this book. Drawing on a wide range of post-war texts published or substantively written and researched between 1948 and 1958, and on the intellectual archaeologies those texts depend on, as well as on more recent accounts of political space, the book's focus is nonetheless on a core set of key works. These are: the Universal Declaration of Human Rights (1948); Arendt's *The Origins of Totalitarianism* (1951, second edition 1958) and *The Human Condition* (1958); Charles Olson's works of the period, starting in 1950 with his manifesto 'Projective Verse', and including the first volume of his major work *The Maximus Poems* (substantively completed by 1958 and published in 1960); key contemporary histories of the post-war crisis of forced migration, notably those by Jacques Vernant and Malcolm Proudfoot (1953 and 1957); and Frantz Fanon's *Black Skin, White Masks* (1952), *Studies in a Dying Colonialism*, and *The Wretched of the Earth*, the last two of which, though published in 1959 and 1961, respectively, were products of research completed by 1958. In addressing this range of texts, I am in grateful dialogue with a number of exceptional commentators on the history of rights, the intersection of rights with literature, and the history and culture of the post-war period, most notably Samuel Moyn, Mark Greif, Lyndsey Stonebridge, and Joseph Slaughter.[41] In particular, I share Stonebridge's acutely balanced judgement that 'for literary ethics to amount to something more than literary humanitarianism, it [...] must reckon with political and moral judgement' but also that we can, and must, look to literature 'in order to imagine blueprints for a different politics of belonging'.[42] Both of these statements seem crucial to me, as does Stonebridge's methodological impulse, brilliantly unfolded in her study of mid-century attempts to arrive at a 'style capable of responding to the new rightlessness', that the condition of post-war statelessness was such that it touched on, and was touched upon, by a whole range of writers for whom it might not have seemed an immediate concern.[43]

Where this book differs from such commentaries is in its singular, sometimes obsessive preoccupation with the category of space and where that preoccupation derives from, as a reading of the post-war context, is Olson. Like Stonebridge, I make no apology for drawing a poet into discussions about the spatiality of post-war non-personhood. What that spatiality amounted to, focused as it was in the foreclosures of mid-century camps, was a profound failure to imagine geopolitical relations, international human spaces, in ways that meant non-personhood did not occur. Olson's significance in this context can be gauged by two facts. The first fact is that before he was a poet he was a politician. During the Second World War, he worked in the Office of War Information, rising to a senior level in Roosevelt's administration, while immediately after the war, having chosen poetry, not politics, as his career, he worked as a lobbyist (in particular, for Polish interest groups) at the fledgling United Nations. The second fact is that Olson was shocked into his most significant early poetry by direct reportage from the camps. 'La Préface' was written in response to a series of unflinching drawings made by Corrado Cagli during his participation, with the US army, in the liberation of Buchenwald. When Olson set out his poetics, most notably in his ground-breaking 1950 manifesto 'Projective Verse', the sensibility at work was formed directly out of the overwhelming concerns of contemporary geopolitics. Drawing on the language of the Universal Declaration itself, what Olson called for was writing capable of 'a whole series of new recognitions', and how he framed that writing was as a medium whose fundamental category was 'space'.[44]

What that meant in practice will be considered in Chapter 2, 'Writing Against Expulsion', where I will show how the various authors in this study sought to arrive at forms of thought and writing from which no person might be forced out. The larger aim of this book, however, is to show what happens when we take such a politically motivated emphasis on space back into the post-war discourse of which it was a part. And what happens, I argue, is that the underpinning spatiality of that discourse opens up, that we understand key authors of the period—the drafters of the Declaration, Arendt, historians of forced human movement, Fanon—as working desperately to reimagine the spaces by which the catastrophe of geopolitical non-personhood had been produced.

That the Universal Declaration is fundamentally spatial in intent is apparent in the fact that its underlying objective (however compromised it might have become) is to enable movement across and between sovereign territories. For Arendt, such a concern with spatiality is focused in her discussion of what she terms, in *The Human Condition*, 'the space of appearance', where the objective is to arrive at a form of political setting in which a person's appearance might be guaranteed. For Olson, the category was entirely foundational to post-war poetry and poetics, witness (among many expressions of this commitment to a writing underpinned by spatiality) his declaration, in 'Projective Verse', of what he termed a poetry of the 'open field'.

To draw Fanon into this discourse is, of course, to force an encounter with a radically different and seemingly separate context. Thus, whereas Arendt, Olson, and the authors of the Universal Declaration can be taken broadly (if by no means exclusively) to occupy a European–US discursive environment, the context in which Fanon's reading of spatiality was principally formed was the Algerian War of Independence.[45] Although hardly without implications for the European imaginary, this inclusion of a decolonizing context is nonetheless a jarring geopolitical move and one which is perhaps discomfiting to all the critical interest groups. It is, however, as the book suggests, a necessary step.

It is necessary in part because, as Arendt herself insisted, it is historically insufficient to present the production of geopolitical non-personhood in a European context without registering its continuity with the production of non-personhood in the colonial space. Nobody was more aware of this than Fanon, who, in *The Wretched of the Earth* in particular, insisted repeatedly on the continuity between the expulsions effected by fascism and the displacements produced by colonialism, in order to open the latter to the implications of human rights. In Algeria, he would observe time and again, the domination of indigenous Algerians was totalitarian in its spatial expression: in its segregation, its policing, and its denial of movement. As Sekyi-Otu observes, Fanon replaces Marxism's preoccupation with temporality and its 'denunciation of capital's [. . .] heartless prolongation of the working day, with a condemnation of the "totalitarian" ordering of lived and living space'.[46]

From which encounter with European domination in a colonial context, Fanon became one of the most subtle and far-reaching post-war commentators on the politics of space. This is apparent in his accounts of the micro-management of colonized space, where the mechanisms of spatial control bear directly, brutally, and on a daily basis, on the contours of the individual whose personhood is at stake. It is apparent in his accounts of the colonized person's animating desire, of their hopes and dreams, for a different lived experience of space. And it is apparent in his political reimagining, in the fact that, almost without fail, Fanon sought to extend the expectations of a national politics by identifying it in terms of a 'new humanity'.[47] The argument of *Writing Against Expulsion* is that we need all these mid-century accounts of space to understand how geopolitical non-personhood is produced and how the logics of displacement interlock in order to develop the conditions whereby such foreclosures might come to be prevented.

On the Production of Expulsive Space

In bringing these authors and texts together, and in providing an account of the interlocking spatialities of the mid-century discourse of non-personhood, *Writing Against Expulsion* both draws on and resists—and in the process, I hope, complements—the major theory of space to emerge from the post-war period, Henri Lefebvre's *The Production of Space*. The principal value of Lefebvre's account in this context is precisely its overarching intention to historicize space, to show that 'social space', by which he means the space or spaces of human interaction and domination, is not neutrally given but politically and economically produced. Without proposing a chronology as such, *The Production of Space* thus circles through moments in the history of political economy in which both the lived experience of space and its representation were decisively altered. One such defining moment was the Renaissance, when, as Lefebvre observes, '*some* artists and men of learning arrived at a very different *representation* of space: a homogeneous, clearly demarcated space complete with horizon and vanishing point'.[48] A second such moment, the critical spatial moment of modernity, is to be found in the 'historic' role of the Bauhaus, which, in its architectural practice (he doesn't refer to other aspects of the Bauhaus programme), did not merely 'locate space in its real context or supply a new perspective on it: it developed a new conception, a global concept, of space'.[49] The argument here is that the mid-century period in question (broadly speaking the decade 1948–1958) constituted a further decisive moment of spatial production, a moment that Lefebvre almost, but not quite, names: the moment in which expulsion was registered both as lived reality and in which, to borrow his terms, authors looked to arrive at a different representation of space.

That Lefebvre almost, but not quite, names expulsion as a mode of spatial production owes to the history of his own theoretical development. Published in 1974, *The Production of Space* sets out to consider 'what has been happening in the second half of the twentieth century, the period to which "we" are witness'.[50] The name Lefebvre gives to the mode of spatial production that has shaped this period is 'abstraction', it being the abstractions of lived space epitomized by Bauhaus design that represent and enact the homogeneity of global capitalism. Lefebvre is hardly wrong in this characterization and therefore not wrong when he proposes that 'modern spatial practice' might be defined by 'the daily life of a tenant in a government subsidized high-rise housing project'.[51]

There is, however, another story of post-war spatial production that one can tell through Lefebvre, and which one glimpses here in his insistence on 'daily life'. A seemingly neutral term, 'daily life' derives theoretically from Lefebvre's major post-war work *Critique of Everyday Life*, published in 1951. The purpose of that no less ground-breaking text was to establish the study of what Lefebvre called 'lived experience' as a gauge and ongoing critique of the reality of alienated social relations.[52] In that respect, the abstract organization of space that Lefebvre takes to characterize late-twentieth-century capitalism is continuous with his immediate post-war work, crushing as such spatiality is of the specificity and difference that might constitute lived experience in its richest form. There is, however, a darker aspect to Lefebvre's mid-century critique that, by the time he writes *The Production of Space*, has quite largely dropped from his view. Where one sees that darker aspect is in the final chapter of *Critique of Everyday Life*, in which, through a reading of various testimonies by survivors of the camps, he identifies a link between abstraction and expulsion. Drawing in particular on David Rousset's *L'Univers Concentrationnaire*, a text that was crucial to both Arendt and Olson, Lefebvre identifies the logic by which abstraction becomes expulsion:

> And yet, how many times do we feel ourselves carried away by some enormous power, absurd and yet fearfully rational. In factories, government offices, courts of law, barracks, or simply in cities, an implacable mechanism is at work. And human Reason appears only as a terrifying, distant,

dehumanized reason: scientific barbarity [...] But the dominant, essential meaning appears to be this: if Fascism represents the most extreme form of capitalism, the concentration camp is the most extreme and paroxysmal form of a modern housing estate, or of an industrial town.[53]

To excerpt Lefebvre like this is to risk simplification, where, in fact, his identification of an 'implacable mechanism' comes at the end of a long and patiently argued text. He is not, in other words, implying an inevitability of transition from capitalism to fascism. What he is indicating, however, in his incipient theory of the production of space, is that just as space, in the mid-century moment, could be characterized by abstraction and alienation, so also it had to be understood in terms of the propensity to expel. He doesn't name it as such because he hasn't yet arrived at his theory of spatial production, but it is implicit in his argumentation that in the mid-century moment expulsion was suddenly discernible as a means of organizing space. The space produced by expulsion—in other words, the space of mass non-personhood—was as definitive of the mid-century moment as the abstracted constructions epitomized by the Bauhaus that Lefebvre would subsequently identify as producing 'global space'.

Reading Lefebvre's relation to the mid-century moment in this way opens up various implications that are important for this book. In one sense, it is to observe that by the time he formulated his theory of space in the early 1970s, the underlying logic of expulsion had receded from view. It is all too clear now, once again, that such logics don't go away, that it would have been better had it been remembered that in the twentieth century one principal mode by which space was organized was through the capacity to expel. It is the opening up of the space of expulsion that Agamben saw in the executive order that permitted the arbitrary detention of people held at Guantanamo Bay. In the United Kingdom, as elsewhere, that failure to remember is ongoing as policymakers continue to produce impossible spaces whereby people present might be deemed outside. At the same time, what Lefebvre's larger periodizing logic permits—his sense, precisely, of the *production* of space— is an account of the mid-century moment whereby expulsion, the mass production of non-personhood, was understood at the time as a new condition of space. What one finds accordingly, across the range of authors and texts addressed in this book, are interlocking attempts both to register the new reality of expulsion *and* to articulate space and the way people lived and experienced space such that the production of geopolitical non-personhood might not occur.

It is, in fact, precisely because expulsion was understood as a new mode of spatial production—because authors came to see continuities between the non-personhood of the concentration camp, forced displacement, and colonial segregation—that it is both possible and necessary to address the range of texts and authors that *Writing Against Expulsion* frames. Always dialectical, Lefebvre's approach is to describe the new material reality through which social space had been reconfigured and to identify key cultural figures whose achievement was to recognize and also reimagine emergent spatial forms. In addition to the pioneers of the Bauhaus, he names Picasso and Frank Lloyd Wright as Modernist creators capable of rethinking space. Olson, this book proposes, was an equivalent figure for the mid-century moment, whose standing as poet by the end of the 1950s rested precisely on his understanding that a new articulation of spatiality must be integral to the poet's concerns. That Olson arrived at this mid-century understanding of the importance of space was itself, in part, a legacy of the Bauhaus, the closure of which by the Nazis—as Chapter 3 will explore— contributed to the founding of Black Mountain College, the experimental arts college in which Olson honed his early thought. It was, moreover, precisely his understanding of the need to rethink space that Donald Allen, the most influential poetry editor of the period, identified when he positioned Olson as the leading figure in his field-defining anthology *The New American Poetry 1945–1960*. As Allen put it in his preface, 'Olson's 'Projective Verse' essay and his letter to Elaine Feinstein present the dominant new double concept: 'composition by field' and the poet's 'stance toward reality'.[54]

The argument here, to reiterate, is not that Olson, or any other single figure, defined the discourse discussed in *Writing Against Expulsion*. Rather, that such was the brutality of the logic of mid-century expulsion—the degree to which, in expulsive settings, social space was foreclosed—that in writers as diverse as Arendt, Fanon, the authors of the Universal Declaration, and the many authors on whom these figures drew, one finds interlocking efforts to re-articulate and reimagine lived relations to space that might prevent the production of the geopolitical non-person. Olson's 'stance toward reality' was his own, but in his drive to reimagine social space, he was responding to a logic of expulsion that was definitive of the mid-century moment.[55]

In one sense, then, the evidence that the spatiality of geopolitical non-personhood became a condition of mid-century thought lies in the range of writers, texts, disciplines, and modes in which one discerns the concern. The writers and texts in question are linked, as Lefebvre would suggest, by period and by a period-defining mode of spatial production. A further way of calibrating the force of shared realization, however, is that it is possible to trace a discourse of mid-century spatiality across the writers and texts in question *notwithstanding* the major differences between them and the differing ideological limitations of their stances and writings. One way to dramatize this is outside the period itself, in Arendt's discussion of Fanon in her highly problematic volume *On Violence*, published in 1970. Arendt's engagement with Fanon in her short text is both disingenuous and strictly partial. It is disingenuous in the sense that, as she concedes in a footnote,

> I am using this work [*The Wretched of the Earth*] because of its great influence on the present student generation. Fanon himself, however, is much more doubtful about violence than his admirers. It seems that only the book's first chapter, 'Concerning Violence' has been widely read.[56]

There is a dishonesty in this position only amplified by the fact that throughout her treatment of Fanon's consideration of violence she at no point reflects on the violence of the French colonial regime. It is a form of blindness to the political reality of Fanon's writing context that elsewhere in the text displays itself as racism, as when, in her discussion of the influence of the Black Power movement on US campuses, she resorts to a racist slur. As she puts it,

> In America, the student movement has been seriously radicalized wherever police and police brutality intervened in essentially nonviolent demonstrations: occupations of administration buildings, sit-ins et cetera. Serious violence entered the scene only with the appearance of the Black Power movement on the campuses. Negro students, the majority of them admitted without academic qualification, regarded and organized themselves as an interest group, the representatives of the black community. Their interest was to lower academic standards.[57]

I reference Arendt's racist argumentation in *On Violence* in part simply because anybody writing about her must acknowledge this aspect of her thought. What her subsequent discussion of Fanon shows, in fact, is how important it is to place his discussion of mid-century expulsion alongside hers. Thus, for all that she wrote at length about the racist logic of colony and empire, and for all that her accounts of the lived experience of statelessness remain urgent in the understanding of non-personhood they present, it is apparent from subsequent pronouncements on race conflict in the United States that she held reprehensible views on race. No account of mid-century expulsion could rest exclusively, or even principally, on Arendt, and precisely what her later texts make apparent is the need, in thinking about post-war geopolitical non-personhood, to engage seriously with Fanon. Writing from a colonial context, shaped by the immediate memory of fascism, and from a conflict, as he repeatedly reminds us, that was producing refugees, Fanon provides a crucial intersectional account of mid-century geopolitical non-personhood, of the lived experience of space of people racially denied rights.

In writing about Arendt, then, I share Etienne Balibar's view that it is necessary

> to think with Arendt beyond Arendt herself: this is to suggest that what exterminist processes, and more generally the product of 'non-persons' on a mass scale, demonstrate is the reciprocity and the mutual inherence of universalistic notion of human rights and the belonging [...] to a *political community*.[58]

As Balibar implies, Arendt remains an essential thinker on the question of 'exterminist processes' and on the production of '"non-persons" on a mass scale'. Throughout this book, however, it will be necessary to think beyond her not only on the question of race but also on the question of the political agency required to resist such processes and, in particular, on the question of the agency required to animate a politics of rights. Arendt becomes most interesting when placed in dialogue with those who contest or radicalize her thought; witness the work of Jacques Rancière or Ayten Gündoğdu.

Arendt's function in this book, then, is as an always necessary, but never entirely sufficient, witness to the mid-century production of expulsive space. By focusing on her work of the period 1948–1958 and by situating her in relation to a range of writers and texts also grappling with that expulsive condition, the book both sharpens and re-aligns key dynamics in her thought. As with Olson, Fanon, and Lefebvre, we see her constantly seeking to articulate the mechanics by which the conditions of expulsion and also non-expulsion are achieved. Critically contextualized by such contemporaries, the book shows Arendt in sustained negotiation between the territory and the map, where the map is contemporary geopolitics ruthlessly partitioned and bordered and where the territory is a set of lived relations through which such expulsive cartographies can be resisted and reframed. What emerges from this account of Arendt is a period-specific body of work—principally *The Origins of Totalitarianism* and *The Human Condition*—which, while it continuously contemplates the politics of expulsion and non-expulsion, also invariably stops short at the brink of political engagement. Arendt, for whom the act of dialogue is the fundamental marker of political belonging, is herself rendered political by critical engagement with others.

Paul Mason is right, therefore, that 'Reading Arendt Is Not Enough'. In his short, brilliantly speculative essay on Arendt in *Clear Bright Future: A Radical Defence of the Human Being*, Mason recognizes Arendt as 'a courageous opponent of tyranny' and considers that her 'descriptions of the dynamics of the totalitarian movement hold good' but proposes that 'instead of deifying her we should understand her ideas in their context'.[59] This is not a question, for Mason, simply of registering Arendt's milieu since what is ultimately at issue is an account of human rights that places them 'on more solid foundations than the ones currently under attack'.[60] Rather, she must be read in critical relation to her moment, constantly challenged and extended where her thinking stops short. For Mason, what principally she didn't grasp was the 'working-class project of collaboration, equality and human-centred society', a failure this book addresses in Chapter 4 in its discussion of the right to work.[61] More broadly what Mason affirms is precisely what Balibar insists on, that it is necessary to think 'with Arendt beyond Arendt herself'. She must be understood as a crucial observer of the politics and mechanics of expulsion, but her thinking on such questions must be dialectically situated and extended at every turn. The way this book contributes to that thinking is to place her work in sustained dialogue with significant contemporaries and, through such thickened historical contextualizing of her inquiries into expulsion, rights, movement, work, and speech, to repeatedly identify what was and remains politically at stake. The method, in other words, is radical contextualization, where the aim is re-cognition of the politics of rights.

To extend Balibar's phrase, as *Writing Against Expulsion* repeatedly argues, all of the authors in question must be thought with and beyond. Fanon has to be followed beyond his immediate arguments for a national consciousness, always conditionally made, to his attempt across various modes of lived experience to arrive at a politics of what he calls 're-humanisation'. Olson's articulations of space must be critiqued, as Rachel Blau DuPlessis has argued powerfully and undeniably, for their invariably gendered constructions.[62] The Universal Declaration of Human Rights must repeatedly be framed to allow the implied agency and relationality of its provisions to come through and thereby to resist that reading of the document, which the document itself permits, that focuses its meaning on the category of the disempowered individual.

The argument in bringing these interlocking texts together, in other words, is not that we should subscribe to the propositions of any given writer, or that the differences between writers can be elided, or that we can overlook the prejudices and ideological limitations of any of the writers concerned. The argument, rather, is that across these differing texts, in a way that Lefebvre's sense of spatial production would suggest and which is, in fact, more pronounced for the multiple differences that apply, the fact of mid-century expulsion, and the desire to articulate a non-expulsive space, was a defining concern. It was a concern, moreover, which called, and still calls, for an expanded intellectual frame. What Arendt clearly understood in *The Origins of Totalitarianism,* even though subsequently she lost her grip on this fact, was that if there was to be a satisfactory account of the mid-century production of non-personhood, that account must register the different but interlocking geopolitical settings in which non-personhood was made. It was necessary, in other words, to document the intersections between fascism, colonialism, and the intensified function of sovereignty, where one key point of intersection was the refusal of a language of rights. It is towards such an expanded frame that *Writing Against Expulsion* looks to point, invoking as it does, at various points, a second theory of spatiality with its roots in the mid-century moment, which is to say Paul Gilroy's conception of *The Black Atlantic.*

Without drawing directly on the specifics of his findings, *Writing Against Expulsion* is influenced by Gilroy in its sense that any account of mid-century expulsion, and of the counter articulations of space it generated, must register the intersections of modernity and race framed by the various movements of the Black Atlantic. What *Writing Against Expulsion* thus seeks to arrive at, as it pivots between texts produced in Africa, Europe, and the United States, is an understanding of how spaces in which human rights are denied reproduce themselves and how, therefore, what is required is a constant reassertion of the agency implied by rights precisely at the level of lived experience. There is, therefore, across all of the texts discussed, a double sense of contemporary space. On the one hand, what all of the texts demonstrate is a geopolitical scale, a clear and motivating understanding of the way the organization of geopolitical space had resulted in the radically foreclosed spaces of expulsion and non-personhood. On the other hand, and in response, one finds a commitment to articulations of 'lived experience' across the different texts and contexts that have the implication of transforming social space. As Lefebvre himself put it in 1958, in the foreword to the second edition of *Critique of Everyday Life*: 'socialism (the new society, the new life) can only be defined *concretely* on the level of everyday life, as a system of changes in what can be called lived experience'.[63]

That sense, Lefebvre's sense, of 'lived experience' is worth pausing on here. His reason for introducing the term in *Critique of Everyday Life* was to provide a measure for larger social structures of reality: 'socialism (the new society, the new life) can only be defined *concretely* on the level of everyday life'. Building on this precise calibration of the value of lived experience, one claim of *Writing Against Expulsion* is that if we are to arrive at regimes of political space that are not expulsive, we need to pay deliberate attention to those aspects of lived experience in which expulsion is acutely felt. It is for this reason that the book follows mid-century writers in addressing the realities and settings of detention, movement, work, and speech. It is crucial, in other words, as Lefebvre's own mid-century text asserts, that we understand the production of space not just as abstract historical categories but as 'lived experience' of 'everyday relations', where the experience itself can be changed and remade.

What *Writing Against Expulsion* proposes, then, is not a theory of space as such because the thinking with which it is concerned had not yet hardened into theoretical form. Instead, what it looks to present is a discourse in which various writers addressed the reality of a newly visible mode of the production of space, suddenly aware, as they were, of the scope and brutality of the mass production of non-personhood and determined to articulate the relations of lived experience in such a way that the expulsion of persons might not occur. That discourse is a resource. We are living through a new moment of expulsion. We need to know what writers occupied by an earlier moment of expulsion imagined and thought.

Politically speaking, what the book helps to express, and what all of the authors and texts concerned sought at various points to articulate, are the fundamental and always potentially radicalizing contradictions of human expulsion.[64] It is with such contradictions that Lefebvre is ultimately concerned, with the potential, in contradiction, for radical change, where 'fragmented reality (dispersion, segregation, separation, localization) may on occasion overwhelm political power, which for its part depends for sustenance on continual reinforcement'.[65] What *Writing Against Expulsion* looks to express, through its recovery of an interdisciplinary, interlocking, and international discourse of spatiality, is the fundamental human contradiction inherent in the production of expulsive space. The purpose of the book is to detail the impossible contours of the space of geopolitical non-personhood *and* to use the writers in question to articulate a lived experience of space whereby such non-personhood would not occur.

Exactly how the language of the Universal Declaration figures in this argument will become apparent as the book unfolds. It is crucial to say at the outset, however, that the aim here is in no sense to stage a defence of the international regime of rights that can be said to have followed the promulgation of the Declaration, much less so the globalized humanitarianism that has been carried out in its name. The aim, rather, is to revisit the human relationality that the series of articles itself sought to articulate and which is properly visible when the document is thought of in terms of space. From its inception, the Universal Declaration has been both significantly over- and under-sold. It is oversold when it is understood as a political *deus ex machina*, a guarantee from elsewhere that persons will be recognized as such. There are surely few lessons the world has learned more fully in the ongoing age of geopolitical non-personhood than that there are no such external guarantees; that sovereign politics is brutal in its expulsions and that the capacity of the state to inure itself and its citizenship to other people's suffering knows little or no limitation. But, and in the same breath, precisely what the overselling of the Universal Declaration has led to, as Jacques Rancière argues, is a misunderstanding of the necessary agency of rights.[66] Rights might not be guaranteed (they certainly are not), but they can be claimed, they can both enable and legitimize struggle. And in a world once again defaulting brutally to the practice of arbitrary detention, the enduring possibility of such a claim has to be defended.[67]

Broadly speaking, then, this book tells a story. In the first part, I show how the writers in question addressed and characterized the world they inherited. Chapter 1, 'The Non-Place', shows how, variously, the authors in question (including the drafters of the Declaration) articulated the nature of the non-place, the setting in which non-personhood is produced. Chapter 2, 'Writing Against Expulsion', considers how, in different but crucially intersecting ways, the texts contemplate the political reality of expulsion and how they intersect in their concern to arrive at expressions of space from which no person might be expelled. Olson's image of the open field is crucial in this respect, making vivid as it does the post-war aspiration for a spatialization of expression, the drive towards forms of articulation from which no person might be expelled.

The purpose of the second part of the book is twofold. In the first place, I use the writers in question to detail the effects of particular prohibitions by which geopolitical non-personhood is produced and reinforced. But secondly, and crucially for the argument of the book, the purpose of Chapters 3, 4, and 5—on 'Moving', 'Making', and 'Speaking'—is to show how the authors sought to establish the practicalities of a sustainable human space. Drawing on their explicit preoccupations with the defining human practices of movement, work, and speech, the second part of the book shows how, for all the authors, the intention was not simply to call, in the abstract, for a new kind of political space. What they looked to articulate more concretely was a series of practical human commitments that could hold such a respectful political space open, that might prevent a reversion to non-personhood by establishing forms of relation, of lived experience, that constituted the basis of a common ground. In order to arrive at new spatial imaginaries, the writers separately understood, it was necessary to arrive at new expressions of those forms of agency by which humans shape and participate in shared space. What *Writing Against Expulsion* thus aims to provide is two kinds of intellectual resource. In the first place, what one finds in key writers and works of the post-war period are concerted attempts to understand what it means to the individual and society in question to create and inhabit the spaces in which geopolitical non-personhood is produced. In the second place, in response to that understanding, fundamentally sharpened as it was by the catastrophe of the war, one finds far-reaching attempts to articulate counter-spaces, non-national spaces, spaces not defined by expulsion; spaces in which personhood and the movement of persons might be secured.

In aiming to provide this account, the book draws throughout on a range of disciplinary threads: legalized international declaration, histories of human movement, poetry and poetry manifestoes, philosophy, and postcolonial theory. That such a range of texts is necessary, and that the authors themselves found it necessary in their own practices to draw on a range of disciplines, owes to the axiomatic character of the question at issue. The historical emergence of the systematic production of non-persons, the realization after the war that such a category had become symptomatic of modern geopolitical space, touched any number of disciplines and practices. If the objective was to arrive at forms of thought and language from which no person might be allowed to fall, then the resulting discourse would inevitably draw on the widest range of expressive resources.

In looking to indicate that expressive range, *Writing Against Expulsion* necessarily also engages a number of connected critical and theoretical traditions. At various points, as the discussion unfolds, the argument addresses the intersection of literature and law, in particular in Chapter 2, as I discuss Joseph Slaughter's account of the fictional personality he takes to be at the centre of the conception of human rights. Similarly, in Chapter 4, as I discuss the relation between political and economic modes of belonging, I address the discourse of sovereignty, notably Seyla Benhabib's critique of the modern state, and the cartography it entails, in *The Rights of Others*. At all points, however, and unapologetically, the argument draws also on the potentialities of the poem. To draw on that resource, to insist on the importance of poetry and poetics in the face of the mid-century crisis of geopolitical spatiality, is to draw on the animating commitments of the writers concerned. As Stonebridge writes of Arendt,

> Poetic language and literary history mattered to Arendt in her thinking about community because they told a story about how political worlds, whether bound by nation states or by international laws and treaties, traffic with the worlds we imagine and create.[68]

It is a claim that has its echo in Ato Sekyi-Otu's account of Fanon's politics of spatiality, where, as he reads it,

> perhaps the single most important literary source of this metaphorics of space in Fanon's texts—perhaps the single most important influence on his entire representation of racial and colonial bondage—is Aimé Césaire's *Cahier d'un retour au pays natal*.[69]

Olson himself reflects the underlying importance of the poem as a means of reimagining space by reversing the direction of the dialogue. Where Arendt and Fanon drew on poetry and poetics to help articulate their political philosophy, Olson (with his political career already behind him) turned to the poem as the setting in which questions generated by history and politics might be worked out. For Olson, driven by a radical understanding of the divisions of intellectual labour, it was crucial to the development of post-war politics that disciplines with which the poem was in dialogue should also grasp the intellectual value of the poem. Where that value lay, how the potentialities of the poem helped shape the political imaginary, is perhaps best summarized by Édouard Glissant, Fanon's contemporary and friend at the Lycée Schoelcher, where Césaire himself taught. For Glissant, the value of the poem lies in its capacity for the articulation of relationality—in its enduring potential, through its multiple modes of patterning, to articulate how persons, peoples, and histories relate. As he puts it in 'The Open Boat', the first chapter of *Poetics of Relation*,

> Not just a specific knowledge, appetite, suffering and delight of one particular people, not only that, but knowledge of the Whole, greater from having been at the abyss and freeing knowledge of Relation within the Whole.[70]

It was through poetry's capacity for articulating the complexity and possibility of relations, as radically extended by Olson in 'Projective Verse', and as drawn upon by Fanon and Arendt, that poetics contributed to the mid-century reimagining of geopolitical space. From which it follows, as I argue in Chapter 2, that we need a reading of the Universal Declaration of Human Rights tuned to mid-century developments in political poetics that hears the degree to which that defining mid-century document was a reimagining of human relations in space.

To the Future

To read writings from the immediate post-war period is to come across voices that call forward, voices shaped by the reality of the post-war world that call to some unspecified future moment. Writing in 1999, the poet Ed Dorn identified such a call in the work of his late friend Charles Olson. Olson's work, he proposed, 'anticipates a millennium already underway in 1950—a period marked by "terror as pandemia".[71] This is not to suggest that Olson was prophetic. Not at all. One must be deeply wary of any poet who identifies with prophecy. It is to propose that in certain texts authored in the period 1948–1958, one finds readings of the post-war world that, in their attention to emergent historical realities, resonate deeply with the moment we are living through.

INTRODUCTION: MAKING SPACE FOR THE HUMAN   33

Consider, in a different register, John Hope Simpson's 'Preface' to Malcolm Proudfoot's exhaustive contemporary history *European Refugees: 1939–1952: A Study in Forced Population Movement*. Writing in 1956, a year before the book was published, Simpson set out patiently to explain the value of Proudfoot's text:

> This work has a value apart from and additional to that of an accurate, detailed, and documented record of events, in many of which its author was personally concerned. The problem of refugees and of displaced persons of the Second World War, and the methods adopted to solve those problems, indicates the chief difficulties which arose, and provides valuable lessons for the future. Throughout the world there is everywhere the cherished hope that the Second World War was the final instance of the settlement of international differences by force. Throughout the world, however, preparations are, at the same time, being made to increase and to perfect armaments, in case that cherished hope proves to be ill-founded. Should war come again, it will result, without question, in the emergence of just such problems as are dealt with in this volume, and it is essential that steps should be taken in advance to provide adequate machinery for their solution.

'All who are interested,' Simpson concludes,

> in refugee matters are indebted to the colossal labour entailed on its author in the production of this volume. It not only provides an authoritative historical record of a period now past, but also describes difficulties which, had they been foreseen, might have been avoided. This work is thus of practical value for operations in the future.[72]

Simpson's address is conscious and explicit: he is directing the future to Proudfoot's book. Like Proudfoot, he himself had written a history of mid-century forced population movement and was therefore intimate with what he called, in his agonized grammar, 'difficulties which, had they been foreseen, might have been avoided'. Here, too, there is nothing prophetic. What one hears, rather, in Simpson's framing of Proudfoot's history is what one might term an anticipatory address. It is a similar anticipatory address that Dorn hears in Olson and that readers of various kinds hear in Arendt. Documenting the realities of the post-war moment, such writers, in their different modes, anticipated an emerging geopolitics, a geopolitics in which the production of non-personhood would shape the future.

The conclusion to this book will address one future such post-war voices were seeking to anticipate, which is to say the moment we currently find ourselves living through—a moment once again defined by the figure of the geopolitical non-person, by an international failure, as Arendt put it, to allow displaced persons a home. What the body of the book will have documented, in its consideration of the post-war period, can be taken to be a pre-history of this present time. Which is not to smooth away the manifest structural differences, the singular decisive factor, for example, that we are no longer living in the order of the Cold War. It is to observe, rather, that as we consider the re-emergence of the geopolitical non-person, there are demonstrable ways in which we continue to live through conditionalities framed and consolidated in the post-war moment. This is apparent in certain specific ongoing histories of juridical non-personhood that date to the period in question: the ongoing displacement of the Palestinian people inaugurated by the 1948 Nakba; the continued scandal of the British establishment's seemingly unceasing effort to turn the generation that came over on the Windrush back; the ongoing insistence, inscribed in 1953 by the European Convention on Human Rights, that Europe's commitment to rights ends with its borders. Such enduring conditionalities are apparent also in the continued expansion of those settings in which geopolitical non-persons are warehoused and their lives suspended: the detention centres and the removal centres that constitute the obscured coordinates of a once again failing international map. It is a map, one might argue, of expulsion, an expanding cartography of expulsive space, a cartography pictured by the Global Detention Project's 'map view' of detention centres—whether 'administrative', 'ad hoc', 'criminal', or 'unknown'—across the world.[73] What that map documents is a logic the latest expression of which, as this book is completed, is the UK government's plan to offshore the processing of people seeking asylum to an asylum processing centre in Rwanda. Against the backdrop of the crisis of mass forced displacement caused by the Russian invasion of Ukraine, an occupation that plainly recalls post-war geopolitics, the UK government's intention to offshore so-called 'illegal' asylum claims is in direct contravention of its commitment, as a signatory, to the 1951 Convention Relating to the Status of Refugees. Above all other documents, as Chapter 2 observes, it was the 1951 Convention that named the need, in the post-war moment, to imagine and establish a non-expulsive political space. More than ever, and more even than might have been imagined when I

INTRODUCTION: MAKING SPACE FOR THE HUMAN 35

started working on this book, the logic of expulsion has once again taken hold.

The fact that such conditions of geopolitical non-personhood are once again with us means that voices from the post-war moment have a particular resonance in the present. We hear their difference, of course, in all kinds of tones and cultural assumptions, but as we read back a series of speech acts carry particular force. The first is a form of warning, the anxious articulation of the risks that follow from the production of non-personhood on an industrial scale. Such warnings were numerous and detailed, as Chapter 1 will indicate, but nobody projected from the post-war moment quite as forcefully as Arendt. Consider, for instance, her account of the signs it would be necessary to register:

> In comparison with the insane end-result—concentration camp society — the process by which people are prepared for this end, and the methods by which individuals are adapted to these conditions, are transparent and logical. The insane mass manufacture of corpses is preceded by the historically intelligible preparation of living corpses. The impetus and what is more the silent consent to such unprecedented conditions are the products of those events which in a period of political disintegration suddenly and unexpectedly made hundreds and thousands of human beings homeless, stateless, outlawed and unwanted, while millions of human beings were made economically superfluous and socially burdensome by unemployment [...] The first essential step on the road to total domination is to kill the juridical person in man. This was done, on the one hand, by putting certain categories of people outside the protection of the law and forcing at the same time, through the instrument of denationalization, the nontotalitarian world into recognition of lawlessness; it was done, on the other, by placing the concentration camp outside the normal penal system, and by selecting its inmates outside the normal judicial procedure in which a definite crime entails a predictable penalty.[74]

Although not all of these conditions currently apply, and although the purpose of Arendt's project is to determine how history need not repeat itself, the points of comparison with the present moment are alarming. In particular, what needs to be underlined is the intersection of 'superfluousness' and 'lawlessness'. To read writings from the period 1948–1958 is to find oneself warned.

A second speech act clearly audible in the writings of the period is the act of definition. When John Hope Simpson refers to the 'methods adopted' to solve the problem of 'displaced' persons, he refers the reader in part to the apparatus of categorization that evolved in the immediate aftermath of the war. The most prominent manifestation of that evolving apparatus was the 1951 Convention Relating to the Status of Refugees, affording as it did crucial protections to certain categories of people who found themselves displaced. At the same time as it protected, however, the language evolved in response to geopolitical non-personhood produced its own critical exclusions, not least along the fault line of political and economic migration. To go back to the writings of the period is thus to document the development of a language of non-personhood that continues to underpin the international asylum regime and to register how, in their rapid evolution, the definitions could have been otherwise.

The third kind of speech act is the act, in language, of making space for the human. In all of the texts in question, and in many of the texts they drew on, one finds serious attempts to articulate cartographies that did not subordinate personhood and the movement of persons to the borders of the state. One sees this in part in an opening of language to the scale of the new geopolitical condition; one sees it in Arendt's sense of the 'common world', in Fanon's preoccupation with a 'new humanity', in the Universal Declaration's adverbial constructions, its insistence on 'everyone everywhere'; one hears it in Hope Simpson's call for an adequate international machinery, and one sees it in Olson's commitment to a geographical imagination. Underpinning these expansive locutions are detailed considerations of the constitutive elements of a reimagined geopolitical space, forms of agency capable of re-opening the map. To make space for the human called for forms of relation *not* dependent for their validation on the national imaginary but on the participatory practices, as post-war authors understood it, of movement, making, and speech. *Writing Against Expulsion* goes back to a moment when the geopolitical non-person became visible, to a moment when it was necessary to understand what it meant to produce non-personhood on a global scale and to imagine political spatialities from which no person might be expelled.

Notes

1. Behrouz Boochani has written extensively about the realities of the Australian immigration system. See, in particular, his novel *No Friend but the Mountains*, both for its brilliant detailing of the structures of immigration detention and for

the counter spaces he seeks to open up. Behrouz Boochani, *No Friend but the Mountains*, tr. Omid Tofighian (London: Picador, 2019).
2. Daniel Wilsher, *Immigration Detention: Law, History, Politics* (Cambridge: Cambridge University Press, 2012), p .88.
3. Home Office, 'Immigration Statistics, Year Ending 2019', updated 3 March 2022, https://www.gov.uk/government/statistics/immigration-statistics-year-ending-december-2021/how-many-people-are-detained-or-returned (accessed 22 April 2022).
4. For an overview of US immigration detention statistics, see: Global Detention Project, 'United States', https://www.globaldetentionproject.org/countries/americas/united-states (accessed 22 April 2022).
5. Global Detention Project, 'United States'.
6. Chloe Chaplain and Emily Ferguson, 'Inside the Rwanda Centre Which Will House Asylum Seekers and UK Channel Migrants', iNews, 14 April 2022, https://inews.co.uk/news/politics/inside-rwanda-centre-asylum-seekers-uk-channel-migrants-1575640 (accessed 22 April 2022).
7. UNHCR (United Nations High Commissioner for Refugees), Global Trends: Forced Displacement in 2020, p. 2, https://www.unrefugees.org.uk/wp-content/uploads/Global-Trends-2020.pdf (accessed 22 April 2022).
8. UNHCR, Uganda: Refugee Policy Review Framework Country Summary as at 30 June, p. 9, https://reporting.unhcr.org/document/1907 (accessed 22 April 2022).
9. Giorgio Agamben, *State of Exception*, tr. Kevin Attell (Chicago, IL and London: University of Chicago Press, 2005), pp. 2–3.
10. For an outstanding account of the implications of the US detention practices at Guantanamo Bay, see William Watkin's chapter 'Reading Guantanamo or Camp as Coercion', in *Bioviolence: How the Powers That Be Make Us Do What They Want* (London: Routledge, 2021), pp. 174–190.
11. UNHCR, Global Trends: Forced Displacement in 2015, https://www.unhcr.org/uk/statistics/unhcrstats/576408cd7/unhcr-global-trends-2015.html (accessed 29 April 2022).
12. Peter Gatrell, *The Unsettling of Europe: The Great Migration, 1945 to the Present* (London: Allen Lane, 2019).
13. Daniel Cohen, *In War's Wake: Europe's Displaced Persons in the Postwar Order* (Oxford: Oxford University Press, 2011).
14. Hannah Arendt, *Origins of Totalitarianism*, 3rd edn (New York: Harcourt Brace Jovanovich Publishers, 1979), p. 287.
15. Maya Goodfellow, *Hostile Environment: How Immigrants Became Scapegoats* (London and New York: Verso, 2019), pp. 56–57.
16. For a full account of the Windrush scandal, see Amelia Gentleman, *The Windrush Betrayal: Exposing the Hostile Environment* (London: Guardian Faber Publishing, 2019).
17. Goodfellow, *Hostile Environment*, p. 57.

18. Arendt, *Origins*, pp. 293–294.
19. Thomas Nail, *Theory of the Border* (Oxford: Oxford University Press, 2016), pp. 96–98.
20. Cited by Wilsher, *Immigration Detention*, p. 13.
21. Wilsher, *Immigration Detention*, pp. 19, 20.
22. Cited by Wilsher, *Immigration Detention*, p. 37.
23. Wilsher, *Immigration Detention*, p. 37.
24. Cited by Wilsher, *Immigration Detention*, p. 37.
25. Cited by Wilsher, *Immigration Detention*, p. 40.
26. To detain in the manner described was to breach both *Magna Carta* and habeas corpus, where what both documents articulated was the imperative that incarceration could only follow what the Fifth Amendment of the American Constitution would term 'due process'. As Chapter 39 of *Magna Carta* had it: 'No free man is to be arrested, or imprisoned, or disseised, or outlawed, or exiled, or in any way destroyed, nor will we go against him, nor will we send against him, save by the lawful judgement of his peers or by the law of the land': *Magna Carta*, with a new commentary by David Carpenter (London: Penguin Books Ltd, 2015), p. 53. The purpose of this provision was to defend the individual against tyranny or, as it would subsequently come to imply, against the unfettered authority of the State.
27. Wilsher, *Immigration Detention*, p. 42.
28. Carl Schmitt, *Political Theology: Four Chapters on the Concept of Sovereignty*, tr. George Schwab, foreword by Tracy B. Strong (Chicago, IL and London: University of Chicago Press, 2007), p. 5.
29. Schmitt, *Political Theology*, p. 5. There has been no shortage of commentary on Schmitt since Agamben revived his thinking to explain the politics underlying the establishment of Camp X-Ray at Guantanamo Bay. The value of Schmitt here lies in the way he allows one to track the history whereby the non-person comes into view. Crucial, in this respect, is Schmitt's advocacy of 'arbitrariness' as a principle of decision-making. Writing about attempts to exclude 'arbitrariness' from jurisprudence, Schmitt offers the following view: 'This pattern of thinking is characteristic of the natural sciences. It is based on the rejection of all "arbitrariness" and attempts to banish from the realm of the human mind every exception' (Schmitt, *Political Theology*, p. 41). What we are offered here is a glimpse of the logic of the border. Whereas frequently, and not erroneously, the person at the border is shown to be in the grip of an excessive bureaucracy, what Schmitt underlines is that the decision at the border is also always, in some respect, arbitrary. His value as a thinker is precisely that he is not an apologist for sovereignty and all it entails but a believer, and as a believer, he says it how it is. Sovereignty is sovereignty because it is willing to act arbitrarily, to create exceptions; to cast persons into the outermost sphere.

30. For a compelling account of Arendt's lived experience of the transit camp at Gurs and of the ways that experience shaped and informed her writing, see Lyndsey Stonebridge, *Placeless People: Writing, Rights, and Refugees* (Oxford: Oxford University Press, 2018), pp. 46–69.
31. Arendt, *Origins*, p. xiv.
32. Arendt, *Origins*, p. 244.
33. Arendt, *Origins*, p. 275.
34. Arendt, *Origins*, p. 275.
35. Arendt, Origins, p. 269.
36. As the UNHCR reported, 'the current number of displaced globally is nonetheless the highest since the aftermath of World War II'. UNHCR, Global Trends: Forced Displacement in 2015.
37. Arendt, *Origins*, p. 466.
38. Arendt, *Origins*, p. 284.
39. Charles Olson, *The Collected Poems of Charles Olson (Excluding the Maximus Poems)*, ed. George Butterick (Berkeley, Los Angeles, CA and London: University of California Press, 1987), p. 46.
40. For discussion of such questionnaires and the larger discourse of 'eligibility', see Malcolm Proudfoot, European Refugees: 1939–1952 (London: Faber and Faber, 1957), pp. 240–248. The discussion is taken up here in Chapter 3: Moving.
41. See Samuel Moyn, *The Last Utopia: Human Rights in History* (Cambridge, MA: Harvard University Press, 2012); Mark Greif, *The Age of the Crisis of Man: Thought and Fiction in America, 1933–1973* (Princeton, NJ and Oxford: Princeton University Press, 2016); Stonebridge, *Placeless People*; Joseph Slaughter, *Human Rights, Inc.: The World Novel, Narrative Form, and International Law* (New York: Fordham University Press, 2007).
42. Stonebridge, *Placeless People*, pp. 14, 21.
43. Stonebridge, *Placeless People*, p. 20.
44. Charles Olson, *Collected Prose*, ed. Donald Allen and Benjamin Friedlander, intro. Robert Creeley (Berkeley, Los Angeles, CA and London: University of California Press, 1997), p. 240.
45. The qualifiers are important. As Stonebridge observes, and as I discuss at length in Chapter 2, 'The drafting committee of the UDHR was geographically, ethnically, politically and ideologically diverse. If the document still resonates powerfully now, this is as much because of the political and moral imagination, not to say the tenacity of progressives from the South, as anything else': Lyndsey Stonebridge, *Writing and Righting: Literature in the Age of Human Rights* (Oxford: Oxford University Press, 2021), p. 37.
46. Ato Sekyi-Otu, *Fanon's Dialectic of Experience* (Cambridge, MA: Harvard University Press, 1996), p. 87.

47. As Fanon puts it in the closing paragraph of *Studies in a Dying Colonialism*, 'The revolution in depth, the true one, precisely because it changes man and renews society, has reached an advanced stage. This oxygen which creates and shapes a new humanity—this, too, is the Algerian Revolution': Frantz Fanon, *Studies in a Dying Colonialism*, tr. Haakon Chevalier, intro. A.M. Babu (London: Earthscan Publications Ltd, 1989), p. 181.
48. Henri Lefebvre, *The Production of Space*, tr. Donald Nicholson-Smith (Oxford: Blackwell Publishing, 1991), p. 79.
49. Lefebvre, *The Production of Space*, p. 124.
50. Lefebvre, *The Production of Space*, p. 23.
51. Lefebvre, *The Production of Space*, p. 38.
52. Henri Lefebvre, *Critique of Everyday Life: Volume 1*, tr. John Moore (London, New York: Verso, 1991), p. 49.
53. Lefebvre, *Critique of Everyday Life*, pp. 243–245.
54. Donald Allen (ed.), *The New American Poetry, 1945–1960* (Berkeley, CA: University of California Press, 1999), p. xiv.
55. I am conscious, of course, in making this argument, that for the reader who might come to this book through an engagement with Arendt, or Fanon, or the history of rights or from the vantage of the various disciplines concerned with the politics of human movement the book invokes, Olson will seem an unexpected point of reference. This is explained in part by the marginal position of poetry in the intellectual division of labour, as if poetry's insights were a subset concerned all but exclusively with the development of the practice itself. I would further suggest, however, that Olson's relative marginality is also explained by the act of partial cultural forgetting that allowed the impulses towards a post-war reimagining of space themselves to become obscured. He should be considered a significant figure in that process of reimagining, not to the exclusion of other writers and their concerns but because, in ways the book articulates, he had an understanding of the need to think the question of his moment, the question of expulsion, in spatial terms. It was this that Donald Allen, the most influential editor of the period, understood about Olson's work and which makes him, in our moment of intensified expulsion, a still significant resource.
56. Hannah Arendt, *On Violence* (New York: Houghton Mifflin Harcourt Publishing, 1970), p. 14.
57. Arendt, *On Violence*, p. 18.
58. Etienne Balibar, 'On the Politics of Human Rights', *Constellations* 20:1 (2013), 24–25.
59. Paul Mason, *Clear Bright Future: A Radical Defence of the Human Being* (London: Allen Lane, 2019), pp. 106, 110. Mason's polemic is wide-ranging and his discussion of Arendt is only a short interlude in the discussion. His argument is compelling throughout, not least his concluding statement that:

> Living the antifascist life involves putting your body in a place where it can actually stop fascism, and having done so, to hold a tiny piece of liberated space long enough for other people to find it, populate it and live. The radical defence of the human being starts with you.

Mason, *Clear Bright Future*, p. 300. All of the arguments in this book go in that direction, towards a physical holding open of an antifascist space.
60. Mason, *Clear Bright Future*, p. 112.
61. Mason, *Clear Bright Future*, p. 110.
62. See Rachel Blau DuPlessis, 'Olson and His *Maximus Poems*', in David Herd (ed.), *Contemporary Olson* (Manchester: Manchester University Press, 2015), pp. 135–148.
63. Lefebvre, *Critique of Everyday Life*, p. 49.
64. Some of the strongest work on contemporary forced migration is concerned with precisely this sense of the contradictions, or paradoxes, of displacement. See, e.g. Judith Kohlenberger, *Das Flucht Paradox: Über unseren widersprüchlichen Umgang mit Vertreibung und Vertriebenen* (Vienna: Kremayr & Scheriau, 2022); Ayse Dursun and Birgit Sauer, 'The Asylum–Child Welfare Paradox: Unaccompanied Minors in Austria', Humanities and Social Sciences Communications (September 2021), https://doi.org/10.1057/s41599-021-00886-8 (accessed 6 June 2022).
65. Lefebvre, *The Production of Space*, p. 321. In both the work of Kohlenberger and of Dursun and Sauer, the articulation of the manifest contradictions of the lived experience of displacement constitutes a necessary step towards a new political space. These arguments were richly explored at an interdisciplinary workshop on the subject of *Refugee Tales* hosted by Sandra Mayer and Sylvia Mieszkowski at the University of Vienna (20–21 May 2022). As the present book considers, the question increasingly is how the state responds to the manifest contradictions of the stance it takes towards people who are compelled to move. One possibility is that such contradictions—for example, the extreme gesture of offshoring immigration detention—become the trigger for progressive political change. Another possibility is that states come to live with such contradictions at their border and in their midst, a condition of double standards we should recognize as a form of neo-colonialism.
66. See Jacques Rancière, 'Who Is the Subject of the Rights of Man?' South Atlantic Quarterly 103 (Spring/Summer 2004), 297–310.
67. To situate the Universal Declaration of Human Rights like this, as one text, albeit a key text, in a post-war discourse is to come up against the arguments of Samuel Moyn. Moyn's claim, in *The Last Utopia*, is that commentators have got the history of human rights wrong. Powerfully argued and carefully researched, his thesis is that the concept of human rights gained little uptake in the late 1940s and nor did it constitute a significant idiom in the de-colonial struggles that

shaped the decade after. Rather, as he claims, universal rights became a dominant discourse in the 1970s when competing internationalist paradigms were seen to have failed. It is not my argument that Moyn's history of the uptake of human rights is wrong; rather, as we look back now, from a moment in which non-personhood has once again emerged as a defining issue, there is a different kind of story it has become necessary to tell. The point, to put it bluntly, is that we are the future to which the warnings of so many post-war texts and authors addressed themselves. Which is not to suggest that we have not needed the Universal Declaration and the discourse of which it was part at intervening moments in history. It is to propose that in the moment in which we find ourselves, as regimes of all kinds default to the politics of geopolitical non-personhood, as we detain and deport on a mass scale, the need for the insights of that post-war discourse has become acutely pressing.

68. Stonebridge, *Placeless People*, p. 50.
69. Sekyi-Otu, *Fanon's Dialectic*, p. 80.
70. Édouard Glissant, *Poetics of Relation*, tr. Betsy Wing (Ann Arbor, MI: University of Michigan Press, 1997), p. 8.
71. Cited in Tom Clark, *Charles Olson: The Allegory of a Poet's Life* (Berkeley, CA: North Atlantic Books, 2000), p. xiv.
72. John Hope Simpson, 'Foreword', to Proudfoot, European Refugees, pp. 17, 18.
73. Global Detention Project, 'Detention Centres: Map View', https://www.globaldetentionproject.org/detention-centres/map-view (accessed 26 April 2022).
74. Arendt, *Origins*, p. 447.

1
The Non-Place

Via the Non-Place

The argument of this book starts with the image of a non-place. Or rather, it starts with an account of the impossible spatiality in which, as mid-century authors recognized, geopolitical non-personhood had come to be produced. The reason the book starts there, with the contradictory contours of the non-place, is that it is with the force of that negative impression that the post-war political imaginaries in question begin. In all of the bodies of writing considered here, in Arendt, in the Universal Declaration, in Olson, in Fanon, one finds at the beginning of their thought, or as a shaping trace in their project, an account of the impossible spatiality of the non-place to which their attempt to articulate a space for the human becomes a response.

The fact that some such account of the impossible space of geopolitical non-personhood can be found at the base of, or as defining trace within, the mid-century political imaginaries in question does not mean, necessarily, that the argument has to dwell there. One could state, as would be true, that such a negative spatiality was a condition of thought for all the authors in question, and then one could move on to the better imaginaries they sought to articulate by way of response.[1] This, however, would be to miss the point. It would be to miss the point because it would miss the hold such negative spatiality had on each imagination. It would miss the force with which, at some point in each body of work, the authors undertake to detail the implications of such a negative space. It would miss the fact that, for all the authors in question, it mattered that the contours of such a space should come through, that the topography of the space of non-personhood should be adequately registered.

In setting out to recover how the writers in question arrived at that topography, in showing how, through various texts and their inter-texts, a detailed architectonics of the non-place emerged, the aim in this chapter is to document three kinds of shared and overlapping intention. In the first place, the intention in detailing the impossible topography of the non-place was to begin to discern the basis on which a better political imaginary should exist.

It was necessary to go via an account of the space of non-personhood—to describe and name its contours—in order to arrive at articulations of space which did not result in expulsion. It was with this logic that Olson opened 'La Préface', the inaugurating poem that accompanied Corrado Cagli's drawings on witnessing the liberation of Buchenwald. As Olson put it:

> The dead in via
>   in vita nuova
>   in the way
> You shall lament who know they are as tender as the horse is
> You, do not you speak who know not.[2]

It is only, Olson proposes, via an understanding of the non-place that the lines of a viable spatiality, of the 'vita nuova' (the 'new life') will emerge. Or as Fanon puts it, introducing his own topography in *The Wretched of the Earth*,

> This approach to the colonial world, its ordering and its geographic layout, will allow us to mark out the lines on which a decolonized society will be organized.[3]

One finds this move in each of the bodies of work in question and in many of the texts they draw on, the authors tracing the outlines of spaces of non-personhood in order to articulate spatialities in which such non-personhood would not occur.

The Universal Declaration of Human Rights is exemplary in this respect and the chapter opens with an account of the way certain of its articles carry the negative impress of the non-place, how its prohibitions and expectations bring a carefully specified spatial dysfunctionality into view. The Universal Declaration, this is to say, gives us names for the non-place, names that it is crucial, whenever we see such spaces re-emerging, that we should continue to use.

A second kind of intention in detailing the topography of the non-place lay in mid-century authors' desire to warn. As various commentators sought to insist, the geopolitical conditions that underlay the mass production of non-personhood up to and during the Second World War continued to obtain after the war ended. Such warnings were carefully articulated and have to be carefully understood. Thus, as David Rousset would argue in his account of his experience at Buchenwald, exceptional as the scale and brutality of the genocidal crimes of the Second World War demonstrably were, the conditions that allowed spaces of non-personhood to be produced had hardly been eliminated with the war's end. Rousset was important to various mid-century writers, Arendt included, and difficult as such a warning was to hear, there was an understanding that it had to be registered and interpreted. The way this chapter frames such warnings is first by considering Olson's reading of the space of non-personhood as he found it rendered both by Cagli and by Rousset himself. The chapter then considers accounts of two settings in which, in the immediate aftermath of the war, the spatialities of non-personhood continued to exist: the displaced persons camps that resulted from post-war forced migration, as presented by Arendt, and the space of colonial non-personhood as documented by Fanon. It was Fanon's point that such settings for the production of non-personhood should not be thought separately, that their logics interlocked and intertwined. To trace that interlocking, as the chapter argues, is to register the full force of such warnings as Rousset's and to understand the significance of continuing to bring the negative spatiality of geopolitical non-personhood into view.

A third intention authors had in detailing the topography of the non-space was to articulate the impact of such spatialities on people themselves. Such impacts are documented throughout the discourse since to talk about the space of geopolitical non-persons is to talk about how such spaces are lived and felt. In particular, however, the final part of the chapter considers how, for Arendt and Fanon, it was crucial to document the lived, recurrent, daily experience of the spaces of non-personhood; the way such coercive spatialities intruded on, inhibited, and held in suspense basic human actions and forms of relation; the way, as both writers would document, such spaces made personhood all but impossible to sustain.

To describe such spaces—spaces in which personhood is all but impossible to sustain—as non-places is not to invent a term; rather, it is to enter the same kind of loop of conceptualization and forgetting one encounters when considering Henri Lefebvre's thinking about space. Thus, if the term 'non-place' can be said to have been conceptually established at any point, that moment was the publication of Marc Augé's *Non-Places: Introduction to an Anthropology of Supermodernity*. First published in 1992, Augé's essay on the non-place, like Lefebvre's much more rigorous inquiry into the production of spatiality, is an attempt to map a kind of space that he takes to be symptomatic of what he calls *supermodernity*. In the process, he arrives at moments of conceptual clarity that are helpful in framing the concerns of the present book. As he puts it,

If a place can be defined as relational, historical and concerned with identity, then a space which cannot be defined as relational, or historical, or concerned with identity will be a non-place.[4]

The question of non-relationality, in particular, is crucial to the understanding of the non-place this book looks to articulate, and Augé was right in his claim that such 'non-places are the real measure of our time'.[5]

Where Augé was wrong, or where his angle of vision was historically limited, was in his understanding of what such a 'measure' implied. Thus, as he puts it,

> In one form or another, ranging from the misery of refugee camps to the cossetted luxury of five-star hotels, some experience of non-place (indissociable from a more or less clear perception of the acceleration of history and the contraction of the planet) is today an essential component of all social existence.[6]

Augé's late-twentieth-century account of space and modernity is valuable, like Lefebvre's, in identifying certain geopolitical logics. It must be said, however, that only an essay written in the grip of postmodernism could propose a concept that incorporated both refugee camps and five-star hotels. In that sense, even as he names a term it is crucial to retain, he also commits an act of forgetting that must be registered as a cost of postmodernism's dislocation from history. Agamben, writing only a few years later, would begin the necessary act of recovery, bringing the historical meaning of the setting of geopolitical non-personhood into contemporary view. As he put it, in *Homo Sacer: Sovereign Power and Bare Life*,

> The camp as dislocating localization is the hidden matrix of politics in which we are still living, and it is this structure of the camp that we must learn to recognize in all its metamorphoses into the *zones d'attentes* of our airports and certain outskirts of our cities.[7]

Writing ten years before *State of Exception*, the text in which he reflected on the establishment of the camp at Guantanamo Bay, Agamben substantially re-oriented understanding of the non-place, what he called the 'dislocating localisation', proposing not a structural analogy between the camp and the hotel but the camp as 'hidden matrix of politics in which we are still living'.[8] When he refers to that politics, Agamben means, at some level, the politics we have been living since the Second World War—albeit a politics that, for a while, commentators allowed to slip from view. And when he refers us to the non-place (the 'dislocating localization') as the hidden matrix of that politics, he is referring to a logic that, even if in plain sight, remains hidden still. Still, only more so, sovereign states are effecting regimes of expulsion to which the non-place is both instrumental and the primary indicator. We need to understand the topography of the non-place because we need to know what, as a political matrix, it always tells us about where we are heading, and to grasp that topography, it is crucial to consider the discourse of the mid-century moment.

To recover the way that mid-century discourse looked to process the space of non-personhood is to make something approaching a theoretical move. Or rather, it is to catch interlocking accounts of the non-place before the term hardened into a theoretical counter. What one finds, in other words, in the mid-century moment are emergent understandings, all the more forceful because of their historical immediacy, of a political reality at the moment at which it comes into view. It is to recover what the non-place means through a network of writers who were in the process of grasping its implications. It is also, however, to find a different, less binary, less intellectually mechanical spatial response.

To read Augé, writing at a moment when the broad category of the non-place was conceptually visible but when its real historical significance had been allowed to slip from view, is to find oneself in a set of binaries that very quickly become corrosive on contemporary thought. The non-place, as he defines it, is to be understood as the opposite of the anthropological 'place' with its easily understood values of identity, history, and relationality. By this logic, to detail the destructive topography of the non-place would be, by implication, to shore up an account of place that, in turn, produces the polarity of belonging and otherness on which the act of expulsion can all too easily depend. Where this can quickly lead is to the degraded rhetoric of the so-called 'somewheres' and 'anywheres' that is the divisive frame for David Goodhart's polemic against human movement.[9] By contrast, to recover a discourse in which the reality of the non-place was adequately grasped— when it implied not a general category of itinerant spaces but a setting in which non-persons were produced—is to find thinking about the politics of space that does not default to the simplicity of opposition but which actively searches for, and feels towards, humanly sustainable modes of thought. As the subsequent chapters will argue, we need the post-war political imaginaries in question for the ways, as they indicated, a space for the human might be made. What this first chapter sets out to show is that we need such imaginaries also for their combined articulation of the spatiality of the mid-century non-place—a profoundly damaging setting which we are all too ready, in the present moment, to reconstruct and repopulate.

The Universal Declaration and the Outline of the Non-Place

The Universal Declaration of Human Rights was an act of language whose stated intention was to prevent the production of non-personhood. To say so is to evoke a whole landscape of debate—both contemporary with and subsequent to the promulgation of the document—that it is the intention of this book to contribute to and address. As will be detailed in Chapter 2, in particular, this book's argument is that it is necessary to think through the spatial implications of the Declaration if one is to begin to address such questions as those that flow from, for instance, Arendt's critique of the language of rights. To assert that the stated intention of the Declaration was to prevent the production of non-persons, is, however, at least at the level of expression, uncontroversial. As Article 6 puts it, catching an implication of the whole: 'Everyone has the right to recognition everywhere as a person before the law.'[10]

Such a statement is itself immediately spatial, with the key qualifier 'everywhere' signalling a requirement, at some level, to recalibrate geopolitical space. In so far, that is, as the Declaration's objective was to prevent the production of non-persons, so it had also to arrive at a presentation of political space according to which the settings in which such non-personhood was produced—the juridical non-space—would not exist. Such an exercise in mapping called for two guiding operations. On the one hand, it required the expression of certain basic consistencies of recognition across and also, ideally, between territories; consistencies whose intention was to guarantee that juridical suspensions did not come into force. On the other hand, what was required was an image, in outline, of the non-place itself, both as a reference against which to determine good practice and as a political warning. The complex question of the Declaration's consistency, a question which goes in part to the history of its composition and to the make-up of its authorship, will be considered in Chapter 2. What needs to be understood here are the ways in which, as it articulated the principle of juridical consistency, the Universal Declaration also outlined the non-place whose existence it was formulated to prevent. In so far, that is, as the authors of the Declaration collectively imagined a new kind of polity, so, at the same time, several articles combine to bring the dynamics of the non-place into view. Consider:

> Article 5. No one shall be subjected to torture or to cruel, inhuman or degrading treatment or punishment.
> Article 6. Everyone has the right to recognition everywhere as a person before the law.
> Article 9. No one shall be subjected to arbitrary arrest, detention or exile.
> Article 12. No one shall be subjected to arbitrary interference with his privacy, family, home or correspondence, nor to attacks upon his honour and reputation. Everyone has the right to the protection of the law against such interference or attacks.
> Article 14. (1) Everyone has the right to seek and to enjoy in other countries asylum from persecution.
> Article 15. (1) Everyone has the right to a nationality. (2) No one shall be arbitrarily deprived of his nationality nor denied the right to change his nationality.[11]

It could be argued that all articles of the Universal Declaration contribute, by implication at least, to an outline of the juridical non-place. By describing rights, and therefore a preferred polity, so, by definition, they articulate those elements the non-place lacks. Of the articles identified here as speaking more directly to the dynamics of the non-place itself, Article 6 is included because it specifies an absence that defines the non-place: the absence of 'recognition before the law'. In all the other instances, what is specified is a concrete reality of the non-place, a defining element of its topography and fabric: torture, cruel, inhuman, or degrading treatment; arbitrary arrest, detention, or exile; arbitrary interference with privacy; persecution; arbitrary deprivation of nationality. What this list constitutes is the Declaration's internal description of the non-place, a working sketch against which future political practice should be formed. Properly to understand that description, however, and the values that underpin it, one needs to perform two kinds of archaeology; the first, to indicate the discussions that informed key articles; the second, to bring forward those earlier foundational documents that the authors drew on to underpin their formulations.

Discussions informing the formulation of two articles, Articles 6 and 9, indicate the nature of the debates. Article 6, as Johannes Morsink observes, did not appear in any form in early drafts of the Declaration and only has an equivalent in two of the constitutions the principal drafter, John P. Humphrey, encountered in his preparatory survey: the Belgian and the Greek.[12] The Greek formulation of the issue is especially dramatic, announcing that, by its provision, 'civil death is abolished'. What Article 6 means to establish is what Humphrey termed 'legal personality', the point being to assert that no person might at any point, in any context, be held outside of—expelled from—legal consideration. The force of this point was not immediately felt, with the United Kingdom, the United States, and India each at some point proposing to vote against the article on the grounds that the concept underpinning it was either too legally technical, or too vague.[13] It was in the Third Committee that the underlying issue became apparent, when the Canadian delegate H.H. Carter drew on recent historical experience to clarify the issue. It was, he said, 'important to keep in mind [. . .] the possibility that certain persons might be deprived of their juridical personality by an arbitrary act of their government. Nazi Germany offered a recent example.'[14] To deprive a person, or group, of their juridical personality, Carter pointed out, just as the Nazi regime had stripped Jews of their citizenship rights, was the necessary preliminary to the other abuses that shaped the non-place. Only after that deprivation had been effected could the state justify such actions to itself.

The discussions informing Article 9, framed to prevent 'arbitrary arrest, detention or exile', were less sceptical since it was clearly understood that some such provision was necessary. The question, in this case, was how the right should be formulated. Early versions of the statement referred to the law, and therefore the given legal context, as a guarantee against the kind of deprivation entailed. The limitation of any such formulation was pointed out by Franz Bienenfeld, representative of the World Jewish Congress. As he observed, 'Under the Nazi regime thousands of people had been deprived of their liberty under laws which were perfectly valid', a set of processes Arendt would come to detail as part of her assessment of Eichmann's role in the Nazi genocide in *Eichmann in Jerusalem*.[15] The question was, therefore: if, as recent history demonstrated, reference to the law did not, in and of itself, guarantee protection against the kind of deprivation of liberty envisaged, how was such a protection to be formulated? The term taken to catch that meaning was 'arbitrary', signalling that form of treatment that might, in extreme circumstances, be permissible within a given legal framework but which nonetheless fundamentally offended against the principles enshrined in a declaration of rights. As the Lebanese delegate, Charles Malik, observed, the word 'arbitrary' thus carried a great deal of weight in the article, as elsewhere in the Declaration, becoming the document's key qualifier.[16]

How we are to understand the term 'arbitrary' as it appears in the context of the Declaration is thus a matter of some importance, it being the term against which a contemporary articulation of rights was posed. What it specified in the moment of the declaration's composition was a defining dynamic of fascism, whereby people rendered beyond juridical recognition were subject to treatment for which no account was deemed due. As a descriptor in a high-level, legal-political document, the term 'arbitrary' is at a considerable remove from historical reality, from the appalling brutality it intends to reference but does not catch. Its value, at that remove, is partly that it places us on the alert, that at the point at which we discern the arbitrary in politics, then, at some level of administration, a practice traceable to fascism has started to emerge. In another sense, however, the term has to be understood against a long view of human considerations of agency. In practice, that long view took the form of Humphrey's survey of national constitutions, a process that implicitly addressed the question of how attributes such as rights might be derived. While it gestured, in its preamble, to the rhetoric of natural rights, in its methodology, what the Declaration spoke to was the history of ideas.

The history in question was the convention of the founding legal-political statement, out of which the Declaration's emphasis on the arbitrary emerged. To invoke that tradition is, at some level, to draw on *Magna Carta*, the lasting importance of which is that it provides an articulation of what modern law understands as 'due process'. As the Fifth Amendment of the Constitution of the United States has it, no one shall be 'deprived of life, liberty or property without due process of law'.[17] The ostensible purpose of the Fifth Amendment, as with *Magna Carta*, is to provide protection: protection against the law by ensuring that the law itself respects the rights that are owed to the individual person. Such protection is intended to apply in all contexts, but in particular what it is designed to guard against is the arbitrary deprivation of liberty. To be placed outside of such protection, to be held beyond the reach of the given framing document, is be forced into a situation in which the arbitrary prevails.

It is helpful, here, to provide a definition. That which is arbitrary is based on random choice or personal will, and as it relates to power or a ruling body signifies the autocratic. Etymologically, it derives from the Latin, *arbiter*, which gives us the word arbitration but which, in its original sense, means 'judge, supreme ruler' out of which combination of meanings we discern the outline of the non-place that the authors of the Universal Declaration had in mind when they articulated their series of rights. What that non-place consists in, where it finds its dynamic, is in the condition of the arbitrary, a political space governed by a judge who acts on whim. It wasn't the role of the authors of the Declaration to detail such a space, only to name it as that which they intended to counter. Such pictures existed, however, at the moment of writing, one such being David Rousset's highly influential text *L'Univers Concentrationnaire*—an account of the non-place of the camp in which the topography itself denotes arbitrariness and where the name given to that operating principle is *Ubu Roi*.[18]

Rousset's Warning

In his invaluable study, *Charles Olson's Reading*, Ralph Maud records that among the texts by which Olson sought to orient himself in the immediate post-war moment, *L'Univers Concentrationnaire* was crucial. As Maud notes, although Olson didn't own a copy of Rousset's book, it is clear from his correspondence with Robert Creeley that he had read it and that he 'knew the book in French, before its translation as *The Other Kingdom*'.[19] For Maud, this reading was part of a wider commitment on Olson's part. As he puts it, 'We have to assume that Olson was conversant with all current political writing in the period 1939–45, and by instinctive habit beyond that.'[20] This is a large and significant claim, placing Olson at some kind of self-appointed intersection in the emergent political discourse of his moment. Even so, it was not through writing that Olson first registered the physical reality of the camps. That first understanding was via the drawings of Corrado Cagli, an Italian artist forced into exile by Mussolini, who served with the US army towards the end of the war. Cagli was in the Third Army Division that liberated Buchenwald and, working partly from a photographic record, he undertook to draw what he saw. As Maud puts it, Cagli 'had brought back the biggest and most ghastly news of all time in the form of drawings he had made at Buchenwald when his artillery unit had opened up the camp'.[21] Not given to overstatement, Maud's view is that, for Olson, the sight of the drawings (no doubt intensified by the fact that he was in the presence of the man who had made and, as it were, witnessed them) was utterly transformative. 'From that stop', as Maud observes, Olson set out to 'know a new beginning.'[22]

What Olson saw when he first looked into Cagli's drawings is well articulated by Glen Sujo in his essay *Legacies of Silence*. As Sujo writes of Cagli's 1945 pen-and-ink drawing, 'Boy in the Camp',

> an emaciated figure stares intently through dilated eyes, well aware of his own destitute state [...] Barbed-wire mules stretch out to infinity and a thin line marks out an otherwise vacant horizon.[23]

It is formally important to Cagli's composition that he opted not simply to present the situation photographically but, instead, to draw it. The effect of the drawing, as Sujo observes, is that he emphasizes not just the boy in the camp but the boy's distorted space, the wire coiling to infinity, the vacant horizon. A similar composition shapes Cagli's sketch 'Lying Corpses', where, as Sujo observes, the 'fidelity' of the artist's line 'so elegantly describes the sinuous matter, skeletal forms and strewn clothing, the repeated vertical of the receding fence and crematoria in the distance'.[24] More generally, as Sujo describes it, such depictions 'restore a link between the living and the dead and draw us into the space of the victim and the persecuted'.[25] Not to press the point too hard, but the news that Cagli brought back was not just of the catastrophic fact of the production of non-personhood on a genocidal scale but of the space, which is to say the non-place, in which such dysfunctional personhood had been constructed.

Fully to understand the impact of Cagli's images on Olson, it is helpful to understand exactly where Olson was, or at least how he was positioned politically, when he encountered them.[26] Having resigned his post at the Office for War Information (OWI) in May 1944, due, as he reported in a press release, to censorship by his superiors, Olson took up a series of short-term political positions. The first of these was on the Foreign Nationalities Division of the Democratic National Committee, charged, as his biographer Tom Clark notes, with 'getting out the ethnic vote'.[27] This was important work for Olson, 'formed' as he was 'by immigrant working class values' and deeply engaged as he was by post-war arguments for free human movement, notably J.C. and R.G. King's *Manifesto for Individual Secession into World Community*.[28] Olson's campaigning work was a success, contributing to a strong turnout among immigrant and working class voters in support of Roosevelt in the 1944 election, and when the role came to an end, though increasingly imagining a career as a writer, he continued to undertake political responsibility. Having maintained contact with Adam Kalikowski, a Polish exile with whom he had worked at the OWI, and with

Oscar Lange, who would become Polish Ambassador to the United Nations, Olson became an unofficial representative for Polish concerns. This had started towards the end of the war, with Olson informing Roosevelt about the situation in Nazi-occupied Poland, but became formal in 1946, when, as Clark reports, he took up a 'temporary position as lobbyist on behalf of Polish interests at early meetings of the United Nations Security Council'.[29]

As Ralph Maud states, it is important to be clear about the intensity of Olson's engagement with politics at the end of the war, the moment at which he transitioned to poetry. Through his role at the United Nations, following his work at the OWI, Olson was close to post-war international deliberations and to efforts, in that immediate aftermath, to arrive at global commitments. That such proximity to international politics informed his emergent thinking about poetics would become apparent when, in a speech he gave to the Pacific Northwest Writers' Conference in Washington (state) in August 1947, Olson, speaking under the title 'Poetry and Criticism', tested his apparently restricted brief. As he told his audience,

> What [...] angers me as much in writing as in foreign policy, are those who clutch old answers in a new, terrifying world. It is the act of the middle-aged, the reactionary [...] word-maker as well as policy-maker.[30]

For Olson, it was instinctive at this time to think writing and foreign policy in the same breath and to grasp the need for new expressions in relation to both.[31]

It was in this context of intense political engagement that Olson had written a short piece for the Socialist monthly, *Survey Graphic*, entitled 'People v. The Fascist, U.S. (1944)', in which he had considered the prospects for successful legislation against the kind of group defamation that defined fascist rhetoric. Informed by the arguments of the sociologist David Riesman, with whom he had taught at Harvard while he was a graduate student, and identifying 'Nazi anti-Semitic agitation' in particular, Olson's article concluded with a call to action:

> To depend today only upon civil liberties or the government to meet the evils of group libel is to avoid the battle. For the field of the fight is the people, that large and mobile public opinion which is the controlling force in politics. Defamation is aimed at the people. Give the fascist devil his due. He works there and there he must be met. He attacks opposing groups – "labor," for example, and weakens them in the eyes of the community as a

whole – and even in their own eyes. Or, instead of attacking the prevailing system, he cunningly shifts his defamation to relatively powerless scapegoats – Negroes, Jews, Mexicans. The Fascist manipulates group against group, and wedges in. He must be stopped there, and only a vigorous people can stop him.[32]

Here, again, it is important to be clear about the degree of Olson's engagement. His article against fascism is not a poet's complaint but a clearly formulated expression both of the space in which the fascist devil operates—'the field of the fight is the people'—and of the intensification of popular agency required to oppose the threat—'only a vigorous people can stop him'. As he transitioned form politics to poetry, this is to say, Olson was a theoretically informed anti-fascist, envisaging long-term strategies through which its development in the United States might be stopped. Even so, the images Cagli brought back from Buchenwald were transformative in their impact. What Olson found in the drawings was a negative construction of space that would continue to inform and shape his writing long into the post-war period. It was the force of this impression that led Olson to collaborate with Cagli on his first poetic publication, the chapbook *Y & X*, in which five drawings by Cagli were accompanied by five of Olson' s poems. It was the same impression of negatively constructed space that would motivate his viscerally polemical micro-essay, 'The Resistance'. What Cagli also necessitated, however, was further reading, a key text being Rousset's *L'Univers Concentrationnaire*.

Like the Universal Declaration, and like Arendt's *Origins of Totalitarianism*, *L'Univers Concentrationnaire* was projective in intent.[33] Its aim was to burn an impression of the fascist non-place so deeply into the language that its outline would be discernible in the event that its structures should ever begin to reappear. Having worked before the war as professor of philosophy, and having been active in the early organization of the French Resistance, Rousset was first imprisoned at Fresnes, near Paris, before being held for 'sixteen months in the concentration camps of Buchenwald, Helmstedt, Neuengamme and Wöbbelin.'[34] As Ramon Guthrie notes in the introduction to his text, having been freed by the US 82nd Airborne Division in May, 1945, 'He returned to Paris weighing 114 pounds.'[35] Presenting his experiences in an associative poetic prose whose effect is cumulative and profound, Rousset understood it as his task to write with such force from the present moment that the post-war future might register the non-place should it begin to re-emerge. And like Arendt, whose history of totalitarianism his text informed, Rousset was careful to observe that such a re-emergence was entirely possible, the fascist non-place having its structural underpinning in imperial capitalism. As he put it, by way of conclusion,

> The existence of the camps is a warning [. . .] Germany interpreted, with an originality in keeping with her history, the crisis that led her to the concentrationary universe. But the existence and the mechanism of that crisis were inherent in the economic and social foundations of capitalism and imperialism. Under a new guise, similar effects may reappear tomorrow.[36]

That the 'existence of the camps' was, at some level, inherent in the 'economic and social foundations of capitalism' would be emphasized by Fanon, as discussed below, in his brilliantly detailed account of the negative spatiality of the colonial non-place in *The Wretched of the Earth*. It was precisely Fanon's point, as it would be Arendt's point, that 'Under a new guise, similar effects may reappear tomorrow.' Where the prospective lesson was to be found, as Rousset understood it, was largely in the spatiality of the setting itself. Witness the fact that he opens with a short account of the space of the camps in which he was incarcerated. Thus, for instance,

> Helmstedt: long concrete sheds in a circle, camouflaged with their own suppuration of filth, cases of bombs and torpedoes stacked in the fields of wheat and mustard and, on the plain, gaunt silhouettes of derricks black against the sky [. . .] freight cars, strewn at random on the ruined tracks beyond the lifeless stones in the sprawling gaps of hunger, pierced from time to time by the clamor of a war close at hand but never grasped.[37]

By starting with a description of the space in which non-personhood is produced, Rousset's objective is to show how the spatial organization itself is constructive of that condition. At various points within the text, we are presented with startling disjunctions: a Christmas tree at Dora, which the prisoners were allowed to admire while standing half-naked in the snow; the brothel at Buchenwald situated opposite the hospital; the Buchenwald zoo established across the road from the camp. What such details disclose is an orchestration of the relation of person to space such that personhood itself is difficult to sustain. Rousset's name for the principle of that orchestration is Ubu Roi, taken from Alfred Jarry's character:

> The camps are the realm of King Ubu. Buchenwald lives under the sign of a monstrous whimsicality, a tragic buffoonery.[38]

What that 'monstrous whimsicality' amounts to is what the authors of the Universal Declaration called the arbitrary, that condition which is the opposite of the rights-based polity, the non-place of the camp constituting a setting in which the space itself is arbitrarily composed.

The substance of Rousset's textual warning can be seen to rest in the conduct the arbitrary spaces of the camp give rise to, the spatiality bearing on the way persons comport themselves and are conveyed. Human movement itself bears the impress of the setting's monstrous whimsicality, such that men,

> blinded by blows that catch them off guard, reel back, stumble against each other, shove, jump and land, tottering on their bare feet in the dirty snow, hobbled with fear, their stiff, nightmare gestures like rickety automatons.[39]

Here, spatiality informs physicality, a series of uncoordinated movements constituting a person's passage across the camp. Elsewhere, the process is administrative, or quasi-legal, rather than physical:

> a case is never finished, never closed. The trial goes on, expands, fattens upon personages born of itself, without any reason ever being formulated. An order arrives. A simple decision without any commentary or explanation.[40]

It is in such symptoms as these that one hears the force of Rousset's warning, with the logic of the concentrationary universe disclosed not in its most terrifying excesses but in the procedural distortions through which non-personhood is routinely produced. Similarly, then, where work was a factor, it was introduced into the regime, 'without ever losing sight of the principal and primary purpose of the camps. It was only a new and inexhaustible source of incongruities.'[41] One might note the fact that whereas people currently seeking asylum in the United Kingdom are not permitted to work and can therefore be first imprisoned and then detained if they are found to have taken employment illegally, they are nonetheless allowed to work within a detention centre at a rate of pay of £1/hour. One effect of such contradictory regulations is corporate profit, with detainees working to maintain the privatized centres they are held in at a fraction of the minimum wage.[42]

A further function, however, is to generate incongruity, such incongruity being axiomatic to a setting in which non-personhood is maintained.[43]

What Rousset presents his post-war reader with, in other words, is a topography of the non-place whose dynamics bear directly on the way personhood is dismantled and broken down. What determines those dynamics is something like an environmental assault on continuity, with each new advance, whether spatial or temporal, bringing discontinuity and rupture. At which point, we are tending towards the idea of personality, and the trope of personal development that, as is discussed in Chapter 2, underpins Joseph Slaughter's account of the language of rights. What should be underlined, however, is that, in Rousset, the argument always comes back to space, to the spatiality through which non-personhood is produced. Thus, just as character cannot be shown to see its way ahead, so the space itself is without continuity. The people detained are

> conscious only of having lost a world which must have been unique and which lies hidden perhaps just beyond the network of electrified barbed wires, far beyond the unhorizoned void of tangled rails.[44]

As in Cagli's drawing of the 'Boy in the Camp', there is, in Rousset's text, no discernible horizon. The non-place, Rousset wants us to be reminded, is rendered fundamentally spatially dysfunctional; dysfunctional to the point of impossibility.

The Resistance

Olson's distillation of the lessons he learned from Cagli and from Rousset (as well as from other witness accounts of the Camps such as Louis Martin-Chauffier's *L'Homme et La Bete*) took the form of his condensed essay statement 'The Resistance'. Written in 1949, 'The Resistance' was dedicated to Jean Riboud who, like Rousset, was an early organizer of the French Resistance and who was also, for that reason, incarcerated at Buchenwald. As with so many of Olson's most important statements, in prose and poetry, 'The Resistance' first found expression in a letter (to Natasha Goldowski of Black Mountain College) and was eventually published in 1953, in Vincent Ferrini's magazine *Four Winds*.[45] Only six paragraphs long, it was nonetheless a defining early statement for Olson; foundational, one can argue, to his subsequent thinking about space and movement.

The value of Olson's essay-statement in the context of these discussions—of Rousset, of Cagli, of the apprehensions of the Universal Declaration of Human Rights—lies in its intention of outlining a non-arbitrary relation between person and environment. As the essay starts by stating,

> This is eternity. This now. This foreshortened span. Men will recognize it more easily (& dwell in it) when we regain what the species lost, how long ago: nature's original intention with the organism that it live 130 years. Or so Bogomolets' researches into the nature of connective tissue seem to prove. True or not, with or without aid from his own biosis, man has no alternative: he accepts his mortal years as his eternity. It is the root act.[46]

In outlining what it means for people to 'dwell' in the space in which they find themselves, which is to say to arrive at a sustainable mode of existence, Olson's principal objective is to show that not everything is possible. For both Rousset and Arendt, that slogan, 'everything is possible' constituted the motif of totalitarianism, bearing the meaning that anything can be done to or with the human form. From which it follows that the moment had come to re-establish limits. And, as Olson sees it, confronted by accounts of all kinds of brutally arbitrary operations and arrangements, such a limit had to be established in the shape and extent of the human form itself.[47] An acceptance of the non-arbitrariness of the mortal span was, as Olson understood it, 'the root act'.

The more crucial element of the statement, however, presents the human 'biosis' not in temporal but in spatial terms. As Olson puts it, in paragraphs four and five,

> Man came here by an intolerable way. When man is reduced to so much fat for soap, superphosphate for soil, fillings and shoes for sale, he has, to begin again, one answer, one point of resistance only to such fragmentation, on organized ground, a ground he comes to by a way the precise contrary of the cross, of spirit in the old sense, in old mouths. It is his own physiology he is forced to arrive at. And the way—the way of the beast, of man and the Beast.
>
> It is his body that is his answer, his body intact and fought for, the absolute of his organism in its simplest terms, this structure evolved by nature, repeated in each act of birth, the animal: man, the house he is, this house that moves, breathes, acts, this house where his life is, where he dwells against the enemy, against the beast.[48]

As a marker of Olson's transition from politics to poetry, 'The Resistance' should be understood as the equivalent in poetics of the explicitly political statement of 'People v. The Fascist, U.S.'. What identifies 'The Resistance' as such—as an anti-fascist statement in the form of poetics—is Olson's reference to the practices of reducing the bodies of those exterminated to 'fat for soap, superphosphate for soil'. Olson's reference is to the non-place of the camp via the practices that most define its genocidal realities, where the task, by way of response, is to arrive at an 'organized ground'. To trace Olson's thinking in 'The Resistance' back through his encounter with Cagli and his reading of Rousset, through to his depiction of the site of anti-fascist action in 'People v. The Fascist U.S.', is to register the force of the spatiality of the non-place on his imagination and therefore to appreciate why a politics framed as poetics should take the form of a commitment to the re-articulation of human space.

The key move in 'The Resistance' thus lies in the assertion of the spatiality of human physiology itself: 'this house that moves, breathes, acts, this house where his life is, where he dwells'. It is an assertion that subsequent theories of space would come to take for granted. As Lefebvre would observe in *The Production of Space*, 'Human beings—why do we persist in saying "man"?—are in space; they cannot absent themselves from it, nor do they allow themselves to be excluded from it.'[49] Or, as Augé would write, in his discussion of *Non-Places*,

> This magical effect of spatial construction can be attributed without hesitation to the fact that the human body itself is perceived as a portion of space with frontiers and vital centres, defences and weaknesses, armour and defects.[50]

In the mid-century, it could not be taken as read that human beings were 'in space' and would not be expelled from it, since spatial settings had been produced in which expulsion was precisely the effect. Against the intrusions and distortions that constitute the non-place, and which result in the appalling fragmentation that sees bodies broken and commodified, Olson thus asserts the physical presence of the person as the basis for their recognition, it being the person's spatiality, their relation to space, that must, as a matter of urgency, be defended. That humans have to be reinserted in the space they occupy is evidence of the 'intolerable way' by which recent history has travelled. Where that 'way' has ended up is in the juridical non-place, a place in which a person's relation to space, and the space itself, is rendered fundamentally dysfunctional, where, by the ongoing equivalent of the 'entry fiction', a person's physical presence is discursively denied. Olson's project, like the various contemporary projects being documented here, was to establish, or recover, or somehow formulate an understanding of spatiality in its largest sense according to which personhood might be adequately recognized and therefore adequately protected. To envision such a non-expulsive space would involve the sustained articulation of forms of human agency and relationality, as the second part of this book (Chapters 3, 4, and 5) will come to discuss. What such an envisioning required as a kind of ground, however, was a reassertion of the body in space, an expression of space from which, as Lefebvre would argue, the human form could not be absented.

Olson's transition, between 1944 and 1949, from the writer of 'People v. the Fascist U.S.' to the writer of 'The Resistance', is a measure of the importance of engaging with political imaginaries that take poetic form. He had a set of legal-political terms to articulate the shape of opposition to the fascist threat – the threat, of group defamation, the threat of 'Nazi anti-Semitic agitation' - a set of terms that would remain useful. What he came also to understand was the necessity for what can, in good faith, be called a poetic response, a response in which poetry's grasp of relationality, its capacity to situate persons in relation to their environment, might be a basis for resisting the production of the non-place. Fully to understand his intentions for 'The Resistance' itself, however, one needs to know just a little about the circumstances of its publication, Olson finally publishing the piece in 1953 in Vincent Ferrini's journal *Four Winds*.

Already based in Gloucester at the time Olson began to write his epic poem in relation to the place, Ferrini can be understood (or disregarded) as the poet Olson had somehow to credit, or at least engage, before embarking on *The Maximus Poems*. What this misses is the fact that, as Ammiel Alcalay documents, by the time Olson located him, Ferrini had an established literary project of his own, grounded in a long history of activism both as a member of the Communist Party and as labour organizer.[51] His poetry spoke to that historical reality and, though limited in technical and rhetorical range, nonetheless brought with it an implicitly international world view.[52] That Olson related to Ferrini in this way, as somebody to whom to address his literary-political objectives, is apparent from a letter he wrote Ferrini from Washington D.C., dated 23 May 23 1950; a letter which, as was often the case with Olson, unfolded to become a poem:

> the only object is
> a man, carved
> out of himself, so wrought he
> fills his given space, makes
> traceries sufficient to
> other's needs
> (here is
> social action, for the poet,
> anyway, his politics,
> his news)⁵³

The poet's politics, Olson tells Ferrini, his 'social action', is to carve out for the person their given space. Olson's language here is gendered, just as, as Susan Howe has clearly stated, his larger project was all too frequently gendered, it being crucial, as Howe makes clear in interview, to be explicit on the question of his misogyny.⁵⁴ At the same time, in the same breath, Howe insists on recognizing Olson's generative handling of space. Describing, as Lytton Smith notes, 'George Butterick's carefully-spaced editing of Olson's poetry as "one of the most generous gifts to poetry in my time"', Howe suggests that the 'feminine is very much in his poems in another way', in the 'sound forms. The Fractured syntax, the gaps', it being Butterick's achievement, as Olson's editor, to *print* the poet's space.⁵⁵ Crucial as he was to her own feminist historical inquiries, Howe is explicit and unrelenting in documenting the gendered quality of Olson's text. What we need to not *not* hear, however, she argues, is his insistence, as he puts it in his letter to Ferrini, on a 'given space', on the 'traceries sufficient to other's needs'. In the face of the news of the non-place, the news that Cagli brought back from Europe, the poet's politics, their 'social action', as Olson tells Ferrini, is to seek to re-establish the person in space.

Qualifying Persons: Arendt and the Post-War European Non-Place

David Rousset closed *L'Univers Concentrationnaire* with a warning. The 'existence and mechanism', he stated, of the crisis that had led Germany to the concentrationary universe, 'were inherent in the economic and social foundations of capitalism and imperialism'. It therefore followed that, 'Under a new guise similar effects may reappear tomorrow.'⁵⁶ Rousset's phrasing was judicious, and it is important to be careful in echoing his observation. His point was not to predict an imminent reversion to the methods of the concentration camp (though neither did his closing remarks preclude such a possibility). His observation, more precisely, was that since the underlying logic of the camps lay in the 'economic and social foundations of capitalism and imperialism' (with both conjunctions being critical to the point), therefore a comparable development remained immanently possible. To identify what he carefully termed 'similar effects' was thus to put the post-war world on the alert. The danger, as he saw it, was less likely to lie in a precise replication of Nazi methodology but rather in the reproduction of the structural circumstances out of which the concentrationary itself had emerged. What this meant was the re-emergence of the non-place, that setting in which the protections that, in theory, underwrote the relation of the individual to the state were held in suspense or abeyance.

One setting in which the structural circumstances of the non-place re-emerged in the immediate aftermath of the war was the territory to which the obligations of human rights should most clearly have been extended. Arendt herself has proved the most enduring commentator on this circumstance, observing of what she termed the 'internment camp' that while

> human rights [...] are enjoyed only by citizens of the most prosperous and civilized countries [...] the situation of the rightless themselves [...] has deteriorated just as stubbornly, until the internment camp—prior to the second World War the exception rather than the rule for the stateless—has become the routine solution for the problem of domicile of the 'displaced persons'.[57]

Writing in 1957, with the 'number of stateless people [...] larger than ever', with 'one million "recognized" stateless' and more than 'ten million so-called "*de facto*" stateless', Arendt observed the paradox that 'the moment human beings [...] had to fall back upon their minimum rights, no authority was left to protect them and no institution willing to guarantee them'.[58] Abandoned to 'the barbed-wire labyrinth into which events had driven them', what the post-war stateless demonstrated, in the non-places they were compelled to occupy, was that 'no one seems able to define with any assurance what these general human rights, as distinguished from the rights of the citizen, really are'.[59]

Arendt's account of the pathology of the post-war internment environment is critical to our ongoing understanding of the human reality of the non-place. Few commentators worked harder than she did to grasp and articulate the meaning of the non-personhood such settings produced.⁶⁰ She is crucial, also, in consolidating Rousset's logic: that the *univers concentrationnaire* established a set of spatial practices towards which politics was disposed to default, the structure of the camp as such, if not in its genocidal excesses, proving a defining element of the post-war geopolitical environment.⁶¹ Where Arendt was in error, I want to suggest, was in the way, as a consequence, she assessed the implications of human rights. Rather, arguably, than a lack of clarity on the question of general human rights, what the procedures governing the non-place demonstrated was a certainty about the principles being breached. Where one finds this immediately after the war is in the way the question of rights was handled in a European context and, in particular, in two texts relating to the question of qualification: the first in the context of the displaced persons camp, the second bearing on the European colony.

As Gerard Daniel Cohen has documented, the US term 'displaced person' was applicable to great numbers of people across the globe in the immediate aftermath of the war: between 24 and 40 million people in China could be said to be displaced; up to 12 million people in Japan.⁶² What the term came principally to refer to, however, under the auspices of the United Nations, were those displaced in Europe, with approximately 8 million so-called 'DPs' occupying Germany at the end of the war. Of those, some 6–7 million people were quickly repatriated, often, as Cohen reports, with tragic consequences. Where post-war political practice came to settle and develop was in relation to those still displaced at the beginning of 1946, the so-called 'last million', the future of whom was understood to be predictive of the post-war international environment. As the *New York Times* editorial of 2 February 1946 put it, 'the fate and status of hundreds of thousands of human beings' was 'clearly an international responsibility', a sense of obligation that triggered far-reaching pronouncements. Witness Emanuel Mounier's declaration that France was '"a country where an exiled, desolate, and desperate man will always find a hand stretched out to him with no questions asked"'.⁶³ That there was a genuine desire to arrive at a language whereby an exiled person would be received with no questions asked will be demonstrated in Chapter 2. It was out of this desire that the political imaginaries with which this book is concerned were born, the Universal Declaration giving rise to the protections (however compromised) of the 1951 Convention Relating to the Status of Refugees. In practice, however, in the immediate aftermath of the war, many questions were asked.

Where the questions occurred was at the point of definition. The key task in the context of the DP camp was, as an International Refugee Organization (IRO) handbook outlined, to determine '"Who is a genuine, bona fide and deserving refugee?"'[64] Inscribing administrative practice that would inform much subsequent policy towards human movement, the *Manual for Eligibility Officers* issued detailed advice to IRO staff on how to identify the 'non-genuine' claimant. First published in 1948 and running to 160 pages, the manual constituted the formalization of a policy the IRO inherited from its predecessor organization, the United Nations Relief and Rehabilitation Administration (UNRRA). As Cohen documents, under the auspices of the UNRRA, 'Allied screenings' of displaced persons 'borrowed from denazification proceedings' conducted under the auspices of the Nuremberg Trials. Thus,

> Just as German citizens filled out much-despised questionnaires designed by Allied occupiers to uncover active supporters of Nazism, their DP neighbours were handed 'eligibility questionnaires' issued by UNRRA to verify nationalities, dates of displacement, and wartime personal histories.[65]

The purpose of such questionnaires was to determine the question of jurisdiction itself, to establish who, having been genuinely displaced, was permitted then to be relocated. To answer satisfactorily was to be granted juridical standing, recognition somewhere before the law. Not to answer satisfactorily was to have such recognition thrown into doubt, to be held in the suspense of what Arendt termed 'internment', the quasi-juridical process determining jurisdiction. What this meant in reality was prolonged deprivation, not least because residency in the camps invariably entailed a prohibition on work. Reporting on the situation of the DP camps in 1953, the Council of Europe confirmed Arendt's view. As the authors put it,

> The conscience of the peoples of Europe should revolt at the fact that among them are living millions of persons bearing the label of 'surplus' [...] What of the mental outlook of these beings cast out by society? What of the young people, whose earliest impressions are of the wretchedness of refugee camps or of permanent unemployment.[66]

The fact that such institutionally sponsored suspension of personhood, 'wretchedness' as the Council of Europe termed it, occurred at the point at which the obligations entailed by rights ought properly to have been invoked, is what prompted Arendt to diagnose an indefinability at the heart of the discourse. In fact, what institutional practice demonstrated was something like the reverse, the process of interrogation regarding eligibility disclosing a sure understanding of the commitments the recognition of rights entailed. As the British-based Refugee Defence Committee report 'Is It Nothing to You?' put it 1949, 'It does not need a complicated system of legal jurisdiction such as that set up by IRO to discover the fact that a person is a Refugee.'[67]

What the processes of sifting and interrogation that shaped the post-war environment of the displaced person can be taken to demonstrate is not the weakness and incoherence but rather the substance of the concept of general rights. Such was the force of the implied claim that a whole new jurisprudence had to be created, the express purpose of which was to establish that a recognizable entitlement did *not* apply. To observe the procedures of the non-place, this is to suggest, is to register a setting generated by an identifiable act of institutional denial.[68] Where such denial was writ largest in the post-war moment, as Marie-Benedicte Dembour has documented, was in the institution of Europe itself, which is to say in the formulation of the European Convention of Human Rights.

Drafted in the two years following the Universal Declaration, and adopted in 1950, the object of the Convention, as Dembour describes it, was

> to defend citizens—not any human being—against arbitrariness by the state. The hope was that the revolutionary mechanism put in place, with complaints by mere individuals allowed for the first time in history to be adjudicated by an international court, would make it possible to avoid another European descent into anything resembling Nazism or fascism.[69]

Where the Convention differed from the Universal Declaration was in its intended usability, the purpose of the document being to effect protection rather than simply outline in what such protection should consist. From which it followed that the question of scope and of extent was more sharply drawn, focusing in particular on whether the articulation of rights inscribed by the document extended as far as the colonial setting.

Dembour describes in detail the arguments that shaped the drafting process, noting that, in its first iteration, the understanding was that a Convention that did not apply in the colonies was 'politically unfeasible'.[70] For the Belgians, who held to this basic view, the object with respect to the overseas territories was to secure an acknowledgement of what was termed 'local needs and the standards of civilization of the native population'.[71] For the British, repeating arguments they had first made during the drafting of the Universal Declaration, what was required was an acknowledgement of the 'autonomy which its dependent territories constitutionally enjoyed' and therefore the inapplicability, via British endorsement of the final document, of the extension of rights to its colonial regimes.[72] What resulted, despite arguments to the contrary that clearly spelt out the contradictions, was a clause (Article 63) that accommodated the colonial position, subsequently termed the 'Colonial Clause'. Thus,

1. Any State may at the time of its ratification or at any time thereafter declare by notification addressed to the Secretary General of the Council of Europe that the present Convention shall, subject to paragraph 4 of this Article, extend to all or any of the territories for whose international relations it is responsible.
2. [Provides for a one-month delay before this declaration comes into force.]
3. The provisions of this Convention shall be applied in such territories with due regard, however, to local requirements.
4. Any State which has made a declaration in accordance with paragraph 1 of this article may at any time thereafter declare on behalf of one or more of the territories to which the declaration relates that it accepts the competence of the Court to receive applications from individuals, non-governmental organisations or groups of individuals as provided by Article 56 (now 34) of the Convention.[73]

Clauses 1 and 4 entitle the signatory power, should it so wish, to extend the convention to territories for which it is 'responsible', not declaring explicitly because the document doesn't like to, that such an extension need not apply. Clause 3, on the other hand, allows for 'due regard ... to local requirements', which phrase cuts irremediably across the geopolitical consistency to which the Universal Declaration aspired. What Article 63 enters, in other words, is a qualification, just as the IRO handbook sought a qualification, generating a circumstance, a non-place, in which the protections entailed by a general concept of rights do not apply. The document, in other words, and the institution, Europe, for which it stands, is compelled to enter into a contradiction, producing a non-place, a space in which the principles in question are suspended, at precisely the juncture at which the extension of rights ought properly to obtain.

The Colonial Non-Place

What needs to be understood here is what, in reality, the qualifications of Article 63 referred to, what really were the local requirements that a curtailment of the Convention's geographical extent was intended to meet. To which end, one might consider a footnote in *The Wretched of the Earth*, in which the reality of the so-called Colonial Clause is plainly delineated; in which the non-place delineated by the qualifying article is shown to be brutally maintained.

As Fanon puts it, quoting his own article in *Résistance Algérienne* No. 4, dated 28 March 1957,

> It was then agreed (in the Assembly) that savage and iniquitous repression verging on genocide ought at all costs to be opposed by the authorities: but Lacoste replies, 'Let us systematize the repression and organize the Algerian man-hunt'. And, symbolically, he entrusts the military with civil powers, and gives military powers to civilians. The ring is closed. In the middle, the Algerian, disarmed, famished, tracked down, jostled, struck, lynched, will soon be slaughtered as a suspect. Today, in Algeria, there is not a single Frenchman who is not authorized and even invited to use his weapons. There is not a single Frenchman, in Algeria, one month after the appeal for calm by the UNO, who is not permitted, and obliged to search out, investigate and pursue suspects.
>
> One month after the vote on the final motion of the General Assembly of the United Nations, there is not a European in Algeria who is not party to the most frightful work of extermination of modern times. A democratic solution? Right, Lacoste concedes; let's begin by exterminating the Algerians, and to do that, let's arm the civilians and give them *carte blanche*. The Paris Press, on the whole, has welcomed the creation of these armed groups with reserve. Fascist militias, they've been called. Yes; but on the individual level, on the plane of human rights, what is fascism if not colonialism when rooted in a traditionally colonialist country?[74]

The reason for quoting Fanon at such length is that here, in a single explosive footnote, all the discourses and operations that inform the construction of the non-place are brought to bear in a moment of defining violence. Against the backdrop of United Nations discussions intended to extend human recognition, Robert Lacoste, the French governor general, suspends the law, bringing into force a state of emergency in which every European becomes a member of the militia.[75] With 'the ring closed', and at the centre of the action, Algerian citizens occupy the topography of the non-place. Calling to mind Rousset's account of men making their way across the environment of the camp, Fanon presents actions compromised by arbitrariness, 'the Algerian, disarmed, famished, tracked down, jostled, struck, lynched'. What this constitutes, as Fanon understands, in its rendering and production of non-personhood, is a practice clearly recognizable as structurally fascist. And what he further understands, just as Rousset indicated, is the synergy of fascism and colonialism. As he puts it, triangulating the key elements of the discourse, 'on the individual level, on the plane of human rights, what is fascism if not colonialism when rooted in a traditionally colonialist country?'

Fanon's footnote draws *The Wretched of the Earth* into deep connection with the discourse of the non-place outlined so far. In the image of the ring closed around the Algerian resistance, in flagrant breach of the United Nations' assertion of minimal human rights, Fanon identifies an inevitable concentration of the colonial topography that, at the outset of his text, it is his intention to analyse. 'The colonial world', as he puts it, outlining the basis of all subsequent actions, 'is a world cut in two. The dividing line, the frontiers are shown by barracks and police stations.'[76] What the line divides are different juridical zones, the settler zone where the law applies and the native zone where it is arbitrarily enforced. Thus,

> All that the native has seen in his country is that they can freely arrest him, beat him, starve him: and no professor of ethics, no priest has ever come to be beaten in his place, nor to share their bread with him. As far as the native is concerned, morality is very concrete: it is to silence the settler's defiance, to break his flaunting violence—in a word, to put him out of the picture. The well-known principle that all men are equal will be illustrated in the colonies from the moment that the native claims that he is the equal of the settler.[77]

In Fanon, in other words, what becomes 'savage and iniquitous repression' in the moment of resistance is entirely inherent in the colonial organization of space: the arbitrariness with which the 'native' can be treated—'they can freely arrest him, beat him, starve him'—establishing the basis where, as the colonial regime deems necessary, 'the most frightful work of extermination will be carried out'.

What such a logic produces is a form of non-personhood from which, as Fanon insists, only violence can be the end result. To make the point, he quotes Aimé Césaire, from *Les Armes Miraculeuses,* published in 1946:

> THE REBEL (harshly): My name—an offence; my Christian name—humiliation; my status—a rebel; my age—the stone age.
> THE MOTHER: My race—the human race. My religion—brotherhood.
> THE REBEL: My race: that of the fallen. My religion ... but it's not you that will show it to me with your disarmament....[78]

The Rebel's prosody is familiar. Compare and contrast Olson's speaker in 'La Préface':

> 'I will die about April 1st...' going off
> 'I weigh, I think, 80lbs...' scratch
> 'My name is NO RACE' address
> Buchenwald   new Altamira cave.

The resemblance is striking. Olson's speaker echoes Césaire's Rebel in addressing a series of questions, documenting name and race and locating himself in what Césaire calls 'the stone age', which is to say 'new Altamira cave'. Two possibilities emerge. The first is that, in 1946, both Césaire and Olson arrived at the questionnaire as their way of communicating identity, with both speakers articulating a subject position in relation to questions issuing from an administrative procedure designed to establish, or deny, their worth. The second, more likely I suspect, is that Olson (in his voracious reading and determination to find a form equal to contemporary circumstance) came across Césaire and adopted his mode. Either way, what one has here is a consolidation of the outline of non-personhood, differently situated but projecting a shared mode of expression that serves, if nothing else, to dramatize the intersection of the colonial and the fascist, 'on the individual level, the plane of human rights'.

Nowhere, perhaps, is the logic of the non-place more clearly formulated than in Fanon's footnote. The discourse of human rights exists to preclude the construction of settings in which arbitrariness is the organizing principle. It proposes a set of relations which, by definition, extend across space and which intend to guarantee an environment in which personhood is recognized. To suspend the implications of that discourse, to suspend its entitlements and obligations, is to intend to produce such a non-place. It is not the case, therefore, as Arendt proposed, that 'no one seems able to define with any assurance what the general human rights [. . .] really are'. Rather, such rights are understood so clearly that where their claim is to be denied, they have to be actively suspended. The issue, in other words, is not lack of clarity. The issue, rather, is that what the discourse embodied in the Universal Declaration promises to open up is a radical political space, a space that challenged decision-makers at every level, and not least those decision-makers responsible for the European Convention. The following chapters will pursue these spatial implications, considering in particular how the political imaginaries in question sought to reimagine geopolitical space. What that work of reimagination came out of was a deep consideration of the non-place, both as an immediate fact and as an immediate legacy of the Second World War. What needs to be considered before proceeding, however, is what that non-space meant for people, how in the writing of the period the lived experience of non-personhood was understood and presented.

'A Being Hemmed In'

In their different ways, in their different contexts, Hannah Arendt and Frantz Fanon each experienced the juridical non-place. Having fled Germany in 1933, precisely at the moment the Nazi party enacted a state of exception, Arendt, who had faced persecution as a Jew in Germany, was detained in France in 1940 as an enemy alien, interned at the transit camp at Gurs prior to the fall of Paris. It was out of this experience that she wrote 'We Refugees'. Having served in Algeria during the war, Fanon secured an appointment at the psychiatric hospital at Blida-Joinville in 1953. There, he worked principally with French soldiers who experienced trauma after carrying out torture as a means of suppressing anti-colonial resistance but also with their Algerian victims. Resigning his post in 1954, Fanon first worked alongside and then joined the *Front de Libération Nationale*, out of which experience he wrote *Studies in a Dying Colonialism* and *The Wretched of the Earth*. To go back to Arendt and Fanon is, as we have seen, to recover detailed accounts of the topographies of the non-place, of how the spatialities of such settings were constructed and enforced. It is also to recover, in each case, what we might call a phenomenology of geopolitical non-personhood. For both writers in their specific but, as they separately understood, geopolitically interlocking spaces, it was crucial to describe not only the apparatus of non-personhood but also the lived experience, as Lefebvre termed it, of being held outside.

Where one finds that lived experience most searchingly expressed in Arendt is in the dialogue between her major works of the 1950s, *The Origins of Totalitarianism* and *The Human Condition*, the latter being best understood in relation to the former, not least because Arendt was revising *Origins* whilst formulating *The Human Condition*. Writing about the origins, the effects but also the legacy, in statelessness and internment, of totalitarianism, Arendt identifies as her object of study, 'groups of people to whom suddenly the rules of the world around them had ceased to apply'.[79] To begin to account for the lived experience of such a condition, as Arendt understood it, was to start with the non-application of the rules themselves, Arendt's straightforward observation being that to hold a person outside the law is, in effect, to compel them towards illegality. Thus, as she put it in 'The Decline of the Nation-State and the End of the Rights of Man', 'The stateless person, without right to residence and without the right to work, had of course consistently to transgress the law'.[80] For Arendt, there was to be no ambiguity: to render a person rightless and therefore outside the law was to cause them to transgress it. This lived reality had two significant aspects. The first, perversely, was that criminality afforded a degree of protection. Thus,

> The same man who was in jail yesterday because of his mere presence in the world, who had no rights whatever and lived under threat of deportation, or who was dispatched without sentence and without trial to some kind of internment because he had tried to work and make a living, may become almost a full-fledged citizen because of a little theft.[81]

Such an improvement of circumstance should not to be overstated, not least because, as Malcolm Proudfoot cited John Hope Simpson as reporting, the commitment of a crime, for all that it invoked certain due processes, frequently resulted in the penalty of deportation.[82] The juridical personhood afforded by criminality, in other words, was short-lived.

A second consequence of compelling people to live outside the rules that apply to the world around them, of legal expulsion, is the power it accords those who enforce the law. Again, Arendt is unambiguous: 'This was the first time the police in Western Europe had received authority to act on its own, to rule directly over people.'[83] From which it followed that one consequence of statelessness was 'the danger of a gradual transformation into a police state.'[84] Fanon, addressing the production of legal non-personhood in the European colony, makes the same point:

> In the colonies it is the policeman and the soldier who are the official, instituted go-betweens, the spokesmen of the settler and his rule of oppression [. . .] In the capitalist countries a multitude of moral teachers, counsellors and 'bewilderers' separate the exploited from those in power. In the colonial countries, on the contrary, the policeman and the soldier, by their immediate presence and their frequent and direct action maintain contact with the native and advise him by means of rifle-buts and napalm not to budge. The intermediary does not lighten the oppression, nor seek to hide the domination [. . .] he is the bringer of violence into the home and into the mind of the native.[85]

What one sees here, in the combined commentaries, is a form of mutual reinforcement. To set a person outside the law, to designate them illegal, is both to render them permanently vulnerable to the intrusions of the police and, at the same time, greatly to enhance police power. And what results is increasing levels of violence against the individual.

It is not sufficient, however, as both Arendt and Fanon observe, to describe the structural effects of juridical non-personhood. What had to be understood also was the affective reality of such a circumstance, the way it feels to the individual whose status is in suspense. For Arendt, what has to be grasped is that the segregated space takes its character from the fact that legality is consequential not on action but on status. Thus, as opposed to a framework 'where one is judged by one's actions and opinions', the juridical non-place entails

> the loss of the relevance of speech (and man, since Aristotle, has been defined as a being commanding the power of speech and thought) and the loss of all human relationship (and man, again since Aristotle has been thought of as the 'political animal', that is one who by definition lives in a community), the loss, in other words, of some of the most essential characteristics of human life.[86]

That such essential characteristics have been lost is due to the fact that the individual's status is unrelated to their actions. Nothing they have done or said, nor anything they can do or say, determines their situation. It was a situation that was intended to have its obverse in what Arendt calls 'the space of appearance', her account of a polis, in *The Human Condition*, founded in her determination to outline a situation in which non-personhood might not apply. Here again, as if writing across from one text to the other, what she points to is the absence of consequence. It is, 'With word and deed we insert ourselves into the human world, and this insertion is like a second birth.' From which it follows that 'A life without speech and without action [...] is literally dead to the world; it has ceased to be a human life because it is no longer lived among men.'[87]

Arendt's focus is on the denial of consequentiality, on the implications of a life 'without speech and without action'. Such a life ceases to be a human life because, in the breakdown of relationality it entails, it is no longer in a meaningful sense lived among persons. Fanon's focus, by contrast, as he details the non-places the colonizer produces, is the way such a coercive and criminalizing experience of spatiality determines movement. In this respect, it is difficult to imagine a more fine-grained account. As Fanon puts it in *Studies in a Dying Colonialism*, under the heading 'Algeria Dispersed',

> The tactic adopted by French colonialism since the beginning of the Revolution has had the result of separating the people from each other, of fragmenting them, with the sole objective of making any cohesion impossible. This effort was at first concentrated on the men, who were interned by tens of thousands [...] The Algerian woman, suddenly deprived of a husband, is obliged to find a means of feeding her children. She finds herself having to go from place to place, to run her errands, to live without the man's protection. Sometimes she will go and visit her husband interned a hundred or two hundred kilometers from his home.[88]

It is difficult, at this point, not to look forward, to the fact that in the United Kingdom in the present moment the Home Office operates a practice it terms 'dispersal', whereby a person who is seeking asylum but who is not detained can, at short notice, be 'dispersed' from one part of the country to another, the effect being to break up any forms of social cohesion they might have begun to develop.

Really to feel the force of the point, however, it is important to stay in Fanon's moment, in the context of his response. As he puts it, describing an approach that informed all his writings of the late-1950s,

We must try to look more closely at the reality of Algeria. We must not simply fly over it. We must, on the contrary, walk step by step along the great wound inflicted on the Algerian soil and on the Algerian people. We must question the Algerian earth meter by meter, and measure the fragmentation of the Algerian family, the degree to which it finds itself scattered.[89]

Drawing on the work of Ato Sekyi-Otu, Stefan Kipfer has written with impressive clarity on Fanon's meticulously spatialized account of colonial violence, on his determination to map the situation 'step by step'. As Kipfer observes, 'Fanon encountered the stark realities of segregation in the colonial city less in Martinique and more in Algiers and Blida, first as an employee of the French authorities [. . .] then as a member of the FLN.'[90] Out of which experiences, as Kipfer observes, Fanon detailed the degree to which 'colonial time/space has a profound impact on the imaginary worlds and bodily experience of the colonized'.[91]

It is there, in that impact on the bodily experience of the colonized, quite as much as in his articulations of revolutionary strategy, that Fanon's writing has its enduring force. And what he details, time and again, is the impact on the colonized person's passage through space; on the way, in that spatiality, the juridical non-person is compelled to move. To quote selectively but indicatively from a long account of the colonized person's movement in *The Wretched of the Earth*,

> The native is a being hemmed in; apartheid is simply one form of the division into compartments of the colonial world. The first thing which the native learns is to stay in his place, and not to go beyond certain limits. This is why the dreams of the native are always of muscular prowess; his dreams are of action and aggression [. . .] The native is always on the alert, for since he can only make out with difficulty the many symbols of the colonial world, he is never sure whether or not he has crossed the frontier. Confronted with a world ruled by the settler, the native is always presumed guilty. But the native's guilt is never a guilt which he accepts [. . .] The native's muscles are always tensed.[92]

As in Arendt's account of juridical non-personhood, the consequence of inhabiting a setting in which 'the rules of the world around them had ceased to apply' is that the rules around them always apply. It is there, in the constant applicability of rules that seemingly don't apply, that one observes the extent of the impossible spatiality of the mid-century non-place. 'Confronted with a world ruled by the settler', as Fanon puts it, the indigenous person is always presumed guilty. For Arendt, what the observation of this condition gives rise to is a pressing account of non-consequentiality, of a life without speech and action. In Fanon, by contrast, what we find are meticulously detailed accounts of the way the spatiality of the non-place makes a person move. They are 'a being hemmed in', where the impossibility of their spatial circumstance is a bodily condition, the lived experience of a space in which it is all but impossible to move.[93]

Conclusion

This chapter has dwelt on the spatiality of mid-century non-places. In so doing, it has documented three kinds of intention in the authors with whom *Writing Against Expulsion* is concerned. The first intention, principally specified here through the Universal Declaration, was to provide a language for the topography of the non-place, the spatiality of non-personhood, in order to begin to determine the outline of a space in which such expulsions would not occur. The second intention was to warn, to give an account of the spatiality of geopolitical non-personhood in order that if and when such spaces began to re-emerge, there would be an understanding of their meaning and implication. That warning was heard from David Rousset, in Rousset's reception in Olson, and in accounts of post-war non-places in Arendt and Fanon. The third intention was to try to articulate the lived experience such spaces of non-personhood produced. This third intention, the desire to provide a language for the lived experience of geopolitical non-personhood, takes us back to the first. As the second half of this book will argue, it is in the coordinates Fanon and Arendt arrive at for the experience of geopolitical non-personhood—in their clear emphasis on movement, making and speech—that post-war writers set out to map a space for the human. To read the production of non-personhood as a spatial question, as all of the writers discussed here do, is to clarify the forms of agency by which a space for the human might be made.

Before addressing those forms of agency, however, and before exploring how they intersect with the language of rights, it is necessary, in the next chapter, to register a shared desire across the authors and texts concerned to arrive at a language that might prevent expulsion. We have started to hear that language already, in one of the period's tropes. Thus, it was crucial for Arendt to register that the non-place compromised speech and action because, as she put it, it is 'with word and deed we insert ourselves into the human world'. Fanon, speaking about the collective rather than the individual, arrived at a comparable image. As he puts it at the end of the first chapter of *The Wretched of the Earth*,

> This huge task which consists of reintroducing mankind into the world, the whole of mankind, will be carried out with the indispensable help of the European peoples, who themselves must realize that in the past they have often joined the ranks of the common masters where colonial questions were concerned.[94]

Where Arendt speaks about inserting persons into the human world, and where Fanon speaks about reintroduction, Olson, it will be recalled, described it as the poet's action to enable a person to fill their given space. These are large statements, expressing serious ambitions, registering the urgency in the post-war moment of countering the realities of the non-place, of the need to assert, not assume (as Lefebvre would come to assume) that 'Human beings [. . .] are in space.'[95] It is in such statements that we find the force of the post-war imaginaries in question, in their drive towards a language in which space for the human might be made.

Notes

1. 'The better imagined' is Ali Smith's phrase. As she wrote in 2016, in her statement as patron of the *Refugee Tales* project: 'Imagine if every city, if every country, greeted refugees with signs which said in many languages the word welcome, and the words you are safe, like Vienna did last summer. We will tell it like it is, and we will work towards the better imagined.' See Ali Smith, 'A Welcome from Our Patron', https://www.refugeetales.org/about (accessed 5 May, 2022).
2. Charles Olson, *The Collected Poems of Charles Olson (Excluding the Maximus Poems)*, ed. George Butterick (Berkeley, Los Angeles, CA and London: University of California Press, 1987), p. 46. Olson's sense that there was no choice, in the immediate aftermath of the war, but to go *via* an understanding of the non-place is echoed in his essay 'The Resistance', discussed below, in which his starting point for comprehension is that 'Man came here by an intolerable *way*.'
3. Frantz Fanon, *The Wretched of the Earth*, tr. Constance Farrington, preface John-Paul Sartre (London: Penguin Books, 2001), p. 29.

4. Marc Augé, *Non-Places: Introduction to an Anthropology of Supermodernity*, tr. John Howe (London: Verso, 1995), pp. 77–78.
5. Augé, *Non-Places*, p. 79.
6. Augé, *Non-Places*, p. 119.
7. Giorgio Agamben, *Homo Sacer: Sovereign Power and Bare Life*, tr. Daniel Heller-Roazen (Redwood, CA: Stanford University Press, 1998), p. 175.
8. For an extended discussion of the connection between Augé and Agamben, see Sarah Sharma, 'Baring Life and Lifestyle in the Non-Place', *Cultural Studies* 23:1 (2008), 129–148. For a searching discussion of Agamben's understanding of the site of exception as 'dislocating localization', see William Watkin's chapter 'Reading Guantanamo or Camp as Coercion' in *Bioviolence: How the Powers That Be Make Us Do What They Want* (London: Routledge, 2021), pp. 174–190.
9. See David Goodhart, *The Road to Somewhere: The Populist Revolt and the Future of Politics* (London: Hurst and Company, 2017).
10. United Nations, Universal Declaration of Human Rights (Paris: United Nations General Assembly, 1948), https://www.un.org/en/about-us/universal-declaration-of-human-rights (accessed 3 May 2022).
11. UN, Universal Declaration.
12. Johannes Morsink, *The Universal Declaration of Human Rights: Origins, Drafting, and Intent* (Philadelphia, PA: University of Pennsylvania Press, 1999), pp. 43–44.
13. Morsink, *Origins, Drafting, and Intent*, p. 44.
14. Morsink, *Origins, Drafting, and Intent*, p. 44.
15. Morsink, *Origins, Drafting, and Intent*, p. 50. For Arendt's account of the process whereby under the Nazi regime Jews were legally deprived of their liberty, see, in particular, chapters IV, V, and VI on 'The First Solution: Expulsion', 'The Second Solution: Concentration', and 'The Final Solution: Killing': Hannah Arendt, *Eichmann in Jerusalem: A Report on the Banality of Evil* (London: Penguin, 2006), pp. 56–111.
16. As Morsink reports, 'Arbitrary arrests did happen and they had to be "condemned", which is why he thought that the word "arbitrary" was "probably the most important word in the entire article and must be retained"': Morsink, *Origins, Drafting, and Intent*, p. 50.
17. National Constitution Center, The Constitution of the United States, Amendment V, https://constitutioncenter.org/media/files/constitution.pdf (accessed 3 May 2022).
18. David Rousset names the concentrationary universe 'The Realm of King Ubu' in Chapter 7 of *The Other Kingdom*, tr. Ramon Guthrie (New York: Reynal and Hitchcock, 1947), pp. 72–78.
19. Ralph Maud, *Charles Olson's Reading: A Biography* (Carbondale and Edwardsville, IL: Southern Illinois University Press, 1996), p. 265. For further discussion of Olson's reading of Rousset and his relationship with Cagli, see

Mark Byers, *Charles Olson and American Modernism: The Practice of the Self* (Oxford: Oxford University Press, 2018), pp. 20–44.
20. Maud, *Olson's Reading*, p. 258.
21. Maud, *Olson's Reading*, p. 70.
22. Maud, *Olson's Reading*, p. 70.
23. Sujo's essay appears in the catalogue for an exhibition of Cagli's work at the Imperial War Musuem. See Glen Sujo, *Legacies of Silence: The Visual Arts and Holocaust Memory* (London: Philip Wilson Publishers, 2001), p. 90.
24. Sujo, *Legacies of Silence*, p. 91.
25. Sujo, *Legacies of Silence*, p. 91.
26. As Maud reports, Olson was commissioned by Cagli to write the poem for the catalogue for the New York and Chicago exhibitions of the drawings (Maud, *Olson's Reading*, p. 70). Cagli returned the favour by providing illustrations for Olson's first pamphlet, *Y & X*. For a further discussion of the influence of Cagli's drawings on Olson's poem, see Robert von Hallberg, *Charles Olson: The Scholar's Art* (Cambridge, MA and London: Harvard University Press, 1978), p. 8.
27. Tom Clark, *Charles Olson: The Allegory of a Poet's Life* (Berkeley, CA: North Atlantic Books, 2000), p. 86.
28. Maud, *Olson's Reading*, p. 269.
29. Clark, *Olson*, p. 112.
30. Clark, *Olson*, p. 124. For an extended consideration of Olson's thinking about the relation of poetry to foreign policy, see David Herd, '"From Him Only Will the Old State-Secret Come"': What Charles Olson Imagined', *English* 59.227 (Winter 2010), 375–395.
31. For further discussion of Olson's thinking about poetry and foreign policy see Ben Hickman, 'Slipping the Cog: Charles Olson and Cold War History', in his *Crisis and the US Avant-Garde: Poetry and Real Politics* (Edinburgh: Edinburgh University Press, 2015), pp. 66–90.
32. Charles Olson, 'People v. The Fascist, U.S. (1944)', *Survey Graphic* (August 1944), pp. 337, 368.. For a full unfolding of the logic of group defamation Olson outlines in his essay, see Philippe Sands' brilliant history, *East West Street: On the Origins of "Genocide" and "Crimes Against Humanity"* (New York: Vintage Books, 2017)
33. For an extended consideration of Rousset's articulation of the concentrationary universe, see Griselda Pollock and Max Silverman's important edited volumes *Concentrationary Memories: Totalitarian Terror and Cultural Resistance* (London: Bloomsbury, 2015) and *Concentrationary Imaginaries: Tracing Totalitarian Violence in Popular Culture* (London: Bloomsbury, 2020). These volumes grow out of Pollock and Silverman's Arts and Humanities Research Council (AHRC) project, 'Concentrationary Memories: The Politics of Representation', the purpose of which was to explore 'the connections between

aesthetics and politics in the formation of what has become known as the cultural memory of the Holocaust and what is not fully grasped through that term: namely the concentrationary which relates to the political event of totalitarianism' ('Concentrationary Memories: The Politics of Representation', https://ahc.leeds.ac.uk/fine-art/dir-record/research-projects/761/concentrationary-memories-the-politics-of-representation (accessed 3 May 2022).
34. Rousset, *The Other Kingdom*, p. 16.
35. Rousset, *The Other Kingdom*, p. 17.
36. Rousset, *The Other Kingdom*, pp. 171–172.
37. Rousset, *The Other Kingdom*, p. 28.
38. Rousset, *The Other Kingdom*, p. 29.
39. Rousset, *The Other Kingdom*, p. 30.
40. Rousset, *The Other Kingdom*, p. 102.
41. Rousset, *The Other Kingdom*, p. 112.
42. In January 2018, the *Daily Record* reported of Dungavel Immigration Removal Centre that,

   > There are 64 detainees working up to 30 hours a week in Dungavel. The jobs include cleaning, hairdressing and gardening—much of it vital for the running of the detention centre. New figures reveal that the detainees received just £130,919 for 128,742 hours worked between November 2014 and April last year. Paying detainees the minimum wage, which rose from £6.50 to £7.05 for over 21s, would have cost an estimated £727,607 extra.

   Phil Miller, 'Dungavel Detention Centre in Slave Labour Shame as Asylum Seekers Paid Just £1 an Hour for Work', Daily Record, 15 January 2018, https://www.dailyrecord.co.uk/news/scottish-news/dungavel-detention-centre-slave-labour-11851052 (accessed 5 May 2022).
43. A measure of the incongruity that informs the asylum seeker's lived experience is the fact that in March 2019, high court judge Mr Justice Murray ruled that 'wages of £1 an hour paid in immigration detention centres are lawful'. As *The Guardian* reported,

   > The pay rate is less than one-seventh of the legal minimum wage and was described by detainees as 'slave labour wages'. However, the judge ruled the rates were acceptable because the purpose of the types of jobs being done, such as cleaning, hairdressing and welfare support, was 'to provide meaningful activity and alleviate boredom'.

   Diane Taylor, 'Judge Rules £1/Hr Wages for Immigration Detainees Are Lawful', The Guardian, 27 March, 2019, https://www.theguardian.com/uk-news/2019/mar/27/judge-rules-1hr-wages-lawful-for-immigration-centre-detainees (accessed 6 May 2022). As Chapter 4 will observe, no such apparent

consideration for the need for 'meaningful activity' is given in framing employment rights for people seeking asylum when not detained.
44. Rousset, *The Other Kingdom*, p. 31.
45. For details of the composition and publication of 'The Resistance', see Ralph Maud (ed.), *A Charles Olson Reader* (Manchester: Carcanet, 2005), pp. 3–4 and Maud, *Olson's Reading*, p. 266.
46. Charles Olson, *Collected Prose*, ed. Donald Allen and Benjamin Friedlander, intro. Robert Creeley (Berkeley, Los Angeles, CA and London: University of California Press, 1997), p. 174.
47. For a searching account of the theme and language of 'limit' in Olson, see chapter 2, 'Finding Out for Oneself' of Stephen Fredman, *The Grounding of American Poetry: Charles Olson and the Emersonian Tradition* (Cambridge: Cambridge University Press, 1993), pp. 26–46.
48. Olson, *Collected Prose*, p. 174.
49. Henri Lefebvre, *The Production of Space*, tr. Donald Nicholson-Smith (Oxford: Blackwell, Publishing, 1991), p. 132.
50. Augé, *Non-Places*, p. 60.
51. See Alcalay's essay on the early contexts of Ferrini's work in Ammiel Alcalay and Kate Tarlow, *Vincent Ferrini: Before Gloucester* (New York: CUNY Poetics Document Initiative: Lost and Found, 2014).
52. It was the implied scope of his writing, that made Ferrini worth addressing from Olson's point of view. What Olson meant to mark with 'The Resistance' was the origin of a substantial undertaking, one that might reckon with the scale of the political calamity that had found its expression in the fascist non-place. To publish it in Ferrini's magazine, however small, was to signal an intention to address the scale of the contemporary problem, to arrive at a mode of thought and writing that understood the requirement of arriving at a geopolitical reach.
53. For the letter in which Olson's poem appears, see Charles Olson, *Selected Letters*, ed. Ralph Maud (Berkeley, CA and London: University of California Press, 2000), pp. 108–109.
54. Susan Howe, *The Birth-Mark: Unsettling the Wilderness in American Literary History* (Middletown, CT: Wesleyan University Press, 1993), p. 180.
55. Lytton Smith, 'Projective Citizenship: The Reimagining of the Citizen in Post-War American Poetry', unpublished PhD thesis, Columbia University, 2012, p. 33; Howe, *Birth-Mark*, p. 180.
56. Rousset, *The Other Kingdom*, p. 173.
57. Hannah Arendt, *Origins of Totalitarianism*, 3rd edn (New York: Harcourt Brace Jovanovich Publishers, 1979), p. 279.
58. Arendt, *Origins,* pp. 279, 292.
59. Arendt, *Origins,* pp. 292, 293.
60. Arendt's articulation of the non-personhood entailed by the logic of the camp took numerous forms, including, as Lyndsey Stonebridge has documented,

literary criticism. Witness 'Reading Statelessness: Arendt's Kafka', in Lyndsey Stonebridge, *Placeless People: Writings, Rights and Refugees* (Oxford: Oxford University Press, 2018), pp. 29–45.

61. Always, in this strand of the argument, the discussion hovers close to Agamben's conceptualization of 'biopolitics' as presented in particular in Part III, Section 7 of *Homo Sacer*, 'The Camp as the "Nomos" of the Modern'. See Agamben, *Homo Sacer*, pp. 95–101. Where my argument seeks to depart from Agamben is in seeking out logics by which the process of encampment can be resisted. That intention to explore modes and principles of resistance takes different forms across the different chapters. Here, it is crucial that Rousset guides Arendt in relating the production of the camp space to the processes of imperial capital, opening as it does a political-economic response to Agamben's political pessimism.
62. Gerard Daniel Cohen, *In War's Wake: Europe's Displaced Persons in the Postwar Order* (Oxford: Oxford University Press, 2017), p. 14.
63. Cohen, *War's Wake*, pp. 13, 16.
64. Cohen, *War's Wake*, p. 35.
65. Cohen, *War's Wake*, p. 37.
66. Cited in Cohen, *War's Wake*, p. 123.
67. Cited in Cohen, *War's Wake*, p. 41.
68. This is to follow Nancy Fraser's lead in tracing the question of recognition to specific institutional settings, Fraser's point being that the refusal to grant political recognition is best understood not as a generalized disposition but as a set of decisions in practical and material contexts. See Nancy Fraser, 'Rethinking Recognition', *New Left Review* 3 (May–June 2000), pp. 107–120.
69. Marie-Benedicte Dembour, *When Humans Become Migrants: Study of the European Court of Human Rights with an Inter-American Counterpoint* (Oxford: Oxford University Press, 2015), p. 1.
70. Dembour, *When Humans Become Migrants*, p. 67.
71. Dembour, *When Humans Become Migrants*, pp. 67–68.
72. Dembour, *When Humans Become Migrants*, p. 68. For a concrete account of how, in the immediate post-war period, the UK government reneged on public commitments to human rights when they conflicted with ongoing colonial imperatives, see Philippe Sands's outstanding history of the UK's expulsion of the Chagossians from the Chagos archipelago, *The Last Colony* (London: Weidenfeld & Nicholson, 2022).
73. Council of Europe, European Convention of Human Rights—Convention for Protection of Human Rights and Fundamental Freedoms (Strasbourg: Directorate of Information, 1952), cited in Dembour, *When Humans Become Migrants*, p.70.
74. Fanon, *Wretched of the Earth*, p. 71.
75. This book will return at various points to the intersection between fascism and colonialism in French policy towards Algeria and to the contradictions,

therefore, in the French government's contemporary pronouncements on human rights. In particular, in Chapter 5, the argument addresses Joseph Slaughter's account of the French use of torture against Algerians, the visible effects of which in psychiatric settings were causal in Fanon's politicization. See Joseph Slaughter, 'A Question of Narration: The Voice in International Human Rights Law', *Human Rights Quarterly* 19:2 (May 1997), 406–430.

76. Fanon, *Wretched of the Earth*, p. 29.
77. Fanon, *Wretched of the Earth*, p. 34.
78. Fanon, *Wretched of the Earth*, p. 68.
79. Arendt, *Origins*, p. 267.
80. Arendt, *Origins*, p. 286.
81. Arendt, *Origins*, p. 286.
82. The point is clarified by John Hope Simpson, quoted by Malcolm Proudfoot:

    The refugee finds himself deprived of legal protection [...] For practical purposes he is outlawed by his country of origin; in his country of refuge, he has a measure of ordinary legal protection in any decently-governed State, but he suffers under all sorts of disabilities [...]; above all, he has no claim as of right to continued legal residence, and he is liable to expulsion if his presence for any reason is no longer desired.

    Malcolm Proudfoot, *European Refugees: 1939–1952* (London: Faber and Faber, 1957), pp. 22–23.

83. Arendt, *Origins*, p. 287.
84. Arendt, *Origins*, p. 288.
85. Fanon, *Wretched of the Earth*, p. 29.
86. Arendt, *Origins*, pp. 296, 297.
87. Hannah Arendt, *The Human Condition*, 2nd edn, intro. Margaret Canovan (Chicago, IL and London: University of Chicago Press, 1958), p. 176.
88. Frantz Fanon, *Studies in a Dying Colonialism*, tr. Haakon Chevalier, intro. A.M. Babu (London: Earthscan Productions, 1989), pp. 118–119
89. Fanon, *Dying Colonialism*, p. 119.
90. Stefan Kipfer, 'Fanon and Space: Colonization, Urbanization, and Liberation from the Colonial to the Global City', *Environment and Planning D: Society and Space* 25 (2007), 709.
91. Kipfer, 'Fanon and Space', p. 711.
92. Fanon, *Wretched of the Earth*, pp. 40–41.
93. In Abdulrazak Gurnah's wonderful novel of the contemporary refugee experience, *By The Sea*, Gurnah describes the contemporary refugee's lived experience of hostile political space in comparable terms, the feeling, as the narrator Saleh Omar describes it, of being 'hemmed in and observed': Abdulrazak Gurnah, *By the Sea* (London: Bloomsbury, 2001), p. 4.
94. Fanon, *Wretched of the Earth*, p. 84.
95. Lefebvre, *The Production of Space*, p. 132.

2
Writing Against Expulsion

Against Expulsion

In Chapter 1, I considered how, in the period following the Second World War, the authors with whom this book is centrally concerned, and the writers and artists on whom they drew, sought variously to articulate the spatialities of the mid-century non-place. Such non-places took various forms, the chapter detailing responses to the concentrationary universe as articulated by David Rousset, the displaced persons camps as reported on by Arendt, and the colonial exclusion zone as documented by Fanon. To dwell on the reality of such impossible spaces, and on the way different forms of the non-place interlocked, was to understand the degree to which contemporary geopolitics was grounded in the expulsive act. In the mid-century moment, geopolitical space could reasonably be thought to be shaped by expulsion and by the non-places those expelled were compelled to occupy.

The purpose of the present chapter is to begin to consider how the same post-war authors, whether writing separately or (as in the authorship of the Universal Declaration) as a collective, set out to counter and reimagine such an expulsive construction of space. The second half of the book (Chapters 3, 4, and 5) will focus on certain specifics of such re-imaginings, on the way authors dwelt on the shared human practices of moving, making, and speaking. The theme of the present chapter is more abstract, and therefore more difficult to pin down, but is not, I think, any less pressing for that. What I want to show is how, in their different ways, the writers in question sought to articulate a non-expulsive understanding of space. To say this is not simply to contend that in such mid-century writing one finds arguments against forms of politics by which persons find themselves expelled: Fanon's argument against settler-colonialism, for example, or Arendt's argument against the fascist state. It is to suggest, also, that in certain key texts of the post-war moment, one finds a drive, in writing, towards forms of expression whose intention was that nobody should be forced outside. There was a period after the war, this is to say, in which the drive to establish a non-expulsive spatiality constituted a condition of language itself. To say so is to recall Lefebvre and his insistence that we register what he calls the production of space. Faced with the material realities of the non-place and all that such settings implied, various mid-century authors sought to articulate a non-expulsive understanding of space.

That non-expulsion as such was an explicit impulse in mid-century thought is demonstrated by one of the period's defining documents, the 1951 Convention Relating to the Status of Refugees. In that document, as this chapter will discuss, Articles 32 and 33 name 'Expulsion' as the political condition the Convention is written against. As Article 33 puts it, under the heading 'Prohibition of Expulsion or Return ('Refoulement'),

> No Contracting State shall expel or return ('refouler') a refugee in any manner whatsoever to the frontiers of territories where his life or freedom would be threatened on account of his race, religion, nationality, membership of a particular social group or political opinion.[1]

The 1951 Convention is a complicated document, but Article 33 could not be more clear. It names a mid-century drive towards a non-expulsive understanding of space that found further expression across an interlocking discourse of different disciplines and modes. One could cut into the discourse at any point, perhaps, but one place to start is with recent framings of the document that underpinned the 1951 Convention, the Universal Declaration of Human Rights.

Taken on its own terms, the Universal Declaration was an attempt in language to underwrite the relation between an individual person and the human collective. Following the genocidal crimes of the Second World War, issuing as they did from the Nazi production of non-personhood, the aim of the document was to formulate a set of relations between persons and the collective such that no individual or group would be forced out. It can hardly be argued that, in so far as it articulated such an objective, the Universal Declaration has succeeded in its intended effects. From Arendt's mid-century discussion of the failure of the language of rights to secure those, the stateless, who were most in need of its protection, to Jacques Rancière's account of the pattern of rights abuse that has shaped the period since the end of the Cold War, through to Samuel Moyn's account of the way the language of human rights has excluded political alternatives, numerous commentators have documented circumstances in which the Universal Declaration has not done its work.[2] This must be a matter of grave concern, of course, and it is the aim of the present book to help address that concern. But it must also be understood that, from the outset, the Declaration was, in certain obvious respects, historically conditioned to struggle not to fail. In its twentieth-century form, the nation state had learned to determine itself by the production of non-personhood such that those processes of production—in the camp, at the border, in the colonial environment—had become integral to the state's conduct and self-definition. While, that is, the Declaration was called into being by the most catastrophic of historical outrages, certain political-economic logics from which those outrages issued, as David Rousset warned, both preceded and post-dated the event. What those logics constituted, in other words, was an historical development (the systematic production of non-personhood) that both made some such statement of rights or mutual recognitions internationally necessary and also made it inevitable that any such statement could only struggle not to fail.

How one proceeds from that inherent difficulty, whether one tends to emphasize the necessity of the Declaration or to observe its periodic failure, is dependent, in part, on the contemporary urgency of the question of non-personhood itself, on how pressing it seems at any given moment as a political issue. To certain writers after the war, there was no more pressing concern than the fact that, on an alarming scale, people had been rendered non-persons, in the transit camps that housed the stateless that Arendt was not alone in estimating at 10 million people.[3] One has to be wary of straightforward cross-reference, of course, but it is clearly the case that in the present moment the question of geopolitical non-personhood is with us once again. At the time of writing, for example, the UK government has recently secured royal assent for the Nationality and Borders Act, legislation which contains two provisions whose intention is to expel. By the terms of the Act, it has become 'illegal' to request asylum at the UK border, the only 'legal' route to asylum being government-selected resettlement from a third-country space such as a refugee camp. More explicitly still, the Act proposes that detention under immigration rules will, in the future, take place not in the United Kingdom but, where the government can find international partners, offshore. Both provisions, as the former Secretary General of the United Nations Ban Ki-Moon has written, are in breach of the 1951 Refugee Convention and in breach, therefore, of the principles of human rights.[4] Exactly why the UK government is now systematically disassembling its commitment to human rights must be a matter of conjecture, but it is perhaps not conspiratorial to observe that, in advance of the mass forced displacement of people the climate emergency is likely to effect, the United

Kingdom is dismantling its international obligations by breaking its commitment to human rights. It is officially sanctioning a global environment in which persons can be expelled.

All of which is to say that, at the time of writing, our relation to the Universal Declaration has once again changed. Where it had become possible, until even very recently, for commentators to regard the Declaration as an historically remote document whose failings might be enumerated with critical equanimity, we are now once again in a moment when its guiding impulses make sense. One way to register this is via two substantial and properly high-prolife commentaries on the Declaration and its related discourses, from both of which this book has learned a great deal but from both of which it departs in a significant respect. The first is Joseph Slaughter's *Human Rights, Inc: The World Novel, Narrative Form and International Law*, published in 2007, and the second is Mark Greif's *The Age of the Crisis of Man: Thought and Fiction in America, 1933–1973*, published in 2015.

Slaughter's argument, underpinned by extensive research in the discursive histories of human rights and international law, is that in the model of the person (or more specifically the human personality) embedded in the articles of the Declaration, one finds an homology with the model of personality development inscribed in the *Bildungsroman*. It is an argument that has significant strengths, both as exposition of the Declaration and also as critique. One of Slaughter's starting points is Article 22, where it is proposed that

> Everyone, as a member of society, has the right to social security and is entitled to realization, through national effort and international co-operation and in accordance with the organization and resources of each State, of the economic, social and cultural rights indispensable for his dignity and the free development of his personality.[5]

The key phrase here, as Slaughter interprets it, is the last, 'the free development of his personality', in which, as Slaughter not unreasonably argues, there is encoded a novelistic understanding of a person's relation to the world. Drawing on the involvement in the drafting of the Declaration of the French aesthetic philosopher and natural law advocate Jacques Maritain, Slaughter argues that in the development of human rights discourse and the growth of the world novel, one finds mutually reinforcing accounts of the individual's progress through society grounded in the structure of the *Bildungsroman*.[6] It is true, of course, that the model of personality articulated by the Declaration is a construction, and Slaughter provides good reason for drawing on the novel as the basis of his account. As he observes, he focuses his inquiry into the Declaration's account of personality on prose narrative ('rather than on poetry or drama for example'), in part in line with Hayden White's proposition that '"narrative in general [. . .] has to do with the topics of law, legality, legitimacy, or more generally, authority"'.[7]

It is unquestionably the case that the claim on the protections articulated by the Universal Declaration (which, with the publication of the 1951 Convention, would become the claim to refugee status), has to do with narrative. As Gerard Daniel Cohen observes of the situation of displaced persons following the Second World War, '[A]s the Cold War intensified, access to the DP world became increasingly dependent on a decipherable and convincing narrative of persecution.'[8] As I have registered elsewhere, the claim to asylum remains profoundly contingent on narrative, with the appellant's 'story' subject to extraordinary scrutiny and pressure.[9] This fact can be framed in numerous ways, and this book's argument will come back to the question of story in Chapter 5. In so far, however, as the telling of their story is a structural element of the displaced person's experience, constituting as it can the transition from geopolitical non-personhood to personhood, then Slaughter is justified in tracing an homology between rights discourse and the *Bildungsroman*. Drawing equally on the idea of 'incorporation' into the body politic and 'enfranchisement' into the realm of citizenship, Slaughter suggests that

> Like contemporary international human rights law, the affirmative *Bildungsroman* offers a narrative model for enfranchising the disenfranchised, for unproblematising the disenfranchised, for unproblematising the problematic individual, for keeping the broken emancipatory promise of the Enlightenment by repairing the citizen-subject divide.[10]

In human rights practice and the *Bildungsroman*, one thus has a model of social or political enfranchisement, where the story is the vehicle by which the individual appeals for incorporation into and by the state. As description and critique of the structure of human rights, this unquestionably has an accuracy: the precariously poised individual tells their story and the political collective decides on its worth. Finally, however, for all the quality of its reading, my suggestion is that Slaughter's account of the Universal Declaration becomes caught in the complicities it describes. Thus, while it is certainly the case that human rights law can assume the structures of the novel, which is to say of bourgeois individualism, and while such a sense of rights calls for a critique which identifies such shared narrative ground, so also what it calls for is a reading of the Declaration that does not foreground the particular personality in this way, an account, in other words, that does not privilege a novelistic encounter with the world.[11]

The second reading of the Universal Declaration that helps greatly in arriving at the framing of the document this book proposes is provided by Mark Greif. Greif's argument is subtle and wide-ranging and as such is not concerned centrally with the Universal Declaration but with that document as an instance of a wider discourse. His central theme is captured in his conclusion, where he argues,

> My feeling [...] is that, for my own time, I want to tell my contemporaries: Stop! Anytime your inquiries lead you to say, 'At this moment we must ask and decide *who we fundamentally are*, our solution and salvation must lie in a new picture of ourselves and humanity, this is our profound responsibility and a new opportunity'—just stop [...] Answer, rather, the practical matters, concrete questions of value, not requiring 'who we are' distinct from what we say and do, and find the immediate actions necessary to achieve an aim.[12]

There is no part of Greif's conclusion with which this book is in disagreement; it is precisely with an understanding of the concrete value of what people do and say that the second part of the book is concerned. Greif's argument, throughout, is that the 'discourse of man' (located in books by Ronald Niebuhr, Lewis Mumford, Dwight Macdonald, Jean-Paul Sartre, Herbert Marcuse, and Arendt among others) erred, in general, by setting out, in the face of mid-century political crisis, to arrive at a redefinition of the essence of 'man'. Greif establishes this error very clearly, not least as he proceeds to read mid-century crisis discourse through the identity politics and poststructural interrogations that constituted the 1960s response. I am broadly in agreement also with Greif in his assessment of Arendt, whose contemporary value, as he puts it, lay in her willingness 'to simultaneously give the direst practical critique of the pretensions of the rights of man and to speak of the necessity for their new or renewed basis'.[13]

The fact that both Slaughter and Greif remain principally content to critique the Declaration rather than, as Arendt proposes, to seek to renew it, has, in part, to do with chronology. While both can be heard to offer powerful recent accounts of the discourse of the human and of human rights, neither writer, in our rapidly evolving political moment, is precisely contemporary; not contemporary, at any rate, with the re-emergence of the question of geopolitical non-personhood. Since they wrote, our vantage has altered: a new politics of expulsion is being unfolded before our eyes and, as a consequence, perspectives on the language of human rights have changed. Where previously it was possible simply to provide critique, now, as it is systematically dismantled across political settings of all kinds, it is clear that the language of human rights has to be heard anew. We have to hear not what kind of individual the Universal Declaration might have been looking to present nor what kind of definition of humanity, but how, in common with a cluster of contemporary texts, it sought to address the mid-century question of expulsion, how it sought to articulate a non-expulsive space.

To approach the Universal Declaration in this way, as one text alongside others wrestling with the question of expulsion, is to hear anew the emergence of key mid-century terms. One such term was 'recognition', a concept which, as Anita Chari has observed in connection with Fanon, can all too easily reproduce the compromised model of enfranchisement that Slaughter identifies in his novelistic account of rights. As Chari writes, building on Judith Butler, to seek 'recognition' is to 'struggle to be recognized within the terms of a dominant and dominating discourse'.[14] This chapter does not propose a 'politics of recognition' for precisely this reason.[15] What it offers, instead, is an account of the way the mid-century writers in question reached repeatedly for a sense of what Fanon called 'reciprocal recognitions' as a means of initiating an understanding of a non-expulsive space. In each case (for Fanon, for Olson, for Arendt, for the authors of the Universal Declaration), the idea of recognition would be exceeded by their attention to struggles and practices at the level of lived experience, at the level, as this book argues, of moving, making, and speaking. 'Recognition', in other words, was a transitional term, a means of beginning to address the mid-century realities of non-personhood and of starting to articulate a non-expulsive space. What we find, in each case, is what might be called, following the political philosopher James Ingram, a series of 'images' of non-expulsion, where the imaging itself is necessary to more substantive accounts of human relationality and to which the term 'recognition' emerged historically as a necessary resource.[16]

At every point, however, it is that drive towards a space of non-expulsion we have to keep in mind. It is not enough to argue for recognition, or even for rights, to make either recognition, or even rights, the political end. What has to be argued for, as Rancière understands, is the space, physical and political, in which rights and reciprocal recognitions are claimed. To go back to the mid-century moment, to authors and texts faced with the reality of non-personhood, is to recover the significance of that larger frame. Recognitions mattered, just as rights mattered, because they could be instrumental in articulating a non-expulsive space. What the texts in question sought to articulate, in other words, was not (as a novelistic reading of rights would suggest) the individual claim but rather (as mid-century open-field poetics help us to see) a space from which persons would not be expelled.

On the Question of Scope

To raise the question of expulsion in relation to the Universal Declaration is immediately to focus on the process of its composition. The definitive account of that process is given by Morsink in *The Universal Declaration of Human Rights: Origins, Drafting, and Intent*, a text which sets out the degree to which a document that claimed universality was partial in respect of its authors and signatories. Two facts in particular establish that partiality. In the first place, from a United Nations membership of fifty-eight nations, while forty-six signed, there were also eight abstentions (with two nations, Yemen and Honduras) failing to vote.[17] Of the eight abstaining, South Africa and Saudi Arabia could be characterized as rogue states, nations for whom it was straightforwardly not desirable that a notion of human rights should apply. The other six were Soviet nations: the Union of Soviet Socialist Republics (USSR), the Ukrainian Soviet Socialist Republic, the Byelorussian Soviet Socialist Republic, Czechoslovakia, Yugoslavia, and Poland. On the face of it, in other words, for the Communist world, the principles of the Universal Declaration did not apply. The second fact was colonialism. Following Lenin's 1914 calculation, Morsink estimates that at the moment of the Declaration's promulgation, 50 per cent of the world's population lived under colonial rule, covering 75 per cent of the world's territories.[18] This is reflected in the make-up of the Declaration's signatories, twenty-one of which were from North and South America and sixteen from Europe, whereas from Asia there were fourteen signatories and from Africa four. Without question, the Declaration's claim to universality was deeply compromised by historical reality and principally by the fact that a number of the European signatories were operating brutal, two-tier jurisdictions across great swathes of the globe.

At which point, one might reasonably opt to disregard the Declaration as the product and imposition of western liberal democratic ideology.

Why not? The document was authored, or at least signed, by colonial, anti-communist forces; how could it possibly assert the universality it claimed to pronounce? This, however, would be to misread or, more precisely, to underestimate the document's implications; to which end, two historical caveats are necessary. The first is Morsink's carefully documented observation that although, finally, the Communist powers abstained from the document (on the grounds that it presented a relation of individual-to-state to which they would not subscribe), they were, nonetheless, actively involved in its drafting. Where that participation is keenly felt is in the assertion, throughout, of the principle of non-discrimination and therefore in the language (best indicated by the pronouns) of inclusivity.[19] Thus, while the six Communist abstentions formally undermine the Declaration's claim to anything like universality, the principles of equality and inclusivity that underpin that claim were owed, in no small part, to Soviet delegates as well as to Latin American socialist contributions.

The second caveat concerns colonialism and requires a different framing—a framing to which, in this context, Fanon repeatedly speaks. Thus, while it is a matter of fact that colonized African and Asian countries were not involved in the drafting process of the Universal Declaration, it is also the case that the document makes provisions that the colonizing nations both resisted and would find impossible to sustain. One way to contextualize this is with reference to the European Convention on Human Rights (ECHR). As Marie-Benedicte Dembour has detailed (and as was discussed in Chapter 1), the drafters of the European Convention interpreted the implications of human rights as necessitating, in their own context, what became known as a 'colonial clause'.[20] The principle of that colonial clause (originally Article 63 of the ECHR) was that colonial powers were granted the discretion either to extend or not extend the rights enshrined in the European Convention to those territories in which they had imposed jurisdiction. This is by contrast with Article 2 of the Universal Declaration, where the issue of scope, and therefore of consistency, is articulated without qualification:

> Everyone is entitled to all the rights and freedoms set forth in this Declaration, without distinction of any kind, such as race, colour, sex, language, religion, political or other opinion, national or social origin, property, birth or other status. Furthermore, no distinction shall be made on the basis of the political, jurisdictional or international status of the country

or territory to which a person belongs, whether it be independent, trust, non-self-governing or under any other limitation of sovereignty.[21]

Human rights, as formulated in 1948, as opposed to European rights, as formulated in 1950, were to apply with no distinction across all kinds of territory. This contrast of approaches to the question of scope of application between the Universal Declaration and the European Convention tells us three things about the earlier document. First, written as it was with the realities of the Second World War still so vivid as to shape political intentionality but also just before the politics of the Cold War hardened into shape, the Universal Declaration articulated principles of equality of application that even only two years later certain international policymakers would be seeking to restrict. Second, the contrasting statements help us to focus the real force of the Declaration, to understand where its principles should be addressed. Precisely at the moment the Declaration established the scope and consistency necessary to prohibit such expulsions as fascism had produced, so among the political relations most compromised was settler-colonial rule.[22] The geopolitical fault line most challenged, in other words, by a Declaration of Human Rights was that which insulated sovereign European states from equal engagement with other parts of the world. Which is not to argue that the Universal Declaration called for decolonization but to observe that, in so far as the principles of scope and consistency inscribed in the Declaration promised to open geo-political space, it was the colonizers who set out to resist such opening. Third, what the contrast between the Universal Declaration and the European Convention brings into focus is the perceived importance, in the immediate post-war moment, of the relation between language and geopolitical space. If there were not to be geopolitical non-persons, then there must not be settings in which non-personhood was to be produced, from which it followed that a language had to be arrived at which ensured basic continuities of recognition across political space. Partial as its compositional process unquestionably was, the Universal Declaration instituted a language of political relation that, in its scope and proposed application, had the potential, if mobilized, to radicalize geopolitical space.

That 'recognition' was core to such a language, that it constituted one of the terms by which the urgencies of contemporary politics had come to be expressed, is apparent from the Declaration's 'Preamble', witness the clause by which the document introduces its concerns:

Whereas recognition of the inherent dignity and of the equal and inalienable rights of all members of the human family is the foundation of freedom, justice and peace in the world.[23]

There are other key nouns that describe actions in the Declaration, for instance, 'protection' as regards individuals and their rights and 'realisation' as regards the development of the individual. 'Recognition' is crucial, however, in the reciprocity it proposes to introduce to the discourse. Thus, whereas both 'protection' and 'realisation' imply both an individual and also a society to which the individual relates, so in both cases the relationship is asymmetrical: some agency has to do the protecting; there must be some social context in which the individual personality might be realized. It is this kind of asymmetry that Joseph Slaughter has in mind when he likens the image of the person in human rights discourse to the image of the person in the *Bildungsroman*. The individual rights bearer secures membership of society by petitioning the structures of the state. The term 'recognition', by contrast, at least as it is positioned here, seeks to establish a mutuality of participation. This is why it occurs as the first substantive term in the Declaration, with the 'recognition' in question serving to underwrite both the rights of individual members of 'the human family' and the 'foundation' of the collective itself.

The term is mentioned three more times in the document, each time at a strategic moment. The first is in the closing clause of the 'Preamble', where all individuals, groups, and organs of society are exhorted 'to promote respect for these rights and freedoms and by progressive measures, national and international, to secure their universal and effective recognition'.[24] The second occurs in Article 29, part 2 of which reads

> In the exercise of his rights and freedoms, everyone shall be subject only to such limitations as are determined by law solely for the purpose of securing due recognition and respect for the rights and freedoms of others and of meeting the just requirements of morality, public order and the general welfare in a democratic society.[25]

The third further reference occurs in Article 6, perhaps the most comprehensive of the Declaration's pronouncements, where it is stated that: 'Everyone has the right to recognition everywhere as a person before the law.'[26] Both Articles, 29 and 6, have particular importance within the document. It is in Article 29 that the authors of the Declaration set out most clearly to articulate the human collective implied by rights, it being in that statement that obligations to others and the collective are set forth. As Morsink reports, Humphrey originally intended that Article 29 should appear as Article 2, an ordering that would certainly have altered future readings.[27] Article 6, on the other hand, is the first of the Declaration's seven statements on legal rights (Articles 6–12) and serves to underpin both that series of statements itself and the document as a whole. The 'right to recognition everywhere as a person before the law' is the closest the document comes to what Arendt termed 'the right to have rights'.[28] Above all articles, it is through the 'recognition' afforded by Article 6 that the status of non-personhood was intended to be precluded.

To register the Declaration's articulation of 'recognition' is to observe the degree to which the document is a spatially orientated text, that its concern, finally, is not with the development of personality or the preservation of human essence but with people in their relationality. Where this is most apparent is in Article 6 itself, the earlier draft of which was not so pithy, reading instead: 'Everyone has the right everywhere in the world to be recognized as a legal person.'[29] What that clunky early draft lacked, as in some sense the authors must have appreciated, was the dynamic spatialization that eventually they arrived at in the final version. What, by contrast, that final version—'Everyone has the right to recognition everywhere as a person before the law'—establishes, through the combination of 'everyone', 'everywhere', and the preposition 'before', is that recognition is fundamentally a function of space. For people to be recognized as such, for there not to be non-personhood, then, as the authors of the Declaration understood, it was necessary to articulate a non-expulsive political space. This was, as it remains, an immensely difficult task since the principal geopolitical space in question was the nation state and since both the geopolitical non-person and the non-places which they are forced to inhabit and in which they are produced had come to be a defining aspect of the international order. Immensely difficult, but not impossible; witness the document the Universal Declaration gave rise to, the 1951 Convention Relating to the Status of Refugees.

That the adoption of the 1951 Convention constituted a defining mid-century moment is evident in various respects. It was the first 'human rights treaty to be adopted in the wake of the Universal Declaration of Human Rights', arising directly from Article 14 of the Declaration on the right to seek and enjoy asylum.[30] It was also the first international document to articulate a 'universal definition of the term refugee', its predecessor documents, the 1933 and 1938 conventions formulated under the auspices of the League of Nations, having presented 'group-based ad hoc approaches to addressing forced displacement situations'.[31] Though not without its restrictions on extent, limited as its provisions were to events prior to 1951 and principally, but not exclusively, to European situations (limitations overridden by the 1967 Protocol), even so, in the generality of its approach to the question, the Convention broke new ground. As Terje Einarsen puts it, commenting on the 1946 session of the General Assembly of the United Nations at which the idea of the Convention was first proposed,

> It was decided to start the work of a general convention for the protection of refugees and stateless persons. The international spirit had changed and was significantly more visionary than before.[32]

What the 1951 Convention envisioned—above and beyond its careful detailing of the obligations signatory states would have to refugees (provisions the argument will come back to in subsequent chapters)—was a different relation of persons to political space. As the third Recital puts it,

> It is desirable to revise and consolidate previous international agreements relating to the status of refugees and to extend the scope of and protection accorded by such instruments by means of a new agreement.[33]

Where the protection accorded by earlier conventions extended to particular groups of displaced people, it was the intention of the 1951 Convention to generalize such protection and therefore significantly to extend its scope.

It is in the body of the document itself, however, that the most radical reconfiguration of political space was proposed:

Article 32
Expulsion

1. The Contracting States shall not expel a refugee lawfully in their territory save on grounds of national security or public order.

Article 33
Prohibition of expulsion or return ('refoulement')

1. No Contracting State shall expel or return ('refouler') a refugee in any manner whatsoever to the frontiers of territories where his life or freedom would be threatened on account of his race, religion, nationality, membership of a particular social group or political opinion.[34]

The 1951 Refugee Convention is not predicated on a world in which persons are not expelled; precisely in addressing the status of refugees, the Convention is addressing itself to the reality of expulsion. It does, however, picture a world in which, to all intents and purposes, re-expulsion, or as the document puts it, *refoulement*, does not occur. It is of great importance that the French term was preserved. The verb *refouler* means to force or to push back, deriving from the nineteenth-century noun *refoulement*, being the instance of 'water being forced back into the channel of a river'. Or say a channel of any kind. Say the English Channel, for instance, back across which the UK government now seeks to force those who seek refuge.[35] The French term is necessary, in other words, because it preserves a palpability of space, because it tells us what we do when we repel those who seek asylum. Difficult as it was for commentators to imagine in the face of the production of geopolitical non-personhood that followed the Second World War, and difficult as it is, once again, to imagine now, in the mid-century moment, thinkers of various kinds, but crucially the authors of the 1951 Convention, became capable of imagining a non-expulsive space. To imagine such a space, to articulate it, does not guarantee that it comes into being. But it does indicate, as variously the writers with which this book is concerned wanted to indicate, that such a space can be envisioned.

A Whole Series of New Recognitions

When Charles Olson published the essay 'Projective Verse' in *New York Poetry* in the Spring of 1950, he issued a set of findings that had been long in development. Although with only one slim volume of poetry, *Y & X*, to his name, and with his first major poem, 'The Kingfishers', still awaiting publication, by the time he laid out the principles of what he variously termed (in his subsequent 'Letter to Elaine Feinstein') 'Projective Open or Field Verse', Olson had given extensive thought to the situation of contemporary poetry.[36] In part circumstantially, but also characteristically, Olson's thinking about poetry had crossed and been informed by various intersecting practices and disciplines. As a graduate student at Harvard in the 1930s, he had altered the field of Melville studies, both as archivist (re-assembling Melville's library) and through his radical re-contextualization of *Moby-Dick*.[37] The resulting book, *Call Me Ishmael*, published in 1947, dug deep into the political economy of mid-nineteenth-century New England, presenting Melville's novel as the period's focal point.[38] Between graduate study and the publication of his research, Olson was politically engaged in the war effort, rising to a position of seniority in Roosevelt's Democratic Party. In October 1948, he was appointed visiting lecturer at the experimental arts institute Black Mountain College, an institution (as will be discussed in Chapter 3) shaped, from its inception, by the expulsion in 1933 of leading German artists from the Bauhaus. *Y & X*, published in 1949, was a co-publication with Corrado Cagli, to whose drawings of Buchenwald Olson's poems issued a response. Written and revised in collaboration with Robert Creeley and Frances Boldereff, 'Projective Verse' appeared in *New York Poetry* on 3 April 1950. Noting the essay's moment of publication in his introduction to Olson's *Selected Writings*, Creeley observed: 'The date is significant.'[39]

In insisting on the significance of the date, Creeley, writing in 1965, was in part underlining Olson's own assertion, in correspondence with Donald Allen, that the year 1950 (not some earlier Modernist moment) was the appropriate start date for what Allen (not Olson) would call the New American Poetry.[40] Indebted as it undoubtedly was to Modernist models, Olson's view was that poetry after the war had to be understood to be irrevocably different from what had gone before. There were continuities, but unquestionably, also, there had been a rupture, in the description of which Olson coined the term 'post-Modern'.[41] But when Creeley wrote, without qualification or explanation, of the publication of 'Projective Verse', that the date was significant, it was not primarily to underscore a literary historical narrative. What mattered, as he saw it, was simply that with the appearance of the essay a change had been effected, that the possibilities of poetry, and creative thought more generally, had been altered.

Looking back from the present vantage point, after the many readings and counter-readings generated by the essay's welter of terms, and with knowledge of the major body of work that emerged out of it, it can be difficult to get a fix on Olson's central findings, on what he was really introducing when he announced his new approach. It is useful, therefore, to go back to the central term itself, to the 'field', the metaphor on which all of Olson's innovations hinged. A glance at the dictionary gives a series of partly overlapping, partly disconnected meanings that, in the combination of their relatedness and unrelatedness, speak to Olson's aesthetic intent. A field, to work from the ground up, is an 'area of open land', though one might note immediately that the designation of a given 'area' is at some level at odds with the definition's basic assertion of openness. An important sub-meaning of this first definition, stepping away from the term's pastoral implication, is that of land 'rich in a natural product such as oil, or gas'. A second meaning of the term is that of 'a branch of study or sphere of activity'. A third meaning indicates 'the space or range within which objects are visible from a viewpoint or through a particular apparatus'. In sport, not to be disregarded, the field means 'all the participants in a given event'. In physics, the term defines the region in which 'a force such as gravity or magnetism is effected'. In mathematics, it points to 'a system subject to two binary operations analogous to those for the multiplication and addition of real numbers, and having similar commutative and distributive laws'.[42]

When Olson used the term 'field', when in his essay he spoke of 'the moment' the poet 'ventures into FIELD COMPOSITION' (Olson's emphasis), all of the above meanings were, in some measure, in play.[43] As in his book about Melville, in which he presented it as the 'central fact', he meant to make space (the space of the page and the space of the person inscribing the page) central to the new poetics, both as a common property and as a site of potential conflict.[44] He meant to signal diverse spheres of practice and knowledge and, more particularly, their connections and intersections. He meant to raise the limitations and difficulty registered by the fact of a framing view. He wanted to emphasize the idea of shaping forces, drawing on the term's meaning in physics. He wanted, crucially, to establish the poem as a means of attending to 'all participants'. To say it in a single sentence: what Olson set out in 'Projective Verse', following the catastrophic abuse of personhood that culminated in the Holocaust, and building on his cross-disciplinary study of political and economic space in nineteenth-century literature, was a conception of the poem grounded in relations, an aesthetic that made relatedness (of people, objects, and ideas) axiomatic to the poem's form and creative practice.

That Olson's essay warrants such attention, limited as its circulation was at the moment of publication, would have seemed entirely plausible by 1958. By that point, Allen was already planning the shape and contents of *The New American Poetry*, an anthology that would come to define poetic work of the post-war period and in which Olson was the principal aesthetic presence.[45] That Olson himself, on the other hand, felt he had arrived at a form of expression worthy of consideration is evident from the tone of the essay's opening sentence. As he put it, laying the credibility of the art form on the line,

> Verse now, 1950, if it is to go ahead, if it is to be of *essential* use, must, I take it, catch up and put into itself certain laws and possibilities of the breath, of the breathing of the man who writes as well as his listenings.[46]

It suited Olson to say, of course, that everything was at stake. But as he saw it, following the war, everything *was* at stake. 'Projective Verse', this is to observe, had the force of a declaration, and what that declaration rested on was Olson's expression of three interlocking terms: 'recognition', 'listening', and the term they opened on to, 'space'.

Olson has many terms in play in 'Projective Verse', terms that criticism has dwelt on at length: 'breath', 'projection', 'geometry', 'kinetics', 'composition by field', 'stance towards reality', 'objectism'. There are two ways, not mutually exclusive, in which one can think about such a profusion of terms itself. In the first place, in setting out to open a new field of poetic inquiry, Olson is trialling concepts, looking to see which of his various forms of expression has purchase. At the same time, however, there is clearly a sense in which he wants his reader to think with all the terms he brings forward. What is required at this point is a new set of coordinates, a way of envisioning space so that all the elements and relations it consists in are understood to belong. It is towards that new spatial mapping that Olson puts his welter of terms into circulation.

But if all of Olson's terms are significant to the picture of the open field he is looking to introduce to mid-century thought and practice, the idea of recognition appears integral to the act of writing itself. Setting out to describe the process he variously calls 'open field poetics' or 'COMPOSITION BY FIELD', Olson sets out to address, 'the problem which any poet who departs from closed form is especially confronted by'. What that problem 'involves', as he puts it, is

> a whole series of new recognitions. From the moment he ventures into FIELD COMPOSITION—puts himself in the open—he can go by no track other than the one the poem under hand declares, for itself. Thus he has to behave, and be, instant by instant, aware of some several forces just now beginning to be examined.[47]

Olson's tone is characteristically urgent. We are to understand that we are on the brink, or in the midst, of a discovery. We are also to understand that the process being discovered is intensely demanding, requiring of the poet an 'instant-by-instant' attention to the work in hand. Integral to this process is what Olson calls 'a whole series of new recognitions', out of which, as he goes on to say, a new understanding of the compositional process begins to emerge. Thus, as he puts it, in a single sentence that aims to bring everything into view,

The objects which occur at every given moment of composition (of recognition we can call it) are, can be, must be treated exactly as they do occur therein and not by any ideas or preconceptions from outside the poem, must be handled as a series of objects in field in such a way that a series of tensions (which they also are) are made to *hold*, and to hold exactly, inside the content and the context of the poem which has forced itself, through the poet and them into being.[48]

Here is a conceptualization of space, albeit written space, from which it is envisaged nothing is forced out. Objects are to be treated 'exactly as they do occur [. . .] and not by any ideas or preconceptions from outside'. The word for this mode of engagement, as he tells us, is 'recognition', a term which, here, is synonymous with 'composition'. To write, or to compose, in the open-field manner Olson is proposing is to engage, fundamentally, in the act of recognition.

To observe the intersection at the point of 'recognition' between 'Projective Verse' and the Universal Declaration is not to argue in any simple way that Olson's essay was influenced by the Declaration: that he read the Declaration then he wrote 'Projective Verse'. It is to argue, rather, that 'Projective Verse' was shaped by, and emerged out of, the knowledge, concerns, dynamics, and impulses that called the Universal Declaration into being. There was no question, in the years following the war, that the state-sponsored production of expulsion, of expulsive space, was a defining political issue, and therefore that all forms of intellectual enterprise should arrive at—or more precisely, perhaps, contribute to—a response. If, as Olson says, verse in 1950 was to be 'of essential use', then what that meant was developing some kind of apparatus whereby 'recognition' might be possible, a term that the Modernists had not emphasized but which the Universal Declaration had entered into international circulation. To read the two documents in relation to one another is thus to register that, as much as 'Projective Verse' was at one level a guide to poetry and poetics, so also, in so far as it proposed a new 'stance toward reality', what it sought to articulate was a cognitive, or imaginative, ideal.

My observation here is not simply that Olson alights on the term 'recognition' as the name for his new mode of composition but that, in 'Projective Verse', what he articulates is something like a whole apparatus of recognition, where in its every aspect the open-field poem's purported objective is to render things apparent. As regards expression, Olson's emphasis and attention fall principally on the syllable, it being 'by their syllables that words juxtapose in beauty'.[49] The demand of such attention is high ('the exaction must be so complete') and requires, as Olson frequently reminds us, 'daily work'. The aim of that work is an intensity of listening that draws out the syllables in the beauty of their juxtapositions so that each syllable, like each of the poem's objects, is allowed to hold its place. By the same token, the poem must make it its objective to allow its elements to give the writing shape. One of the takeaway phrases of the manifesto, attributed to Robert Creeley, is that 'FORM IS NEVER MORE THAN AN EXTENSION OF CONTENT'. The principal aim of the poem's form is not to direct but to disclose the materials it brings forward.[50]

To appreciate what is implied here, it is useful, I think, to register an analogy in Arendt, from her chapter 'The Decline of the Nation-State and the End of the Rights of Man'. As Derrida notes in his discussion of hospitality in 'On Cosmopolitanism', in that chapter (contemporary with 'Projective Verse'), Arendt offered, as a counter to the image of the expulsive spatiality of the modern nation state, a medieval principle of a person's relation to territory. As Derrida remarks, 'Arendt recalls that this right [of asylum] has a "sacred history", and that it remains "the only modern vestige of the medieval principle of *quid est in territorio est de territorio*"'.[51] As the Latin puts it, 'that which is in the territory is of the territory'. There is not some separate place, or non-place, to which things or persons might find themselves expelled. It is in this way that Olson and Creeley want the reader to think about the poem; or rather, it is in this way that they want the reader to use the poem to think. What Olson wanted the reader to imagine, through open-field poetics, just as Arendt wanted her reader to imagine, through the medieval principle she cites, is a setting from which no element is excluded, a non-expulsive comprehension of space.

'Projective Verse' is in two parts. The first part concentrates on what Olson calls 'the new stance toward the reality of the poem itself'. In other words, in that part of the essay, Olson aims to show how the writing of poems has to change. The second part of the essay, by contrast, is concerned with 'the degree to which the projective involves a stance toward reality outside a poem'.[52] It is this second, less discussed part of the essay, that bears the real weight of Olson's thought. His aim, as he stated at the beginning of the piece, was to ensure that verse in 1950 should be of 'essential use', and what that meant, for Olson, was that the poem should permit or enable a different relation between persons and space. What this calls for, as Olson describes it, is the act of 'listening'. As he puts it, and to quote at length,

If [the poet] sprawl, he shall find little to sing but himself, and shall sing, nature has such paradoxical ways, by way of artificial forms outside himself. But if he stays inside himself, if he is contained within his nature as he is participant in the larger force, he will be able to listen, and his hearing through himself will give him secrets objects share. And by an inverse law his shapes will make their own way. It is in this sense that the projective act, which is the artist's act in the larger field of objects, leads to dimensions larger than the man [...] It is projective size that the play, *The Trojan Women*, possesses, for it is able to stand, is it not, as its people do, beside the Aegean—and neither Andromache or the sea suffer diminution [...] I would hazard the guess that, if projective verse is practiced long enough, is driven ahead hard enough along the course I think it dictates, verse again can carry much larger material than it has carried in our language since the Elizabethans.[53]

Olson takes his reader as far as he can here. The task of the poet is not to 'sprawl', not to extend themselves, but to 'listen', and in that act of 'listening', which is an act of 'recognition', to become capable of articulating 'the larger field of objects', of imagining on a different 'scale'. He does not say quite what this means in the mid-century moment because as a poet at an early stage in his career he does not yet entirely know. He can, however, point to historic examples: to Adromache, for instance, in *The Trojan Women*, bringing the Aegean into view. It is by such gestures, Olson considers, that verse in 1950 can be of use. The intention, in the face of brutal spatial foreclosures, is to change the dimensions, to enable thinking about the human to take place on a different scale. The aim, however compromised it would become in practice, is to envision what might properly be called a space of recognition, a dimensionality in which people are visible as participants.

To Live Outside the Common World

In the closing paragraphs of 'The Perplexities of the Rights of Man', Hannah Arendt set out to picture the world that had emerged and was emerging through the geopolitical production of non-personhood. Seeking to provide an image that captured both the scale of the situation and its defining dynamics, Arendt drew, in this concluding assessment, on an older rhetoric of displacement. As she put it,

> The great danger arising from the existence of people forced to live outside the common world is that they are thrown back, in the midst of civilization, on their natural givenness, on their mere differentiation. They lack that tremendous equalizing of differences which comes from being citizens of some commonwealth and yet, since they are no longer allowed to partake in the human artifice, they begin to belong to the human race in much the same way as animals belong to a specific animal species. The paradox involved in the loss of human rights is that such loss coincides with the instant when a person becomes a human being in general—without a profession, without a citizenship, without an opinion, without a deed by which to identify and specify himself—*and* different in general, representing nothing but his own absolutely unique individuality which, deprived of expression within and action upon a common world, loses all significance.[54]

With this passage, Arendt aims to bring the condition of mid-century non-personhood to a moment of high visibility. To observe 'people forced to live outside the common world', 'some commonwealth' as she puts it, is to draw on early modern dislocations, moments in the history of capitalist expansion and extraction when accumulation was achieved through eviction. To be 'thrown back' is effectively to be thrown off or thrown out, forcibly removed from an area held in common. What Arendt draws on, in other words, as she seeks to visualize the reality of global non-personhood, is the process the contemporary border theorist, Thomas Nail, names as 'expulsion', a concept he derives from Marx's account of 'primitive accumulation'.

Noting that whereas Adam Smith mythologizes the earliest form of accumulation in order to obscure its basic criminality, Nail recalls how

> Marx identifies this process with the expulsion of peasants and indigenous peoples from their land through enclosure, colonialism and anti-vagabond laws in sixteenth-century England. Marx's thesis is that the condition of the social expansion of capitalism is the prior expulsion of people from their land and from their juridical status under customary law.[55]

Nail hardly disagrees that such 'expulsion' is instrumental to the initial expansion of private property and therefore capital. He does, however, want to insist that expulsion takes, and has come to take, different forms. As he goes on to argue,

Expulsion does not simply mean forcing people off their land, although in many cases it may include this. It also means depriving people of their political rights by walling off the city, criminalizing types of persons by the cellular techniques of enclosure and incarceration, or restricting their access to work by identification and checkpoint techniques. Expulsion is the degree to which a political subject is deprived or dispossessed of a certain status in the social order.[56]

Arendt's image, at the end of 'The Perplexities of Human Rights', of people forced outside the common world is her attempt to encapsulate what she takes to be the post-war moment's defining condition. The world had organized itself to generate a new form of expulsion, the production of the juridical non-person, where such non-personhood, which is to say existence outside the commons, was variously observable on an extraordinary scale. No mid-century commentator articulated the scale of that expulsion more forcefully than Arendt, from which it followed that, as much as any contemporary, she understood the imperative to find forms of expression from which nobody was expelled, the language of rights providing a prominent model.

Arendt's attitude towards that language, or rather towards the concept of human rights, was complex: not despairing quite of the concept's potential but in her attempts, as Mark Greif observes, to express the need for its renewal, subtly but significantly out of date. Thus, on the one hand, as she detailed forcefully in the essay on interwar statelessness she folded into *The Origins of Totalitarianism*, the concept of rights had been seen to fail at precisely the juncture and with respect to precisely the people it was apparently intended to address. As she puts it, in one of several such formulations, 'The Rights of Man, supposedly inalienable, proved to be unenforceable [. . .] whenever people appeared who were no longer citizens of any sovereign state.'[57]

Writing after the promulgation of the Universal Declaration but, crucially, with respect to the phenomenon of statelessness that followed the First World War, Arendt's point was that the discourse of rights had failed precisely at the perimeter of the sovereign state, that no understanding of rights had been arrived at that would extend their application beyond that point. This was to alter in the year Arendt's text was published, with the formulation of the 1951 Convention Relating to the Status of Refugees. But Arendt's commentary concerned the interwar moment and the limitation in the language of rights the history of that period disclosed.

Arendt's bleak, if hardly unreal, assessment of the interwar period is largely reflective of her thinking in the first edition of *The Origins of Totalitarianism*. Committed as she was to what Ayten Gündoğdu calls the 'equivocality and contingency' of history (the fact that history could have been otherwise), Arendt nonetheless provides such a compelling account of the consequences of the development of the sovereign state that it is difficult for her to imagine human relationality otherwise.[58] It is a position she gradually adjusts, hence the different rendering of political space she offers in *The Human Condition*. Even in the earlier book, however, it is possible to observe moments of latitude in her thought, witness the understanding of rights she articulates in 'Totalitarianism in Power'. Providing a synoptic account of the crimes of the Second World War, Arendt observes, in a moment of devastating rhetoric, the ways in which

> The insane mass manufacture of corpses is preceded by the historically and politically intelligible preparation of living corpses. The impetus and what is more important, the silent consent to such unprecedented conditions are the products of those events which in a period of political disintegration suddenly and unexpectedly made hundreds and thousands of human beings homeless, stateless, outlawed and unwanted [...] This in turn could only happen because the Rights of Man, which had never been philosophically established, but merely formulated, which had never been politically secured but merely proclaimed, have, in their traditional form, lost all validity.[59]

It is crucial, in considering Arendt's assessment of the value of 'the Rights of Man'—and, given her influence over the discourse, crucial in considering their value more generally—that we hear the balance of this statement right. There is a reading of Arendt's remark that can construe it as identifying the 'rights of man' or, more particularly, their failure, as the cause of what she terms the insanity of the camps. Precisely by designating a bare humanity that it could not protect, the concept of rights (so the logic of this reading goes) exposed the non-person whose security it could not guarantee. To be a claimant of rights, in other words, was to be identifiable as existing outside the sovereign state, membership of which was all that actually secured recognition. In its unenforceability, the effect of the language of rights is to identify but not to ameliorate vulnerability, therefore, in practice, compounding the original condition. This, broadly speaking, is Rancière's reading of Arendt's critique of rights, and although, as I will observe, Rancière is compelling in his broad response to Arendt's thinking about rights, his assessment of her critique is, I think, a misconstruction.[60]

How one hears that critique turns on one's reading of the complicated final sentence:

> This in turn could only happen because the Rights of Man, which had never been philosophically established, but merely formulated, which had never been politically secured but merely proclaimed, have, in their traditional form, lost all validity.

There is an ambiguity at work in this statement that exemplifies what Gündoğdu means by the 'equivocality' of Arendt's thought. While Arendt clearly wants to observe that, in the interwar period, history has demonstrated the fallibility of the concept of rights (that 'in their traditional form' they have 'lost all validity'), she allows the possibility that such rights might yet be philosophically established, that they might be politically secured. What looks like a statement on Arendt's part is also, implicitly, a question. There is a significant difference of intention, as James Ingram documents, between philosophical and political justifications of rights—between the question 'why we have them' and the problem, which he is much more interested in, 'of putting human rights into practice'—and arguably it is Arendt's mistake that she allows her inquiry to hover between the two.[61] What we need to hear in the first instance, however, is that, for Arendt, the question of whether rights might be established was real.

Arendt's answer to her implied question lies in the linkage she proposes between the non-personhood of statelessness and the non-personhood of the camps, which by her own account indicates a linkage between two dysfunctionalities of space. Statelessness was the effect of the organization of geopolitical space according to the principle of sovereignty, the consolidation of which meant that millions of people were rendered without a home. In consequence of which, the state came actively to produce a non-space, a setting to house those persons whom statelessness had rendered superfluous or void. It was this condition of spatial dysfunctionality to which the language of rights was intended as a response. From which it followed that if rights were to be philosophically established (not merely formulated) and politically secured (not merely proclaimed), it was towards a recalibration of space that intellectual energy had to be devoted.

The text in which Arendt undertook such a recalibration of political space was *The Human Condition*. Stepping outside the immediate pressures of history but looking to address the logic of expulsion that recent history had produced, *The Human Condition* set out to provide an image of the form of human relationality that any articulation of the political realm ought to seek to protect, her term for that image being 'the space of appearance':

> It is the space of appearance in the widest sense of the word, namely, the space where I appear to others as others appear to me, where men exist not merely like other living or inanimate things but make their appearance explicitly [...] [This] space of appearance comes into being wherever men are together in the manner of speech and action, and therefore predates and precedes all formal constitution of the public realm and the various forms of government, that is the various forms in which the public realm can be organized.[62]

The strongest readings of Arendt understand, with Balibar, that she must be thought with and beyond, or as Ingram puts it, that her work must be 'productively extended'. Invariably, this is to observe, in Arendt's thought there is a step towards agency that either she doesn't register or she doesn't take. What she doesn't register in *The Human Condition*, even as she articulates the necessity of a non-expulsive space, is that the 'space of appearance' is, to all intents and purposes, the space of rights. For Ingram, what this means is that 'the space of appearance' is the setting for what Arendt famously, but only speculatively, designated, 'the right to have rights', where that underlying right amounts, as Balibar argues, to the 'right to have politics'.[63] That Arendt would not have seen it this way—that she took the thinking of *The Human Condition* to be a departure from, not a supplement to, her critique of the concept of rights—owes in part to the particular historical pressures to which she was responding. She grasped the scale of mid-century statelessness because she had documented the histories of interwar statelessness, a period in which individuals had been failed by the concept of rights, where, as she put it, 'the loss of human rights [...] coincides with the instant when a person becomes a human being in general—without a profession, without a citizenship, without an opinion, without a deed by which to identify and specify himself'.

What Arendt critiques here is not any actual statement of human rights but the concept of human rights in general. She reads that general concept through the history of the interwar period, and, not unreasonably, she finds the concept to have failed, with individuals abandoned to their individuality. What she failed to register, because she was reading rights in the abstract not in their written expression, was that this was precisely the problematic the authors of the Universal Declaration were seeking to address. To read that document in its mid-century moment, alongside texts, including Arendt's, which shared its commitment to a language of non-expulsion, is to grasp its intention to articulate a relational space: a set of recognitions and relations that constitute a commons, a space from which, where they operate, no person might be expelled. This is what Thomas Nail means when he extends the Marxian notion of expulsion (as eviction from land held physically in common) to include 'depriving people of their political rights by walling off the city, criminalizing types of persons by the cellular techniques of enclosure and incarceration, or restricting their access to work by identification and checkpoint techniques'. The Declaration of Human Rights, this is to underscore, was written against expulsion, an image of a commons articulated in the context of a mid-century discourse seeking urgently to imagine a non-expulsive space.

Which is, of course, to beg the question. Human rights are not always in operation; if they were, it would not be necessary to write them down. The crucial point, however, is that unless we understand them as articulating a set of relationalities, a space of recognitions, they cannot have the force we need them to have. This, finally, is Rancière's response to Arendt, when he sets out what he calls the politics of human rights. As Rancière puts it, and to quote him at length,

> There is no man of the Rights of Man, but there is no need for such a man. The strength of those rights lies in the back-and-forth movement between the first inscription of the right and the dissensual stage on which it is put to test. This is why the subjects of the Soviet constitution could make reference to the Rights of Man against the laws that denied their effectivity. This is also why today the citizens of states ruled by a religious law or by the mere arbitrariness of their governments, and even the clandestine immigrants in the zones of transit of our countries or the populations in the camps of refugees, can invoke them. These rights are theirs when they can do something with them to construct a dissensus against the denial of rights they suffer. And there are always people among them who do it. It is only if you presuppose that the rights *belong* to definite or permanent subjects that you must state, as Arendt did, that the only real rights are the rights given to the citizens of a nation by their belonging to that nation, and guaranteed

by the protection of their state. If you do this, of course, you must deny the reality of the struggles led outside of the frame of the national constitutional state and assume that the situation of the "merely" human person deprived of national rights is the implementation of the abstractedness of those rights.[64]

It is instructive to read Rancière's commentary back into the mid-century moment to which ultimately it refers. When the authors of the Universal Declaration inscribed the preamble and thirty articles that constituted the series of human rights, they produced a setting 'outside of the frame of the national constitutional space'. What that setting amounts to, as Rancière puts it, is a dissensus, a space that it is always possible to claim precisely because it has been written down, where the act of claiming is the act of putting rights to use. To read the Declaration in the moment of its composition, alongside texts that were similarly written against expulsion, is to register the degree to which, as a mid-century document, it understood itself to be addressing spatial concerns. To understand the document this way, in the context of its production, is to appreciate the degree to which human rights are always a disruptive concept. In their inscription, and in the possibilities of enactment that inscription continues to produce, they call on and require a reimagining of political space.

Fanon's Mid-Century Anti-*Bildungsroman*

To read Fanon alongside such defining mid-century documents as the Universal Declaration of Human Rights and the Convention Relating to the Status of Refugees is, in one sense, to correlate texts that were worlds apart. Whereas the Declaration and the Convention were issued with all the authority of the United Nations (relocated for the occasions from its Headquarters in New York to Paris and Geneva, respectively), Fanon situated the preamble to *Peau Noire, Masques Blancs* as if writing from the void:

> Why write this book? No one has asked me for it.
> Especially those to whom it is directed.
> Well? Well, I reply quite calmly that there are too many idiots in this world. And having said it, I have the burden of proving it.

> Toward a new humanism ...
> Understanding among men ...
> Our colored bothers ...
> Mankind, I believe in you ...
> Race prejudice ....
> To understand and to love ....[65]

The publication history of *Peau Noire, Masques Blancs* confirms the speculative tone of Fanon's introduction. First published in Paris in 1952 by Editions de Seuil, the book was not translated into English until it came out with Grove Press in New York in 1967. As Paul Gilroy notes, this lag in the book's translation underlines Fanon's invisibility in 1952. It also had an impact on his reception, with the English-language edition of *Black Skin, White Masks* appearing after the translations of *Wretched of the Earth* and *Studies in a Dying Colonialism*. The sequence was consequential because, as Gilroy observes, Fanon's first work established the scope and theme of his ongoing inquiry in significant ways. As Gilroy puts it,

> *Black Skin, White Masks* attracted little interest and few reviews when it was first published in 1952. It appeared in an environment that was still reverberating with the aftershocks of the Second World War, a conflict which had restricted legitimate struggle against racism exclusively to the anti-Nazi effort. Adapting and extending that geopolitical morality, Fanon turned towards the flowering of demands for independence from colonial rule.[66]

The fact that, at the age of twenty-seven and as a debut author, Fanon was able to adapt and extend the geopolitical morality that had constituted the 'anti-Nazi effort', owed in part to his institutional upbringing. Taught by Aimé Césaire at the leading Martinique High School Lycée Schoelcher, Fanon's thought and writing was partly framed by Césaire's *Discours sur le Colonialisme* (published in 1950 by Éditions Réclame), *Black Skin, White Masks* opening with an epigraph from Césaire's text that establishes both writers' relation to the history of racism:

> I am talking of millions of men who have been skillfully injected with fear, inferiority complexes, trepidation, servility, despair abasement.[67]

It was in Césaire, also, that Fanon found the basis for a complicated extension of the language of rights. As Césaire put it,

This is the great thing I hold against pseudo-humanism: that for too long it has diminished the rights of man, that its concept of those rights has been—and still is—narrow and fragmentary, incomplete and biased and, all things considered, sordidly racist.

I have talked a good deal about Hitler. Because he deserves it: he makes it possible to see things on a large scale and to grasp the fact that capitalist society, at its present stage, is incapable of establishing a concept of the rights of all men, just as it has proved incapable of establishing a system of individual ethics.[68]

When Fanon spoke, as he did throughout his career, about what in the opening sentences of *Black Skin, White Masks* he called 'a new humanism', Césaire's articulation of 'pseudo-humanism' was among his points of reference. Césaire was crucial, in other words, in setting out the implications of the 'concept of the rights of all men' for the colonial context, in drawing the link between the assertion of such rights, the struggle against fascism, and the ongoing institutionalized racism of settler-colonial capitalism. But if his early reading brought him to this point, to the need to extend and adapt emergent geopolitical morality, so too, critically, did his lived experience. Drawing deeply on his upbringing in Martinique, not least on his experience of the Nazi-inflected colonialism of the Vichy regime, and framing that experience through the lens of his arrival and residency as a student and trainee psychiatrist in France, Fanon's text can be read as something like a theoretical anti-*bildungsroman*. As he exposes the colonial constructions that result in what he terms psychopathologies, Fanon's critique stops well short of the moment of acceptance that is the genre's intended denouement. 'European civilization and its best representatives are responsible for colonial racism' and it will take more than a declaration of universal values to 'make possible a healthy encounter between black and white'.[69] Where Fanon's anti-*bildungsroman* concludes is precisely with the complex race politics of the scene of recognition, his chapter on 'Le Nègre et la Reconaissance' being the most searching of mid-century inquiries into the meaning of the term.

To draw attention to Fanon's extended consideration of 'recognition' in *Black Skin, White Masks* is to make an historical as much as a theoretical point. I am not arguing, this is to say, as Anita Chari warns we should not, that Fanon can be represented as a theorist of recognition. Chari is right to read him in opposition to a late-twentieth century politics of 'recognition' in which 'the struggle' amounts to 'a struggle to be recognized with the terms of a discourse that is dictated largely by the colonizer'.⁷⁰ She is wrong, however, while identifying that resistance in Fanon himself (a resistance on which he could not be more explicit), to propose that his inquiry into 'recognition' can simply be bypassed. It is in his negotiation with the term, his determination to think through it, that Fanon first extends and adapts the 'geopolitical morality' that had emerged, as Gilroy puts it, in the 'struggle against racism' constituted by the anti-Nazi effort. To hear Fanon thinking through 'recognition', this is to argue, is to observe his engagement with a concept that had presented itself historically as a means of articulating a non-expulsive space. The task, as he well understood, was to grasp the term dialectically: not to petition for cultural recognition in the manner of the protagonist of the *Bildungsroman* but to articulate the political space, the field of relations, that a reciprocal articulation of recognition could be taken to imply. It is entirely right, as Chari suggests, that Fanon exceeds recognition as a category. It is equally true that in order to proceed to frame an anti-racist, non-expulsive lived experience, Fanon engaged a category that in the mid-century moment enabled an extension of the discourse of rights.

In 'Le Nègre et la Reconaissance', Fanon provides what one might think of as alternative endings: two versions of the scene of recognition that between them draw a distinction that goes to the core of this chapter. Beginning with 'Le Nègre et Adler', Fanon identifies a process of recognition according to which the individual presents him- or herself for approval. As he observes, according to this model,

> The Martinicans are greedy for security. They want to compel the acceptance of their fiction. They want to be recognized in their quest for manhood. They want to make an appearance. Each one of them is an isolated, sterile, salient atom with sharply defined rights of passage, each of them *is*. Each one of them wants to *be*, to *emerge*. Everything that an Antillean does is done for The Other [. . .] because it is The Other who corroborates him in his search for self-validation.⁷¹

It is important to register the specific gravity of Fanon's terms here. In his image of the Martinican wanting to make an 'appearance', Fanon presents a framing of the rhetoric of recognition that amounts to a strictly limited human event. The problem rests on the model of 'rights' with which the principle of recognition is here shown to intersect. The 'rights of passage', as Fanon describes them, making use of the pun, are rights whose function is to allow entry into a given social setting, where the possibility of appearing is entirely on that society's terms. The kind of recognition that comes of such a 'right' is that which the narrative structure of the *Bildungsroman* expresses. Or as Fanon puts it, referring back to Adler,

> In effect, Adler has created a psychology of the individual. We have just seen that the feeling of inferiority is an Antillean characteristic. It is not just this or that Antillean who embodies the neurotic foundation, but all Antilleans. Antillean society is a neurotic society, a society of 'comparison'. Hence we are driven from the individual back to the social structure.[72]

In an account of recognition that limits itself to the 'psychology of the individual', the individual must petition the society by which they have been produced. In a colonial context, that would mean petitioning a racist structure. Witness the ending that Fanon presents as one version of the scene of recognition: 'At the climax of his anguish there remains only one solution [. . .] furnish proofs of his whiteness to others and above all to himself.'[73] Fanon could not be more clear. The model of recognition grounded in the psychology of the individual, where the individual who is colonized must 'furnish proofs of his whiteness', cannot be transformative. It cannot be on this basis that the geopolitical morality of rights might be adapted and extended.

The counter ending is presented in the section of the chapter called 'Le Nègre et Hegel', where the implications of 'recognition' are much more fully worked out. As he opens by observing,

> Man is human only to the extent to which he tries to impose his existence on another man in order to be recognized by him. As long as he has not been effectively recognized by the other, that other will remain the theme of his actions. It is on that other being, on recognition by that other being, that his own human worth and reality depend. It is that other being in whom the meaning of his life is condensed.[74]'

There is no escaping the conflict in this passage, derived in part from Hegel and in part from the lived experience of colonialism—an experience that would ultimately shape the case for conflict set out in *The Wretched of the Earth*. But it is important also to hear in his passage precisely how Fanon situates recognition at the centre of his mid-century discourse. Recognition, as Fanon wants to describe it, is necessary to humans because humans are relational animals. 'It is on [. . .] recognition by that other being' [where that other is not now capitalized, but might be just another person] 'that his own human worth and reality depend.' Fanon wants to say this because he wants his reader to understand what is stake in non-recognition, that state of expulsion in which personhood is denied. The situation might be summarized as follows. What the discourse of human rights extends is the quality of recognition. What recognition acknowledges is the fact that personhood is a relational act. Not to be recognized, to be held outside, is to be denied that possibility of relation through which personhood forms. Rights are human because they institute a quality of recognition upon which the relationality of being human depends.

Fanon is clear: to insist on 'recognition' is to insist on a quality of relationality on which personhood depends. Still, however, the task is to identify a model of recognition according to which such relationality might be underwritten. As he puts it,

> At the foundation of Hegelian dialectic there is an absolute reciprocity which must be emphasized. It is in the degree to which I go beyond my own immediate being that I apprehend the existence of the other as a natural and more than natural reality. If I close the circuit, if I prevent the accomplishment of movement in two directions, I keep the other within himself. Ultimately, I deprive him even of this being-for-itself.[75]

What Fanon finds in Hegel is a model of recognition where recognition is, by definition, a reciprocal act. With apologies for the terminological repetition (which I think is necessary): Fanon's meaning here is that to recognize a person is to recognize their capacity for recognition; it is to understand that just as their personhood is in part constituted by the recognition you extend, so your personhood is likewise constituted in reverse. Recognition, as Fanon understands it, is thus, fundamentally, a 'movement in two directions'; what Olson, describing the dynamics of open-field poetics, would call 'chiasmus'. The aim, in other words, of the scene of recognition in Fanon's text is not simply that the individual will be recognized but that the necessity for recognition will shape the situation itself. As he goes on to observe,

> As soon as I *desire* I am asking to be considered. I am not merely here-and-now, sealed into thingness. I am for somewhere else and for something else. I demand that notice be taken of my negating activity insofar as I pursue

something other than life; insofar as I do battle for the creation of a human world—that is, a world of reciprocal recognitions.[76]

The language of recognition can quickly become dense as writers using it seek to articulate the loops of relationality on which personhood depends. What must be acknowledged here, however, is that as Fanon drills down into the meaning of his central term, he arrives at a formulation upon which mid-century authors converged. To identify the 'creation of a human world' as the creation of 'a world of reciprocal recognitions' is to articulate a model of political relationality from which no person might be expelled, an expression, as Fanon hopes, of a non-expulsive space. To hear 'recognition' playing through and across texts and discourses in this way is thus to observe a defining term of the post-war period coming into view. Olson, who was keen on temporal markers, was among the earliest writers to propose a period he called the post-Modern, by which he meant to observe the historical rupture of the Second World War. What that rupture called for was 'recognition', the value of which term for Fanon, as Gilroy implies, is that it carried the weight of the international community's response to fascism. To adapt and extend that 'geopolitical morality' was to insist on the underlying principle's inherent scope. Understood as a reciprocal act, the logic of recognition, and of the human rights framed to secure it, had the potential to transform. It was why, where they could, the signatory authorities smuggled in a colonial clause.

Fanon's extension of the language of recognition and of rights must not be simplified, or rather, it must be heard with its anticipatory notes. As the final sentence of 'Le Nègre et la Reconaissance' puts it, 'To educate a man to be *actional*, preserving in all his relations his respect for the basic values that constitute a human world, is the prime task for him who, having taken thought, prepares to act.'[77] To act, as Fanon explains in *Black Skin, White Masks*, was, for the black person, to risk their life. In an abstract, existential sense, he considered that risk to be necessary since it was in the act of risking their life that a person demonstrated their refusal to live a bare existence. A bare existence was not a human existence precisely because it didn't entail or insist on recognition. If recognition was refused, then, at some level, it had to be fought for. It was a position—however controversial Arendt would subsequently claim to find it—that in the mid-century moment was broadly understood. Or at least, in so far as they claimed to voice such a broad understanding, the authors of the Universal Declaration understood that it was a form of action that followed from the articulation of rights. As the third recital of the Preamble put it,

Whereas it is essential, if man is not to be compelled to have recourse, as a last resort, to rebellion against tyranny and oppression, that human rights should be protected by the rule of law.[78]

The recital is clear. Where human rights were not protected, which is to say enshrined, by the rule of law, then people would be compelled to rebellion against tyranny. Where people were not to be heard, this is to say, where they could not leverage the voice enshrined by rights, they would be compelled, as a last resort, to 'leverage their bodies'.[79]

Such a situation, as Fanon explained in detail in 'Concerning Violence', obtained in Algeria. The purpose of that opening chapter of *The Wretched of the Earth* was to document the lived experience of those expelled by the French State and to detail the processes and apparatuses by which, on a daily basis, such expulsion was maintained. Those processes have been considered already, in the discussion of Fanon's articulation of the colonial non-place, but it is worth recalling how in practice, in the daily life of the person unrecognized by the law, the law intrudes:

> It is obvious here that the agents of government speak the language of pure force. The intermediary does not lighten the oppression, nor seek to hide the domination; he shows them up and puts them into practice with the clear conscience of an upholder of the peace; yet he is the bringer of violence into the home and into the mind of the native.[80]

This is what it means, as Fanon came to know from lived experience, to be held outside a law that protected human rights. These were the forms that expulsion would take, from which it followed, as Fanon saw it, that in the colonial context the forces effecting the expulsion had to be removed. Having patiently described how the colonial world is a world cut in two, allowing a marking out of 'lines on which a decolonized society will be reorganized', Fanon articulates the compulsion to what the authors of the Universal Declaration called 'rebellion': 'The destruction of the colonial world is no more and no less than the abolition of one zone, its burial in the depths of the earth or its expulsion from the country.'[81]

In the context of a discussion of mid-century writing against expulsion, these remarks steer towards a contradiction. What must also be recalled, however, in Fanon's case, is that his writing is driven by, and constantly returns to, the scene of recognition. By which I mean not the moment when the expelled person petitions the authorities for entry but the setting in which recognition is the shaping principle. It is a motif in Fanon's writing, bordering on a rhetorical reflex, that invariably when he mentions the Algerian revolution, or when he describes the claim to sovereignty that is the revolution's immediate political ground, he promptly extends the horizon to reference what, from the opening sentences of this first book onwards he called 'a new humanism' and where what that horizon constitutes is a setting of recognition. Witness the final remarks of *The Wretched of the Earth*:

> No, we do not want to catch up with anyone. What we want to do is go forward all the time, night and day, in the company of Man, in the company of all men. The caravan should not be stretched out, for in that case each line will hardly see those who precede it; and men who no longer recognize each other meet less and less together, and talk to each other less and less [...] For Europe, for ourselves, and for humanity, comrades, we must turn over a new leaf, we must work out new concepts, and try to set afoot a new man.[82]

For Fanon, it remained axiomatic that the non-expulsive political space was, at some level, a space of recognition. His image for that space was the caravan. He wrote, as we will see in Chapter 3, in order to set the new humanism afoot.

Conclusion

As we once again find ourselves in a geopolitical environment in which policy is being explicitly framed to produce expulsion, it is of value to reconsider what it meant, in the mid-century moment, to seek to envision a non-expulsive space. To do so is to recover histories and dimensions of terms whose implications have been obscured by familiarity and use. When Fanon, Arendt, Olson, and the authors of the Universal Declaration figured their thought in terms of recognition, their objective was to articulate a non-expulsive space. Recognition was a necessary coordinate within mid-century rights discourse, but rights discourse itself was a means of envisioning non-expulsion, a means of articulating a space from which—as the insistence on *non-refoulement* has it—people would not be pushed out or back. When we hear talk of rights and recognitions, in other words, in the present moment, and in particular when we observe rights and their implicit recognitions being degraded and abused, we have to picture the spaces those terms intended to keep open and the spatialities of expulsion they mean to prevent.

At the same time, and in the same breath, we have to understand that, as Chari says of Fanon, all the authors in question went beyond the expression of recognition, necessary as reciprocal recognitions were to a space shaped by rights. What they understood, and what their intersecting mid-century discourse shows, is that, as James Ingram argues, rights and the recognitions they imply 'are not in the first instance a matter of philosophical or moral ideas, state guarantees or legal declarations' but 'are created from the bottom up, through practices of communication and interaction'.[83] Just as, this is to say, in the texts and authors in question we find an intersecting commitment to envisaging a space in which reciprocal recognitions apply, so also that space is framed constantly in terms of human action and practice.

Two contemporary commentators on recognition help us to understand what this emphasis on action and practice mean. The first is Nancy Fraser, whose argument in 'Re-thinking Recognition' is that if we are to arrive at an understanding of the politics of recognition that allows 'parity of participation in social life', then it is necessary to specify the settings (by which she means the institutions) in which material mis- or non-recognition occurs. As she puts it,

> To be misrecognized [...] is not simply to be thought ill of, looked down upon or devalued in others' attitudes, beliefs or representations. It is rather to be denied the status of full partner in social interaction, as a consequence of institutionalized patterns of cultural value that constitute one as comparatively unworthy of respect or esteem.[84]

In the case of legal non-personhood, this could not be more true. Such status is not, in other words, just the result of an attitude or representation, of racism broadly maintained; it is the consequence of clearly formulated and knowingly executed racist policies which bear directly and destructively on the practices of personhood itself. The second theorist is Ingram, for whom 'a space of political freedom, a realm in which people can be recognized as interlocutors' does not 'consist principally in laws or institutions but is achieved through practice', by 'the practices of interaction and mutual recognition, conflict and cooperation, through which people construct a common public-political sphere'.[85]

To seek to envision, as various intersecting mid-century authors did, a spatiality of non-expulsion, was to insist on spaces in which rights and recognitions applied. But it was also to argue not simply for concepts but for practices, practices through which recognitions and rights are sustained. The question for the authors with whom this book is concerned—for Olson, for Arendt, for Fanon, for the authors of the Universal Declaration of Human Rights—was not only how they might articulate the desire for a space from which nobody might be expelled but also how such a form of commons could be effected. In each case, the writers understood that to get beyond the aspiration towards a generalized space of recognition, it was necessary to identify human practices through which such a space might be sustained. The discussions that informed the drafting of the Universal Declaration are a record of this understanding as well as a documenting of precisely those junctures where such an opening was blocked. The second half of this book addresses itself to such specific junctures, to settings and practices via which, as these authors understood it, a space of 'parity of participation' might be achieved. Through far-reaching considerations of the acts of moving, making, and speaking, mid-century writers sought to establish how a space for the human might be made.

Notes

1. UNHCR (United Nations High Commissioner for Refugees), Convention and Protocol Relating to the Status of Refugees (Geneva: UNHCR, 2011), p. 29, https://www.unhcr.org/uk/3b66c2aa10 (accessed 12 May 2022).
2. See Hannah Arendt, *The Origins of Totalitarianism* (San Diego, CA, New York, and London: Harcourt Brace Janovitch Publishers, 1979), pp. 267–269 and Jacques Rancière, 'Who Is the Subject of the Rights of Man?', *South Atlantic Quarterly* 103 (Spring/Summer 2004), 297–310. For further discussion of historical failures of the discourse of rights, see Samuel Moyn, *The Last Utopia: Human Rights in History* (Cambridge, MA: Harvard University Press, 2012), pp. 44–83 and Bridget Anderson, *Us and Them? The Dangerous Politics of Immigration Control* (Oxford: Oxford University Press, 2013), pp. 54–57.
3. For a detailed account of the scale of the post-war refugee crisis, see Jacques Vernant, *The Refugee in the Postwar World* (London: George Allen and Unwin Ltd, 1953). The bulk of Vernant's book is an account of the global refugee situation on a country-by-country basis, providing detailed information on the circumstances, treatment, and number of refugees in 40 countries. For a recent summary of the numbers involved, see Cohen's discussion of 'The Last Million' in *In War's Wake: Europe's Displaced Persons in the Postwar Order* (Oxford: Oxford University Press, 2011), pp. 3–12.

4. Ban Ki-Moon, '70 Years Ago, the World Made a Pact to Protect Refugees. Too Many of Our Leaders Are Failing to Uphold That Promise', Time, 26 July 2021, https://time.com/6083151/1951-refugee-convention-anniversary/?utm_source=twitter&utm_medium=social&utm_campaign=social-share-article&utm_term=ideas_world-affairs (accessed 12 May 2022).
5. United Nations, Universal Declaration of Human Rights (Paris: United Nations General Assembly, 1948), https://www.un.org/en/about-us/universal-declaration-of-human-rights (accessed 12 May 2022).
6. For his account of Maritain's involvement in the shaping of the concept of personality articulated by the Declaration, see Joseph Slaughter, *Human Rights, Inc.: The World Novel, Narrative Form, and International Law* (New York: Fordham University Press, 2007), pp. 55–56.
7. Hayden White, *The Content of the Form: Narrative Discourse and Historical Representation* (Baltimore, MD: John Hopkins University, 1987), pp. 13–14, cited in Slaughter, *Human Rights Inc.*, p. 41.
8. Cohen, *In War's Wake*, p. 34.
9. David Herd, 'Afterword' in David Herd and Anna Pincus (eds), *Refugee Tales I* (Manchester: Comma Press, 2016), pp. 133–143.
10. Slaughter, *Human Rights Inc.*, p. 134.
11. In one sense, the question arising from Slaughter's reading of the framework of rights concerns the extent to which the imagination addressing rights-based relations should allow itself to become organized by the conventions of the Romantic novel. Lyndsey Stonebridge poses a version of this question when she observes:

> This is no straightforward analogy between fiction and law: when the UN drafters got into a fight about the limits of self-determination in the writing of Article 29, it was to Daniel Defoe's *Robinson Crusoe* (1719) that they turned. *Crusoe*, Slaughter claims memorably was the Declaration's principal 'enabling fiction'. This was in 1948, and it was as though neither Modernism nor Kafka had ever happened.

Lyndsey Stonebridge, *Placeless People: Writings, Rights and Refugees* (Oxford: Oxford University Press, 2018), p. 36. Stonebridge's argument is that the discourse of rights looks very different if we approach it though a different, more contemporary cultural paradigm, her criticism being, in part, that in so far as the drafters of the Declaration looked to the novel to underwrite their thinking, their reading was neither sufficiently wide nor contemporary. Kafka, in other words, presented a model of the relation between individual and state that anybody addressing rights discourse should certainly have considered. My argument, along comparable lines, is that to read the Universal Declaration in relation to its most conservative cultural referent is to predetermine a culturally limited account of the text. It is also, in this case, to over-privilege the

Declaration's reference to 'personality', a term that by no means structures the political relationality of the whole text.

12. Mark Greif, *Age of the Crisis of Man: Thought and Fiction in America, 1933–1973* (Princeton, NJ and Oxford: Princeton University Press, 2015), p. 328.
13. Greif, *Age of the Crisis of Man*, p. 90.
14. Anita Chari, 'Exceeding Recognition', *Sartre Studies International* 10:2 (2004), 113.
15. For a full expression of the 'politics of recognition', see Axel Honneth, *The Struggle for Recognition*, tr. Joel Anderson (Cambridge, MA: MIT Press, 1996) and Charles Taylor, 'The Politics of Recognition' in Amy Gutmann (ed.), *Multiculturalism: Examining the Politics of Recognition* (Princeton, NJ: Princeton University Press, 1994). Nancy Fraser provides a materialist critique of these positions in her article 'Rethinking Recognition', *New Left Review* 3 (May–June, 2000), 107–120. For an excellent account of how to mobilize 'recognition' within a democratic politics of rights, see James D. Ingram, 'What Is a "Right to Have Rights"? Three Images of the Politics of Human Rights', *American Political Science Review* 102:4 (November 2008), 401–416.
16. Ingram, 'What Is a "Right to Have Rights"?', 402.
17. Johannes Morsink, *The Universal Declaration of Human Rights: Origins, Drafting, and Intent* (Philadelphia, PA: University of Pennsylvania Press, 1999), p. 21.
18. As Morsink puts it, 'In 1914 Lenin calculated that "more than half of the world's populations lived in colonies, which together covered ¾ of the world's territory," a calculation that was still roughly correct at the end of the 1940s': *Origins, Drafting, and Intent*, p. 96.
19. Morsink makes this vivid by collating the occurrence of inclusive pronouns in the universal declaration. See *Origins, Drafting, and Intent*, p. 129.
20. For her discussion of the 'colonial clause', see Marie Benedicte-Dembour, *When Humans Become Migrants: Study of the European Court of Human Rights with an Inter-American Counterpoint* (Oxford: Oxford University Press, 2015), pp. 66–71. The questions raised by this clause are considered in Chapter 1.
21. United Nations, Universal Declaration.
22. How the principles articulated in the Universal Declaration intersected with decolonization is a matter of historical debate captured in two books published in 2010. For Samuel Moyn, the appeal to the principle of self-determination, and therefore sovereignty, that necessarily in part shaped decolonial struggles had the effect of rendering the principle of universal rights temporarily obsolete (see Moyn, *The Last Utopia*, pp. 84–119). A more focused and fine-grained account of the intertwining histories of rights and decolonization is provided by Roland Burke in *Decolonization and the Evolution of International Human Rights* (Philadelphia, PA: University of Pennsylvania Press, 2010). 'Using UN transcripts, archives, and the personal papers of key historical actors,' Burke

'provides a detailed narrative of decolonization's effects on thirty years of UN human rights debates', demonstrating not only that key decolonial actors drew on rights discourse but also that they contributed significantly to its shaping (see Burke, *Decolonization*, p. 3). It is against the background of such an historical analysis that this book reads Fanon.
23. United Nations, Universal Declaration.
24. United Nations, Universal Declaration.
25. United Nations, Universal Declaration.
26. United Nations, Universal Declaration.
27. Morsink, *Origins, Drafting, and Intent*, pp. 244–246.
28. The statement was historically crucial since, as was observed by the Canadian delegate, H.H. Carter, 'certain persons might be deprived of their juridical personality by an arbitrary act of government'": Morsink, *Origins, Drafting, and Intent*, p. 45. Carter's intervention is discussed in chapter 1. His point was that the Nazi regime had stripped Jews of their citizenship rights as a preliminary to the abuses that led to the Holocaust.
29. Morsink, *Origins, Drafting, and Intent*, p. 44.
30. Erika Feller, 'Foreword' to Andreas Zimmerman (ed.), *The 1951 Convention Relating to the Status of Refugees and Its 1967 Protocol: A Commentary* (Oxford: Oxford University Press, 2011), p. vii.
31. Feller, 'Foreword', p. vii.
32. Terje Einarsen, 'Drafting History of the 1951 Convention and the 1967 Protocol', in Andreas Zimmerman (ed.), *The 1951 Convention Relating to the Status of Refugees and Its 1967 Protocol* (Oxford: Oxford University Press, 2011), p. 45.
33. UNHCR, Convention, p. 13.
34. UNHCR, Convention, p. 30.
35. Following the death of twenty-seven Kurdish refugees in the English Channel, the UK prime minister called on the French government to 'take back' any person who crossed by boat to request asylum in the United Kingdom. The Channel was thus designated, by the UK government at least, a site of expulsion. See Doug Faulkner, 'Channel Migrants: PM Calls on France to Take Back People Who Make Crossing', 26 November 2021, https://www.bbc.co.uk/news/uk-59423245 (accessed 12 May 2022).
36. Charles Olson, *Collected Prose*, ed. Donald Allen and Benjamin Friedlander (Berkeley and Los Angeles, CA: University of California Press, 1997), p. 250.
37. For a detailed account of Olson's life, see: Tom Clark, *Charles Olson: The Allegory of a Poet's Life* (Berkeley, CA: North Atlantic Books, 2000).
38. Charles Olson, *Call Me Ishmael* (New York: Reynal and Hitchcock, 1947).
39. Charles Olson, *Selected Writings*, ed. Robert Creeley (New York: New Directions, 1966), p. 6.

40. Allen refers to Olson's letter in his 'Afterword' to the 1999 edition of the anthology: Donald Allen (ed.), *The New American Poetry 1945–1960* (Berkeley, CA and London: University of California Press, 1999), p. 448.
41. Olson first used the term, referring to the 'post-modern world', in a letter to Creeley dated 9 August, 1951. See Charles Olson and Robert Creeley, *Charles Olson and Robert Creeley: The Complete Correspondence, Volume 9*, ed. Richard Blevins (Santa Barbara, CA: Black Sparrow Press, 1990), p. 71.
42. References are to the *Concise Oxford English Dictionary*.
43. Olson, *Collected Prose*, p. 240.
44. As Olson writes in *Call Me Ishmael*, 'I take SPACE to be the central fact to man born in America, from Folsom cave to now.' See Olson, *Collected Prose*, p. 17.
45. As Allen wrote of 'Projective Verse', the essay with which he opened the 'Poetics' section of his anthology, it articulated 'the dominant new double concept: "composition by field" and the poet's "stance toward reality"'. See Allen, *The New American Poetry*, p. xiv.
46. Olson, *Collected Prose*, p. 239.
47. Olson, *Collected Prose*, p. 240.
48. Olson, *Collected Prose*, pp. 243–244.
49. Olson, *Collected Prose*, p. 241. For a searching comparative discussion of Olson's attention to syllable as opposed to his contemporary Jack Spicer's attention to the phoneme, see Daniel Katz, 'From Olson's Breath to Spicer's Gait: Spacing, Pacing, Phonemes', in David Herd (ed.), *Contemporary Olson* (Manchester: Manchester University Press, 2015), pp. 77–88.
50. Olson, *Collected Prose*, p. 240.
51. Arendt, *Origins*, p. 280, cited in Jacques Derrida, 'On Cosmopolitanism', in Stephen Cairns (ed.), *Drifting: Architecture and Migrancy* (London: Routledge, 2003), p. 56.
52. Olson, *Collected Prose*, p. 246.
53. Olson, *Collected Prose*, pp. 247–248. It is worth noting that the image of physical containment outlined in 'Projective Verse' echoes the articulation of the relational nature of the human form presented in 'The Resistance' (as discussed in Chapter 1). In both cases, the limits of the body are understood as the basis, or ground, of human relationality. It is through an understanding of the limits of physicality, in other words, that (as Olson suggests in 'Projective Verse') the possibility of listening and participation arise. I am grateful to Stephen Collis for pointing out the connection between these two texts.
54. Arendt, *Origins*, p. 302.
55. Thomas Nail, *Theory of the Border* (Oxford: Oxford University Press, 2016), p. 22.
56. Nail, *Theory of the Border*, p. 23.
57. Arendt, *Origins*, p. 293.

58. Ayten Gündoğdu, *Rightlessness in an Age of Rights: Hannah Arendt and the Contemporary Struggles of Migrants* (Oxford: Oxford University Press, 2015), p. 29.
59. Arendt, *Origins*, p. 447.
60. See Rancière, 'Who Is the Subject?', 297–299.
61. Ingram, 'What Is a "Right to Have Rights"?', 402.
62. Hannah Arendt, *The Human Condition*, 2nd edn, intro Margaret Canovan (Chicago, CA and London: University of Chicago Press, 1958), pp. 198–199.
63. Etienne Balibar, *Masses, Classes, Ideas: Studies on Politics and Philosophy before and after Marx*, tr. James Swenson (London: Routledge, 2004), p. 212.
64. Jacques Rancière, 'Who Is the Subject?', 305–306.
65. Frantz Fanon, *Black Skin, White Masks*, tr. Charles Lam Markmann, intro. Paul Gilroy (London: Pluto Press, 2017), p. 1.
66. Paul Gilroy, 'Introduction' to Frantz Fanon, *Black Skin, White Masks*, p. vi.
67. Fanon, *Black Skin, White Masks*, p. 1.
68. Aimé Césaire, *Discourse on Colonialism*, tr. Joan Pinkham, intro. Robin D.G. Kelly (New York: Monthly Review Press, 1972), p. 37.
69. Fanon, *Black Skin, White Masks*, pp. 72, 63.
70. Chari, 'Exceeding Recognition', 110.
71. Fanon, *Black Skin, White Masks*, p. 181.
72. Fanon, *Black Skin, White Masks*, pp. 181–182.
73. Fanon, *Black Skin, White Masks*, p. 183.
74. Fanon, *Black Skin, White Masks*, p. 185.
75. Fanon, *Black Skin, White Masks*, p. 186.
76. Fanon, *Black Skin, White Masks*, p. 187.
77. Fanon, *Black Skin, White Masks*, p. 191.
78. United Nations, Universal Declaration.
79. I am grateful to Stephen Collis for this clear-sighted phrase, the implications of which are further discussed in Chapter 5. In that context, as Collis helps us to understand, the violence that may be consequential upon the denial of recognition (i.e. the denial of rights) is not infrequently self-directed.
80. Frantz Fanon, *The Wretched of the Earth*, tr. Constance Farrington, preface Jean-Paul Sartre (London: Penguin, 2001), p. 29.
81. Fanon, *Wretched of the Earth*, p. 31.
82. Fanon, *Wretched of the Earth*, pp. 254–255.
83. Ingram, 'What Is a "Right to Have Rights"?', 410.
84. Fraser, 'Rethinking Recognition', 113–114.
85. Ingram, 'What Is a "Right to Have Rights"?', 410.

3
Moving

A Crisis of Movement

To read mid-century histories of forced human movement is to hear a proleptic note. The crisis of displacement resulting from the Second World War triggered an extensive international response. The work itself was demanding and harrowing for those involved and, as the commentaries show, deeply consuming. There was no more urgent task in the post-war moment than the resettlement of those who had been displaced. Also pressing, however, as some of those involved realized, was the need to report on the difficulties and consequences of the operation. Those reports were for the future and were deliberately addressed as such, as documents of a circumstance that could not be allowed to take shape again. As John Hope Simpson put it, writing the preface to Malcolm Proudfoot's survey, *European Refugees: 1939–52. A Study in Forced Population Movement*,

> [This book] not only provides an authoritative historical record of a period now past, but also describes difficulties which, had they been foreseen, might have been avoided. This work is thus of practical value for operations in the future.[1]

Proudfoot himself, who had been directly involved in the operations, made the same observation, only with more force:

> It seems almost certain that a refugee problem far more formidable than any so far encountered would be a concomitant of a third world war [...]. It may well be that the experiences reviewed in this book should be regarded as a dress-rehearsal for a tragic drama not yet begun.[2]

Proudfoot was a careful, often painfully eloquent writer. When he describes the operations he reports on in his study of forced movement as 'a dress rehearsal', he wants the future reader to understand that, in outline at least, the tragic drama to which they might find themselves witness has already been enacted.

Published in 1957, Proudfoot's history was based, in part, on his work with the Supreme Headquarters Allied Expeditionary Force (SHAEF), one aspect of whose role was to work with the United Nations Relief and Rehabilitation Administration (UNRRA) on the crisis of displacement resulting from the war. Over and above this direct involvement, Proudfoot's research was exhaustive, drawing on the records of the many agencies involved in the crisis as well as on a series of mid-century studies and surveys that sought similarly to document the scale of the problem such that the future might take note. His text set out to continue the history that Simpson had initiated with *The Refugee Problem*, published in 1939 and made extensive use of Jacques Vernant's *The Refugee in the Postwar World*, a comprehensive international survey commissioned by the United Nations High Commissioner for Refugees (UNHCR). The purpose of these and other reports and histories was fourfold: to document the unprecedented scale of the forced movement of people in the mid-century moment, to record the efforts of multiple intersecting agencies to address the situation, to observe the geopolitical conditions which made the fact of such human displacement so acute and difficult to remedy, and to suggest ways in which the conception of that geopolitical order would have to alter if such displacement was not to occur again. What one finds in the histories, in other words, is the documentary basis of a discourse according to which the politics of human movement might be reconceived.

The scale of the forced movements involved can be gauged, in part, through the array of statistics that underpinned the documentation. Necessarily, the reports proliferate numbers as the authors record the impact of various forms of expulsion on different territories and national groups. Certain high-level statistics, however, quickly convey the global magnitude of the effects. As Proudfoot observes, during the course of the war itself 'some 60 million European civilians were forced to move'.[3] Of that number, 8,615,000 foreign workers were deported to Germany as forced labour for the Nazi war machine.[4] At the point at which the war ended, by broad agreement, the number of people estimated to be displaced worldwide was 30 million.[5] This figure covers all forms of displacement, internal and external, from the deportation of Jews from countries occupied by the Nazi regime to the forced return of expatriate Chinese nationals to China in the face of Japanese occupation in the Far East. Across Belgium, Denmark, France, Germany, Austria, Luxembourg, the Netherlands, and Norway, some 10,366,000 people were found to be displaced at the end of the war. Of these, 2,405,000 were refugees, according to SHAEF categorizations, while 7,961,600 were displaced persons. By the beginning of 1946, the number of people still displaced in Europe and receiving assistance from UNRRA stood at 1,676,000.[6] By 1951, the year in which the Convention Relating to the Status of Refugees was signed, the European Office for Refugees (established by the Council of Europe) estimated that 4.5 million refugees were not yet 'absorbed' and 5 million not 'economically established'.[7] Some 400,000 people within that number had no fixed status whatsoever, with around 130,000 'still living in camps awaiting resettlement or re-establishment'.[8] Two years later, in 1953, the UNHCR recorded its responsibility for 2 million refugees.[9] Human displacement, as Proudfoot observed as he completed his history in 1955, was unquestionably a continuing problem.

Devastating as this weight of statistics clearly is, it is not in the tables and the graphs that the mid-century histories communicate the intensity and scale of post-war movement. Where one feels those dimensions more forcefully is in the writers' descriptions, where the effort to represent the volume and degree of displacement compels a series of statements that inscribe the new reality as a form of thought. Here is Proudfoot, for instance, on the kinds of forced movement experienced during, and immediately after, the war:

> The following kinds of forced movement all occurred, and each, except the last, involved millions of civilians: flight to avoid religious and political persecution; forced transfer and exchange of ethnic groups; flight or evacuation associated with military action; deportation for forced labour; deportation for extermination; air-raid evacuation; repatriation movement; expulsion of ethnic groups; resettlement movement; and exodus resulting from the memory of persecution and extermination, and the fear of its recurrence.[10]

Frequently, amid the statistical analysis and accounts of particular organizations and operations, Proudfoot provided descriptions of the ways in which people, in huge numbers, found themselves forced to move. As, for instance, with the movement into France ahead of the advancing German armies, when people fled 'on foot, by bicycle, motor-car or any other means of transport available'.[11] Or in the case of the large numbers of Poles, Czechs, Yugoslavs, and Greeks making their way back across the lands scorched by both Soviet and German armies, 'either walking or hitching rides on military transports'.[12] Or witness the 'spectacular mass movement' that constituted the 'repatriation of Europe' in the months immediately after the war ended, when

> open railway cars and boxcars, and all manner of improvised, uncovered, and unheated transport such as army supply trucks, river barges, and small boats, could be used.[13]

In his exemplary recent history of the period, *The Unsettling of Europe*, Peter Gatrell quotes the Canadian historian Modris Ekstein's attempt to capture the same phenomenon:

> Beyond the corpses, beneath the rubble, there *was* life, more intense than ever, a human anthill, mad with commotion. A veritable bazaar. People going, coming, pushing, selling, sighing—above all scurrying. Scurrying to survive. Never had so many people been on the move at once. Prisoners of war, slave labourers, concentration camp survivors, ex-soldiers, Germans expelled from Eastern Europe, and refugees who had fled the Russian advance [...] A frenzy.[14]

Ekstein's account is Brechtian in its record of dazed, traumatized, intersecting migrations. Repeatedly, and at every juncture, post-war historians presented people in transit, each reiteration establishing forced, improvised, desperate movement as a basis of the mid-century, post-war condition.

However, at the same time as the histories convey the fact of people in transit, so do they also work hard to articulate the reality of persons held in suspense. As Vernant presented that situation,

> Very often having neither house nor work nor means of support, he may count himself lucky if he is put into a camp. There he waits weeks, months, even years, for his future to be decided, until some country or other agrees to take him. Even if the reception country grants him a residence permit— nearly always temporary—and a work permit, he will live in constant fear of losing this privilege, for he knows that often it needs little—an unfavourable police report—for him to be expelled, and to be liable to imprisonment because no other country would accept him.[15]

The picture here is not of movement but of precarious stasis, where the camp is the principal setting but where, even in the event of work being permitted, the person is constantly vulnerable to expulsion or re-incarceration. Proudfoot echoes and, in the process, sharpens the account:

> The refugee finds himself deprived of legal protection, mutual support, the access to employment, and the measure of freedom of movement which happier mortals take as a matter of course. In an ordered world, this legal protection and mutual support [...] is enjoyed by the nationals of a sovereign State. Security is extended to them, not only at home, but when they move about the world in other countries. The refugee [...] has no such security, but exists in any country on sufferance [...] above all, he has no claim as of right to continued residence, and he is liable to expulsion if his presence for any reason is no longer desired.[16]

Such accounts of the status of the refugee and the displaced person in the post-war polity take us back to the discussion of the non-place in Chapter 1. What Vernant and Proudfoot describe is the state of exception that defines non-personhood, where the individual is rendered fundamentally vulnerable to the law. As both writers document, it is a status that fades ambiguously into the realm of criminality and which is structured fundamentally by the permanent possibility of expulsion. Equally, however, such images of the refugee's status have to be understood in terms of movement; not the forced movement that compelled them into that position of vulnerability in the first place but the deeply restricted and compromised nature of their movement once they have been displaced. They lack 'the measure of freedom of movement which happier mortals take as a matter of course'. They cannot, as Proudfoot puts it, 'move about their world'.

What we observe, when attention is focused in this way, is the degree and extent to which the post-war moment understood itself as conditioned by a crisis of movement. One aspect of that condition, clearly, was the desperate mass transit in which forced movement was manifest, all those perilous human flows and forms of transportation that Proudfoot, in particular, records. Fully to grasp the condition in question, however, we need to register the other pole of displacement: that people, having been forced to move, then find themselves unable to do so or to do so only in ways that are profoundly (one can say existentially) compromised, whether by actual physical limitations (say the perimeter of a camp) or by a vulnerability to expulsion that renders every step treacherous. It was in this double and compounding sense that the post-war world faced, or was constituted by, a defining problematics of movement, a contradiction of forced mobility and forced stasis that should properly be understood as a dialectic of displacement. As the war ended, up to 30 million people were compelled to move by the fact of expulsions, but so too, at the other pole of the experience, were millions of people prevented from doing so. Human movement in the post-war moment, whether forced or stopped, was deeply and intractably in crisis.

One way to grasp the implications of these urgent material pressures is in terms of the argument outlined by Thomas Nail in *The Figure of the Migrant*. The object of Nail's analysis is, in part, to observe the historical processes of expulsion and displacement by which the migrant, as an historical personage, has been produced. In this respect, *The Figure of the Migrant* is concerned with the causes of migrancy, with the histories of political and economic decisions and factors that bring migrancy into being. By his term 'figure', however, Nail means not just to point to the person of the migrant. Drawing on the term's rhetorical implication, he means also to indicate what one can term the imaginaries that emerge from the condition of movement. It is equally Nail's intention, therefore, to register the new forms of thought and practice emerging from the work and actions of migrants themselves. That is to say, the migrant, while rendered deeply vulnerable by the processes of expulsion that form their condition, is not just, or not exclusively, the product of historical reality. They are also, through their movement and in their thought and action relating to that movement, generators of new formations that challenge the realities by which they have been exposed. The suggestion here is that as one considers the post-war crisis of displacement, one sees such refiguring as Nail proposes on an international scale. Such was the extent of both the displacement of people and their subsequent containment that the question of movement became axiomatic to a range of disciplines and forms of thought. What emerged was a figuration of migrancy writ large, a multidisciplinary attempt to think through the problematics of movement that constituted a shaping discourse.[17]

The underlying argument of this chapter is thus that the crisis of movement, clearly articulated through post-war histories of displacement, was understood to be so fundamental as to constitute a condition, a defining dialectic, of mid-century thought. To assess this in reverse, consider how, in the present moment of forced migration, the question of human movement is with us as an urgent consideration in all forms of thought and practice. At the same time, in the case of all the authors in whom this book has its focus, their emerging imaginary was directly or personally motivated by expulsion or displacement in some form: Olson, whose father, as a first-generation Swedish immigrant experienced institutional exclusion, whose mother was a second-generation Irish immigrant from County Cork, and whose defining intellectual experience took place in the exiled community of Black Mountain College; Fanon, whose education and activism took him from Martinique to Paris and to the Algerian Revolution; the authors of the Universal Declaration, for whom the necessity of human movement was a shaping factor of their geopolitical imaginary; Arendt as an émigré German Jew who was twice expelled and, as the Germans entered Paris, herself experienced internment. In all of these writers, and across their work, one finds the fact of human movement, both as individual experience and as post-war condition, giving shape to what Nail terms 'alternative[s] to social expulsion'.[18]

Broadly speaking, two tendencies emerge in these writings about movement. In the first place, in Fanon and Olson in particular, one finds an attempt to relearn the language of human movement itself. So destructive had mid-century geopolitics become on a person's relation to their own movement—whether in the form of expulsion or stasis—that a new or a restored lexicon of movement was required. It had to be understood what it meant to a person to move, how their movement and its prohibition was in and of itself a measure, at the level of physicality, of their recognition. Second, what one finds across the authors in different ways is a series of figurations of movement through and across the world in which the category of nation is not the mediating fiction. In each case, the pressure of that category is never far from view such that we understand the writing in question to be historically formed. In each case also, however, a sustained counter-imaginary is proposed, providing terms in which human movement can be recalibrated. The production of mid-century geopolitical non-personhood was a function of how people on an unprecedented scale were both forced and also not permitted to move. One way or another, the conditions of human movement had to be reimagined.

Decolonizing Movement

Arguably, the writer in whom one finds the most exacting development of the mid-century lexicon of human movement is Fanon. Across each of his texts, but in *The Wretched of the Earth* and *Studies in a Dying Colonialism* in particular, one finds a language acutely tuned to the way the production of non-personhood bears upon, and frames, the act of moving through the world. It is a language, as we will come to see, that remains all too useful in describing how, in the present moment, hostile asylum regimes construct non-personhood through the micromanagement of the way individuals are permitted, and not permitted, to move. To read Fanon now is to register how colonial processes of restriction have been re-imported through asylum regimes and how, therefore, more generally, the neoliberal state domesticates previously external frameworks. The nation state, this is to argue, is fundamentally colonial in nature, it being by practices developed in colonial settings that internally bordered environments are maintained. The implications of Fanon's lexicon, however, and in particular the precision with which his writing documented the link between the production of non-personhood and movement, have tended to be overlooked in the scholarship.

Stephanie Clare has commented on the relative absence of discussions of movement from critical consideration of Fanon's work. While there is, as she observes, a well-developed commentary on spatiality in Fanon, beginning with Ato Sekyi-Otu's rereading of his politics in terms of the colonial organization of space, less has been said about his evocation of the lived experience of such space, about the way, in daily practice, such space was inhabited and moved through. As Clare reads it, Sekyi-Otu restricts himself to a discussion of colonial spatiality as such, where the emphasis is on stasis, not on movement because, in such a static situation, 'there is no space for politics; the colonized can only make space through violence'.[19] For Clare, such an account of Fanon is reductive, failing to observe, or failing to make visible, other modes of transformation which are core to his writing. I will argue that an understanding of Fanon's language of movement is critical in this respect, not least because it ties his explicitly decolonizing texts to the arguments for recognition he articulates in *Black Skin, White Masks*. To not allow a person to move in the world is to prevent their recognition. To follow Fanon's commentary on human movement is thus to realize the necessity of rights to move.

Clare's account of Sekyi-Otu's static reading of Fanon's spatiality provides one explanation for the relative inattention to Fanon's lexicon of movement. A second explanation lies in the tendency to disaggregate Fanon from his wider mid-century context. There are good reasons for this move. The immense achievement of Fanon's body of work, and of *The Wretched of the Earth* in particular, was, plainly, to inaugurate a theoretical framework whereby the dynamics of colonialism could be both articulated and resisted. In emphasizing that achievement, commentary has understandably tended to concentrate on the singularity of Fanon's setting and the specific force with which he addresses the brutalities of colonial practice. To read Fanon this way, however, is not to tell the whole story or, rather, is not to convey the whole story that Fanon looks to tell. As he puts it, in *The Wretched of the Earth*, tying his discourse to broader contemporary themes,

> For centuries the capitalists have behaved in the under-developed world like nothing more than war criminals. Deportations, massacres, forced labour and slavery have been the main methods used by capitalism to increase its wealth, its gold or diamond reserves, and to establish its power. Not long ago Nazism transformed the whole of Europe into a veritable colony. The governments of the various nations called for reparations and demanded the restitution in kind.[20]

Here, as elsewhere, as Paul Gilroy underlines, Fanon's intention is to frame the colonial context in terms of the broader practices and trajectories of mid-century geopolitics. One hears the force of such a framing not least in Fanon's discourse of human movement and, in particular, in his account of the larger structures by which, in the Algerian situation, the actions of the settler state bear on individual movement.

What the history of those larger state structures and actions represents is a continuation and intensification of precisely the crisis of movement that mid-century historians of displacement were concerned to warn against. As Peter Gatrell summarizes the situation,

> The French government poured troops into Algeria in a military migration of 512,000 soldiers by 1956. Around 1 million civilians were rounded up and incarcerated, and 250,000 more fled to neighbouring Tunisia and Morocco. These refugees, who did not come under the aegis of the 1951 UN Refugee Convention, relied upon local and international charities for basic subsistence. Freedom fighters and their supporters moved abroad to continue the struggle.[21]

Fanon, whose work as a psychiatrist at the psychiatric hospital at Blida-Joinville led him to join the Front de Libération Nationale, bore witness to all aspects of this crisis of forced and prohibited movement, of the dialectic, as visible in Algeria as elsewhere, of mid-century displacement. As he reports on the situation of Algerian refugees, in *The Wretched of the Earth*,

On the Moroccan and Tunisian frontiers, there are to be found something like 300,000 refugees since the decision of the French government to practise their burnt-earth policy over hundreds of kilometres. The destitution in which they exist is well known. International Red Cross committees have repeatedly paid visits to these places and after having observed the extreme poverty and precariousness of living conditions there have recommended increased aid to these refugees from international organizations.[22]

Here, as elsewhere, Fanon's intention was to internationalize the Algerian situation, in this case, by amplifying calls for international agencies to assist those experiencing the precariousness of the camps.

Fanon's account of the way detention was used to dismantle Algerian communities was similarly detailed, witness his description of the impact of the French policy of dispersal by internment under the heading 'Algeria Dispersed'. As he put it,

The tactic adopted by French colonialism since the beginning of the Revolution has had the result of separating the people from each other, of fragmenting them, with the sole objective of making any cohesion impossible.[23]

It is important, in passing, to underline the enduring quality of the colonizer's terms. In the present moment, the UK government practices its own official policy of 'dispersal', moving asylum seekers from one part of the country to another at short notice in order to prevent the development of local associations and ties. Fanon continues,

This effort was first concentrated on the men who were interned by tens of thousands. It is well known that in 1955–6, the number of internment centers multiplied rapidly over the national territory. Lodi, Paul Cazelles, Berrouaghia have held fathers and husbands captive for years.[24]

It was a policy that produced forced movements of its own, suddenly obliging an Algerian woman, 'to go from place to place, to run her errands [...] [to] visit her husband interned a hundred or two hundred kilometers from his home'.[25] As a policy of containment, it also compounded the phenomenon of displacement since, as Fanon reported, 'in order to flee the regroupment camps', as well as to escape repeated aerial bombardment, 'tens of thousands of families have taken refuge in Tunisia and Morocco'.[26] In these and other discussions (for instance, his account in 'The North African Syndrome', of the way North African immigrants to France engaged with the medical profession), Fanon presents co-ordinates of displacement that map directly onto the mid-century discourse of the crisis of movement. It is a crisis experienced specifically through the colonial regime but is nonetheless continuous with the broader dialectic: of people compelled to move and simultaneously forced to stop.

Where Fanon's account differs, where his analysis is uniquely accentuated, is in the degree to which he specifies the intimacy of the connection between non-personhood and the state-structured capacity, or incapacity, to move. Time and again, what one finds in Fanon's prose is the most detailed consideration of the way in which the Algerian is obliged to move through space. It is the quality of that articulation that we need to consider, the care with which Fanon inscribes movement, but it is important also to be clear who Fanon is writing about. Writing typically about a single figure, as if tracking an individual's progress, Fanon's term for the person he presents is frequently the 'native'. The value of the term, clearly, is that it contrasts and opposes the term 'settler'. In another sense, however, it doesn't capture the condition Fanon has elsewhere described. The individual in question is displaced, expelled by the colonial act; they might at any moment be detained, and, to avoid detention, they might be forced to leave their home. By any measure, in other words, what Fanon presents is a figure of the migrant, the movements of a person who has been, or at any moment might be, compelled to move. What he thus provides, more than any other mid-century commentator but in ways that his connections with mid-century contemporaries allows one to see, is a language for human movement that, precisely in the clarity of its articulation, underscores the politics of the right to move.

The story Fanon tells about the intricacy of the connection between juridical non-personhood and the lived experience of restricted movement has its origin in his repeated accounts of political space. Consider, for instance, his description of the impact of urban zoning:

> French colonialism had marked off certain zones as forbidden, and within these zones people's movements were strictly controlled. Thus the peasants could no longer go freely to the towns and buy provisions. During this period, the grocers made huge profits. The prices of tea, coffee, sugar, tobacco and salt soared. The black market flourished blatantly. The peasants who could not pay in money mortgaged their crops, in other words

their land, or else lopped off field after field of their fathers' farms and during the second phase worked them for the grocer.²⁷

Even here, as Fanon dwells on the organization of space, he wants to bring the reader to a comprehension of what it feels like to move through such strictly controlled spatiality. What the Algerians experience as they go about the daily business of securing their provisions is a double displacement. They are compelled to make their way through territories which have been characterized as hostile while being forced to depend on the black market because they are excluded from the cash economy. For individuals to move within such a restrictive regime, Fanon thus wants it to be understood, is to feel themselves continuously expelled: from the urban space, which has been rendered a hostile environment, and from the land, which has to be bartered away in order to meet inflated demands.

The strength of such accounts of human movement in the Algerian context lie, in part, in the way they deepen across iterations so that the reader's understanding of the colonized person's relation to space accumulates across the text. Thus, if, in material terms, the reader is to understand that to move through zones is to be displaced, so Fanon also wants the reader to grasp the constant quality of the experience:

> The native is always on the alert, for since he can only make out with difficulty the many symbols of the colonial world, he is never sure whether or not he has crossed the frontier. Confronted with a world ruled by the settler, the native is always presumed guilty. But the native's guilt is never a guilt which he accepts; it is a rather a kind of curse, a sort of sword of Damocles, for, in his innermost spirit, the native admits no accusation [...] The native's muscles are always tensed.²⁸

It is here, in the production of an environment in which the juridical border is ubiquitous because not clearly demarcated—and where, therefore, the person's presence is always tantamount to a criminal act—that Fanon begins to specify the relation of colonial non-personhood to movement. What his intensely detailed description conveys, with its carefully calibrated articulation of inter-relation, is the fact that non-personhood is reinforced and re-established step by step. The border is always present because always moving, always at the threshold of the colonized person's body. The Algerian's muscles are 'always tensed' because to move as a juridical non-person is constantly to invoke guilt. It is in the act of moving that the expelled individual finds their non-personhood established.

What we are noticing here, to reiterate—or rather, what we are invited to notice—is the quality of Fanon's inscription, the care with which the movement of those whose actions are meant to be invisible is written down. It was a descriptive attention Fanon had first established in *Black Skin, White Masks*, where he documents his own actions. On the one hand, then, what he hopes for in 'The Fact of Blackness', is 'to be a man among other men. I wanted to come lithe and young into a world that was ours and to help to build it together.'[29] What he finds instead, in white French culture, is that he is denied 'the slightest recognition', a denial that, as he describes it, bears directly on his capacity to move: 'I move slowly in the world, accustomed now to seek no longer for upheaval. I progress by crawling. And already I am being dissected under white eyes, the only real eyes. I am *fixed*.'[30]

Where the language of movement in *The Wretched of the Earth* comes to differ from Fanon's earlier text is in the degree of physical specificity he evokes. Attention to the pressure of musculature thus becomes a refrain, Fanon observing how, in the colonial context,

> That impulse to take the settler's place implies a tonicity of muscles the whole time; and in fact we know that in certain emotional conditions the presence of an obstacle accentuates the tendency towards motion.[31]

The colonial regime, Fanon wants repeatedly to assert, is fundamentally a condition of movement, a dialectic of forced and prohibited motion, where the displacement has to be understood not as a single episode but as a lived and living fact. Here, as elsewhere, what that lived fact produces is a physiology of resistance, what Clare calls 'resistance [. . .] entrapped in muscular tension', where 'the tendency towards motion' is held in a state of active suspense.[32] Elsewhere, however, and notably in his discussion of 'Colonial War and Mental Disorders', what Fanon finds is human physicality in a state of collapse. Under the heading of 'Generalized contraction with muscular stiffness', Fanon documents the case of the patient for whom the prohibitions on movement have rendered him unable to move:

> These symptoms are found in patients of the masculine sex who find it increasingly difficult [. . .] to execute certain movements: going upstairs, walking quickly or running [. . .]. It is an extended rigidity and walking is performed with small steps. The passive flexion of the lower limbs is almost

impossible [. . .]. The patient does not seem able to 'release his nervous tension'. He is constantly tense, waiting between life and death. Thus, one of such patients said to us: 'You see, I'm already stiff like a dead man.'[33]

In reading Fanon in the context of the mid-century crisis of movement, one finds the relation between juridical non-personhood and movement intricately articulated. In the case of the patient diagnosed as experiencing debilitating contraction and muscle stiffness, their condition is directly correlated to their expulsion by the state, the condition of constant containment in which they find themselves, the way they are unable to move without tensing up, leaving them 'stiff like a dead man'. This is what it can be like, Fanon wants the reader to know, to be constantly restricted in one's movements. For some people, ultimately, it will render them unable to move. The question is, how might such an account of movement extend beyond critique, how might another mode of movement be imagined? Fanon poses the possibility this way:

> Decolonization never takes place unnoticed, for it influences individuals and modifies them fundamentally. It transforms spectators crushed with their inessentiality into privileged actors, with the grandiose glare of history's floodlights upon them. It brings a natural rhythm into existence, introduced by new men and with it a new language and a new humanity.[34]

That the new language, and the new humanity, decolonization articulates will be predicated on movement is apparent from the suggestion that a new 'rhythm' will be brought into existence. Where settler colonialism is dependent on the racialized production of non-personhood, and where the index of such status is the lived experience of restricted movement, so a new mode of movement, a different rhythm, will constitute decolonized life. The question is, where human movement is so brutalized, how can such a rhythm be brought into effect?

At which point, it is helpful to draw again on Thomas Nail, offering, as he does in *The Figure of the Migrant*, alternative ways of thinking about the situation Fanon documents. Telling an abstracted history of movement that works in grand sweeps and phases, where the phases are determined by what he takes to be a defining mode of expulsion, Nail identifies one such as the period of political expulsion, which is to say expulsion from the apparatuses of politics itself. Broadly identifying this period with the ancient world, and referring to the figure who experiences political expulsion (following the terms of the dominant culture) as 'the barbarian', Nail notes that such 'social movement' takes two forms. The first is the refuge, it being at the moment of political exclusion that the principle of asylum emerges, witness, as Nail observes, 'the laws of asylia' and the 'vast networks of temples dedicated to asylum' that emerged in Ancient Greece.[35] Equally definitive, however, of the movement against political expulsion, was the revolt:

> Revolts across the ancient world [...] attest to the socially, ethnically and linguistically diverse organization of barbarian groups in contrast to the bordered, divided and centralized societies of empire [...]. Under this kinetic pressure the slaves revolted against their containment, and the transport of social disturbance was released in a wave of destruction.[36]

Historically speaking, as Nail describes, the revolt is a figure of the migrant, a form of action he characterizes as a 'wave', which has been a response to expulsion from the political realm. Such a revolutionary social disturbance, plainly, is one of the modes of transformation Fanon outlines, against the 'bordered, divided and centralized' 'containment' that is the experience of empire.

There is, however, a further way in which Nail can help us think about the articulation of movement in Fanon. The underlying purpose of Nail's theoretical commentary is to establish the correlation between personhood and movement. Where that correlation is most clear is in the value he places on 'pedesis', being the mode of movement in which human expression finds its basic form:

> Pedesis (from the PIE root * ped-, meaning 'foot') is the first motion of autonomous self-transport: the motion of the foot. Pedetic motion is the force of the foot—to walk, to run, to leap, to dance.[37]

Always, in his historical theorizing, Nail wants to take us back to 'the force of the foot'. It is there, in that motion of 'autonomous self-transport'—in walking, running, leaping, dancing—that the multiple imaginaries of the migrant have their value. Such motion, the motion of the foot, has value even when simply written down; or rather, to write such motion is constantly to be instructed in its value. Fanon, famously, correlates personhood and movement in comparable terms. Thus, it is a consequence of the prohibitions the Algerian experiences that, as he asserts,

> the dreams of the native are always of muscular prowess; his dreams are of action and of aggression. I dream I am jumping, swimming, running, climbing; I dream that I burst out laughing, that I span a river in one stride or that I am followed by a flood of motor-cars which never catch up with me.[38]

It is important to be clear what I take Fanon to be asserting here, given how much was at stake, historically, in the context of his utterance. In the first place, then, what must be acknowledged is that Fanon's imaginary is, at this point, explicitly masculine. Across his work of the mid-to-late 1950s, he would write carefully, if by no means always unproblematically, about the movement and movements of Algerian women, not least in 'Algeria Unveiled', where, as Stefan Kipfer suggests, he describes the politicization of Muslim women as 'a transformation of the relationship between body and world order'.[39] The string of verbs Fanon presents, in other words, do not necessarily operate—perhaps do not claim to operate—across genders. In the particular movements they identify, they are not the whole of the Algerian imaginary. People have different dreams. They dream of different movements.

What Fanon's dream principally underscores is not the value of particular movements, or even, I think, the value of the fact of moving, but the value of picturing a person as moving in the world. It is that value, the value of presenting a person moving, that explains the care with which Fanon writes about movement in his texts. He inscribes human movement as carefully as he does, works so hard to formulate an adequate lexicon, because to present a person moving is to recognize their participation in the world; because where a regime wants to sustain non-personhood, then, first and foremost, it has to prevent those persons from being seen to move. The new language that brings a new humanity is therefore already embedded in Fanon's text. To read the care with which he presents the colonized person as moving, however difficult that movement is made, is to establish the possibility of recognition, the claim to juridical personhood asserted by the right to move.

The Wretched of the Earth ends with 'the motion of the foot'. One could cite any number of paragraphs from Fanon's remarkable conclusion, but here is the last:

> For Europe, for ourselves and for humanity, comrades, we must turn over a new leaf, we must work out new concepts, and try to set afoot a new man.[40]

Here, in his final sentence, Fanon loops together his various strands. The final page of his book must lead to the writing of the next (to the turning over a new leaf), where the new concepts will be predicated on an understanding of human movement. What that understanding requires is inscription. The movement of people must be written down because it is in the presentation of movement that personhood is recognized. To inscribe human movement (as Rancière says about rights), is to begin to make a space in which movement is possible; it is to refute those hostile environments in which the person moving is rendered invisible.

The Universal Declaration and the Language of Movement

To understand the implications of the mid-century crisis of movement, the modes of imagining it brought forward and foreclosed, it is instructive to consider the intensity with which, in decision-making contexts, the terms of such movement were subject to scrutiny. Just as, for Fanon, it was crucial to specify precisely the manner in which, in a colonial environment, it was possible for persons to carry themselves through space, so, in contexts in which a transition from one jurisdiction to another was at issue, the formulations by which people might move came under intense pressure. Which is not to suggest that, in any uncomplicated sense, movement is a function of language, but it is to observe that to revisit key mid-century decision-making contexts is to gain a sharpened sense of the different imaginaries of movement the period was bringing into view. It mattered intensely, in the immediate aftermath of the war, how movement was framed, and it is instructive to register, as they emerged, the different coordinates of human movement such framings made possible.

What needs to be understood here, first, is how, in the context of post-war displacement, persons seeking to move were becoming categorized and, in particular, how such categorization evolved through the administration of the international resettlement operation. Where quickly, if not almost immediately, the administrative thinking about the repatriation and resettlement operation settled was on the question of what SHAEF documents called 'eligibility'. To draw attention to this question is not to deny its contextual force. What needs to be understood, rather, is how quickly the question of 'eligibility' comes to exercise a grip on the administrative imagination and how, as the authors of the Universal Declaration sought to express, it was equally necessary for the question to be suspended.

The role of the 'Eligibility Officer' was core to the work of the International Refugee Organization (IRO) from its inception in 1947, the function of the post being to determine whether or not the applicant came within the organization's mandate. What 'eligibility' entailed, in this context, was permission or entitlement to move since the purpose of the IRO was principally to resettle those who had become displaced. To fall within the IRO's mandate, in other words, was to be entered into a process the end result of which might be relocation. In exercising such scrutiny, however, the IRO was operating in line with protocols already established by the UNRRA and by SHAEF, whose processes and guidance relating to the question of eligibility were extensive. Core to that system of protocols was the distinction established in the SHAEF Outline Plan, drawn up prior to the invasion of Normandy, according to which those displaced were to be categorized as either refugees or displaced persons. As the plan sets out,

> *Refugees* (are) civilians not outside the national boundaries of their country, who desire to return to their homes, but require assistance to do so, who are: (1) temporarily homeless because of military operations; (2) at some distance from their homes for reasons related to the war.
>
> *Displaced Persons* (are) civilians outside the national boundaries of their country by reason of the war who are: (1) desirous but are unable to return to their home or find homes without assistance; (2) to be returned to enemy or ex-enemy territory.[41]

In the light of contemporary conventions, this distinction is counter-intuitive since those 'outside the national boundaries of their country' are not deemed to be refugees. Either way, this initial categorization proliferated processes driven by considerations of eligibility.

For the person seeking assistance, the symbols of those processes were two cards, a Registration Record Card and an Assembly Registration Card: the first '5 by 8 inches in size, to be filled out in duplicate with one card to accompany the refugee until finally repatriated or resettled'; the second '3 by 5 inches in size, to be used for administrative purposes in Assembly Centres'.[42] The administrative framework within which these cards were used was captured by a detailed UNRRA document in the form of a table entitled: 'UNRRA and Military Eligibility Criteria for Displaced Persons to Receive or be Denied Assistance in the Western Zones of Germany: July 1946 to July 1947'.[43] The table consisted of three columns: Category of Displaced Persons, UNRRA Action Indicated, and Military Action Indicated. There were fifteen categories of displaced person in all, grouped variously by nationality or immigration status, each entailing carefully formulated actions, and it was the work of the eligibility officers to determine the category into which the individual applicant fell.[44] As an aid to that determination, applicants would come to complete an eligibility questionnaire. It was in answer to the requirements of just such a questionnaire that Olson's speaker presented himself as he laid out his claim on humanity in 'La Préface'.

To focus attention on the procedures determining eligibility is not to underestimate the work of the successive organizations concerned. In so far as we are now living through the kind of further crises of displacement post-war commentators anticipated, there is no equivalent international intervention to assist those displaced and much to learn from those earlier operations.[45] Equally, however, it is necessary to register the implications and contradictions attendant on a handling of displacement through the procedures of eligibility. In the context of the operation itself, those contradictions were keenly felt. As early as July 1946, Review Boards were established to scrutinize applicants for displaced person status on the basis of their questionnaires. This coincided with a tightening of centre regimes. Thus,

> The granting of leave permits for residents of the centres was further restricted, and early curfews became the general rule [...] Life in the centres became even more monotonous, rations became smaller, and to an increasing degree, the residents were isolated, if not virtually imprisoned.[46]

Those living that life, the residents of the centres, quickly came to resent 'the tendency to accuse them, unfairly for most, of the prevalent crime' and they 'feared the repeated registrations and interrogations made to ascertain their eligibility'.[47] The ironies of this experience of the operation to address displacement were hardly lost on those concerned—from the careful sifting of national origins, through the registration by number, to the barbed wire, and the curfews, and the routine accusations of crime. Nor should those contradictions be lost sight of now, when the aspect of the post-war international resettlement operation certain jurisdictions have been most keen to retain is the apparatus for ascertaining eligibility. It is there, in fact, on the grounds of eligibility, that the hostile environments of the present moment have taken shape. The implication of that rhetoric, in other words, installed at the beginning of the period of mid-century mass displacement has been profoundly negative.[48]

Natural, because naturalized, as the apparatus for ascertaining eligibility has come to seem, it hardly seemed inevitable to mid-century commentators. An example of what, in their theory of bordering, Sandro Mezzadra and Brett Neilson call 'filtering',[49] the eligibility in question was the eligibility to move, it being precisely such apparatus that J.C. and R.G. King drew attention to in their *Manifesto for Individual Secession into World Community*, a text which, as is discussed below, figured in Olson's post-war reading. The value of such texts, written in the moment of the emergence of post-war languages of movement (and so before those languages had hardened into place) is that the counter-imperative is equally plainly felt. 'The ultimate right', as the *Manifesto for Individual Secession* put it, was 'to walk out on political persecutions'.[50] The Universal Declaration was one such text, the overriding aspiration of which was to articulate a response to the fact and possibility of expulsion such that the question of eligibility did not arise.

How that aspiration was articulated, and where also, in the form of intense terminological pressure, it broke down, can be heard in the first of two groups of articles identified as protecting 'special international rights' but which can equally be designated, in their cross-nationality, in terms of 'movement'.[51] The second group, which calls for 'international cooperation', is comprised of Articles 22, 28, 29 and 30, concerned as they are, respectively, with: social security at a national and international level, an international order capable of securing rights; social responsibility and duty in line with the principles of the United Nations; and the obligation on all states and individuals not to destroy the rights and freedoms set forth in the Declaration. The first group of international rights consists of Articles 13, 14, 15, with the first two of these pressing directly on the question of movement. As Article 13 puts it,

> (1) Everyone has the right to freedom of movement and residence within the borders of each state. (2) Everyone has the right to leave any country, including his own, and to return to his country.[52]

Article 13 captures much that is definitive of the Declaration. In the first place, in its first clause, it installs as a principle 'the right to freedom of movement'. In the particular case, that freedom might seem relatively uncontroversial, specifying, as it does, 'movement [...] within the borders of each state'. Except, of course, that in the mid-century moment, such a stipulation carried considerable force. As much as it addressed totalitarian regimes of movement, so also it spoke to colonial regimes and to settings in which displaced persons were themselves contained. What the authors understood, as Fanon understood, was the fundamental value of movement, that to not permit movement was to effect non-recognition. Witness, in the present moment, the proliferation of sites of detention and the multiple modes of restricted movement that constitute asylum regimes. To establish the 'right to freedom of movement [...] within the borders of each state' was to enable persons to come into view.

The article's second clause is not less important in the right of freedom of movement it inscribes, articulating, as it does, what the Kings, in their manifesto, called 'the ultimate right to walk out on political persecution', 'the right to leave'. Equally significant, however, is the article's manner of address, it being in the document's determining pronouns that the Declaration most directly refuses the categorical distinctions through which the question of eligibility forms. The implications of that address require a moment's consideration. Insisted on in the drafting process by Soviet Communist and South American Socialist representatives, it is the document's repeating pronouns—'All', 'Everyone', 'No one'—that govern the Declaration's rhetorical shape. To make the point, Morsink lists the whole series of their iterations, a catalogue which, in its repetition, reads like a conceptual poem:

> 'All human beings' (Article 1), 'Everyone' (2), 'Everyone' (3), 'No one' (4), 'No one' (5), Everyone (6), 'All' (7), 'Everyone' (8), 'No one' (9), 'Everyone' (10), 'Everyone' and 'No one' (11), 'No one' (12), 'Everyone' (13), 'Everyone' (14), 'Everyone' (15), 'All men and women' (16), 'Everyone' (17), 'No one' (18), 'Everyone' (19), 'Everyone' and 'No one' (20), 'Everyone' (21), 'Everyone' (22), 'Everyone' (23), 'Everyone' (24), 'Everyone' (25), 'Everyone' (26), 'Everyone' (27), 'Everyone' (28), 'Everyone' (29), and 'In no case' and 'Nothing' (30).[53]

Thomas Nail helps us to understand what such an insistent address implies. Among the terms by which he looks to capture counter-understandings of movement, figures in the history of migration through which movement can be positively expressed, is 'the wave': a physical and political process in which, as he observes, 'the social bond of solidarity unites [...] in a collective and continuous motion without dividing [...] into territories'.[54] Familiar examples of this form of movement are waves of strikes and protest, but Nail also wants to include movements arguing for common property as a response to displacement. He cites the Diggers and their campaign for shared land rights following enclosure as an original example but carries the principle of their action forward into contemporary history. Thus, as he argues, 'common property is a wave distribution insofar as it is an individual (non-private) realm that is collectively transmitted and shared in solidarity with others'.[55] What one finds in the call for common property following displacement is what Nail describes as a 'vagabond egalitarianism', a wave in which equality and an equal relation to the territory is the principle of solidarity upon which the movement is built.

In these ways, and in these terms, following the mid-century catastrophe of expulsion, the Declaration should be understood as a wave. One hears the sound of the wave in the list of pronouns: All, Everyone, Everyone, All. More importantly, what one hears in that sound, in that echoing movement, is an articulation and an understanding of the human as commons, as a shared ground of rights and recognitions through which everyone is entitled to move. For all its flaws, and its flaws were many, the Declaration thus articulated a response to unprecedented human expulsion which consciously and resolutely precludes the categorical distinctions through which the question of eligibility forms.

All of which, as formulated under the auspices of the United Nations in response to the mid-century reality of mass displacement, presents a reimagining of political relations that had conditioned the production of non-personhood. Central to that reimagining was the right of freedom of movement across a shared human ground articulated as commons. The border was by no means abolished (there was a clear outlining of the parameters of each state), but the value of human movement as a condition of appearance was understood. Where the imaginary broke down was in committee, its expression finessed and compromised in Article 14 by the representative of the British state.

The purpose of Article 14 was to complement Article 13. If it was necessary, as the drafters understood, to grant the right to leave any country, it was necessary also that they should have somewhere to go. Not to establish this complementary provision would be to run the risk of instituting an extended state of exception, a global waiting area in which people were constantly categorized and sifted. Accordingly, in committee, numerous national delegates, joined by representatives of prominent non-governmental organizations (NGOs)—by Paul Weiss, for instance, of the IRO, and by A.L. Easterman of the World Jewish Congress—argued for a strong statement of the right to asylum. As Metha, the Indian delegate put it, "'the principle of freedom of movement [...] was a fundamental right'", just as for Santa-Cruz, the Chilean delegate, 'the freedom of movement was the sacred right of every human being.'[56] Eleanor Roosevelt was concerned at raising false hopes, but General Romulo of the Philippines corrected her thinking: '"it was not so much a question of raising false hopes as of establishing a principle to be followed by all"'.[57]

What the argument came down to was a verb, a verb relating to movement. As Romulo proposed the wording, Article 14 was to read thus:

> Everyone shall have the right to seek and be granted asylum from persecution. This shall not be accorded to criminals nor to those whose acts are contrary to the principles and aims of the United Nations.[58]

As Morsink reports, the Second Session upheld this version of the text. It was in the Third Session that the wording was amended, following discussion in a subcommittee on asylum, the key members of which were China, France, and the United Kingdom. The Saudi Arabian amendment proposed the deletion simply of the words 'and be granted', leaving everyone the right to 'seek [. . .] asylum'. Corbett, the British delegate, supported the deletion but proposed a wording to finesse the gap. Accordingly, the first sentence of the article would read 'Everyone has the right to seek and to enjoy in other countries asylum from persecution.'[59] The vote on the Saudi amendment was close, 18 to 14 in favour, with 8 abstentions. The vote on the British amendment passed by 30 to 1, with 12 abstentions, since, at least in that case, the right was not simply to seek. But nothing was 'granted' except that, as the British delegate disingenuously put it, in the event that asylum was secured, a person had the right to 'enjoy' it.[60]

The argument here is that for all that the wording of Article 14 failed to deliver on its most radical implications, on the question of movement, the Universal Declaration ushered a significant imaginary into view. The evasive expression of the right to asylum, of the right to seek and enjoy, reads anomalously in the Declaration because, in the context of the whole, it is an anomaly. The right wasn't expressed as such, but the understanding of the fundamental value of freedom of movement had come clearly into view. If it wasn't honoured in the final articulation, nor was it simply obscured: it was visible, for all to read, albeit under erasure. Even so, there was a breach: people had the right to leave but not, formally, to arrive. It was towards a politics of arrival, I want to suggest, that Arendt pointed mid-century articulations of movement.

Towards a Politics of Arrival

The degree to which the post-war world found itself conditioned by a dialectic of displacement, framed equally by the compulsion to move and by movement's prohibition, is clearly articulated in Arendt. What one finds in Arendt's work of the late 1940s and 1950s, as she draws and redraws the world in which she finds herself, is a picture of geopolitical arrangements in which expulsion is taken to be the defining note. 'Suddenly there was no place on earth where migrants could go without the severest restrictions [. . .] Only with a completely organized humanity could the loss of home and political status become identical with expulsion from humanity altogether.'[61] Driven not least by the fact that she had lived through such expulsion, Arendt's response to the crisis of movement was conducted across both her major texts of the period, *The Origins of Totalitarianism* and *The Human Condition*. What the first undertakes is an extensive inquiry into the interlocking histories that had eventuated in such unprecedented expulsion; what the latter aims variously to articulate is a politics in which the appearance of the newcomer is understood as a defining fact. Arendt thus provided an account of the post-war crisis of movement that both registered its intractability—that human movement had come to be both forced and stopped—and that sought, by way of response, to articulate a political language capable of recognizing the fact that humans, when they move, both leave and arrive. To follow her thinking on that question is to switch registers, from her densely documented, if theoretically, driven history of totalitarianism to the abstractions of political philosophy articulated through *The Human Condition*. A central aim of the later inquiry was precisely to picture how persons arrive, where the idea she came to rest on was 'natality', the principle of entering the world.

Arendt introduces the principle of natality at the point at which she introduces the tripartite division of labour, work, and action that is the organizing schema of *The Human Condition*. We will come on to the differences between these terms in Chapter 4. For now, what needs to be registered is the way that 'natality' underpins all three processes, that Arendt introduces it as her governing term:

> Labour and work, as well as action, are also rooted in natality in so far as they have the task to provide and preserve the world for, to foresee and reckon with, the constant influx of newcomers who are born into the world as strangers. However, of the three, action has the closest connection

with the human condition of natality; the new beginning inherent in birth can make itself felt in the world only because the newcomer possesses the capacity of beginning something anew, that is, of acting. In this sense of initiative, an element of action, and therefore of natality, is inherent in all human activities. Moreover, since action is the political activity par excellence, natality and not mortality, may be the central category of political, as distinguished from metaphysical thought.[62]

That 'natality' should be so central to a political philosophy written in reaction to the recent history of displacement should not be surprising—a history in which expulsion underscored by an obsession with eligibility produced a politics governed by death. It is not only in this historical reversal, however, that Arendt wants to provide a corrective through 'natality'. What she also aims to formulate is an image of politics in which movement is a necessary and desirable fact. To approach politics through the principle of natality is thus to arrive at a language in which 'the influx of newcomers' is understood as generative and therefore welcome.

That 'natality' constitutes a figure of movement is apparent from the way, in an abstract sense, Arendt pictures action. Grounded as it is in the human capacity for initiation, it is a defining feature of human action that its effects are boundless:

> This boundlessness is characteristic not of political action alone, in the narrower sense of the word, as though the boundlessness of human interrelatedness were only the result of the boundless multitude of people involved [. . .] the smallest act in the most limited circumstances bears the seed of the same boundlessness, because one deed, and sometimes one word, suffices to change every constellation.[63]

As images of action go, this is, to be sure, at the high end of abstraction. What Arendt is seeking to do, however, at this level (as she intends throughout her argument), is to provide an understanding of the human condition that never loses sight of its fundamental plurality. To be human is to be among others, as she reminds us that Aristotle had argued, and is therefore to be shaped by networks of actions whose effects cut across bounds. One way to think of this is as an imaging of the earth as common ground across which movement, like the flow of consequence, is understood as a defining condition. Thus, whether immigration policy chooses to recognize it or not, each man is as much an inhabitant of the earth as he is an inhabitant of his country. Men now live in an earth-wide continuous whole where even the notion of distance, still inherent in the most perfect unbroken contiguity of parts, has yielded before the onslaught of speed.[64]

The 'earth-wide continuous whole' has become an historical fact, and therefore a condition of politics, for which new imaginings are necessary and towards which the emphasis on natality is a significant step.

To read *The Human Condition* this way, by underlining its emphasis on the newcomer, is to register the fact of movement as fundamental to Arendt's text. What Arendt also understood, however, because she has registered it in her reading of the discourse of human rights, was that any account of human movement was fundamentally deficient if it did not contain an articulation of how a person might be understood to arrive. Introducing the section of her discussion entitled 'Action', and writing under the heading of 'The Disclosure of the Agent in Speech and Action', Arendt presents an understanding of those processes, action and speech, which constitutes a form of arrival:

> With word and deed we insert ourselves into the human world, and this insertion is like a second birth, in which we confirm and take upon ourselves the naked fact of our original appearance.[65]

How 'we insert ourselves into the human world' is the core concern of Arendt's text. Writing against the backdrop of the mass production of non-personhood and of the spaces in which that non-personhood was produced, her aim is to articulate a political philosophy in which insertion into the human world is the principal consideration. One way to think of this, as Arendt's term 'disclosure' suggests, is how, in practice, people become known to one another. Thus, as she puts it,

> If action as beginning corresponds to the fact of birth, if it is the actualization of the human condition of natality, then speech corresponds to the fact of distinctness and is the actualization of the human condition of plurality, that is, of living as a distinct and unique being among equals.[66]

As Arendt presents it, there are two ways of becoming known, of entering into the human world, the first being action, the second speech. Arguably, in the present moment, we don't need Arendt to tell us this, it being precisely at these intersections that the hostile environments of so many national asylum regimes operate: prohibiting work, which is to say action, and undermining speech through a pervasive culture of disbelief. To be denied the capacity to act and speak is to be denied the capacity to make oneself known, which is to be denied the capacity to enter, which is to be denied the capacity to arrive. It is a combination of suspensions which performs the contemporary equivalent of the 'entry fiction', that borderline impossible situation whereby a person was 'deemed not to have been landed, even if conditionally disembarked'.

The question, then, as Arendt understands, is what should happen at the moment of arrival, how a person should be enabled to enter in. To which the answer, as Arendt explains at length, is that the person should be invited to tell their story. As she puts it,

> Action and speech are so closely related because the primordial and specifically human act must at the same time contain the answer to the question asked of every newcomer: 'Who are you?'.[67]

To understand the force of Arendt's question, we have to understand what that question is not. It is not, 'What are you?', where the answer called for would very likely be in terms of national categories. Nor is it, 'What do you do?', where the answer might relate to professional competence and be subjected to some kind of labour test. Arendt's question is not, in other words, the form of interrogation that was, and remains, conventional in the context of the displaced persons camp, not the kind of questionnaire designed to determine who did and did not come through. Her question, rather, is an invitation to talk, to secure a person's entry into the human world by sharing their story.

The fact that the story is, in practice, so integral to movement as to prepare the ground for arrival is apparent in the lengths to which state apparatuses go to prevent those stories from being told. In the United Kingdom, in the first two decades of the twenty-first century, as political attitudes towards human movement have hardened, so the mechanisms for denying action and speech, and especially story, have become so perfected as to effect an almost complete institutional silence. At the point of entry, it is the individual's story that is not let through, the person, as the entry fiction has it, having entered but not arrived. By contrast, to answer Arendt's question, and more importantly (as we will see in Chapter 5) to create a space in which that question can be answered is to articulate by the process of narration that one has arrived. It is to issue a declaration upon which one's presence is established, it being in that declaration that arrival, and therefore the entitlement to rights, are made plain. Which is not exactly to say that to construct a space, which is to say a politics, in which a migrant's story can be heard is to guarantee their transition from one territory to another. It is to observe, however, that something like the opposite has been achieved: a political space in which expulsion is maintained by silence. To which Arendt can be heard to offer the following, as argument for story as means of arrival:

> In acting and speaking, men show who they are, reveal actively their unique personal identities and thus make their appearance in the human world, while their physical identities appear without any activity of their own in the unique shape of the body and the sound of the voice. This disclosure of 'who' in contradistinction to 'what' somebody is—his qualities, gifts, talents, and shortcomings which he may display or hide—is implicit in everything somebody says or does. It can be hidden only in complete silence and perfect passivity.[68]

Which condition, 'complete silence and perfect passivity', is the state's preferred circumstance for the person seeking asylum and hoping thereby to arrive. From which it follows—and I really think it does follow—that to construct a political relationality in which stories could be heard would be to alter the grounds on which people move.

On Movement's Ground

In 1948, via the offices of Caresse Crosby (poet, publisher, and patron of the arts), Charles Olson received his 'Passeport Citoyen du Monde'. The document was issued by J.C. and R.G. King as a follow-up to their *Manifesto for Individual Secession into World Community*. The pamphlet, which Olson owned, proposed 'issuing passports to identify each citizen who stands with us'.[69] It was simultaneously an eccentric, politically well-informed and entirely serious proposition, the intention of which was to establish a basis for post-national human movement. That Olson received the passport is not evidence precisely that the *Manifesto* itself was influential upon him. What the passport and, more importantly, the *Manifesto* do show, however, is that Olson was participant in a discourse in which the politics of human movement was a live concern, the *Manifesto* framing a set of coordinates that would come to mesh with Olson's conception of the primacy of movement.

Wittingly and therefore, one has to suppose, strategically naïve, the Kings' *Manifesto* is immediately arresting, in part due to the openness of its address. As they put it,

> This effort is dedicated to you. We write only because that seems the most effective way to reach you at the outset; we should have much preferred to make our offering face to face. And perhaps we shall meet. Meanwhile, printed words will have to serve.[70]

The reason for this address, disarming at it proves from the outset, is that central to the *Manifesto*'s argument is the need to establish networks not constituted in the name of what they call 'the national state'. Writing before *The Origins of Totalitarianism* but anticipating Arendt's critique, the Kings start from the fact that, 'We cling tenaciously to all the values of the sovereign national state, an institution as outmoded as cannibalism in this day and far more costly to its adherents.'[71] Like Arendt, they date the moment of that outmoding to the 'era preceding World War 1' when 'human society became too well integrated [...] to be well served by an anarchy of omnipotent and conflicting sovereigns'.[72] The direct cost of that conflict was, as they observed, the capacity to move, such that

> The myth of personal and territorial jurisdiction has served to pinion every living soul in a web of quotas and passport requirements and police registrations and to surround every clod of earth with formidable walls.[73]

It followed that the task was to recover a sense of relation to territory according to which 'our precarious situation' might be 'explored' and 'understood'.[74] What had to be understood was that 'we hold the earth in a precarious life estate', where that felt precarity was the basis of inter-generational inheritance.[75]

What the *Manifesto* was wanting to argue for, in other words, was a territorial commons, critical to which was a mode of address. Thus, 'If this is true—if we are indeed on common ground—then all of us should know about it. We need a test, and the quickest we could devise was this direct address to you.'[76] The purpose of the *Manifesto*'s open address was to establish a basis, or rather perhaps a ground, on which people might move. The headline proposal towards that objective was that, as the title of the pamphlet had it, individuals should secede, where the secession was from the apparatus of nation into the world community. This is variously stated, with different degrees of positivity, the underlying principle being the 'ultimate personal privilege of withdrawing from whatever offends, oppresses, or ceases to merit loyalty'.[77] Or to hear the same thing more affirmatively argued,

> The only community to which absolute allegiance must be given, the only polity from which there can be no right of personal secession, is the community of the whole.[78]

What that polity amounts to is what one could reasonably, in this context, call the community of the open field, where the shared task is to articulate an apparatus from which nobody might be expelled. Where the drive for such a polity rests, however, is in the absolute necessity of a right to move when the state to which one is allied comes to present itself as threat. Thus,

> The ultimate right [. . .] to walk out on political persecutions [. . .] would give all of us the final integrity we lack, in non-exercise as in actual escape.[79]

The issuing of world passports, of the Passeport Citoyen du Monde, was a desperate gesture. Its immediate purpose was not materially to alter immigration or asylum procedures but as a move in a discourse intended to demonstrate the necessity of geopolitical change. As the Kings put it,

> One right that might attach to them as soon as there are enough holders to make it significant would be the basic right of safe physical removal, guaranteed by all the pressures we could bring to bear, for individuals threatened with tomorrow's gas chambers and cremation ovens, whenever some nation sees fit to 'liquidate' innocent human beings again for political, or economic or racial reasons [. . .] Such a right is a logical extension of the human right to secede; its recognition should not perhaps be left to fumbling bureaucrats and indifferent statesmen.[80]

In one sense, one can hear the *Manifesto for Individual Secession into World Community* as a document in the tradition of the modest proposal. It is hardly conceivable, after all, that people might individually secede on the basis of unauthorized global passports. The mere fact, however, that such a proposition has been arrived at is a measure of the reality people had found themselves required to accept. How much more inconceivable should it not be that there is no 'basic right of safe physical removal [...] for individuals threatened with tomorrow's gas chambers and cremation ovens'? Whether or not the *Manifesto* was intended to be heard in this way, as a document in the tradition of the modest proposal, is not necessary to establish. What Olson would have heard, as his own thinking began to find its signature forms and expressions, was the call for modes of thought that started from the primacy of movement and the need for an image of territory as human commons across which such movement could take effect.

The argument here is that, in Olson's poetry and poetics of the later 1940s and 1950s, one finds a body of work which calls on the reader to re-envision movement at every level of human action, from expression of individual physiology to a person's motion across the earth, Olson proposing what can properly be called a kino-poetics.[81] To describe his work in this way is to make explicit a commonality with Thomas Nail and his combined theory of the migrant and the border. The overarching name Nail gives to that theory is kino-politics, being 'the theory and analysis of social motion: the politics of movement'. As Nail puts it, defining his own central concept,

> Instead of analyzing societies as primarily static, spatial or temporal, kinopolitics or social kinetics understands them primarily as 'regimes of motion'.[82]

Kino, as Nail takes time to observe, is from the Greek, *kinetikos*, and from *kinein* to move. Movement, he wants us to understand, is not secondary to place and the societies which form around place but fundamental to the way societies emerge and evolve. To go back to the Greek, to draw on kinetics, is to signal that an understanding of movement must come first. Olson makes a comparable move in 'Projective Verse' when he introduces what he likewise calls 'kinetics'. Thus,

> every element in an open poem (the syllable, the line, as well as the image, the sound, the sense) must be taken up as participants in the kinetic of the poem just as solidly as we are accustomed to take what we call the objects of reality.[83]

Like other major documents of the post-war moment, Olson's manifesto was an attempt to think everything at once. Here, then, as he thinks about 'recognition' and about material presence so, also, he thinks about movement, about what he terms the 'kinetic of the poem'. Everything in the poem is understood in terms of the poem's commitment to presenting and understanding movement, its commitment to articulating a set of relations for which movement was the primary element. How, eventually, Olson would come to develop a geopolitical understanding to which movement was primary will be considered in a moment, when the argument turns to *The Maximus Poems*. Before we arrive at *Maximus*, however, and its deeply layered sense of movement, it is helpful to consider the environment out of which 'Projective Verse' emerged, which is to say Black Mountain College, an experimental educational setting in which the mid-century dialectic of movement was addressed through pedagogy.

Olson first visited Black Mountain in 1948, when he taught in one of the college's famous summer sessions, and from the outset the total intellectual environment of the college was critical to his development. 'It was a place', as Tom Clark, reports, 'uncommonly accommodating to just such groundbreaking work as Olson himself had in mind' and in whose 'willing, attentive students he [...] found his audience'.[84] Olson subsequently described a collaboration with the institution in which he was the major beneficiary. As he put it, overgenerously, 'I came with no ideas; Black Mountain did it all.'[85] It is hardly true that Olson arrived at Black Mountain with no ideas (he was the author, already, of *Call Me Ishmael*, itself a remarkable study of a particular political-economy of movement, the nineteenth-century US whaling industry), but if the college didn't do it all, it did stimulate in him a newly acute sense of physicality and of the need, in its multiple forms, for a new lexicon of human movement.

That physical literacy, the language of movement, was central to the Black Mountain curriculum is traceable to the institution's foundation in 1933 and to many of the institution's signal pronouncements. For Josef Albers, who arrived at Black Mountain in its first year, the point of that programme was to develop the tactile sense. As he put it,

> No wonder a faculty that is so largely unemployed [...] is degenerating. Our materials come to us already ground and chipped and powdered and mixed and sliced [...] No need to get our hands into the dough. No need for us, either, to make our implements, to shape our pots or fashion our knives.[86]

Albers' comment is, in one sense, unremarkable, an instance of generic antimodern Modernism, an articulation of the priority the Bauhaus placed on practical intelligence. What was remarkable was the degree to which Albers's preoccupation shaped the Black Mountain experience, the emphasis given, as a consequence, to, for instance, the crafts of weaving and pottery. More fully expressive of the college's specific physicality was a statement by its founder, John Rice:

> [I]n Black Mountain [education] was round the clock and all of a man. There was no escape. Three meals together, passing in the hall, meeting in classes [...] a man taught by the way he walked, by the sound of his voice, by every movement.[87]

Here again, perhaps, we are in the presence of a trope, Rice articulating for Louis Adamic, the interviewer with whom he was in discussion, the conventional sentiment of a body's absence from modernity. More fully expressive of the college's specific physicality, however, was the inscription of physiological tuition into the centre of the programme. From 1941 to 1944, Elsa Kahl taught eukinetics, a course advertised in the college programme thus:

> Eukinetics tries to help the physical and mental attitude of the student by developing body control and poise as well as an elementary sense of dance movement. Without identifying itself with any particular system of physical or dance training, it is a comprehensive training of the body.[88]

All of which (the insistence on the tactile sense, the comprehensive training of the body), built in, as these were, to the college's sense of itself, added up to an institutional framework that, in the summer of 1948, provided the context for the extraordinary physiological spectacle of Merce Cunningham.

The presence of Cunningham at Black Mountain, and in particular his performance of the piece 'Untitled Solo', brought the need for a new language of movement to the forefront of the institution's thought. As Cunningham explained, describing the physiology of the piece,

> A large gamut of movements was devised [...] for the arms, the legs, the head and the torso, which were separate and equally tensile in character, and off the normal or tranquil body balance. These separate movements were arranged in continuity by random means, allowing for the superimposition of one or more, each having its own rhythm and time length.[89]

The vocabulary was, in one sense, everything, Cunningham's radical objective being, as William Fetterman has suggested, to make his culture movement-literate. Thus, by contrast with the protocols of classical ballet, Cunningham, in the 1950s, listed 'eight basic movements, with variations: bending, rising, extending, turning, sliding, skimming and brushing, jumping, and falling'.[90] Roger Copeland specifies this new assemblage as Cunningham's major contribution to modern dance: 'the evolution of a codifiable technique that forges fresh connections between the dancer's head, back, pelvis, legs and feet'.[91] Watching Cunningham dance, in other words, was an education, a lesson in physiology, transfiguring, as Clark says, 'an audience's perception of space', forging 'fresh connections between [. . .] head, back, pelvis, legs, and feet [. . .] producing strategies for linking together different phases of movement'.[92]

There is a great deal more to be said about the centrality of the language of human movement to the curriculum at Black Mountain College, more than it is possible to document here.[93] What does have to be underlined, however, is the specific relation between that curriculum and the crisis of human movement which, at the level of pedagogy and personal development, it was intended to address. Black Mountain, this is simply and directly to say, was founded, or at least shaped, by an act of expulsion: by the closure of the Bauhaus that was itself one of the Nazi Party's earliest acts. Josef and Anni Albers were thus displaced, and in their displacement they formulated an educational programme to which recognition of human physicality was of principal concern. And what that recognition called for, not least, was an understanding of movement, of the basic fact that to recognize the human was to recognize how, but also simply that, a person moved. As in the kinetics of Olson's projective poetry, in other words, movement at Black Mountain was everything—the medium in which the human might properly be discerned. Olson's own language for human movement would change, becoming an attention to what his 1961 essay called 'Proprioception' (the study of stimuli relating to the position or movement of the body). What the later essay confirms, however, with its intricate consideration of the language of physiology and of the relations between the body in its limitation and possibility and the environment in which it finds itself, is the enduring primacy of human movement to Olson's poetics. As he puts it, under the heading '"ACTION"—OR, AGAIN, "MOVEMENT"',

> [M]ovement or action is 'home'. Neither the Unconscious nor Projection [. . .] have a home unless the DEPTH implicit in physical being—built in

space-time specifics and moving (by movement of 'its own')—is asserted or found-out as such. Thus the advantage of the value of 'proprioception'. As such.[94]

Dedicated to LeRoi Jones, as the poet Amiri Baraka still called himself in 1961 (it being Jones who first published the various parts of the essay in his journals *Yugen*, *Floating Bear*, and *Kulchur*), 'Proprioception' is equal in its appreciation of the necessity of description of movement to those passages in Fanon in which such a language takes centre stage. Movement, as Olson has it, is home, which means that it is through attention to movement that a non-expulsive relation to an environment must emerge.

The degree to which *The Maximus Poems*, building on 'Projective Verse' and Olson's collaboration with Black Mountain College, was informed by a commitment to movement—both at the level of proprioception and at the level of geopolitics—is indicated by the late poem, 'I have been an ability—a machine', at the core of which is an image of human movement prevented by nation:

>   my father a Swedish
> wave of
> migration after
> Irish? like Negroes
> now like Leroy and Malcolm
> X the final wave
> of wash upon this
> desperate
> ugly
> cruel
> Land this Nation
> which never
> lets anyone
> come to
> shore.[95]

Not published during Olson's lifetime but posthumously by George Butterick as part of Volume Three of *The Maximus Poems*, 'I have been an ability—a machine' falls outside the temporal parameters of this book. Written in 1966, a year after the assassination of Malcolm X, and two years before LeRoi Jones (misspelt in the holograph) would convert to Islam and change his name to Baraka, the poem explicitly frames the 'Nation' in terms of the prevention of movement, its status as 'Nation' determined by the cruelty with which it filters and expels. But if 'I have been an ability' is situated against the anti-black race politics of the 1960s, the childhood memory that triggers the poem takes Olson back to a story he first documented in 1948.

The story is a of trip Olson and his first-generation immigrant father took to Plymouth, Massachusetts to attend the 300th anniversary celebrations of the arrival of the Mayflower. In an autobiographical fragment, subsequently entitled 'The Post Office', Olson recalls how his father planned meticulously for the visit and how at the last moment, as an act of retaliation for his union activities, his Post Office bosses cancelled his leave. Olson's father took the trip anyway, in what the poet calls an act of 'resistance', and was subsequently punished for his insubordination, principally by removing him from his long-established route.

'The Post Office' has two principal interweaving themes, the first being movement, the second nation. As Olson details, 'Men worked for years to get the routes they wanted. The routes would open as older men retired and the carriers bid for them, by seniority, in turn.'[96] More damaging, however, than the disregard for his status, was the intrusion on the way Olson's father had learned to move:

> Just to cross the bridge a winter morning and a winter afternoon, or to be part of the boating around it in the summer and the fall, gave his work a freedom he could never have known in any other route in the city.[97]

Always looking for the larger meaning in an event, what Olson saw in the removal of his father from the rhythm of his route was the dispossession of an immigrant by an agency of the state. From which rejection Olson's father was thrown back 'on that other rock of the immigrant, his foreign nationality organizations'.[98] What his father couldn't see, but what Olson wanted to be understood, was that

> With the help of Gloucester, he might have seen his struggle outside both Sweden and America, as part of this ambiguous battle all human society is now, for good and evil, engaged in.[99]

Dwelling on his father's immigrant experience in the immediate aftermath of the war, what Olson sought to picture was a non-national ground, with Gloucester, as port and islanded city, providing the history of human movement out of which such an imaginary might be made. It is the same story Olson tells in 'I have been an ability—a machine', compounded, in the moment of Black Power, by the racist rejection of his friend the poet, LeRoi Jones/Amiri Baraka and his assassinated comrade Malcolm X. The nation is thus defined by its repeated act of expulsion, by the fact that, as Olson's haunting expression has it, it 'never/lets anyone/come to/shore'. What had to be articulated, as Olson saw it, and what Gloucester's situation helped him to imagine, was a geography not conditioned by borders but by movement; 'not this land/not this Nation' but 'the very Earth/here'.

For Jeremy Prynne, *The Maximus Poems* as a whole was an attempt to imagine this non-national ground, to comprehend geography not as a series of bordered regimes but earth, as it were, as condition of movement. As Prynne put it, writing shortly after Olson's death,

> I know for myself that the primary structure of this poem is already complete. And complete in two major movements: the going out, the asking the great questions, the making of the great statements: and the coming back, the coming back across the sea, the coming back through the ocean, coming back to the shore, and then the shore fades into a condition of land, and the condition of land approximates to the condition of the planet.[100]

What that condition constitutes, as Prynne interprets *Maximus* as articulating, is an apprehension of the quality of the planet grasped at the moment lands meet sea; not the specific dynamics of Gloucester, but the condition of coast that those specifics are given to present. It is an image of the poem's trajectory that goes back to its opening statements. As Olson put, in the poem's third 'Letter',

> As the people of the earth are now, Gloucester
> is heterogeneous, and so can know polis
> not as localism, not the mu-sick (the trick
> of corporations, newspapers, slick magazines, movie houses,
> the ships, even the wharves, absentee-owned
>
> and whine to my people, these entertainers, sellers
>
> they play upon their bigotries (upon their fears[101]

Olson's post-war terms are carefully calibrated. Against a 'localism' fostered by corporate manipulation of bigotry, he pictures a heterogeneity which is the condition of people of the earth. Which is not to suggest that Olson does not recognize national difference; his poem addresses the 'Nova Scotians,/ Newfoundlanders,/ Sicilianos,/ Isolatos' who, among others, make up the people of Gloucester.[102] What he resists steadfastly and throughout, however, is that 'slaver' that 'would keep you off the sea, would keep you local'. That 'slaver', as Olson had argued, had disturbing overtones. As he had put it, just a few years before, in the 'The Fascist v. The People, US': 'The Fascist manipulates group against group and wedges in. He must be stopped there, and only a vigorous people can stop him.'[103]

At one level (I would argue, at its defining level), *The Maximus Poems* is an anti-fascist project, critical to which is the principle of freedom of movement. Against the category of nation 'which never/lets anyone/come to/shore', Olson works constantly to sustain an image of the earth across which people might circulate. In Letter 3, he calls it the 'condition of the under-water, the cut-water of anyone'. It is this condition that Prynne wanted readers to see in *Maximus*, what he thinks of as the poem's relation to the planet. In saying so, Prynne hardly conveys all that can be said about Olson and movement. He doesn't register, for instance, as has subsequently quite rightly been registered, that when Olson left the United States and spent time in Mexico, his own movements were a series of human blunders that can certainly be read as carrying an imperialistic charge.[104] Nor does Prynne observe that by no means all the movements Olson documents in *Maximus* are born of the freedoms his phrasing indicates, witness the forced movement of enslaved Africans that, as will be observed in Chapter 5, Olson framed as the origin of the production of geopolitical non-personhood. What Prynne does allow one to register, nonetheless, which is crucial to Olson's project, is that as he imagined *The Maximus Poems*, what he wanted to conceive was a depiction of the ground as condition of movement, as the frame against which human movement should be properly observed. What Prynne saw in Olson, in other words, was the desire, as the J.C. and R.G. King *Manifesto* put it, 'to hold the earth in a precarious life estate', as commons across which persons might move.

Conclusion

To read across disciplines in the way this chapter does is to grasp the extent to which mid-century authors engaged the question of what it meant for persons to move. Faced by an historical circumstance in which human movement, whether forced or stopped, was in crisis and where that crisis had its origins in the politics of expulsion, the writers in question, and those on whom they drew, sought to imagine processes and environments though which movement could occur. I use the word 'imagine' advisably in the knowledge that discussion of human movement couched in terms of reimagining must inevitably seem unequal to the realities the chapter has addressed. What the chapter has hoped to establish, however, which the writers of the period clearly understood, was that the human realities to which they were responding—the dialectic of forced movement and forced stasis produced by expulsion—were themselves consequences of the way politics had imagined geopolitical space. What the situation called for, in other words, was a commitment to reconceptualization, to new thinking at every level about what human movement meant and how it could be enabled. The result, from text to text, and across a range of defining mid-century contexts linked by a deep awareness of the expulsive act, was a series of attempts to relearn and re-establish basic lexicons of human movement, to restate what it meant for a person to leave and to arrive, to walk through an environment, to move across. It was such functions, writers observed, that were thwarted and impeded by expulsion; to be expelled was, in the range of ways documented, to be deeply restricted in efforts to move. Nobody captured the need for a new language of movement more precisely than Fanon, the need for an intimate re-articulation of the way in which the act of moving should be expressed. But across all the texts in question one finds a defining commitment to the expression of conditions of movement, to the articulation of processes and grounds whereby persons could move.

In the present moment, faced by the scale of crisis of movement mid-century historians of displacements sought to warn against, by the realities of mass expulsion and by the mass production of lives held in suspense, there are various ways we might hear mid-century attempts to recover the language of movement. In the first place, we should register the impulse itself. Fanon remains a crucial commentator on hostile environments of all kinds precisely because he repeatedly insists on the connection between the expulsive regime and the ability of a person to move in daily life. We have to be reminded—as Fanon never ceases to remind us—that it is by prevention of movement (among other political practices) that a person's expulsion is effected. For movement to be restricted, as Fanon describes, is to be expelled. Fanon spells this phenomenon out because he wants us always to know it when we see it and to know absolutely, when we see it, that a different regime of movement is required. In the second place, it is crucial to register the care with which the discourse of human rights broadly conceived—where that broad conception includes such critical interlocutors as Arendt—was grounded in movement's basic transitions, in the capacity as a person to leave and to arrive. These processes are not incidental to human rights, they are the grounds in which they obtain, and in the mid-century moment we find political imaginaries that engaged seriously, and at the level of practice, with that fact. Finally, in all the texts in question, and as described here in relation to Olson in particular, one finds sustained attempts to imagine—or as J.C. and R.G. King's *Manifesto* put it, to 'hold'—'the earth in a precarious life estate', as ground as commons across which persons might move. What one observes, in other words, is a collective drive towards figures of movement, political imaginaries grounded in the fact that people move. To read the mid-century writers in question is to understand what it means to deny that fact, to grasp the connection between movement and recognition which constitutes the right to move.

Notes

1. John Hope Simpson, 'Foreword', in Malcolm Proudfoot (ed.), *European Refugees: 1939–1952. A Study in Forced Population Movement* (London: Faber & Faber, 1957), p. 18.
2. Proudfoot, *European Refugees*, pp. 24–25.
3. Proudfoot, *European Refugees*, p. 21.
4. Proudfoot, *European Refugees*, p. 80.
5. Jacques Vernant, *The Refugee in the Postwar World* (London: George Allen and Unwin Ltd, 1953), p. 29.
6. Vernant, *The Refugee*, p. 36.
7. Vernant, *The Refugee*, p. 50.
8. Proudfoot, *European Refugees*, p. 436.
9. Vernant, *The Refugee*, p. 41.
10. Proudfoot, *European Refugees*, p. 22.
11. Proudfoot, *European Refugees*, p. 49.
12. Proudfoot, *European Refugees*, p. 190.
13. Proudfoot, *European Refugees*, p. 229.
14. Cited in Peter Gatrell, *The Unsettling of Europe: The Great Migration, 1945 to the Present* (London: Allen Lane, 2019), pp. 20–21.
15. Vernant, *The Refugee*, p. 14.
16. Proudfoot, *European Refugees*, pp. 22–23.

17. That such a question was pressing upon mid-century thinking is apparent not least in the commentaries that shaped and flowed from the operation to resettle and return displaced persons and refugees. In the form of evolving international agencies, with developing remits (from the High Commission for Refugees, established in 1922, through the Intergovernmental Committee on Refugees established at the Evian Conference in 1938, to the UNRRA established in 1943 by the representatives of forty-four United Nations states, to its successor body, the IRO on 15 December 1946), a series of complex, collaborative operations had sought to effect the movement of displaced persons from one jurisdiction to another. The IRO itself was gradually wound down through the course of 1951, to be replaced by the UNHCR. This shift was politically significant in that the UNHCR, with its minimal operating budget of $300,000, took over a responsibility for which the IRO had received international funding of $161 million. The IRO had done considerable work, having resettled 1,039,601 refugees and displaced persons between 1 July 1947 and 31 December 1951, and so it was arguable that the problem for which it had been established had been quite largely addressed. It was, however, as Proudfoot asserted, 'a grave error to assume that legal protection by an international agency was no longer necessary for individual refugees [...] The refugee, as in the past, remained a stateless foreigner until he acquired a new citizenship [...] An impartial international agency is undoubtedly needed to supply this guardianship' (Proudfoot, *European Refugees*, p. 434). Or, as even a commentator as conservative as Jacques Vernant put it:

> To allow each State to decide in full sovereignty which persons it will recognize as refugees would almost certainly increase the chances of friction and paralyse the international body, for refugees in the eyes of one State might not be refugees in another's [...] an international authority in whose eyes a man remains a man, no matter whence he comes or where he may be, has a most important mission to perform.
> (Vernant, *The Refugee*, pp. 16, 19)

The multi-national response to the post-war crisis of human movement, even as it came to replicate Cold War antagonisms, must be understood as a complex and extensive operation driving practically towards a new form of thought, towards a way of thinking about human movement not predicated absolutely on the category of nation.
18. Thomas Nail, *The Figure of the Migrant* (Stanford, CA: Stanford University Press, 2015), p. 125.
19. Stephanie Clare, 'Geopower: The Politics of Life and Land in Frantz Fanon's Writing', *Diacritics* 41:4 (2013), 68.
20. Frantz Fanon, *The Wretched of the Earth*, tr. Constance Farrington, preface Jean-Paul Sartre (London: Penguin Books, 2001), p. 80.
21. Gatrell, *Unsettling*, p. 127.

22. Fanon, *Wretched of the Earth*, p. 224.
23. Frantz Fanon, *Studies in a Dying Colonialism* (London: Earthscan Publications Ltd, 1989), p. 118.
24. Fanon, *Dying Colonialism*, p. 118.
25. Fanon, *Dying Colonialism*, pp. 118–119.
26. Fanon, *Dying Colonialism*, p. 119.
27. Fanon, *Wretched of the Earth*, p. 153.
28. Fanon, *Wretched of the Earth*, p. 41.
29. Frantz Fanon, *Black Skin, White Masks*, tr. Charles Lam Markmann (London: Pluto Press, 2017), p. 92.
30. Fanon, *Black Skin, White Masks*, p. 95.
31. Fanon, *Wretched of the Earth*, p. 41.
32. Clare, 'Geopower', p. 66.
33. Fanon, *Wretched of the Earth*, p. 236.
34. Fanon, *Wretched of the Earth*, p. 28.
35. Nail, *Figure of the Migrant*, p. 136.
36. Nail, *Figure of the Migrant*, pp. 141–142.
37. Nail, *Figure of the Migrant*, p. 125.
38. Fanon, *Wretched of the Earth*, p. 40.
39. Stefan Kipfer, 'Fanon and Space: Colonization, Urbanization, and Liberation from the Colonial to the Global City', *Environment and Planning D: Society and Space* 25 (2007), 714.
40. Fanon, *Wretched of the Earth*, p. 255.
41. Proudfoot, *European Refugees*, p. 115.
42. Proudfoot, *European Refugees*, p. 110.
43. Proudfoot, *European Refugees*, p. 243.
44. Proudfoot, *European Refugees*, pp. 242–247.
45. It is difficult to evidence an absence, of course, but as a measure of the lack of a contemporary equivalent to the post-war international resettlement operation, we might point to two kinds of failure: the first an act of omission, the second of commission. In the first place, there has been a refusal among refugee-receiving nations to establish what NGOs such as Safe Passage call safe routes out of conflict zones towards situations of asylum. Safe Passage itself was founded in 2015 'to find a legal and safe way to help child refugees to reunite with their families' (Safe Passage, 'Our Story', https://www.safepassage.org.uk/our-story (accessed 31 May 2022). Modest as this objective is, in that it would secure only the safe movement of children with existing family ties, its achievement has been made less likely by recent national government decisions. Witness the UK government's Nationality and Borders Bill, which, rather than establishing safe routes, criminalizes what it terms 'irregular routes'. This increasing tendency to criminalize movement, rather than establish an international basis for safe movement and resettlement, is further evidenced by the criminalization

in numerous national settings of acts of humanitarian assistance and solidarity towards people seeking asylum. For detailed information on these convergent national tendencies, see Dr Lucy Mayblin's forthcoming database of Crimes of Solidarity and Humanitarianism, in which she will document 'legal cases against people helping irregular migrants, known as crimes of solidarity and humanitarianism'. In other words, in so far as recent crises of forced displacement have attracted an international response, that response has increasingly taken the form of a criminalizing of movement.

46. Proudfoot, *European Refugees*, p. 249.
47. Proudfoot, *European Refugees*, p. 250.
48. Consider, as the latest manifestation of the apparatus of 'eligibility', the UK government's initial failure to welcome people seeking refuge following the Russian invasion in Ukraine, an incapacity rooted in its visa procedures. As Enver Solomon, Chief Executive of the Refugee Council, observed:

    > It's clear that the visa schemes which were supposedly designed to ensure the safety of Ukrainians fleeing war and bloodshed are unfit for purpose. Asking Ukrainian families, who are scared, exhausted, and traumatised to fill out a long, and complex visa application is unacceptable and totally out of touch with the terrifying situation they find themselves in.

    Refugee Council, 'Latest Data on Ukrainian arrivals—Refugee Council Response', 8 April 2022, https://www.refugeecouncil.org.uk/latest/news/latest-data-on-ukrainian-arrivals-refugee-council-response (accessed 24 May 2022)
49. Sandro Mezzadra and Brett Neilson, *Border as Method, Or, The Multiplication of Labour* (Durham, NC and London: Duke University Press, 2013), p. 7.
50. J.C. and R.G. King, *Manifesto for Individual Secession into World Community* (Paris: Crosby Continental Editions, 1948), pp. 27–28.
51. Johannes Morsink, *The Universal Declaration of Human Rights: Origins, Drafting, and Intent* (Philadelphia, PA: University of Pennsylvania Press, 1999), pp. 72–73.
52. United Nations, Universal Declaration of Human Rights (Paris: United Nations General Assembly, 1948), https://www.un.org/en/about-us/universal-declaration-of-human-rights (accessed 12 May 2022).
53. Morsink, *Origins, Drafting, and Intent*, p. 129.
54. Nail, *Figure of the Migrant*, p. 133.
55. Nail, *Figure of the Migrant*, p. 152.
56. Morsink, *Origins, Drafting, and Intent*, p. 74.
57. Morsink, *Origins, Drafting, and Intent*, p. 76.
58. Morsink, *Origins, Drafting, and Intent*, p. 76.
59. Morsink, *Origins, Drafting, and Intent*, p. 78. For a clear sight of the way, in the post-war period, the British government reneged on its public commitment to human rights in the privacy of the committee room, see Philippe Sands' account

of the decision-making that led to the expulsion of the Chagossians from the Chagos Archipelago in *The Last Colony* (London: Weidenfeld and Nicholson, 2022), pp. 40–48.
60. You can turn this mid-century verbal disagreement various ways. You could argue that, in the absence of a power to enforce its principles, it cannot finally have mattered what the Universal Declaration's statement on asylum said. However august the body, to inscribe the right to be granted asylum is not the same as actually having that right, as actually, in the moment, having the asylum granted. Rancière would disagree, I think, on the grounds that inscription produces a space of possibility, and perhaps it was this that the British and their allies in the argument implicitly understood. Thus, as Morsink sees it, the extension of the principle of free movement was thwarted by the immediacy of political events. As Article 14 went through committee, hundreds of thousands of Palestinians were forced into exile, causing interconnecting states—Saudi Arabia by its proximity, the United Kingdom by its mandate—to force an amendment on the right to asylum. Which, if it is true, testifies to the power of the inscription of rights, even at the moment those rights were not finally written down. Or you can argue, as Vivek Chibber has, that, for all its failures in execution and sometimes in expression, the Universal Declaration was the 'crowning achievement of the Twentieth Century', which is to argue, I think, that it is impossible to conceive meaningful political-economic change that does not draw on the language of rights and that the language of rights is under constant assault because it makes such change possible. See Vivek Chibber, 'Imperialism, Orientalism and Social Emancipation', lecture given at the University of Kent, 2 April, 2019; https://www.youtube.com/watch?v=1n0STknbrIk (accessed 20 November 2019) .
61. Hannah Arendt, *Origins of Totalitarianism*, 3rd edn (San Diego, CA, New York, and London: Harcourt Brace Janovitch Publishers), pp. 293, 297.
62. Hannah Arendt, *The Human Condition*, 2nd edn, intro. Margaret Canovan (Chicago, IL and London: University of Chicago Press, 1958), p. 9.
63. Arendt, *Human Condition*, p. 190.
64. Arendt, *Human Condition*, p. 250.
65. Arendt, *Human Condition*, p. 176.
66. Arendt, *Human Condition*, p. 178.
67. Arendt, *Human Condition*, p. 178.
68. Arendt, *Human Condition*, p. 179.
69. King and King, *Manifesto*, p. 100.
70. King and King, *Manifesto*, p. 9.
71. King and King, *Manifesto*, p. 22.
72. King and King, *Manifesto*, p. 23.
73. King and King, *Manifesto*, pp. 27–28.
74. King and King, *Manifesto*, p. 13.
75. King and King, *Manifesto*, p. 18.

76. King and King, *Manifesto*, p.1 0.
77. King and King, *Manifesto*, p. 95.
78. King and King, *Manifesto*, p. 96.
79. King and King, *Manifesto*, p. 100.
80. King and King, *Manifesto*, p. 106.
81. Drawing similarly on Thomas Nail, Kevin Potter offers an account of 'kinopoetics' in a contemporary context in his discussion of the Somali British poet Warsan Shire. See Kevin Potter, 'Centrifugal Force and the Mouth of a Shark: Toward a Movement-Oriented Poetics', *Ariel: A Review of International English Literature* 50: 4 (October 2019), 51–78. Potter's argument draws on his excellent doctoral thesis. See Potter, 'Poetics of the Migrant', unpublished PhD thesis, University of Vienna, 2019. The interest of Olson in this context is that he suggests the term himself, his kinetic poetics serving to anticipate Nail's subsequent formulation.
82. Nail, *Figure of the Migrant*, p. 24.
83. Charles Olson, Collected Prose, ed. Donald Allen and Benjamin Friedlander, intro. Robert Creeley (Berkeley, Los Angeles, CA and London: University of California Press, 1997), p. 243.
84. Tom Clark, *Charles Olson: The Allegory of a Poet's Life* (Berkeley, CA: North Atlantic Books, 1991), pp. 142–143.
85. Charles Olson, *The Special View of History*, ed. Ann Charters (Berkeley, CA: Oyez, 1970), p. 2.
86. Christopher Benfey and Mary Emma Harris (eds), *Starting at Zero: Black Mountain College 1933–1937*, (Bristol and Cambridge: Arnolfini and Kettle's Yard, 2005), p. 65.
87. Mary Emma Harris, *The Arts at Black Mountain College* (Cambridge, MA and London: MIT Press, 1992), p. 53.
88. Harris, *Arts at Black Mountain College*, p. 76.
89. Harris, *Arts at Black Mountain College*, p. 238.
90. Roger Copeland, *Merce Cunningham: The Modernizing of Modern Dance* (New York and London: Routledge, 2004), p. 77.
91. Copeland, *Merce Cunningham*, p. 2.
92. Copeland, *Merce Cunningham,* p. 2.
93. I have explored the rich intersection between Olson and Cunningham and the implications of that encounter for Olson's broader poetics of movement in my article: '"From Him Only Will the Old State-Secret Come": What Charles Olson Imagined', *English* 59:227 (Winter 2010), pp. 375–395. doi: 10.1093/english/efq011. For a more extensive inquiry into the importance of dance for Olson's poetics, what she calls his 'choreographics', see also Molly Murray's excellent unpublished thesis: 'Choreographics: Dance in Post-War American Poetry', unpublished PhD thesis, University of Sheffield, 2022. See also Karlien van den Beukel's detailed discussion of Olson and dance in 'Why

Olson Did Ballet: The Pedagogical Avant-Gardism of Massine', in David Herd (ed.), *Contemporary Olson* (Manchester: Manchester University Press, 2015), pp. 286–296.
94. Olson, *Collected Prose*, p. 182.
95. Charles Olson, *The Maximus Poems*, ed. George Butterick (Berkeley, Los Angeles, CA: University of California Press, 1983), pp. 496–497. For an excellent extended discussion of 'I have been an ability—a machine', see Michael Kindellan, 'Poetic Instruction', in David Herd (ed.), *Contemporary Olson* (Manchester: Manchester University Press, 2015), pp. 89–102.
96. Olson, *Collected Prose*, p. 225.
97. Olson, *Collected Prose*, p. 225.
98. Olson, *Collected Prose*, p. 220.
99. Olson, *Collected Prose*, p. 220.
100. Jeremy Prynne, 'Lecture on Maximus IV, V, VI', Simon Fraser University, 27 July 1971, transcribed by Tom McGauley, *Iron* (October 1971); reprinted in *Minutes of the Charles Olson Society* 28 (April 1999), http://charlesolson.org/Files/Prynnelecture1.htm and http://charlesolson.org/Files/Prynnelecture2.htm (accessed 31 May 2022) (no page numbers given).
101. Olson, *Maximus Poems*, p. 14.
102. Olson, *Maximus Poems*, p. 16. Olson's reference to 'Isolatos' refers the poem from its post-war political geography to the temporarily idealized internationalism of *Moby Dick*, where, in chapter 27, Melville observes these Isolatoes 'federated along one keel'. See Herman Melville, *Moby Dick*, ed. David Herd (Ware: Wordsworth Editions, 2004), p. 100.
103. Charles Olson, 'People v. The Fascist, U.S. (1944)', *Survey Graphic* (August 1944), p. 368.
104. For a thoroughgoing critique of Olson's period in Mexico, see Heriberto Yepez, *The Empire of Neomemory*, tr. Jen Hofer, Christian Nagler, and Brian Whitener (Chainlinks, 2013).

4
Making

The Right to Work

To read contemporary histories of the post-war crisis of displacement is to observe a fault line in the discourse of non-personhood that is only too visible again today. Writing under the auspices of the United Nations High Commissioner for Refugees (UNHCR), Jacques Vernant put the issue as clearly as anybody:

> the events which are the root cause of man's becoming a refugee are always of a political nature. But the term 'political events' is not easy to define [...]. The view is steadily gaining ground that the modern state is responsible for the living conditions of its nationals—a perfectly reasonable view given the part played by the state in the organization of and direction of the national economy.[1]

Vernant's observation was born of common sense. How, in reality—in the reality, say, of the displaced persons camp, where motives for movement are being sifted through—can one preserve a distinction between factors which are political and factors which are economic in nature? His 'perfectly reasonable' point was that in the context of the modern state, economic circumstances were often, if not invariably, the consequence of political decision-making. In other words, there is a tangle at the root of displacement where the distinction between the political and the economic is difficult, if not impossible, to sustain. As Vernant put it, writing in 1953, 'Today, more than at any other period, it is difficult to define which [events] are political and those which are not.'[2]

Perhaps at every period it seems more difficult than at any other period to arrive at such a clarity of definition. Consider, in the present moment, the person forced to move because their locale is becoming untenable because of changes to the climate consequent on other countries' politicians' refusal to act. The point here, however, is not to seek to clarify what is political and what is economic migration, who is an economic migrant and who is not. The intention, rather, is to hear the implications of that discourse at the mid-century moment, the moment the distinction was emerging but before it had hardened into place. The fact that Vernant could ask the question in the way he did, with a straightforwardness that contemporary discourse all but forbids, is a consequence of the fact that, in the moment of asking, the validity of the distinction was a live issue.

In part, what made it live, and what permitted the straightforwardness of Vernant's question, was the seeming clarity of definition provided by contemporary international documents. As the Convention Relating to the Status of Refugees determined, on 25 July 1951, 'the term "refugee" shall apply to any person who'

> As a result of events occurring before 1 January 1951 and owing to well-founded fear of being persecuted for reasons of race, religion, nationality, membership of a particular social group or political opinion, is outside the country of his nationality and is unable or, owing to such fear, is unwilling to avail himself of the protection of that country; or who, not having a nationality and being outside the country of his former habitual residence of such events, is unable or, owing to such fear, is unwilling to return to it.[3]

To be a refugee, as this statement proposes, and therefore to qualify for citizenship (or some form of quasi-citizenship) in another country, one has to have been expelled on the basis of some form of politicized identity.[4] From which it follows that the relation of belonging between the person and the sovereign state is understood exclusively in political terms. And so, of course, it has continued such that, in the present moment, there is no line more vigilantly policed by border policy and officials who enact it than the line apparently dividing the refugee from the economic migrant.

At precisely the same time, however, that clarity was established in relation to the category of refugee, so the implications of such categorical clarity for those seeking refuge were becoming all too visible. Not to be granted refugee status, or to be granted only the minimal protection such status might entail, was all too frequently to be held, economically, in a state of suspense. As Vernant himself observed, in a discussion of what he called 'the refugee complex',

> It would be interesting to study the 'complexes' which camp life, humiliation and suffering have caused among many refugees. That they exist

would seem to follow from certain observations made in the United Kingdom where there is apparently a relatively high percentage of mental cases among former displaced persons [...] This failure, partly psychological and partly physical, is most often due to the enforced idleness to which the refugee is condemned, or to the sudden and too brutal rupture with his home and national background.[5]

However difficult it would have been to establish, it is the equivalence here that is striking. The suffering Vernant observes to be produced at high levels among the refugee population in the United Kingdom is a result, to a comparable degree, of both the 'brutal rupture' that is the act of displacement and the 'enforced idleness to which the refugee is condemned'. From which it followed, for Vernant, that the question of work was axiomatic to the question of displacement. 'Legal assistance', as he said, 'is not enough; the refugee must live. And here the problem can be summed up in two words: housing and work.'[6]

Such accounts of what Vernant terms 'enforced idleness' might be documented many times over. Gerard Daniel Cohen draws on various contemporary sources to bring the reality home:

'Is this not an insult to common sense', asked an IRO official in 1949, 'that hundreds of thousands of people reduced to idleness neither consume nor produce at a time when all men and women should be associated with the task of reconstruction and production.'[7]

Or, as contemporary commentator Francesca Wilson observed, intensifying the rhetoric, '"Slaves were needed, whereas large numbers of refugees live in enforced idleness, and their presence is resented."'[8] For Arendt, seeking to summarize the situation, what this amounted to was an intimate connection between juridical personhood and work. As she put it, 'The stateless person, without right to residence and without the right to work, had of course constantly to transgress the law.'[9]

As with Vernant, Arendt's point is not simply about well-being. Just as it is difficult in relation to causes of displacement to preserve a distinction between events which are political and events which are not, so, in the reality of displacement itself, the categories bleed across. It is inevitable, as Arendt sees it, that the person denied the right to sustain themselves will 'transgress the law'. Whatever states, or their representatives, or their treaties might say, in the lived experience of displacement, the political and the economic were deeply implicated.[10]

In fact, of course, at a certain level, the authors of major mid-century international documents understood such complications. For all that the 1951 Convention designated refugee status in strictly political terms, it also specified what the committee structure of the Universal Declaration called social and economic rights. Principal among these, as the Convention set out, was the right to what the document termed 'gainful employment'. As 'Article 17' put it,

> 1. The Contracting State shall accord to refugees lawfully staying in their territory the most favourable treatment accorded to nationals of a foreign country in the same circumstances, as regards the right to engage in wage earning employment.[11]

There is slippage, to be sure, in the phrase 'lawfully staying in their territory', but as regards 'the right to engage in wage earning employment'—as with the right to association in the form of a trades union—there was to be an entitlement to the most 'favourable treatment'. This is less grand, rhetorically, than the language of universal rights, but in so far as it set out to refuse a two-tier practice, the requirement of common 'treatment' had comparable force.

In this respect, as in other crucial respects, the 1951 Convention followed the 1948 Declaration. It is clarifying to note, however, that when it was incorporated into the Universal Declaration, the right to work was a new right. This is hardly to imply that the right to work had not previously been asserted; in one form or another, plainly, it has been an historic claim. The sense in which it was new is in relation to the form of the Declaration itself. Thus, where the Universal Declaration innovated most substantially on, and differed most significantly from, eighteenth-century declarations of rights was in the inclusion, over and above political rights, of a series of economic and social rights, entirely core to which was Article 23: The Right to Work. There are no such rights, for example, in the Declaration of the Rights of Man and of the Citizen, from which it follows that, with respect at least to its development of the form itself, the inclusion of the right to work was distinctive to, and therefore in some sense definitive of, the Universal Declaration.

To frame this slightly differently, in so far as the authors of the Universal Declaration can be understood collectively to have sought to construct a new relation between the individual and the sovereign state (what Seyla Benhabib would call a 'new modality of membership'), the right to work was critical to that relation.[12] This was a far-reaching and, in its potential at least, a transformative demand, the incorporation of which, as with each of the Declaration's thirty articles, was the product of extended argument by various parties. Joined in their lobbying by international workers' organizations, including the UN-sponsored International Labour Organization (ILO) and the more radically constituted World Federations of Trade Unions (WFTU), the aim of the Latin-American socialist alliance in particular was not solely to establish work as right but to enshrine a series of work-related protections.[13] Captured in Articles 23 and 24, the rights relating to work are as follows:

Article 23.

(1) Everyone has the right to work, to free choice of employment, to just and favourable conditions of work and to protection against unemployment.
(2) Everyone, without any discrimination, has the right to equal pay for equal work.
(3) Everyone who works has the right to just and favourable remuneration ensuring for himself and his family an existence worthy of human dignity, and supplemented, if necessary, by other means of social protection.
(4) Everyone has the right to form and to join trade unions for the protection of his interests.

Article 24.

Everyone has the right to rest and leisure, including reasonable limitation of working hours and periodic holidays with pay.[14]

Fundamental as such qualifications and protections were, and indicative as they were of a commitment to the principle of 'the most favourable treatment', it is crucial also not to lose sight of the overarching importance of the incorporation of work in and of itself, nor of the gravity with which its inclusion in the Declaration was weighed. As Pérez Cisneros, the Cuban delegate, observed, it was essential to distinguish a modern declaration of rights from those of previous centuries. The latter had spoken of man as the citizen; today, such a declaration should stress man as a worker.[15]

It is instructive to hear, in the context of the shaping of the Declaration, precisely how carefully Cisneros' commentary on the text was weighed. It has been observed already, with reference in particular to Article 14, how exhaustively in the drafting process any given wording was scrutinized for import. The expression of the right to work was no exception in this regard. Extended consideration, for instance, was given to the question of whether work should be framed as a 'duty' as well as a right; a proposition that was rejected on the grounds of its proximity to forced labour.[16] More broadly, what framed all such discussions around work was the function of labour, and the worker, in the context of Cold War politics. Simply put, to bring a person's relation to work into the committee room was immediately to reference the global political–economic division that made the formulation of the Universal Declaration in 1948 an all-but-impossible task. As much as anybody might, therefore (and as much, for instance, as when the British delegate insisted on the right to 'enjoy' rather than be granted asylum), the Cuban delegate, Cisneros, understood what he was saying.

His term 'essential' can thus be understood in a strict sense. Whereas citizenship is circumscribed by sovereign territory and so, whereas in any claim to citizenship the authority of such sovereignty is re-invoked, to 'stress' the person as worker is to propose a relation to others and to the environment in which such a model of territory is not simply given but, at some level, cut across. To identify the person as worker, rather than citizen, and to make that an essential point of difference for the Declaration, was to underline, as Cisernos saw it, that the capacity to work—which, as this chapter will proceed to argue, following mid-century authors, is the capacity 'to make'—was more fundamental to any characterization of human relations than was the category of national identification. To introduce the right to work, in other words, to a form of declaration that had historically asserted only political rights, is to assert a claim that, in its broadest potential at least, might cut across the divisions and problematics of citizenship. Really to understand what that claim signified, however, to understand the mode of belonging Cisneros took the right to work to imply, we need to understand what work meant, or was coming to mean, at the moment of its inclusion in the Declaration. What, we need to understand, was being claimed in the mid-century moment when the right to work was formally invoked?

It is an answer to that question that this chapter looks to unfold. To do so, the discussion will dwell in particular on two extended mid-century considerations of the meaning of work, both framed by the post-war question of recognition. In the first place, the chapter addresses Arendt's treatment of 'work' in *The Human Condition*. In that context, Arendt distinguishes 'work' from 'labour' and 'action' as part of her extended consideration of the question of belonging that follows her analysis of expulsion in *The Origins of Totalitarianism*. To deepen the mid-century understanding Arendt provides, and to enrich her sense of what work (as opposed to labour) makes, the chapter will turn to Olson's repeated and extended meditation on work in his 1951 essay 'Human Universe', in 'Projective Verse', and in the first volume of his epic of making, *The Maximus Poems*. What matters, in placing Arendt and Olson alongside each other in this way, is how they intersect. Limited as each writer individually is in their expression of work, what they had in common was an understanding, in the post-war moment, of the importance of articulating work as a mode of belonging. With that mid-century understanding of work in place, the chapter turns to two contemporary commentaries on Arendt, those of Ayten Gündoğdu and Jacques Rancière. Gündoğdu's account is crucial in helping to make the link between work and human movement; Rancière makes it possible to see the connection between work and the necessary agency of rights. The chapter then concludes by attempting to show precisely how the denial of the right to work is a mode of expulsion, where work, as Fanon and Henri Lefebvre help one to grasp, constitutes a defining human relation. Fully to comprehend expulsion and the hostile environments in which it is effected, we need to understand what both Fanon and, in particular, Lefebvre understood in the mid-century moment by the Marxist concept of alienation. Where expulsion takes the form of the denial of the right to work, it is in alienation that we find a description of the experience of non-personhood that results.

To hear such mid-century emphases on work in the present moment is once again to discern a kind of warning. For all kinds of pressing reasons, the contemporary discourse around work has turned, in part, to the prospect of a post-work world, with Josh Cohen's *Not Working* offering a brilliant expression of the shape such arguments for transition would need to take.[17] In re-contextualizing the Universal Declaration's insistence on the right to work, however, we hear a different account of the relation between personhood and making. What one finds, first, is that, in terms of the image of belonging framed by a declaration of rights, there is hardly a more significant right than the right to work since it is the right to work that encodes the agency at the heart of rights. This follows from the fact that, as mid-century writers repeatedly sought to demonstrate, one finds an image of belonging in the agency of working and making that can cut across the bounds of citizenship. All of which is driven, as Vernant, Arendt, and numerous other mid-century commentators observed, by the dark sight of the construction of a surplus; of persons made surplus on a mass basis by the prevention of agency through the denial of the right to work. To go back to mid-century commentaries on the nature of work, in other words, is to be reminded that when we think about a world beyond, after, or without work, we must be exceptionally careful what we wish for.

Exactly why, in the midst of this, we need a poet's commentary on work to understand its implications will not, perhaps, be immediately apparent.[18] It is precisely a measure of the importance of Olson's mid-century imaginary, however, that he situated work as centrally to his poetic project as he did. What he grasped, albeit from within the limitations of his identity, but as a consequence of his reading of a mid-century politics of expulsion, was the importance of the act of making to human belonging. How people work, what protections they need, what benefits must accrue, are hardly questions that mid-century discourse closed down. What that discourse allows us to grasp, however, and what mid-century authors understood, is that to stop a person working—as in the present moment people seeking asylum in the United Kingdom are stopped for years and years on end—is to cast them from the commons people collectively can make.

'The Public Realm: The Common'

Invariably, when, in her extended critique of what she calls the Rights of Man, Hannah Arendt aims to identify the moment of that concept's failure, it is in the expulsion from the world of work that she finds her image. As she poses the issue in the opening of her discussion of 'The Decline of the Nation State and the End of the Rights of Man', the image in question comes direct from Nazi anti-Semitic propaganda:

> The Official SS newspaper, the *Schwarz Korps*, stated explicitly in 1938 that if the world was not yet convinced that the Jews were the scum of the earth, it soon would be when unidentifiable beggars, without nationality, without money, and without passports crossed their frontiers. And it is true that this kind of factual propaganda worked better than Goebbels' rhetoric, not only

because it established the Jews as scum of the earth, but also because the incredible plight of an ever-growing group of innocent people was like a practical demonstration of the totalitarian movements' cynical claims that no such thing as inalienable human rights existed [...].[19]

My argument in this book, and in this chapter in particular, is that Arendt's commentary on human rights is in equal parts limited, brutally insightful, and, despite her intentionality, indicative of the real potential of the discourse. It should not be a surprise that her thinking on the question of rights carries all these qualities. To enter into disagreement with the Declaration was to be in dialogue with the logic of the document's principles such that disagreement could, in fact, turn out to be an exploration of the Declaration's larger, if only partially stated, intent.[20] Arendt was not alone in having such a tangled relation to the Declaration and at the centre of that tangle was the question of work.

In the remark cited above, Arendt's brutal insight is that precisely the point at which rights should be triggered is the point at which their failure as a mode of inclusion is confirmed. Following the logic of the Nazi gambit, Arendt argues that expulsion generates expulsion, that to be excluded from a given jurisdiction is to have one's excludability demonstrated. There are various indexes of such excludability, with work, as Arendt's description suggests, unquestionably one of them, the excluded compelled to seek asylum in the guise of 'unidentifiable beggars'. We must heed the warning in this, brutal as it sounds. As much as we would hope to believe and act otherwise, history indicates that where persons (and especially large groups of persons) are expelled from the realm of work, that expulsion can become politically self-fulfilling. It is part of the value of Arendt, in other words, that she is prepared to observe this historical fact.

Arendt is again at the fault line of personhood and work when she addresses the question of criminalization. As she puts it,

> The stateless person [...] was liable to jail sentences without ever committing a crime. More than that, the entire hierarchy of values which pertain in civilized countries was reversed in his case. Since he was the anomaly for whom the general law did not provide, it was better for him to become an anomaly for which it did provide, that of the criminal.[21]

In this case, the fact that juridical non-personhood combines with the absence of the right to work binds the individual inexorably into criminality.

In one sense, the transgression is formal in that the individual's presence is itself an infringement. In another sense, the transgression is materially motivated in that the individual must make some kind of living. The perverse logic of the situation, as Arendt is partially correct in observing, is that to commit an actual crime is to place oneself within the scope of the law. Such recognition, however, is only temporary since any such transgression only raises the likelihood of removal. As Proudfoot observed, the refugee (and therefore much more so the stateless person) is 'liable to expulsion if his presence for any reason is no longer desired'.[22] Prison, in other words, would only be a temporary sanctuary, a temporary status accorded a person otherwise deemed outwith recognition by the law.

It is unquestionably the case that Arendt identifies a profound vulnerability in the person whose political non-personhood is combined with expulsion from the realm of work. The question is whether, in observing that vulnerability, Arendt has therefore demonstrated a contradiction, and with it a failure inherent in the language of rights. The argument here is that Arendt has not established such a contradiction but rather that, in presuming to do so, she has both demonstrated the limitation of her view of the Universal Declaration and also indicated the document's further scope. What, in effect, she brings us to, in the early 1950s, is what Seyla Benhabib, writing in 2003, called the necessity for a new map. As Benhabib put it, in the Introduction to *The Rights of Others*,

> The modern nation-state system has regulated membership in terms of one principal category: national citizenship. We have entered an era when state sovereignty has been frayed and the institution of national citizenship has been disaggregated or unbundled into diverse elements. New modalities of membership have emerged, with the result that the boundaries of the political community, as defined by the nation-state system, are no longer adequate to regulate membership.[23]

Benhabib's argument was that, following the failure of the nation state to regulate political membership, 'we are like travelers navigating an unknown terrain with the help of old maps'.[24] Arendt is important to this argument because of the clarity with which she expresses the tension between human rights and sovereign rights and with which, therefore, she demonstrates the disjunction between the territory and the map.

What Benhabib does not register is quite how urgently Arendt, along with other mid-century writers, was already working to draw the new map and how carefully she was looking to articulate 'new modalities of membership'. Work itself was one such modality. Precisely because expulsion from the world of work was an index, and perhaps a self-perpetuating index, of political expulsion (because it was in economic expulsion that political expulsion became apparent), so it was necessary to explore how work itself constituted a mode of belonging. The paradox of Arendt's position is that while, in her critique of rights, she does not register the significance of the right to work, she deepens our understanding of that right when she follows her exhaustive account of expulsion in *The Origins of Totalitarianism* with her account of the meaning of work in *The Human Condition*.

In focusing to the degree that she does in *The Human Condition* on the meaning of work, Arendt's overarching purpose is to revisit, trouble, and ultimately rewrite the distinction between the political and the economic, that categorical distinction forced so substantially into prominence by its reformulation in defining international documents of the period. Just as for Benhabib, writing in 2003, it was true to observe that, 'we are at such a historical juncture when the problem of political boundaries has once more become visible', so, for Arendt, writing in the mid-century, the boundary between the political and the economic was a salient concern. For this reason, the early part of Arendt's discussion of work is quite largely taken up with historical accounts that insist on, or effect, a sharp demarcation. Her starting point is the distinction between the polis and the household as codified in Ancient Greek culture, according to which 'the very term "political economy" would have been a contradiction in terms: whatever was "economic", related to the life of the individual and the survival of the species, was a non-political, household affair by definition'.[25] It follows that it is a matter of great importance to Arendt that, in contemporary understanding,

> the dividing line [between the political and the economic] is entirely blurred, because we see the body of peoples and political communities in the image of a family whose everyday affairs have to be taken care of by a gigantic, nation-wide administration of house-keeping.[26]

We should not interpret from Arendt's tone here that she hopes to restore an Ancient Greek sense of political–economic division. She can frequently sound dismissive and what she appears to dismiss, here, is the domain of work gendered as 'house-keeping'. Retrogressive as her image is, however, her intention is not to relegate a particular area of life. Her point, rather, is that a constant vigilance is required in any context to achieve a balancing of political and economic imperatives that does not tend towards expulsion. It is on this basis that she revisits Marx, in whom she finds such a re-inscription of the categorical distinction, albeit with different emphasis. As she puts it,

> That politics is nothing but a function of society, that action, speech, and thought are primarily superstructures upon social interest, is not a discovery of Karl Marx but on the contrary is among the axiomatic assumptions Marx accepted uncritically from the political economists of the modern age.[27]

What matters here is not Arendt's reading of Marx, which, as this chapter will come to confirm, is at best schematic. Both Fanon and Lefebvre, as we will see, were much more carefully insightful readers of Marx on the question of work. What matters, rather, is how such a partial reading gets Arendt to her larger point: that it is necessary to contest those understandings of the political–economic distinction which appear to insist on a conceptual separation because, in fact, 'In the modern world, the two realms [...] constantly flow into each other like waves in the never-resting stream of the life process itself.'[28]

Suggestive as this image might be, it is not according to the metaphor of 'flow' or 'wave' that Arendt comes to redescribe the relation of the political to the economic. Instead, what she proposes is a tripartite distinction between labour, work, and action, each term being subject to extended commentary in *The Human Condition*. Within this structure, 'work' operates as the middle term between categories that, broadly speaking, reconstitute the economic–political distinction Arendt seeks, in fact, to recalibrate. Thus, labour is the life process, the process of daily reproduction, that Greek culture assigned to the home (the *oika*), whereas action, whether as word or deed, constitutes the human as political animal. The realm of action, as Arendt describes it, is what she calls 'the space of appearance', that public space in which recognition is secured and conferred and which has its equivalent in the Ancient Greek agora. Both terms—labour and action—are extensively considered and, as has been indicated elsewhere in this argument, provide insights into both the production and prevention of non-personhood. It is arguably in Arendt's understanding of work, however, as distinct in particular from labour, that her argument is most useful, demonstrating as it does how contemporary understanding of human belonging can, and must, be expanded.

The crucial distinction between work and labour, as Arendt tells it, is that in working, or as worker, a person is what she calls *homo faber*. *Homo faber* is the person who fabricates, who engages in the act of making, where making is distinct from reproducing because the thing made outlasts the activity that brings it into being. Arendt is interested in all kinds of making but principally in what making tends towards, which, as she puts it, is the fabric of the human world:

> The man-made world of things, the human artifice erected by *homo faber*, becomes a home for mortal men, whose stability will endure and outlast the ever-changing movement of their lives and actions, only insomuch at it transcends both the sheer functionality of things produced for consumption and the sheer utility of objects produced for use.[29]

The technical interest of this statement lies in the way work operates between and across the functions of labour and action, serving to produce not a space of 'consumption' and 'utility' but 'a home for men during their life on earth', a 'human artifice fit for speech and action'.[30] What really matters here, however, is not the technical function of work in Arendt's scheme but the relation she identifies between making and belonging. According to this logic, to work is to make, where to make is to create the human artifice and where the human artifice is to be understood as a 'home' for mortal persons. There is, in other words, a profound connection between making and being at home. It is through making that such a sense of home is constituted, where home surely entails non-expulsion.

Persuasive as this might seem, the question is how? How are the practice of making and the fact of being at home connected? To which the best answer is to be found not in Arendt's extended treatment of work as making in *The Human Condition* but in the conclusion to her discussion of 'The Perplexities of Human Rights'. 'The great danger arising from the existence of people forced to live outside the common world', so she argues, 'is that they are thrown back, in the midst of civilisation, on their natural givenness [...] no longer allowed to partake in the human artifice, they begin to belong to the human race in much the same way as animals belong to a specific animal species'.[31] What Arendt considers that she has established (in her articulation of what Agamben would call 'bare life'), is the limit point of the concept of human rights. As she puts it here, human rights in their inalienability refer to a person's givenness, whereas human belonging—which rights would claim to guarantee—is achieved not by what is given but by what is made.

What this overlooks, however, is the defining fact that the Universal Declaration includes the right to work—which is the right to make, which is the right to 'partake in human artifice'. Nor should we mis-hear that term 'partake', which can sound like a form of consumption but, when coupled with making, means the act of taking part, the shared act of making a space for humans. From which it follows that to be denied the right to work is to be expelled—to be thrown, in the oldest sense, from the human commons.

Arendt's presentation of *homo faber*, and of the act of making, clarifies our understanding of the right to work in two ways. In the first place, she establishes the connection between working and belonging, where working is making, and where to make is to participate in the artifice which is the human world. It is a meaning it is instructive to recover, not in order to defend any given mode of working or making, nor to propose—just as the authors of the Universal Declaration opted not to propose—that anybody might be compelled to work. It is to observe, rather, the impact of denying the right to work. If working, in its largest sense, is the act of making a human home, then to be banned from working is to be thrown outside. What Arendt helps us understand in the second place, however, is how the right to work transfigures the relation between individual and state. Thus, whereas an exclusive emphasis on political rights serves to re-inscribe the authority of the state (where it is the state, in its authority, that grants belonging), the emphasis on the right to work invokes another image of belonging altogether. It is an image in which that which is belonged to is the human commons and where the fact of belonging is effected through the act of making.

Work in Progress

When Robert Creeley introduced the work of his friend and collaborator Charles Olson, in the 'Preface' to his edition of Olson's *Selected Poems*, he took the reader back to the post-war moment:

> All previous epistemological structures and, even more, their supporting cultural referents were displaced significantly, if not forever, by the political, economic and technological transformations following the Second World War. The underlying causes were well in place at the turn of the century but by 1950 the effects were even more dominant. There could no longer be such a 'father/son' disposition of reality as either Pound or

Williams, tacitly, took as a given of their situation. Olson's displacement echoes painfully in his own undertakings, and nowhere more so than in "I have been an ability – a machine …".[32]

There are few richer assessments of Olson's understanding of the mid-century moment than Creeley's. The fact that he was able to provide such a distilled and capacious account of his friend's grasp of post-war reality owed to his proximity to the work. It is hardly sufficient, in other words, to observe that Creeley collaborated with Olson. More accurate to say that Olson thought through certain of his major texts with Creeley, that Creeley was engaged directly in the emergence of Olson's thought. For which reason, it is highly instructive to hear how he positions Olson at the beginning of his poetic career.[33]

What Creeley doesn't present is a poet who thought in terms of national frameworks. What we are to understand, instead, is a much wider sense of political, economic, and technological rupture that had been emerging since the beginning of the century but that, by 1950, had become dominant. Creeley's word for that rupture is 'displacement', a term he uses carefully and with its full significance. Elsewhere in his preface, written in 1997 but recovering the thought of the earlier moment, Creeley pictures a world of persons on the move. When he talks about displacement, in other words, he means to point to the physical fact of persons compelled to move by the 'shrinking of their physical provision' but also to the reverberations of its underlying political and economic causes. Likewise, when he refers to Olson's displacement, he means to recall his family's immigrant status, but more so, he means to observe that, in the post-war period, displacement, as an ongoing transformation, was a condition of thought. One can hear that reality, Creeley suggests, in what he calls Olson's 'undertakings', one such being an extended consideration of the meaning of work.

Probably Olson's clearest statement on the question of work is in his essay 'Human Universe', drafted in the first half of 1951 during his extended visit to the Yucatan peninsula and first published in the magazine *Origin* in the winter of 1951–52. Emerging from letters he was writing to Creeley from Mexico, and from which Creeley would select to produce *The Mayan Letters*, Olson's essay moves in various directions but central to its logic, and to the evolving poetic to which it contributed, was a clear and, in many ways, surprising statement about work. As he puts it, moving from circumlocution to direct pronouncement:

> For the truth is, that the management of external nature so that none of its virtu is lost, in vegetables or in art, is as much a delicate juggling of her content as is the same juggling by any one of us of our own. And when men are not such jugglers, are not able to manage a means of expression the equal of their own or nature's intricacy, the flesh does choke. The notion of fun comes to displace work as what we are here for. Spectatorism crowds out participation as the condition of culture.[34]

Olson's statement is at the same time straightforward, unambiguous, and complex in its implications. Unambiguously, what he says is that 'work' is 'what we are here for', which might seem to mean that he wants to rule out fun. And indeed, whatever else he was, Olson would not appear to have been 'fun' exactly. For fun in post-war poetry you have to look a little later, in particular to Frank O'Hara, although, even in O'Hara, 'fun' is laced with threat. O'Hara learned a great deal from Olson, much more than he wanted to let on, not least his sense of the urgency of bringing persons and what he called 'Personism' into view, and his articulation of 'fun', for all that he certainly was capable of it, carried an Olsonian charge. As he put it, in an essay about abstract expressionism,

> In a capitalist country fun is everything. Fun is the only justification for the acquisitive impulse [...] Abstract Expressionism is not [fun], and its justifications must be found elsewhere. Not to say it as justification, but simply as fact, abstract expressionism is the art of serious men. They are serious because they are not *isolated*.[35]

The masculinity of this is oppressive, if not entirely representative of O'Hara's engagement with the art world. But, as with Olson, the problem with fun is the distancing it effects. O'Hara's word for that distancing is isolation. For Olson, on the other hand, as for Creeley, the word is 'displacement'. The problem is not fun as such but that fun displaces work, that work, as value or activity is lost from view. The implications of this for both poets are dark and far-reaching. For O'Hara, the result is a cultural justification of the 'acquisitive impulse'. For Olson, not less aware of that impulse but writing earlier in the decade, the effect is that 'the flesh does choke'.

In 'Human Universe', as elsewhere in Olson, and as in Arendt, the word 'work' hovers on the brink of a synonym. In this case, the issue is that 'Spectatorism crowds out participation as the condition of culture', where participation is the synonym for work. It is important not to lose sight of the fact, however, that when Olson says work, he means *work*, which, in part, is to observe that Olson was, to use Peter Gizzi's term, 'class awake'.[36] This is apparent, as we have seen, in 'The Post Office', Olson's account of his father's mistreatment by the US Postal Service following his successful organizing of the Massachusetts branch of the National Association of Letter Carriers (NALC). Olson's interest in that piece is both to record the anti-union practices of the Postal Service as employer and the multiple mechanisms by which it alienated and expelled the individual worker, and, at the same time, to document his father's commitment to the role. It pictures Karl Olsen at work, how, through his routes and his daily contacts, his rhythms and his interactions, he formed a world. In the shrewdness of its detailing, 'The Post Office' thus establishes the primacy of Karl's experience to the poet's world view, as an immigrant worker rendered alien from his working environment for seeking to establish trades union rights.

It is not principally, however, as anecdotal labour historian that Olson is of interest on the question of work but rather as poet for whom work as participation was the condition of culture. Olson, this is to argue, was not simply an observer of work and working practice but also a poet-thinker for whom it was necessary to establish work as his cultural ground. Where this is first apparent is in 'Projective Verse' itself, that brilliantly explosive response to the post-war cultural condition in which he found himself and to which work was pivotal as a means of understanding poetic practice. The purpose of 'Projective Verse', it will be recalled, in which Creeley was an active contributor, was to establish 'recognition' as the principle of linguistic expression. The open field poem was to be a space of appearance. It was to create a setting in which recognition—the 'whole series of new recognitions'—constituted the writing's shaping dynamic. Crucially, however, in arriving at this poetic and therefore cultural ideal, Olson repeatedly insisted in the essay on the necessity and value of work. Any space, whether aesthetic or (as he would come to observe in *Maximus*) real, in which recognition might be possible did not come from nowhere but was the product, as he constantly reminded his reader, of ongoing work. At certain points, what this seems to amount to is a synonym for daily practice, as when, for instance, he describes the improvement of the poetic line:

> And the line comes (I swear it) from the breath, from the breathing of the man who writes, at the moment that he writes, and thus is, it is here that, the daily work, the WORK, gets in, for only he, the man who writes, can declare, at every moment, the line, its metric and its ending.[37]

We should pause for a moment to reflect on the fact that Olson is unusual as a poet in presenting the poetic undertaking as 'WORK'. In doing so, he counters all those images of poetic production that conceal the effort involved, images of inspiration which both separate the poet from the culture and imply their susceptibility to other kinds of force. Olson emphasizes constancy of practice because what, ultimately, we are talking about here is agency.[38] Even so, and the capitalization notwithstanding, when Olson says 'WORK' here, the term is operating by way of an analogy for practice.

Elsewhere, the identification is stronger, as when Olson criticizes the inattentiveness of the contemporary poet:

> The trouble with most work, to my taking, since the breaking away from traditional lines and stanzas, and from such wholes as, say Chaucer's TROILUS or S's LEAR, is: contemporary workers go lazy RIGHT HERE WHERE THE LINE IS BORN.[39]

The difference here is that the poet is being encouraged to identify explicitly as worker; not simply as an artist required to undertake daily practice but as a person whose creativity should be aligned with work. 'It is a matter', as he puts it:

> of, at *all* points (even, I should say, of our management of daily reality as of the daily work) get on with it, keep moving, keep in, speed, the nerves, their speed, the perceptions, theirs, the acts, the split-second acts, the whole business, keep it moving as fast as you can, citizen.[40]

Olson is talking to poets about poetry, but he is also talking to citizens about citizenry. And as he talks to citizens, what he is calling attention to is the daily work that must underpin the practice and politics of recognition. We go lazy at our peril, as Olson observes, and it will be necessary at the end of this section to remind ourselves what, for Olson, that peril was always called. What needs to be contemplated first, however, is the first volume of *The Maximus Poems*, Olson's major undertaking of the decade following the war, and the sequence in which the significance of work was most fully instantiated.

Of the three volumes of *The Maximus Poems* (*The Maximus Poems* (1960), *Maximus Poems IV, V, VI* (1968) and *The Maximus Poems: Volume Three* (published posthumously in 1975), it is the first volume that most clearly bears the impress of Black Mountain College. Shaped by the expulsion of some of its key personnel from the Bauhaus, Black Mountain developed a curriculum that was intended in some sense to cultivate a counter-measure to such expulsive politics, and central to that curriculum was the act of making. As Edmund de Waal has commented, writing about 'Black Mountain College and the Crafts', 'The crafts—principally weaving and ceramics [...] not only shared in the pedagogy of the college that shaped its tumultuous history, but sometimes led it.'[41] Evidence of this commitment to such crafts is that, as de Waal notes, 'three of the key post-war American texts on the crafts had a strong connection with the College': Anni Albers' *On Weaving*, Marguerite Wildenhain's *Pottery: Form and Expression*, and M.C. Richards' *Centering in Pottery, Poetry and the Person*. That such commitments sometimes led the college's pedagogy can be felt in the approach Albers encouraged her students to take to the materials with which they worked. As de Waal observes,

> In order to approach the material anew to activate 'our latent perceptivity of matière', she encouraged students to 'look around us and pick up this bit of moss, this piece of bark or paper, these stems of flowers, or these shavings of wood or metal. We will group them, cut them, curl them, mix them, finally perhaps paste them, to fix a certain order. We will make a smooth piece of paper appear fibrous by scratching its surface, perforating it, tearing it, twisting it [...] what we are doing can be as absorbing as painting.[42]

In the way Albers urged her students to work, and in particular in the way she encouraged them to handle their materials, one hears a clear analogue with *The Maximus Poems*. Olson's materials, his 'matière', were the history and geography of Gloucester, the documents that formed its archive, and the streets and contours that constituted its space. Like Albers' students, he worked with what came to hand, intent not on creating as such but on using and shaping. And what he came to make, in the first volume of *Maximus* in particular, was an extended poetic history of the act of making itself, an epic in which work was visible at every level.

The principal way in which Olson made work visible was by telling the stories that working people told. Sometimes sharing stories that he picked up in conversation, sometimes incorporating accounts he found in the archives, Olson builds his series of poems out of the stories people tell about their working lives. It matters greatly that these are stories people told themselves, that Olson shares them verbatim or as reported speech. What he thus establishes, from poem to poem, and across the whole sequence in progress, is the importance of work not only to the economic maintenance of the community in question but also to the emergence of the community as shared ground. In other words, what Olson presents in *The Maximus Poems* is an expression of value grounded in labour, a labour theory of value, where the act of working has to be made visible at every turn.

In part, where one finds that labour theory of value expressed is in a series of statements that insist straightforwardly on the importance of work. This is nowhere more apparent than in 'Maximus to Gloucester, Sunday, July 19', where the poem opens with what Olson's speaker refers to as 'that bad sculpture of a fisherman':

> and they stopped before that bad sculpture of a fisherman
>
> —"as if one were to talk to a man's house,
> knowing not what gods or heroes are"—
>
> not knowing what a fisherman is
> instead of going straight to the Bridge
> and doing no more than—saying no more than—
> in the Charybdises of the
> Cut waters the flowers tear off
> the wreathes[43]

'Maximus to Gloucester, Sunday, July 19' is a tender poem. It marks the occasion in the calendar when the community honours those in the fishing industry who, in the course of their work, are lost at sea. The poem observes the ceremony, the throwing of flowers onto the water at the Cut, the inlet that separates Gloucester from the mainland. There is a beautiful fragility in the writing, in the way the flowers of the wreathes are torn off, in the way the poem itself memorializes loss. What really matters, however, in Olson's handling of his matière, is that this is an occasion when the act of working is brought collectively into view. Unsatisfactory as it is, the sculpture matters because it as an attempt to represent the fact of work.

Which is not to argue, for all the intensity of its specificity, that Olson's poem has its meaning in the details of a particular industry. Nor is it to simplify the implications of work. The point of Olson's epic undertaking rather, in both a literal but also an allegorical sense, was to show *work* in progress, to show how constantly, on a daily basis, the society in question had to be made and remade. The question throughout Maximus, as the ongoing history of an actual community, is what brought, and continued to bring, that community into being, where the poem is neither naïve in its sense of human motivation nor static in its sense of history, where motivations are always in competition and where the culture and its politics can at any moment become worse. Thus, among its many threads, *The Maximus Poems* tells a history of exploitation by extraction, where people and resources are sacrificed to the drive to profit. Following that motive, there is a line through the poem that follows the history of John Hawkins' extraction of slaves from West Africa (a history I will return to in Chapter 5), to the numerous deaths of fisherman at sea, through to the industrialized overproduction on to which Maximus and Olson look:

> anything
> nature puts in the sea
> comes up,
>
> it is cornucopia
> to see it
> working up a sluggish
> treadle,
> from a ship's hold
>
> to the truck
> which takes it to the De-Hy
> to be turned into catfood,
> and fertilizer, for nature's
> fields[44]

There is a history, in other words, in *The Maximus Poems*, of the brutal consequences of extraction, of work driven not by the desire to shape but to profit.

But to read *Maximus* carefully is to read, as well, another story, a story that emerges through the poem's history of the community's work. Or, more precisely, it is to observe that the stories the community tells itself come through work, that it is through the processes of working with and in the construction of a common environment that the stories that constitute the social fabric are seen to emerge. To make this point, to show these processes in operation as the history of the community shifts back and forth, Olson constantly observes that, while there is no relation more prone to abuse and exploitation than the relation to work, it is nonetheless in the participation of working and making that the commons is both identified and formed.

It is on this balance of possibilities that the poem pivots, on the prospect, always looming, that, at any point, politically and economically, the community can go wrong. Both possibilities exist equally within the frame of the poem. And how those possibilities play out at any given moment depends fundamentally on the relation to work.

What Olson meant to show as he tilted his major poem towards the conditionalities of the mid-century moment, and with such consideration and in such detail that it might be undeniable, was that where one found the makings of a commons, what that commons called for was daily work. It is a most exacting requirement, and the poem itself as an undertaking can be daunting, but what Olson has constantly in mind is how, in the moment at which he wrote, there could be no illusion: the work of reproducing commonality had to be constantly maintained. Constantly, then, and throughout, the poem is trying to gauge what it means to work well. We are told of the resources required to sustain rather than financially to enrich a community. We are shown in detail how people interact to continue such sustainable work. We are told stories, drawn from the archive, of the things people did and saw in the act of working.

Fully to understand, however, why, in the decade following the war, Olson undertook an epic poetic series with work at its heart, one has to appreciate that, at some level, always, Olson's poem functions as allegory. As he put it in the course of his lecture series 'The Special View of History', given at Black Mountain College in 1956, the year before the college closed,

> How to say it, so that it is abundantly clear. It isn't at all unlike Keats' proposition that a man's life (he was speaking of Shakespeare and his plays) is an allegory. It is that one does have a life to live, exactly that much. And because it is that much, and it is one's own, it has a scale.[45]

The Maximus Poems isn't an allegory in the way that *Absalom and Achitophel* is an allegory, with one personage standing in for another. Nor is it an allegory in the way that *Pilgrim's Progress* is an allegory, with any given episode having its meaning in an episode in another text. Olson's poem is an allegory, rather, in the sense that always in the particularity of detail one can discern the operation of principles, where both the particularities and the principles matter in equal measure. What matters in Olson's project is work, where the work on which he dwelt could have taken another form, and the reason work matters is that ultimately what Olson is concerned with is agency: with what human agency required, enabled, and meant.

The reason for such an intensification of agency, and for establishing such an intensification as contemporary cultural ground, is that history had demonstrated what it meant for agency to be denied or overlooked. As Olson had put it, in 'People v The Fascist, U.S',

> To depend today only upon civil liberties or the government to meet the evils of group libel is to avoid the battle. For the field of the fight is the people, that large and mobile public opinion which is the controlling force in politics. Defamation is aimed at the people. Give the fascist devil his due. He works there and there he must be met. He attacks opposing groups—'labor', for example, and weakens them in the eyes of the community as a whole—and even in their own eyes [...]. The Fascist manipulates group against group and wedges in. He must be stopped there, and only a vigorous people can stop him.[46]

What Olson knew, which surely we now know again, is that always, in modern history, the fascists wedge in. They proceed by defamation, they manipulate group against group, and it follows that the field of the fight is always the people. It is there, on that ground, that Olson situated his poem. He shares stories of work because he wants people to understand themselves as makers, as people collectively making the world in which they belong. It is an act of making that had to be made visible because people had to understand their agency, because, in the constant and ongoing fight against the fascist, 'only a vigorous people can stop him'. What Olson sought to show, page after page, was people engaged in the act of making a world. Which means that, as Creeley saw it, the act of making and the act of recognizing were deeply intertwined: 'Always at root is the impelling fact of working to discover, to recover, the radical *presence* of person he felt to have been lost.'[47] To render people non-persons is to displace their agency, to deny their involvement in the community as a whole. Olson's gambit in his poem is that by demonstrating participation, the fascist production of non-personhood can be met. Or as he put it, by way of conclusion to his article, 'A people locked in combat with the fascists must fight on all fronts.'[48]

Articulating the Agency of Human Rights

At the core of mid-century writings concerned to counter expulsion is a subtle, far-reaching, sometimes counterintuitive discourse on the question of agency. Jacques Rancière gets close to the heart of that discourse in his discussion of Arendt's reading of the language of rights. We make a mistake, Rancière says, if we think that rights belong to us. If we think, as the locutions of the Universal Declaration can seem to encourage us to think, that rights belong to us, or to anybody, on the grounds that we are human, then already we, or some other people, have lost those rights. Roughly speaking, when he makes this observation, Rancière is paraphrasing Arendt. As he puts it, presenting Arendt's account of 'The Perplexities of Human Rights' at its most brutal, 'they are the rights of those who have no rights'.[49] As the Arendtian logic goes, the point at which a person is identified as bearing human rights is the point at which any such rights have ceased to apply. To identify that person as bearing those rights, or those rights as belonging to that person, is to observe an individual who has been expelled. It is a brutal message born of a brutal moment. It is not, however, the truth of human rights.

Where the formulation goes wrong, as Rancière sees it in his acute intervention on mid-century rights discourse, is not in the substance of the rights themselves but in the relation we describe people as having to such rights when we speak of belonging or bearing. On the contrary, 'the citizens of states ruled by a religious law or by the mere arbitrariness of their governments, and even the clandestine immigrants in zones of transit of our countries or the populations in the camps of refugees, can invoke them'.[50] What has to be understood, however, is what invoking means. Or, to put it another way, while Rancière's headline question (the title of his essay) is 'Who Is the Subject of the Rights of Man?', what he also asks, crucially, is how we relate to them. As he puts it, 'These rights are theirs when they can do something with them to construct a dissensus against the denial of rights they suffer.'[51] To invoke human rights, as Rancière reminds us—because surely, really, we knew it all along—is not to call up that which belongs to us, or that which we bear, or that which we will be, or have been, granted. To invoke such rights, on the contrary, is to do something with them. It is to assert, claim, activate, or enact them. 'The strength of those rights', he argues, 'lies in the back-and-forth movement between the first inscription of the right and the dissensual stage on which it is put to test.'[52] To invoke rights, Rancière argues, is to use them.

In the context of this book, to hear Rancière arguing that we invoke rights when we 'do something with them', to hear him arguing for their use, is to recall the language of Charles Olson's promptings in 'Projective Verse', his injunction to, 'keep it moving as fast as you can, citizen. And if you also set up as poet, USE, USE, USE, the process at all points.' I think it is neither entirely a stretch nor entirely a surprise to hear these echoes across Rancière and Olson. It is not entirely a surprise because in taking up Arendt's arguments, formed in and against the historical moment in which she wrote, Rancière returns to the discourse that, as this book has argued, it is important to reconsider in the present crisis of geopolitical non-personhood. It is not a surprise also because, in so far as he takes up the question of invocation, Rancière steps squarely into the poet's territory. 'Projective Verse' is all about invocation. Olson wants to bring cultural forms into being that are not already, or are only partly, there. In so far as he invokes, however, he declines all versions of invocation that imply passivity. He does not summon, nor does he seek to be inspired. There is no assumption that he will be given anything or that anything will be granted. Instead, what he offers is an image of intense agency. In this respect, not least, the essay was of its moment. Agency, in the moment of the production of non-personhood, was everything.

It is because she understood this that Arendt, like Olson, devoted such attention to the subject of work. Central to her articulation of the relationships that constitute *The Human Condition* is participation in the human artifice, which is to say the making of that commons that constitutes a human home. Where she goes wrong, as Rancière sees it, is in not bringing this image of agency to her thinking on human rights, in reading such rights in terms of bearing or belonging. But where both go wrong, or at least what they overlook, is that such an image of agency is already inscribed in the Declaration; in Article 23, the Right to Work. What the authors of the Declaration understood, in other words, was not that any given employment practice had to be defended or guaranteed. Nor was it ever part of their assumption, as their various conditions and qualifications make clear, that the working relation was not prone to abuse. What they understood, rather, was the necessity of agency in a 'community of rights'.[53] What Article 23 understands, first and foremost, is that to render people agency-less by denying them the right to work is to effect their expulsion. From which it follows that the right to work, which is the right to make and do, the right to be participant, is axiomatic.

The argument here is that in their reading of the Universal Declaration or, at least, in their reading of the principle of rights the declaration elaborates, both Arendt and Rancière are always playing catch up. In part, this is to observe that when each writer engages the language of rights, it is the general concept, rather than the details of any given article, to which their arguments refer. Which is not simply to say that neither writer reads the text of the Declaration as closely as they might, though there is truth in this statement.

More constructively, what it observes is a convergence, that for both writers there is a necessary connection between recognition and agency that the authors of the Declaration had already sought to encode.

For Ayten Gündoğdu, drawing out the implications of Arendt's thought for what she calls *The Contemporary Struggles of Migrants*, where that connection lands in Arendt is precisely on the question of the right to work. As a reading of Arendt this is not uncontroversial, disruptive as it is of the governing architecture of her post-war writing. Critical to that architecture is the relation Arendt appears to propose between the economic, social, and political realms in her distinction between labour, work, and action. According to that distinction, labour conforms to the economic in so far as it designates the processes of physical reproduction that in Ancient Greek culture were associated with the *oika*. Action, by contrast, the Arendtian category that maps most closely on to the political, is that form of human contact that is shaped through and by public interaction. From which it can be taken to follow that the struggles of the labour movement do not constitute political interventions, concerned as they typically are with material processes; with wages, conditions, and duration of work; with the practices and terms by which physical existence is reproduced.

For Gündoğdu, this is to stage a conservative reading of Arendt, and in so doing significantly to miss the point. Arendt's intention is not to restore or calcify an ancient categorization. Her point, rather, was that in the face of the catastrophe of expulsion that continued to define and shape the mid-century moment, it was necessary to revisit the relation between the political and the economic in order that such expulsion might be prevented from happening again. Work is crucial in this regard, not least because, as Gündoğdu sees it, it is critical to the struggles of migrants. The double bind of rights is that 'it becomes very difficult for those deprived of membership in a political community to be recognized as human beings entitled to rights'.[54] What is at issue, in other words, is not the character of rights but the processes through which entitlement to rights is recognized. Work bears on this question in two principal ways. In the first place, as Arendt articulates in detail, it is through work that humans achieve the forms of stability that people caught in the vulnerability of juridical non-personhood so definitively lack.[55] More precisely, it is work, and the conditions that work constitutes, from which the person who is subject to expulsion finds themselves expelled. As Gündoğdu puts it, 'Reconsidered alongside her analysis of statelessness, Arendt's concept of work assumes a critical force, drawing attention to the conditions that expel refugees from a world that they can inhabit with others.'[56] The intersection is strong. To be expelled is to be prevented from working. From which it follows that, in some sense, or at some level, recognition is conditioned by the right to work.

To understand what it means to argue for such an intersection, between the processes of work and the politics of recognition, it is helpful to consider Nancy Fraser's contribution to such debates. Fraser's intention, in 'Rethinking Recognition', was to observe the tension between the politics of recognition and what she called the politics of redistribution and, in the same breath, to articulate how the different objectives could be squared. Her premise in so doing was that the 'claim for recognition' is principally articulated as a generalized cultural demand and that, as a consequence, the practices by which people are actually excluded or expelled are too often neither specified nor documented. In the case of the person seeking asylum, the task is not simply to call attention to cultural non-recognition and to demand its redress but also to identify those juridical and administrative procedures and decisions—the daily practice—that militate cumulatively and actively against recognition. Where and how, Fraser wants us to ask, does expulsion happen?

For Fraser, two things follow from this set of observations. First, she wants to insist that, 'Redressing misrecognition means replacing institutional value patterns that impede parity of participation with ones that enable or foster it.'[57] Second, she wants any such politics of redress to register the ways exclusionary practices intersect and, in particular, the ways such exclusions are invariably both political and economic. As she puts it,

> [O]nly by considering both dimensions together can one determine what is impeding participatory parity in any particular instance; only by teasing out the complex imbrications of status with economic class can one determine how best to redress the injustice.[58]

Fraser's argument for a rethinking of recognition, and for an attention to the material practices on which such a rethinking must turn, is anticipated by the mid-century texts on which this book has focused. Precisely what Arendt, Olson, and the authors of the Universal Declaration understood was that the politics of recognition was deeply imbricated with those processes of making and participation that constituted the economy out of which a common environment could be formed. There was no clear distinction, in other words, between the economic and the political. To be prevented from working is to be denied absolutely what Fraser terms 'participatory parity'.

From which it follows that work is a kind of ground, a basis of recognition, or, as Arendt might have understood it, a mechanism by which 'rights' might be 'philosophically established' or 'politically secured'.

The Building of a Bridge

There is an image of the act of making in *The Wretched of the Earth* that cuts deep into the discourse of expulsion and agency focused, in mid-century writing, by the right to work. As Fanon puts it, drawing out the question of participation,

> If the building of a bridge does not enrich the awareness of those who work on it, then that bridge ought not to be built and the citizens can go on swimming across the river or going by boat. The bridge should not be 'parachuted down' from above; it should not be imposed by a *deus ex machina* upon the social scene; on the contrary, it should come from the muscles and the brains of the citizens [...] In this way, and in this way only, everything is possible.[59]

Fanon's image of the building of the bridge—reminiscent as it is of the image of landscape with bridge in Heidegger, where, crucially the bridge is not subject to construction, but as if by some *deus ex machina* always already built—is meticulous in its expression of the relation between the environment and work.[60] The 'social scene' of which the bridge might become a part is to be constructed by the 'muscles and brains of the citizens'. Such work, as Stephanie Clare observes, is a visible counter to the colonial 'transformation of the earth' which, as it 'fosters the life of the colonizers', means that, '[t]he colonized, within the eyes of the colonizer, come to blend in with the land itself'.[61] Fanon thus insists repeatedly on the work that is to be done— '"on the houses to be built, on the schools to be opened"'—because such self-directed work constitutes a decolonial act, a relation to the environment in which those who have been colonized are the visible agents of change.[62] Underpinning this image of decolonial transformation, however—of a relation to the environment that is not one of expulsion—is a deeper and more fundamental commitment to the act of making, a commitment that can be traced, as Clare suggests, to Fanon's reading in Marx.

One setting in which one finds that Marxist reading of work systematically articulated is a series of lectures Fanon delivered at the Institut des

Hautes Etudes in Tunis, preserved in *Alienation and Freedom* in the form of contemporaneous notes taken by Fanon's student, Lilia Ben Salem. Ben Salem sets the scene carefully, noting that she was part of a cohort of new students of 'Tunisian, Algerian, French and other nationalities', Tunis having 'welcomed refugees and many militants of the Algerian cause'.[63] It was in this context that, as Ben Salem puts it, Fanon, 'having left Algeria from where he had been expelled, offered—probably at the suggestion of Claudine Chaulet, who was also a refugee [...] to teach a semester course on social pyschopathology'.[64] Fanon's principal subject in his lectures was the programme of sociotherapy he developed at Blida-Joinville, critical to which was an ongoing reflection on work. As he put it, framing the relation he set out to achieve in the Neuropsychiatric Day Centre,

> [T]he patient there has total freedom; he spends the day at the hospital but returns home after 6pm, just as any worker would, going back to civilian life every evening, taking public transport, going to the café, frequenting the mosque, enjoying a family life.[65]

Fanon's emphasis here, apparent throughout his psychiatric writings, on the rhythm of the working day, originates in part in the model of 'internment' he found in colonial psychiatric practice. By contrast with the 'carceral milieu of the psychiatric hospital', as Fanon described it (an expulsive space I will consider in more detail in Chapter 5), '[r]ecourse to social therapy entails that the patient should not be a passive being but must "verbalise, explain himself, take a stance"'.[66] The image of the patient as worker was important, in part, simply because it countered the production of passivity that Fanon encountered in the colonial psychiatric space. But because, for Fanon, that space was emblematic, and because the colonial relation had to be transformed at every level, what the reference to work entailed was an articulation of what one might call a decolonial labour theory of value, what Fanon termed (as Ben Salem recalls), 'Relations between the Colonized and Work in a Colonized Society'.

It is in this concluding lecture at the Institut des Hautes Etudes that Fanon articulates most clearly the relation between expulsion and work. There is no naivety here, no romanticization: Fanon is acutely aware that there are few forms of relation more prone to abuse than the relation of work. He is clear, therefore, that, in a colonial context, such expulsion takes the form both of forced labour and of unemployment, his critical point being that, in both cases, what the regime produces is expendability. At the core of Fanon's argument is precisely the absence of relation, the pure denial within the process of production of recognition. This is what Clare means when she describes how, for Fanon, '[t]he colonized, within the eyes of the colonizer, come to blend in with the land itself'. As Fanon himself puts it, regarding force, 'Forced labour is a logical consequence of colonial society. Since the native can be forced, the understanding is that he can be hit.'[67] In his Tunis lectures, as elsewhere, Fanon seeks constantly to align such refusal of recognition with the mid-century geopolitical morality that, as Gilroy observes, emerged as a dominant mid-century framing of rights. As he states, quoting his poet-teacher, 'Aimé Césaire said that if the Europeans are anti-Hitler it is because Hitler tried to do to them what they did to the peoples that they had colonized.'[68] Fanon's subject here, however, is work, and as much as non-recognition can take the form of forced labour, so also it can take the form of mass unemployment, which, in a colonial context, is barely registered as such:

> Unemployment is not a human problem; it is an everlasting reserve: first, for replacing cases of early senility, or else it is a reserve of blackmail to maintain wages at a paltry level in cases of protest from indigenous employees. The mass of the unemployed does not bother the settlers.[69]

All of which, as an analysis of 'Relations between the colonized and work in the colonized society', with its demonstration of the denial of human relation, could clearly be heard as an argument for not working. Which it is, in so far as Fanon insists that, among other forms of protest, the colonized must strike. Emphatically, however, his argument is not against work as such. Quite the contrary, as he insists by way of conclusion:

> Labour must be recovered as a humanization of man. Man, when he throws himself into work, fecundates nature, but he fecundates himself also. Fecundating relations of generosity must exist; there is a reform of nature, a modification of nature, but because man shapes himself.[70]

This is the theory that underpins Fanon's image of the bridge. The bridge must be built, not parachuted in, because in the act of building the worker shapes themselves. The bridge comes from 'the muscles and the brains' of the colonized. In this way 'and in this way only, everything is possible'.

Fanon's account in his Tunisian lectures of 'The Relation between the Colonized and Work' has a direct equivalence with the argument Lefebvre was making in the second edition of the first volume of the *Critique of Everyday Life*. Written in Paris, which is to say the metropole, from December 1956 to February 1957, Lefebvre's extensive foreword to the 1958 edition of his text includes a section entitled simply 'Alienated Labour', which Lefebvre opens by embedding a lengthy passage from Marx's discussion of 'Estranged Labour'. The point of the passage, as Lefebvre draws out, is in part to clarify how, under capital, when the worker's product is torn from them, it confronts them as '"hostile and alien"', but also, crucially, how such an act of alienation is an '"estrangement of man from man"'.[71] What Marx thus describes, as Lefebvre wants repeatedly to underline (you can picture him in his mid-century Paris apartment, pencil in hand), is that the hostility of alienated labour has its root in the fact that the act of making constitutes what Marx calls the human animal's 'life activity'. As Marx puts it, drawing the argument out at length,

> man reproduces himself not only intellectually, in his consciousness, but actively and actually, and he can therefore contemplate himself in a world he himself has created [...]. An immediate consequence of man's estrangement from the product of his labour, his life activity [...] is the *estrangement of man from man*. When man confronts himself, he also confronts *other* men.[72]

For Lefebvre, summarizing the passage he has framed, Marx's commentary on 'Estranged Labour' shows that 'for Marx work constitutes man's essence as creator'. What he thus notes by way of quotation (which Fanon observes when he insists, emblematically, that the work of building the bridge must come from the 'muscles and the brains' of the colonized), is the understanding that, as Sean Sayers puts it in his discussion of Marx and work, '[W]e are active—productive and creative—beings. We get satisfaction from actively exercising our powers, from overcoming obstacles and being productive. In short, human beings are producers as well as consumers.'[73] For Sayers, as he paraphrases Marx, this creativity matters precisely as it bears on the human relation to the environment since

> Through work we develop a more complex and mediated relation to nature, both to our natural desires and to the natural environment around us [...] Our coming to be at home in our world is not our natural and initial condition; rather it is an *achievement*, a result of human activity and work, both individual and social.[74]

It is here, I think, in this collective insight, that we understand why writers of the post-war moment concerned with the production of non-personhood became so preoccupied with the act of making. Thus, whereas, without question, to work in an alienated fashion is brutal enough, to be banned from working is to be doubly, perhaps definitively alienated. To be subjected to such a ban, to be denied the right to work, is to be prevented from coming to be at home in the world. To be stopped from working is thus to be rendered antagonistic with both one's environment and oneself. It is a contradiction that, in its hostility, produces expulsion.

Conclusion: Lift the Ban

The contradiction that comes of the denial of the right to work is one which policy makers continue to exploit.[75] A contemporary example of such politically generated antagonism is the environment constructed by UK policymakers for people who seek asylum. A ban on work, lasting easily upwards of a decade, has been the lived experience of tens of thousands of people subjected to that environment. To read mid-century discussions of work, and of the relation between non-personhood and work, is to understand the effect of such contemporary prohibitions. By definition, to ban a person from working is to render their environment hostile because it is to ban them from that activity whereby collectively people make their home in the world. It is to prevent them, as Arendt grasped, but as Fanon and Lefebvre articulated more carefully, from participating in the human commons.

Which is to argue that the right to work carries the necessity of a transitional political demand. It is, as Rancière proposes, an inscription that must be put to the test everywhere it doesn't apply. For such a right to be established, where it does not apply, is hardly to answer or to address all possible problems. There is no such single answer or form of address. It is to argue, however, that, in rights and work, and more precisely in their intersection, an image of a human commons can continue to be expressed. It is why it will always be in the interests of capital to minimize the value and appearance of the act of working; why, as Olson puts it, spectatorism is made to displace participation. And it is why those who would produce non-personhood and who would construct environments in which non-personhood is maintained, default so readily to a ban on work. To effect such a prohibition is to throw persons out. It is to expel people to an environment made, by definition, hostile.

Notes

1. Jacques Vernant, *The Refugee in the Postwar World* (London: George Allen and Unwin Ltd, 1953), p. 9.
2. Vernant, *The Refugee*, p. 9.
3. UNHCR (United Nations High Commissioner for Refugees), Convention and Protocol Relating to the Status of Refugees (Geneva: UNHCR, 2011), p. 14, https://www.unhcr.org/uk/3b66c2aa10 (accessed 12 May 2022).
4. A different direction in which to pursue the logic of the politicization of refugee identity articulated here is the argument between individual and group protection established by international law under the competing terms 'genocide' and 'crimes against humanity'. The story of the different development and implication of those terms is compellingly told by Philippe Sands in *East West Street: On the Origins of 'Genocide' and 'Crimes Against Humanity'* (London: Vintage Books, 2017).
5. Vernant, *The Refugee*, p.17.
6. Vernant, *The Refugee*, p. x.
7. Gerard Daniel Cohen, *In War's Wake: Europe's Displaced Persons in the Postwar Order* (Oxford: Oxford University Press, 2011), p. 104.
8. Cohen, *In War's Wake*, p. 112.
9. Hannah Arendt, *The Origins of Totalitarianism*, 3rd edn (San Diego, CA, New York, and London: Harcourt Brace Janovitch Publishers), p. 286.
10. Consider also that, as it suited their requirements, states routinely blurred the seeming distinction between political and economic facts. Thus, while the person petitioning for refugee status in the aftermath of the war had to present themselves in exclusively political terms, reception countries would typically arrive at their decision on economic grounds. As Proudfoot observed:

    > The IRO quickly discovered that, in spite of all the protestations of sympathy, the pivot of national immigration policies in almost all the countries was strictly practical, and closely related to domestic labour requirements. The IRO, in order to fulfil its mission, had, in fact, to function as an international employment agency.

    (Malcolm Proudfoot, *European Refugees: 1939–1952. A Study in Forced Population Movement* [London: Faber & Faber, 1957], p. 418.)
    Le Monde was less forgiving, describing the displaced persons camps as 'a slave market in the heart of Europe' (Cohen, *In War's Wake*, p. 112).
11. UNHCR, Convention, p. 22.

12. Seyla Benhabib, *The Rights of Others: Aliens, Residents, and Citizens* (Cambridge: Cambridge University Press, 2004), p. 1.
13. See Johannes Morsink, *The Universal Declaration of Human Rights: Origins, Drafting, and Intent* (Philadelphia, PA: University of Pennsylvania Press, 1999), p. 169.
14. United Nations, Universal Declaration of Human Rights (Paris: United Nations General Assembly, 1948), https://www.un.org/en/universal-declaration-human-rights (accessed 14 June 2022).
15. Morsink, *Origins, Drafting, and Intent*, p. 188.
16. Morsink, *Origins, Drafting, and Intent*, p. 161.
17. See Josh Cohen, *Not Working: Why We Have to Stop* (London: Granta, 2018).
18. In drawing out Olson's commentary on work, this chapter in fact contributes to a growing critical discourse on the preoccupation in modern and contemporary poetry with the realities and implications of work. For an excellent survey of the issues and questions raised, see: Jo Walton and Ed Luker (eds), *Poetry and Work: Work in Modern and Contemporary Anglophone Poetry* (New York: Palgrave, 2019).
19. Arendt, *Origins,* p. 269.
20. This is to make the same argument about Arendt's relation to the discourse of rights that she makes about Kant's relation to the 'utilitarianism of his time'. As she puts it:

> Kant did not mean to formulate or conceptualize the tenets of the utilitarianism of his time, but, on the contrary, wanted first of all to relegate the means–end category to its proper place and prevent its use in the file of political action. His formula, however, can no more deny its origin in utilitarian thinking than his other famous and also inherently paradoxical interpretation of man's attitude toward [...] works of art.

(Hannah Arendt, *The Human Condition*, 2nd edn, intro. Margaret Canovan [Chicago, IL and London: University of Chicago Press, 1958], p. 156)
21. Arendt, *Origins,* p. 286.
22. Proudfoot, *European Refugees 1939–1952*, p. 22.
23. Benhabib, *Rights of Others*, p. 1.
24. Benhabib, *Rights of Others*, p. 6.
25. Arendt, *Human Condition*, p. 28.
26. Arendt, *Human Condition*, p. 28.
27. Arendt, *Human Condition*, p. 33.
28. Arendt, *Human Condition*, p. 33.
29. Arendt, *Human Condition*, p. 173.
30. Arendt, *Human Condition*, p. 173.
31. Arendt, *Origins*, p. 302.

32. Robert Creeley, 'Preface' to Charles Olson, *Selected Poems*, ed. Robert Creeley (Berkeley, Los Angeles, CA and London: University of California Press, 1997), p. xviii.
33. The evidence of Creeley's importance to Olson, and of the part they played in shaping each other's thought, is to be found (among other places) in their correspondence. See George Butterick (ed.), *Charles Olson and Robert Creeley: The Complete Correspondence*, vols 1–8 (Santa Barbara, CA: Black Sparrow Press, 1980–87); Richard Blevins (ed.), *Charles Olson and Robert Creeley: The Complete Correspondence*, vol. 9 (Santa Barbara, CA: Black Sparrow Press, 1990). Volumes 1–9 cover the poets' correspondence between 1950 and 1952, their most intense period of collaboration. It is to be hoped that the remaining correspondence, from 1952 to 1970, which is equal in importance if not in frequency of exchange, will soon be available to the general reader.
34. Charles Olson, *Collected Prose*, ed. Donald Allen and Benjamin Friedlander (Berkeley and Los Angeles, CA: University of California Press, 1997), p. 159.
35. Frank O'Hara, *Standing Still and Walking in New York*, ed. Donald Allen (Bolinas, CA: Grey Fox Press, 1975), p. 129.
36. I take the term 'class awake' from Peter Gizzi's homage to the poet Kevin Killian 'Thinking about Kevin: In Memoriam Kevin Killian (1952–2019)', Chicago Review, 21 June 2019, https://www.chicagoreview.org/thinking-about-kevin-in-memoriam-kevin-killian-1952-2019 (accessed 27 June 2022).
37. Olson, *Collected Prose*, p. 242.
38. For an extended consideration of Olson's poetics of agency, see Tymek Woodham's as yet unpublished thesis 'Writing Agency: The Material Imaginations of Charles Olson, Langston Hughes, and Frank O'Hara', unpublished thesis, University College London, 2021. Woodham's thesis is not concerned with work as agency but with the way, in the face of a mid-century crisis of agency, Olson, Hughes, and O'Hara opened their writing to aspects of the material environment in order to remake and remodel modes of agency.
39. Olson, *Collected Prose*, p. 242.
40. Olson, *Collected Prose*, p. 240.
41. Edmund de Waal, 'Black Mountain College and the Crafts', in Christopher Benfey and Mary Emma Harris (eds), *Starting at Zero: Black Mountain College 1933–1957* (Bristol: Arnolfini Gallery, 2005), https://www.edmunddewaal.com/essays/black-mountain-college-and-the-crafts (accessed 27 June 2022).
42. De Waal, 'Black Mountain College'.
43. Charles Olson, *The Maximus Poems*, ed. George Butterick (Berkeley and Los Angeles, CA: University of California Press, 1983), p. 157.
44. Olson, *Maximus*, p. 131.
45. Charles Olson, *The Special View of History*, ed. Ann Charters (Berkeley, CA: Oyez, 1970), p. 17.

46. Charles Olson, 'People v. The Fascist, U.S. (1944)', *Survey Graphic* (August 1944), p. 368.
47. Robert Creeley, 'Preface', p. xvi.
48. Olson, 'People v. The Fascist, U.S.', p.368
49. Jacques Rancière, 'Who Is the Subject of the Rights of Man?', *South Atlantic Quarterly* 103:2/3 (Spring/Summer 2004), 298.
50. Rancière, 'Who Is the Subject?', p. 305.
51. Rancière, 'Who Is the Subject?', pp. 305–306.
52. Rancière, 'Who Is the Subject?', p. 305.
53. Morsink, *Origins, Drafting, and Intent*, p. 161.
54. Ayten Gündoğdu, *Rightlessness in an Age of Rights: Hannah Arendt and the Contemporary Struggles of Migrants* (Oxford: Oxford University Press, 2015), p. 26.
55. See Gündoğdu, *Rightlessness in the Age of Rights*, p. 146.
56. Gündoğdu, *Rightlessness in the Age of Rights*, p. 152.
57. Nancy Fraser, 'Rethinking Recognition', *New Left Review* 3 (May–June, 2000), 115.
58. Nancy Fraser, 'Rethinking Recognition', 119.
59. Frantz Fanon, *The Wretched of the Earth*, tr. Constance Farrington (London: Penguin, 2001), p. 162.
60. For Heidegger's discussion of the way the emblematic figure of the bridge shapes a locale, see the first of his lectures published as 'Building Dwelling Thinking' in David Farrell Krell (ed.), *Basic Writings: Martin Heidegger* (London: Routledge, 1999), pp. 347–363.
61. Stephanie Clare, 'Geopower: The Politics of Life and Land in Frantz Fanon's Writing', *Diacritics* 41:4 (2013), 71.
62. Clare, 'Geopower', 71.
63. Frantz Fanon, *Alienation and Freedom*, ed. Jean Khalfa and Robert J.C. Young, tr. Steven Corcoran (London: Bloomsbury Academic, 2018), p. 514
64. Fanon, *Alienation and Freedom*, p. 514.
65. Fanon, *Alienation and Freedom*, p. 516.
66. Fanon, *Alienation and Freedom*, p. 516.
67. Fanon, *Alienation and Freedom*, p. 529.
68. Fanon, *Alienation and Freedom*, pp. 526–527.
69. Fanon, *Alienation and Freedom*, p. 530.
70. Fanon, *Alienation and Freedom*, p. 530.
71. Karl Marx, 'Economic and Philosophical Manuscripts', in Karl Marx, *Early Writings* (London: Penguin, 1975), p. 328, cited in Henri Lefebvre, *Critique of Everyday Life Volume One*, tr. John Moore (London: Verso, 2000), pp. 59, 61.
72. Cited in Lefebvre, *Critique*, p. 61.
73. Sean Sayers, 'Why Work? Marx and Human Nature', *Science & Society* 69:4 (October 2005), 611.

74. Sayers, 'Why Work?', pp. 611, 613.
75. Launched in 2018, 'Lift the Ban' is a campaign instigated by the Manchester-based non-governmental organization Refugee Action that calls for asylum seekers in the United Kingdom to be granted the right to work after six months' residency.

5
Speaking

A New Kind of Human Being

In her now widely cited essay 'We Refugees', first published in the *Menorah Journal* in 1943, Hannah Arendt wrote directly from her lived experience to describe the emergence in geopolitics of a new kind of person. Looking to find terms that would articulate the intersection between her individual life history and the brutal trajectories of world events, Arendt's starting point was a series of negative, or negating, constructions. 'In the first place', as she put it, correcting a silent interlocutor, 'we don't like to be called "refugees".'[1] Instead, looking to change the terms from the outset, 'We ourselves call each other "newcomers" or "immigrants".'[2] Arendt would return to the term 'newcomer' in *The Human Condition*, where it became integral to a lexicon aimed at establishing a new basis for the transition from one political setting to another. It was as a refugee, however, that, in her 1943 essay, Arendt sought to describe her relation to the world.

Crucial to that description was a condition that elsewhere Arendt would refer to as a kind of non-consequentiality.[3] Whereas a refugee 'used to be a person driven to seek refuge because of some act committed or some political opinion held', those on behalf of whom Arendt spoke—'We Refugees'—had 'committed no acts' and most had 'never dreamt of having any radical political opinion'.[4] A similar vulnerability to events characterized the experience of being displaced. To be a refugee, or to be seeking refugee status, was to have only minimal control over critical occurrences in one's daily life: 'we learn from the stars [...] on what day we have the best chance of filling out one of those countless questionnaires which accompany our present lives'.[5] Arendt's existence as a refugee was one in which there was no predictability to the timing of crucial encounters, a mode of daily life that entailed being constantly subject to another person's time. And yet, whereas in all areas of life the experience was of non-consequentiality, it was also a lack of agency constantly rendered politically consequential. As she put it, 'We try the best we can to fit into a world where you have to be sort of politically minded when you buy your food.'[6]

Arendt's account of the negating encounters that constituted the experience of 'We Refugees' in 1943 is once again applicable. Under the policies of the Hostile Environment regime which successive UK governments have developed for people seeking asylum, when a person was to go shopping they would be singled out—Arendt's word would be politicized—by the fact that their means of purchase would not be cash, or cash equivalent, but a form of top-up card reserved exclusively for the person applying for refuge. It is not a badge exactly, but it might as well be a badge. To shop is to be marked as a person held outside. In 'We Refugees', in other words, as Arendt arrived at her terms, she provided a template for a kind of lived experience that has once again been imposed. In so doing, she also documented a way of living, or rather a mode of existence, to which her writing would repeatedly return. It is in 'We Refugees', for instance, that we find the first draft of her account of what, in *The Origins of Totalitarianism*, she would call the political construction of the 'living corpse'. *The Origins of Totalitarianism* is a very different kind of text. Written in full knowledge of the catastrophe of the Holocaust, Arendt's historical account operates at a level of analysis and assertion that she stops short of in 'We Refugees'. Her aim in the earlier text is to begin to find a language, to arrive at descriptions that capture her emerging mode of life. Even there, however, in that short piece, Arendt feels authorized to make an announcement:

> Apparently nobody wants to know that contemporary history has created a new kind of human beings—the kind that are put in concentration camps by their foes and internment camps by their friends.[7]

The new kind of human being contemporary history has created is the human who can be detained, a kind of person, as Arendt observed it, deemed detainable.

Against the background of this necessarily negative account, her personal record of the historical appearance of non-appearance, Arendt sounds one kind of hard-won positive note. As she puts it in her final paragraph,

> Those few refugees who insist upon telling the truth, even to the point of 'indecency', get in exchange for their unpopularity one priceless advantage: history is no longer a closed book to them and politics is no longer the privilege of gentiles. They know that the outlawing of the Jewish people in Europe has been followed closely by the outlawing of most European nations. Refugees driven from country to country represent the vanguard

of their peoples—if they keep their identity. For the first time Jewish history is not separate but tied up with that of all other nations. The comity of European peoples went to pieces when, and because, it allowed its weakest member to be excluded and persecuted.[8]

It is necessary to quote at length because it is important to hear how Arendt's account of the refugee experience is both specific to Jewish history and applicable beyond it. 'The outlawing of the Jewish people in Europe' by fascism is followed closely by the 'outlawing of most European nations'. It is from this position that Arendt speaks. To be precise, she speaks, as she understands it, from what she terms the 'vanguard' of contemporary history, and what she asserts from that vantage is the necessity of story.

It is with the significance, in the context of political expulsion, of narrating experience—of speaking, writing, or sharing story—that this chapter is concerned. What Arendt asserts, from her position at the vanguard of history and outside the polity, is that telling the truth of that position, narrating the experience, gains what she calls a 'priceless' advantage. Somehow, in the face of remorseless historical forces, forces that have generated a whole new kind of human being positioned outside, and rendered detainable, by the state, there is a political utility in the process of relaying story. There is a connection, in other words, between sovereignty, expulsion, political membership, and narration. Somehow, Arendt asserts, story helps.

One way to frame this relationship between story and sovereignty as Arendt begins to describe it in 'We Refugees' is in the terms Paul Gilroy maps out in *The Black Atlantic*. As Gilroy observes, setting out his intentions for his study of *Modernity as Double Consciousness*,

> My concern here is [. . .] with exploring some of the special political problems that arise from the fatal conjunction of the concept of nationality with the concept of culture and the affinities and the affiliations which link the blacks of the West to one of their adoptive, parental cultures: the intellectual heritage of the West since the Enlightenment.[9]

Gilroy's account of the Black Atlantic was crucial in opening the critical space studies such as the present one require. A brilliant commentator on mid-century politics of expulsion, Gilroy widens the frame by showing how such crucial contemporary figures as Richard Wright pressed constantly to read fascism through, and in connection with, the histories of slavery and colonialism. One focus for such extended readings of fascism was the Algerian War of Independence, where, as Gilroy notes, as part of the editorial team generating the resistance newspaper *El Moudjahid*, Fanon constantly identified the French colonial regime as a fascist force.[10] Gilroy's extended historical mapping of the mid-century politics of expulsion is especially important to the present chapter, where Arendt's account of the political importance of story, as framed by her expulsion from Nazi Europe, is set alongside Olson's account of the necessity, in a US context, of recognizing the history of slavery and Fanon's multi-layered account of the importance of story in the context of de-colonial struggle.

Just as important as Gilroy's map of expulsions, however, is his methodological response. Because the 'special political problems' he seeks to address arise from the 'fatal conjunction of the concept of nationality with the concept of culture' (a conjunction on which, though he doesn't reference her, Arendt was herself a crucial commentator), Gilroy proposes a critical practice 'less intimidated by and respectful of the boundaries and integrity of modern nation states than either English or African-American cultural studies have so far been'.[11] In *Black Atlantic*, this determination to disrupt or refuse the national frame leads Gilroy to tell stories of Black American writers and intellectuals that emphasize their deeply woven relation to European traditions of thought. In the present study, what a comparable non-nationalizing intention entails is a reading of authors from different national settings against and alongside one another, where the point of commonality is not shared national culture but an understanding, in the mid-century moment, that the determining cultural fact is precisely what Arendt terms the creation of 'a new kind of human being', a person forced outside by a geopolitical logic grounded in the fatal conjunction of nation and culture. What does it mean, the authors considered in this study each ask, to try to establish an imaginary that addresses and would ultimately prevent the production, by expulsion, of the non-person?

Chapters 3 and 4 have considered, respectively, how, in articulating their different imaginaries, Arendt, Olson, Fanon, and the authors of the Universal Declaration focused on the themes of moving and making (where the act of making was coded as the right to work). The focus of the current chapter is the act of speaking and, in particular, the act of telling or sharing story. To be precise, what all the authors contemplate, thematically and methodologically, is the real material possibility that the act of relaying story produces the weave or infrastructure by which persons can be held within the human community. One way to understand this possibility is in reverse and to observe, simply, that where a person is expelled, they are also silenced, whether in the most obvious sense of being, in some manner, detained, or by other less carceral modes of what Fanon, in his essay on Algerian radio, calls 'jamming'. If expulsion equals silence, so the logic reasonably goes, then non-expulsion must entail speaking or the sharing of story.

The purpose of this chapter, then, is to show how, in a series of carefully articulated, materially imagined settings, the authors in question worked from the premise that somewhere in the process of sharing story is the infrastructure of non-expulsion. In emphasizing how the authors pictured such settings, I am in agreement with the way Lyndsey Stonebridge positions the act of writing in relation to rights. In her recent polemic, *Writing and Righting*, Stonebridge's point, though not to deny literature's capacity sometimes to generate empathy, is that the generation of empathy is neither politically sufficient nor historically effective. On the question of empathy, history shows, literature has failed. Which is not to say that writing has no place in the development and construction of rights. Rather, as Stonebridge puts it, 'writing remains vital to the work [. . .] of creating the political contexts in which it is possible to grant one another what Hannah Arendt first described in 1949 as "the right to have rights".[12] The present chapter considers how the writers in question, in their differing disciplines and imaginaries, sought to create the contexts in which the act of storytelling could have political force.[13]

In considering the different political imaginaries in relation to one another, the aim is neither to advance a single model nor to propose a straightforward synthesis. The objective, rather, is to hear through the different experiments in question what is at stake when, as is frequently the case, the sharing of story is proposed as a way of addressing political expulsion. What this means for Arendt, in *The Human Condition*, is a modern reconstruction of what she terms the polis, a setting in which the act of relaying narrative is a core process. Arendt's model of a storytelling space is hardly without its problems (hence the value of exploring a series of imaginaries in combination), but in its most positive form, what her reimagining of the polis proposes is a space in which individual stories will be heard and, in particular, in which such relaying of stories becomes the basis for movement from one geopolitical setting to another. For Olson, whose whole project can be understood as a gathering and sharing of stories (albeit a range of stories problematically determined by an emphatically masculine world view), the key term is 'feedback'. When Olson writes, in his major post-war poem 'The

Kingfishers', that 'feedback is the law', he seeks to open a field in which stories will be heard in a constant dynamic of recognition. Where Arendt proposes a space in which individuals will be heard, Olson pictures a setting in which recognition will be arrived at through the play of stories in relation to each other and, in particular, where recognition requires a culture to face up to the stories of violence that have brought it into being. For Fanon, the question is how to enable stories to be heard in a situation of domination, where the settings vary from the radio broadcast to the socio-therapeutic environment but where the question throughout is how stories shape and reflect political membership. That unit of membership is, at times, the decolonizing sovereign state. For Fanon, however, as the chapter details, the act of hearing and sharing stories invariably implies a radical sense of shared humanity well beyond the nation. The chapter concludes by returning to the Universal Declaration and to the intimate connection between speech and rights. As Joseph Slaughter has brilliantly demonstrated, with reference precisely to French suppression of the Algerian revolution, human rights are intimately connected to human voice. What the post-war imaginaries in question allow us to consider in detail is how, in a moment shaped by the reality of political expulsion, the sharing of story can propose a shelter within which persons might be held.

Story as Appearance

To understand why, in her 1958 text *The Human Condition*, Hannah Arendt sought to reactivate the Greek term 'polis', with its complicated backstory and historically compromised implications, it is necessary to recall how she concluded *The Origins of Totalitarianism*. This is to take the view that, in its relative abstraction, the later text addresses the political realities that, in her history of totalitarianism, Arendt identified as the legacy of the war. That legacy was 'statelessness, the newest mass phenomenon in contemporary history', the underlying cause of which was the gradual (but as Arendt saw it, now all but complete) identification of the state with the idea of nationality, the effect of which was an international system of governance through which, for the stateless, it had become impossible to move.[14] In the thoroughness of her analysis of the origins (and legacies) of totalitarianism, Arendt had observed, and arrived at, an impasse. So pervasive was the identification between state and national identity ('people–state–territory') that it was difficult, if not borderline impossible, to discern how a different mode of community might form or even be described. Which is to say that when, in *The Human Condition*, Arendt embarks on a discussion of 'the polis', what principally we have to understand about polis is that it is *not* nation.

Arendt's turn, or turn back, to the model of the polis has been much scrutinized and criticized and there can be no reading of her political philosophy that does not engage the force of that critique. Etienne Balibar, one of Arendt's most creative (which is to say most critical) of readers, summarizes that critique well. Referring to what he terms 'the dilemma of the sacralisation of the community', he observes that

> I will entirely grant Habermas and Rancière that *there is* in Arendt a tendency to draw the lessons of the process of extermination in terms of a vindication of *an existing model of the community of citizens* (or rather an imaginary model strangely combining yearnings for the ancient *polis* with and idealization of the 'lost treasure of revolution', i.e. the early modern, not to say the romantic universalistic nation-state). This is especially influential in her resistance to the idea of politically challenging the 'public vs. private' division of social life, possibly because the invasion of the private sphere by political surveillance and ideological constraint was so typical of totalitarian regimes.[15]

There are two related criticisms here. The first is the charge of political nostalgia, that in the face of the 'social production of "non-persons"' Arendt reverts incommensurably to a model of community embedded in the ancient notion of the city state.[16] The second criticism is that, by drawing on a political model that so clearly delineates the public from the private, Arendt precludes consideration of all politics of emancipation rooted in the private sphere. This second criticism does not go away, and Balibar does not seek to obscure the fact that, in so far as Arendt presents an image of rights, it is limited not least on questions of gender and sex. But he also wants to argue that on the urgent issue of 'phenomena like elimination, radical exclusion, and disposable humans [. . .] crucial today more than ever', Arendt remains a necessary commentator, not least if we 'think with Arendt beyond Arendt herself'.[17] Balibar is right, here, to articulate a non-nostalgic sense of Arendt's image of the polis, except that she takes us more directly to that image than he allows. She goes beyond the historical limitations of the polis by refusing the locatedness of the idea and, in so doing, by opening politics to the possibilities of story.

Arendt's main source for her articulation of the polis was Aristotle's *The Politics*, her reading of which both discloses quite precisely the nature of the political question she was posing and departs quite wilfully from the historical implications of the original text. That she turned to Aristotle in the mid-1950s owed to the fact that her political question was fundamental: what was required, she wanted to understand, for a person politically to appear? In his formalism, Aristotle's concern is with political membership, with what it means to be able to participate in political life. In the face of statelessness on an industrial scale, this was, as Arendt saw it, a defining contemporary question. It was also a question on which, given his unqualified endorsement of the function of a slave class, Aristotle, although a necessary, was hardly a sufficient commentator. In her reading of Aristotle, in other words, Arendt was a creative reader, legitimated, as Stonebridge points out, by her lived experience of political events.[18]

Even so, the decision to revisit Aristotle carried a specific historical charge. Read formally, as a foundational account of the actions of humans as political animals ('politikon zoon'), what one finds in *The Politics* is a clarity of description whereby the question of political visibility comes to the fore. 'Polis', interpreted from this point of view, specifies not a particular form of government but simply the idea of a state, where 'the state is a kind of association—an association of citizens in a constitution.'[19] It is in the nature of these terms that they are mutually defining in Aristotle's account. To be a citizen, it follows, is to be a participant in the constitution and the state since, as Aristotle puts it, 'What effectively distinguishes the citizen proper from all others is his participation in giving judgement and in holding office.'[20] The state, then, entails participation and is to be understood as a setting in which participation is taken to be both necessary and good.[21]

Virtuous as participation is for Aristotle, it is not the end to which every person is expected to aspire since it is the function of some, those who are enslaved, to provide material resources in order that others, the citizens, participate in political acts. It is worth observing, in the present moment of non-personhood, that this logic cuts both ways: that to be rendered nonpolitical, in Aristotle's terms, is to have an equivalence to the slave. Arendt's interest, however, is not in Aristotle's archaic hierarchies but with the clarity of his account of the political act. According to that account, to be human is to be political, where to be political means to be in association and where to be in association is to participate—with participation, in turn, being that which the state and/or constitution (politea) are intended to promote. Abstract as this sounds, it is, in fact, precisely the formal quality of Aristotle's account of politics that is its value to Arendt and not least as that turns on the question of 'association'. As Aristotle puts it, 'the state is not an association of people dwelling in the same place, established to prevent its members from committing injustice against each other, and to promote transactions' but, instead, 'an association intended to enable its members, in their households and their kinships to live *well*'.[22] The distinction is subtle but important. While it may well be the case that, in reality, a given state is linked to a given place, it is not the fact of that link to place (and to people 'dwelling in the same place') that defines the state. As Arendt puts it, precisely refusing the connection of political association to place,

> The *polis*, properly speaking, is not the city-state in its physical location: it is the organization of the people as it arises out of acting and speaking together, and its true space lies between people living together for this purpose, no matter where they happen to be. 'Wherever you go, you will be a *polis*.'[23]

Aristotle's importance to Arendt—the value of his insistently formal mode of analysis—cannot be underestimated, not least his foundational move: the definition of the human as political animal. The importance of this move, as is acutely apparent in a moment of non-personhood, lies precisely in the indissolubility of the link. If to be human is, by definition, to be political, which is to say to live in meaningful association, then to be excluded or expelled from the political environment is to be expelled from the human community itself. One hears this Aristotelean logic in Ayten Gündoğdu's application of Arendtian thought in her contemporary account of rights in an age of rightlessness, fundamental to which is the always groundless and always 'revolutionary discovery that human beings appear as subjects entitled to rights only by sharing words and deeds that testify to their equality and freedom'.[24] Where this takes us is to a construction of politics in which story, and more precisely the infrastructural capacity to share story, is integral. As Gündoğdu puts it, indicating how the underlying demand revolutionizes the stakes,

> To the extent that the current human rights framework allows states to deny those rights to migrants who are not authorized to stay in their territories, 'papers for all' is a call that brings to view the limits and exclusions of that framework.[25]

To demand papers is to demand to be heard and, in so doing, to demand the radical alteration of frameworks constructed to deny such hearings.

It was towards such an altered framework that Arendt reactivated Aristotle's account of the 'polis', her revision of which she articulated as the 'space of appearance'. As she put it,

> The space of appearance comes into being whenever men are together in the manner of speech and action, and therefore predates and precedes all formal constitution of the public realm and the various forms of government, that is, the various forms in which the public realm can be organized.[26]

For Balibar, this articulation of the polis as space of appearance, where appearance is constituted by speech and action, constitutes a radical reassertion of the political act. As he argues, steadfastly refusing the backward look,

> In these conditions, the 'community of citizens', which the Arendtian argument calls for, is no longer an *existing* community or an existing *form of community* to be ideally located in the past. It becomes—to put it in quasi-Derridean terms —a 'community to come', or a community without a model, which is bound to appear first as a 'non-community', but *is virtually there* in the struggles themselves. From this point of view, it is tempting to say that human rights are neither 'moral' nor 'juridical', they are *insurrectional*, which means that they are political, but also that the political is not isolated from its 'impolitical' side, the democratic invention of the institution beyond its given limitations.[27]

What Balibar points us to in Arendt is not only a model of community we have not yet arrived at but also a community that, in its principle of insurrection, is capable of change, where change, as Arendt understands it, is intricately connected to story, the act of speech.

Story, and storytelling, enter Arendt's argument at crucial junctures in her construction of a political imaginary in *The Human Condition*. In the first place, she arrives at a consideration of story in the context of her discussion of the way humans make and sustain the world in which their appearance has meaning, as a means of documenting and archiving necessary to the construction and continuation of a shared world. As she observes,

> In order to become worldly things, that is deeds and facts and events and patterns of thoughts or ideas, they must first be seen, heard and remembered and then transformed, reified as it were, into things—into sayings of poetry, the written page or the printed book, into paintings or sculpture, into all sorts of records, documents and monuments. The whole factual world of human affairs depends for its reality and its continued existence, first upon the presence of others who have seen and heard and will remember, and, second, on the transformation of the intangible into the tangible world of things.[28]

The function of this statement is to fix forms of story at the heart of the commons, to establish it as the mode whereby events, in their fragility, are enabled to become real. The basis for such reality is 'the presence of others who have seen and heard and will remember', the community with whom the records and documents resonate. This positions story as document, as a political refusal to allow the historical slate to be wiped clean and, as such, is of no small consideration with regard to the history of non-personhood.[29]

In the context of this insistence on the necessity of forms of document and monument, forms of shared observation, Arendt takes story to be of particular value because of its integrity to the shape of a human life. Thus,

> The chief characteristic of this specifically human life, whose appearance and disappearance constitute worldly events, is that it is itself always full of events which ultimately can be told as a story, establish a biography; it is of this life, *bios*, as distinguished from mere *zōē*, that Aristotle said that it 'somehow is a kind of *praxis*'. For action and speech, which, as we saw before, belonged close together in the Greek understanding of politics, are indeed the two activities whose end result will always be a story with enough coherence to be told, no matter how accidental or haphazard the single events and their causation may appear to be.[30]

It is important to hear how certain key concepts interact here as Arendt circles around the necessity of story to political life. In the first place, she wants to tie story to the framing facts of appearance and disappearance (birth and death), with story taking its form from the fact of these defining events but also being the medium which allows the individual subject to appear. In the second place, such appearance through story is that which distinguishes the human life in question from 'mere *zōē*', which elevates it to '*bios*'. What matters here is the differing relations implied towards events. What story, as an aspect of bios (and as the basis of biography), implies is a relation to events that allows them to be made coherent or to be understood to cohere. The opposite of this, the relation to events entailed by mere existence, is the sense that they are 'accidental or haphazard'—which, in the language of Chapter 1 of this book, is the experience of arbitrariness, which takes us already some way towards an understanding of the function of story in Arendt's understanding of political existence. Precisely what expulsion from the polity invariably (perhaps always) involves is some form of prohibition on the act of sharing story. Thus, just as one finds the arbitrary jutting in brutally at every point in accounts of the circumstance of non-personhood, so, also, always, one finds some kind of institutional blockage on the telling and hearing of stories. A life denied story, this is to say, is a life exposed to the accidental and the haphazard. It is not, as Arendt wants to put it, a life lived within the shelter of human association.

The question was, and is again, if story is, at some level, a measure of the political, if the capacity to share story implies the degree of association on which the political is predicated, how does the person who is excluded secure entry? How, in the face of the global production of non-personhood at the perimeter of the nation state, can story be a factor in enabling a person to cross? There are, I think, a range of possible responses to this question. One would be to observe, as Balibar observes of Arendt's reversion to the polis in the face of the mass production of non-personhood, the sheer incommensurability of the response. To emphasize story in this way is surely to aestheticize politics as if to attend to the act of telling and listening to stories was an alternative to, or a displacement of, the need to attend to more fundamental material requirements. A second response, the polar opposite, is to reiterate the fact that when persons are expelled, rendered expendable, so invariably, at the same time, their stories are erased. Gündoğdu makes the point starkly, referring to the number of unrecorded deaths in the US detention system. Thus,

> The problem of anonymous and unaccounted deaths has resurfaced in the detention centers used for the confinement of asylum seekers and undocumented immigrants. Due to lack of transparency and accountability, immigration detention makes it very difficult to keep an accurate record of these deaths.[31]

Not only is the account of a person's life excluded at the point of expulsion but also the record of their death. Far from aestheticizing politics, in other words, story is entirely material to the expulsive act.

A third kind of response, however—to the question of how story can be a factor in enabling a person to cross from one political setting to another—focuses on the way Arendt ties the act of storytelling to the process of arrival itself, to the principle of new-coming, or as she terms it, 'natality'. Here, again, the argumentative weave is tight. A defining concept for Arendt, 'natality' means not only birth but also the condition of giving birth to. It means the capacity of initiating and therefore proliferating possibility which is fundamental to her account of *The Human Condition*; the capacity to change by making things new, where such new-ness is the experience of human life. The aim of labour, work, and action, as Arendt thus describes it, is to 'provide and preserve the world' for the 'constant influx of newcomers who are born into the world as strangers'.[32] In one sense, what she means here, of course, is children, the constant influx of strangers, capable of initiating and making things new in the world. But she doesn't say children, she says 'newcomers', a term she has used before, in the opening statement of 'We Refugees': 'In the first place', as she insists, 'we don't like to be called "refugee". We ourselves call each other "newcomers" or "immigrants".'

The repetition of the term could not be more important. Arendt's objective in *The Human Condition*, where the condition in question is the political condition, is to address a contemporary geopolitical regime according to which 'there was no place on earth where migrants could go without the severest restrictions'. What was called for, therefore, was not simply a redescription of a given political association but some conception of how persons might insert themselves or be inserted, how they might be understood to make the transition across and between. At some point, of course, this would necessarily be a question of policy. But since it was also a question of participation, of who participates, then it was also, as Arendt understood, a matter of definition. How, that is, might the polity be defined in order that transition and insertion were possible? How could the polis be imagined such that persons might cross?

Arendt's answer was to re-inscribe the value of arrival, the fact of new-coming, which, as she described it, is our constant experience of the world:

> With word and deed we insert ourselves into the human world, and this insertion is like a second birth, in which we confirm and take upon ourselves the naked fact of our original appearance.[33]

Again, Arendt's logic is tight. Humans are political because they must appear to one another, and how they appear to one another is by their actions and by their words. By those words and actions they initiate things, they make things new. It is precisely, then, on the newcomer and the stranger that politics is predicated. Arendt, in other words, writes the influx, the fact of arrival, into the form of politics.

To which, clearly, it can be responded that Arendt's achievement here is no more (if also perhaps no less) than to name new-coming, or arrival, as a *desideratum* of politics. That she has done this is not in doubt and, in itself, should not be underestimated. Against a politics built on the mass production of social death, which is to say the politics of the juridical non-person, Arendt has predicated an account of politics on the principle of birth, in which the stranger, therefore, the newcomer, is the guiding figure. Even so, what one wants to arrive at is more than a new image of political interaction, however appealing or necessary that image might be. In response to which Arendt articulates the political function of story. As she puts it, under the heading 'The Web of Relationships and the Enacted Stories',

> The disclosure of the 'who' through speech, and the setting of a new beginning through action, always fall into an already existing web where their immediate consequences can be felt. Together they start a new process which eventually emerges as the unique life story of the newcomer, affecting uniquely the life stories of those with whom he comes into contact.[34]

The point of this complicated articulation of the interconnected nature of stories, 'the web of relationships' as Arendt puts it, is to affirm the function of the story in communal affairs. It is story, as she observes, that uniquely 'discloses' the individual subject, the 'who' who acts and speaks. It is also through story, however, that any such individual is seen to interconnect and mesh. From which it follows that to deny the individual story or to decline to allow it to be told and heard, is equally to deny both factors in a life: that it has its singularity and that it must be lived among others.

All of which, though Arendt constantly refers to the political, can seem a long way from any actual political reality. In one sense, this is by design since, in the face of seemingly intractable geopolitical realities, Arendt needed to create a space in which the act of reimagining was possible. In another sense, however, as abstract as Arendt's account can sound, its significance to political reality is always coming back. Witness, for instance, Balibar's speech in solidarity with the *sans-papiers* on the occasion of their occupation in Paris of the Church of Saint-Bernard. As Balibar movingly declared, reminding his audience 'What we owe to the *Sans-papiers*',

> We, French citizens of all sexes, origins and professions, are greatly indebted to the '*sans-papiers*' who, refusing the 'clandestineness' ascribed to them, have forcefully posed the question of the right to stay. We owe them a triple demonstration, which also gives us some responsibilities.
>
> We owe them for having broken through the communication barriers, for being seen and heard for what they are: not specters of delinquency and invasion, but workers and families, from here and there at the same time, with their particularisms and the universality of their condition as modern proletarians. They made facts, questions and even oppositions linked to the real problems of immigration circulate in public space, instead of the stereotypes held by dominant information monopolies. Thus, we better understand what democracy is: an institution of collective debate, whose conditions are never imposed from above. People must always conquer the right to speak, their visibility and credibility, running the risk of repression. And they have done this with calm courage, rejecting the use of mediatized violence and sacrifice, even if their situation is often desperate.[35]

It is when those who are hidden speak, in the face of repression, that, as Balibar sees it, we understand what democracy is. It is the moment, in Arendt's abstract terms, when the story of the newcomer uniquely changes the stories of those with whom they come into contact. But that moment is concrete, and as Balibar insists, insurrectional, where what the insurrection requires is solidarity:

> So the Sans-papiers, 'excluded' amongst the 'excluded' [...] have helped us immensely, with their resistance and their imagination, breathing life back into democracy. We owe them this recognition.[36]

The recognition we owe is that the newcomer makes democracy, which we understand when we hear those who have been expelled speak.

Feedback Is the Law

For Hannah Arendt, the story—the act of telling or sharing a story—was a means by which a person inserted themselves into political space. It is a crucial observation, not least because Arendt thus enables us to understand what the state does when it renders a person story-less. What she thus establishes is the connection between the act of sharing, or hearing (or, of course, denying) story and the process of entering a polity. The connection matters because it shows that if we are to imagine a new politics of human movement, then, at some level, policy must settle on the question of story. How, we can reasonably ask, following Arendt, can we ensure that a person is heard since if we don't ensure such a hearing, or listening, then de facto they are shut out. At the same time, however, it is important to hear where the onus in Arendt's account of the function of story falls. The image we are given, in *The Human Condition*, is of a political setting in which, since persons insert themselves through story, story is an act of self or collective assertion. The onus, in other words, rests on those who are coming in, where the reality, as Balibar describes in presenting the situation of the *Sans Papiers*, is that, 'People must always conquer the right to speak, their visibility and credibility, running the risk of repression.' This is, no doubt, part of the logic of rights, that opening of political space Rancière describes as dissensus, but it is not the whole logic of the act of sharing a story. If it is by story that the individual or group assert themselves, then what about the act of listening?

For Charles Olson, who was no less committed to the function of story in the weave of politics, the aim, in the face of the mid-century production of non-personhood, was not so much to emphasize the necessity for the person or group of persons to share their story. His intention, rather, was to create or articulate a space in which stories might be heard. The open field poem, as presented in 'Projective Verse', was fundamentally an act of listening or, at least, it was a poetic apparatus in which listening constituted the principal relation. As he put it in the second part of his essay,

> It comes to this: the use of a man, by himself and thus by others, lies in how he conceives his relation to nature, that force to which he owes his somewhat small existence. If he sprawl, he shall find little to sing but himself, and shall sing, nature has such paradoxical ways, by way of artificial forms outside himself. But if he stays inside himself, if he is contained within his nature as he is participant in the larger force, he will be able to listen, and his hearing through himself will give him secrets objects share.[37]

Olson's question here, as elsewhere in the essay, is how the individual should conceive their relation both to 'others' and to 'nature' in order that they should be, as he puts it, 'participant'. His answer is not, as one might expect of the poet, that they should 'sing' but that they should 'be able to listen', that the act of listening, or hearing, is key. There are many tensions implicit in this statement, and Olson himself was complicit in many contradictions, but in so far as he sought to articulate what he, like Arendt, termed a 'polis', his intention was to generate a space in which, as he puts it in his major early poem 'The Kingfishers', 'feedback is/the law'.[38] Where Olson differs from Arendt, in other words, even as he similarly insists on the intersection between story and politics, is in his emphasis on hearing, on the processes whereby stories are gathered and come through.

Olson's practice as a poet was intimately connected to his complex, compendious, partial, and sometimes controversial practice as a gatherer of stories. Ralph Maud registered this intimacy between the making of poems and the gathering of stories in his assiduous work of scholarly reconstruction, *Charles Olson's Reading: A Biography*. The point of Maud's title was partly that, as a life, Olson's biography was a mesh of relationalities, shaped constantly by his engagement with the stories of others. What Olson understood by the term story, was extensive. As Maud notes,

> In his 1953 freshman handout to students, Olson began by stating flatly that '*fiction* is only one form of storytelling', and with due consideration for where they are starting from, he lists with deliberation the three basic sources for the kind of storytelling he prefers:
>
> 1. the dictionary,
> 2. the encyclopaedia,
> 3. (a) the library card catalogue,
>   (b) Reader's Guide to Periodical Literature.[39]

We should hear various things in Olson's advice to his students. In the first place, we should register and underline the fact that, for Olson, the act of 'storytelling' was pervasive and fundamental. To operate in culture, any culture, was to be constantly engaged with the act and trace of storytelling. The point, as he wanted his students to understand, was to extend the frame. Story was to be found not just in fiction but also in a culture's documentary texts, in the dictionary, for example, or the encyclopaedia. To speak about storytelling, in other words, was not to speak about an incidental creative practice but rather to address the structures within which people might be held. A second thing to notice is that, as Olson advised the first-year students of this experimental college, he was also describing the practice of his major work. In *The Maximus Poems*, his history of a political community, he builds his poetic account precisely by gathering stories that don't present themselves as storytelling, the archive that documents certain relationalities through which, in part, the community was made. Like Arendt, Olson's term for that community was 'polis', and as he considered the question of how the polis was made, so the process of storytelling was axiomatic.

A further thing we must hear, however, is that for all that Olson's understanding of story was in one sense—*his* sense—encyclopaedic, it was also damagingly restrictive. As Lytton Smith observes, with reference to Susan Howe's reading of Olson,

> Women are nowhere to be found within the city poetics of *Maximus* or Olson's letters; instead, symbolic, mythological, objectified Woman appears. Howe, recognizing the innovations of Olson's 'articulation of sound forms. The fractured syntax, the gaps', opts to revise projective verse and the Olsonian conception of citizenship through epistolarity, reinscribing the presence of women by engaging with the way written texts construct versions of citizenship.[40]

Smith's thesis is one of the most dynamic recent accounts not only of Olson's poetics but also of the intersection between poetry and politics in the post-war period. His starting point is Engin Isin's observation, in *Being Political: Genealogies of Citizenship*, that 'poems, as "moments where the relationship between citizenship and alterity is transformed" can record and even achieve change in the statuses of citizen and non-citizen'.[41] Taking up Isin's largely unacknowledged invitation to poetry (that 'there is something about poetic articulation that captures the essence of the political while other forms of expression get tangled up with politics'), Smith identifies in Olson a model of 'projective citizenship' that for certain of his key interlocutors—Howe, Amiri Baraka, Myung Mi Kim—constituted a basis for the reimagining of political space. The principle of exchange in each case, as Smith documents, is a sustained critique of Olson's exclusions grounded in a shared commitment to the possibilities of projective poetics.[42] Howe's point is that both things are irreducibly true, that the actual narrative space, the set of stories Olson tells, is undeniably gendered, but that the poetic principles governing Olson's practice exceed in their implication his imaginative reach. We might understand this in terms of what Miriam Nichols called the 'poetics of outside': that post-war drive in Olson always to be opening the poem.[43]

The composition in which Olson first sought significantly to extend his practice of listening, his sense of the stories that ought to be heard, was 'The Kingfishers', his poem of 1949 in which he arrived at the poetic principles he would subsequently codify in 'Projective Verse'. Still, when one encounters it on the page, 'The Kingfishers' appears as a radical poetic expression, with its disjunctive historical materials distributed spatially across the page. To read it is to encounter an act of writing in which the principle of relationality is everything, in which the question posing itself constantly, as an always live issue, is how the different elements of the poem bear upon one another and relate. For that reason, discussion of the poem can quickly settle on the question of form, on the principles of composition that 'Projective Verse' outlines. To dwell on the question of form, however, can be to miss the poem's politics, where, as the Iraqi scholar Aseel Abdul-Lateef Taha proposes, that politics rests on the history and expulsions of the state. As Taha puts it,

> 'The Kingfishers' is the first anti-imperialist poem written in an apocalyptic era that saw the end of many colonial states and the breakup of the major European empires.[44]

Though we might certainly want to question Taha's claim to primacy, since nothing is ever really the first, his angle of vision is clarifying.[45] Deeply versed as he is in the traditions of European and American poetry, his concern is not principally with the way Olson departs from modernism or ushers in new aesthetic practices. His interest instead, not least as a scholar based in recently occupied Baghdad, is with how the poem set out to position itself in relation to the urgencies of post-war history. From Taha's perspective, 'The Kingfishers' is thus an attempt in poetry to articulate the implications, in the post-war moment, of the long and violent history of the modern state. As he puts it,

> Olson deals with an historically crucial issue which is the betrayal of humanly meaningful modes of life that were discovered before the emergence of the modern state. The European perfection of the state was a triumph of the abstract and imposed on man as a rationally and aesthetically oriented being.[46]

Olson's articulation of this 'historically crucial issue' has two principal frames of reference. In the first place, triggered in the poem by a discussion of the cultural significance of the kingfishers themselves, Olson sets a commentary on the brutality of the conquest of Mexico by Hernan Cortés against the contemporary context of Asian decolonization. The point of these framings, as Taha suggests, is not to detail either historical moment but to bring the history and apparatus of the state clearly into the consciousness of the poem.

It is to that history that 'The Kingfishers' is a response, and so the defining processes of the poem constitute a repeated attempt to arrive at imaginative resources which might open the post-war poem to that which the state expels. Witness, for example, Olson's concluding renunciation, as Taha reads it, 'of the violence and errors of Western tradition, stemming from Greek and Roman civilization', in favour of his identification with 'such rebels as the French poet, Arthur Rimbaud, who left his own country to live in the deserts of the Middle East'.[47] Or witness the poem's demarcation of whiteness, little remarked on by critical commentary, but made visible by a reading of the poem that grasps its relation to the history of colonization. As the poem's speaker puts it,

> The light is in the east. Yes. And we must rise, act. Yet
> in the west, despite the apparent darkness (the whiteness
> which covers all), if you look, if you can bear, if you can,
>   long enough.[48]

Confronted, as Taha puts it, by the 'ugly whiteness of the face of history', 'The Kingfishers' constitutes a series of strategies whereby the post-war imagination might reckon with that which the western state, in its historic racism, has held outside.[49]

It is an impulse one hears at every turn, concerned as the poem is throughout with that which has been rejected, with anything (and by implication everything) the state has expelled. It is what Olson means when, borrowing from Rimbaud's *Une Saison en Enfer*, he arrives at the decision, at the end of the poem, to 'hunt among stones', where the stones are the wreckage of settler-imperial aggression. Taha quotes Maud to establish the point:

> [America] was brutalized from the start by a conquistador who predicted ourselves and our pejorocracy [. . .] we can study the origins of American history and face up to the offences against the aboriginal population, and the cannibalistic-genocidal impulses involved.[50]

Maud is not wrong that 'The Kingfishers' is, among other things, a history of the imperial brutalization of America, a process of racist expulsion that Olson sought to connect to the post-war moment.[51] But Taha is right to insist on the poem's more general intention to delineate the expulsive mechanisms of the state as such, an intention one hears in the lines that close section II and which the poem as a whole has been feeling towards. As the poem puts it, posing a statement in the form of a question:

> with what violence benevolence is bought
> what cost in gesture justice brings
> what wrongs domestic rights involve
> what stalks
> this silence[52]

It is difficult to think of lines which capture more concisely the defining contradictions of the modern state. Focusing his poetic and political intelligence, allowing these realms of understanding to intersect, Olson's intention is to delineate precisely the manner of the state's expulsion while requiring those who benefit from its actions to recognize what it does. Poetically speaking, the guiding formal gesture here—as it was frequently in Olson—is chiasmus, the rhetorical figure whereby grammatical structures in successive phrases or clauses are reversed. The effect of this kind of reversal is to produce a mirror: at the moment of chiasmus, the poem looks back at itself. Thus here, in Olson's poem, as he threads a careful play of sounds through the chiastic arrangement, we hear the '*violence*' by which '*benevolence* is bought', the 'cost in *gesture justice* brings', and crucially, in a line that turns serpent-like upon itself, 'the wrongs domestic rights in*volve*'. This reinforcement by sonic effect is devastating in its enactment of what the poem calls 'involvement'. And at the same time, the political statement could not be more clear. The wrongs involved, as the poem spells out, are the consequence of domestic rights—rights, this is to say, deliberately and explicitly not extended to the space that falls outside the state.

My argument here is not just that by clear implication, a year after the promulgation of the Universal Declaration, Olson delineates a geopolitical order marked by the absence of human rights. His intention, moreover, is to consider how the poem might be conducive to a better imagined space. Part of the answer is indicated in the chiastic play of sound itself, which is to say in the act of listening the poem entails. What the poem requires the reader to hear are the stories the state would silence and which the citizens of any such state must feel compelled to register. Olson, this is to argue, not only details the expulsions and contradictions of the modern state but also seeks to establish a practice whereby a space of recognition might be achieved. The task is to do the listening the state refuses, to hear that which is held outside. Or as he declares in part 4 of the poem, summing up the political-aesthetic practice he is seeking to instantiate: 'feed-back is the law'.

Olson's suggestion that 'feedback is the law' inaugurates a disposition in the writing that would continue to determine his practice at the level of poetic methodology and which, in turn, would allow for the shaping of political spaces the poem could model or make possible. One term for that disposition, for the requirement that any given utterance be exposed to feedback, is what Lytton Smith calls Olson's 'epistolary poetics'. As Smith puts it,

> Beginning in the 1950s, Olson engaged in a series of experiments in the formation of citizenship groups: in and from Gloucester, MA; at Black Mountain College; and in the pages of *Origin*. Writing poems during this time, he eventually developed an epistolary methodology for his projective epic, *Maximus*, in which letter-poems invoke a community of addressees as part of a polis.[53]

As his published correspondences with Cid Corman, Robert Creeley, Ed Dorn, among others, have long since demonstrated, the letter was critical to Olson as a mode of exploration, and indeed, as Maud has observed, the act of writing a letter was as significant in his working day as the act of writing a poem.[54] More recently, published correspondences document how key developments in Olson's project emerged from extended letter exchange. In *Charles Olson and Frances Boldereff: A Modern Correspondence*, Maud and Sharon Thesen trace the evolution of the thinking that Olson would articulate in 'Projective Verse' and towards which his exchange with Boldereff was critical.[55] In *The Collected Letters of Charles Olson and J.H. Prynne*, Ryan Dobran allows us to see how, for both poets, the intensity of correspondence became a means for each of consolidating the poetic trajectories that would come to distinguish their practices in the late 1960s. Olson and his correspondents worked things out in letters.

Smith's point, however, in describing Olson's 'epistolary poetics', is to emphasize not only the importance of Olson's findings as a correspondent to his utterances as a poet but also the principle of letter exchange itself. Setting Olson's development as a poet against contemporary formulations of citizenship in American political discourse, from the internment of Japanese-Americans in War Relocation Centers to the Immigration and Naturalization Act of 1952, Smith identifies in Olson's commitment to epistolary exchange a model of participation that would underpin his insistence on citizenship as a necessarily active process. As he puts it,

> Epistolarity was not just a means of communicating his ideas of citizenship; it was a methodology for acting as a citizen. Through the epistolary, a reader could become a writer, a projective citizen in a polis that was not confined to one place but organised around what Olson called the 'interchange' of letters.[56]

It is in the spirit of such an 'interchange' that *The Maximus Poems*, Olson's history of a political community, is conceived as a series of letters. Situating himself 'Offshore by islands', as the opening of the poem has it, 'Maximus' addresses a correspondence to the people of Gloucester, Massachusetts, in which the content is frequently, whether literally or by implication, the words those whom he has addressed have spoken or written back. It is a writerly method which models a form of political content. *Maximus*, as Smith observes, institutes a process of 'careful listening to others' in which the speaker 'does not claim an authoritative position' but is 'participant' in the field itself.[57] 'Feedback is the law' in *The Maximus Poems* in that the act of listening is the governing practice.

There is, however, a deeper, more troubling, more politically far-reaching sense in which 'feedback' constitutes the compositional principle of *The Maximus Poems*. As much as the poem models an image of active citizenship underwritten by the interchange of correspondence, so it also seeks out stories of those to whom the category of citizen does not apply. Like 'The Kingfishers', Olson's major work is acutely aware of the practices of the state, and like that earlier poem, *Maximus* looks to include the stories of those whom the state expels. What results is a kind of historical chiasmus whereby those held outside by state practice and formation are heard to speak back, an act of recognition that is crucial, as Olson sees it, to the opening of political space.

'Letter 14' is a case in point. Here, as elsewhere, the poem consists of a weave of stories, where those stories take various forms: dream, personal anecdote, excerpt from the *Dictionary of National Biography*, *State Papers*, histories ancient and modern. Structurally, the poem is in three main sections, patterned in a way that is familiar to the early letters of *The Maximus Poems*. Section I, which is in two parts, situates speaker and reader in the present or recent past. Section II becomes abruptly historical in its frame of reference. Section III, where the chiastic manoeuvre takes place, considers how the materials and voices of the past should be heard to speak back.

Against this basic patterning, the poem opens, as Olson poems frequently do, with a remembered dream, where, in this case, the speaker shifts through various city spaces, one of which is Boston, where he recalls leaving a movie house. The second part of the opening section moves from dream to memory, the poet recalling himself and a group of friends in physical training, with the instructor directing them in the development of posture. What connects these opening episodes is the image of the body in space, the dream issuing in a kind of spatial entitlement, 'you had the firmament/over your head', while in the memory the speaker recalls himself 'arms out, legs out, leaping'.[58]

With the beginning of section II, the nature of the storytelling alters. The writing is now shaped not by dream and anecdote but by history and archive. Olson's subject here is the Hawkins family, one of those Anglo families that imperialized the globe, the third generation of which, Richard, made '"perfect discovery"' of the Eastern Seaboard.[59] Richard's father, John, was a slave trader. He traded in the bodies of West Africans in the service of the state. His actions are inserted into the poem through reference to the official record:

> "On board, San Juan de Lua, 57
> Negroes, *optimi generis*, each valued at 160£, or a total of
> 9,120£,
> ("Schedule of Property Lost, *State Papers*, Dom. Elizabeth,
> Iiii")[60]

For the reader of contemporary poetry, Olson's reference to the 'Schedule of Property Lost' recalls M. NourbeSe Philip's brilliant excavation and retelling of the story of the slave ship *Zong*, the captain of which ordered that 'some 150 Africans be murdered by drowning so that the ship's owners could collect insurance monies'.[61] George Butterick, in his *Guide to the Maximus Poems*, glosses Olson's reference to the San Juan de Lua episode thus:

San Juan de Lua is a small island protecting the harbor of Vera Cruz, Mexico, where John Hawkins was attacked by a Spanish fleet in 1568. Hawkins presumably had intended to sell the slaves, the '*optimi generis*' (Latin 'finest products'), at Vera Cruz.[62]

Olson's own comment is to reiterate what, and who, Hawkins's actions were for:

> This
>   was the man broke open
>   the Spanish main,
>   this
>   for England,
>   and for America,
>   for some of those who built
>   white houses.[63]

The purpose of the transaction is made clear: Africans were sold into slavery and death to build white houses; black bodies were brutalized in order to extend whiteness across geopolitical space.

The value of 'Letter 14', as with his earlier poem, 'The Kingfishers'—and what makes it an example not only of Olson's moral outrage but also of his creative method—is the relation it articulates between state and story. John Hawkins' actions as a slave trader are recorded in *State Papers* because, in that trade, he acted on behalf of the state. The poem documents the fact that Hawkins was awarded '"a crest:/"a demi-Moor,/ proper,/in chains", to which Butterick adds, by way of annotation, that 'John Hawkins' slave-trading won him a grant of a coat of arms'.[64] Olson's subject here, in other words, is the state and the state's authorization of processes of expulsion, but his principal concern is with the stories of those who have been held outside. Witness the final section of the poem, where, as is characteristically the case, the speaker draws the themes together and where the story of those excluded is brought back:

> With the gums gone, the teeth
> are large. And though the nose is then nothing,
> the eye-sockets

> And now the shadow
> of the radiator on the floor
> is wolf-tits, the even row of it
> fit to raise
> feral children.
>
> > You will count them all in,
> > you will stay in the midst of them,
> > you will know no law, you will hear them
> > in the narrow seas.[65]

Notoriously, there were times in Olson's career when he didn't listen, when he would talk so long other people would be drowned out.[66] But what the poetry wants to imagine, and what it sometimes achieves, is a space in which listening is dynamic and constant, in which the stories of others as they bear on others are in a continuous process of feeding back. Like Arendt, he takes the act of telling or hearing stories to be axiomatic to the structures of politics and, like Arendt, his concern is with the stories of those the state expels. But where Arendt emphasizes story as claim, the act of speaking as a mode of insertion into political culture, Olson sets out to construct a space of listening. The corpses Olson describes are the bodies of those enslaved. 'You will stay in the midst of them [. . .] you will hear them/in the narrow seas.' The stories of those expelled must be enabled to feed back, and the implications of those stories must be recognized. The state, this is to suggest, only opens up when the stories of those the state expels are actively heard.

Jamming

If, for Olson, it was necessary to recover stories of those the state, in its violence, had expelled, for Fanon, that intersection of story, audibility, and expulsion was structural to his professional experience. In December 1956, having witnessed the damage done to individual Algerians by the sustained violence of the French state, from the torture of members of the *Front de Libération Nationale* to the profound psycho-affective disorders caused by the daily intrusions of the colonial regime, Fanon resigned his post at Blida Joinville. Setting out the reasons for his resignation in an open letter to Robert Lacoste, resident minister and Governor General of Algeria, Fanon stated precisely why his work as a psychiatrist in a colonial setting had become untenable. As he put it,

If psychiatry is the medical technique that endeavours to enable individuals to cease being foreign to their environment, I owe it to myself to state that the Arab, permanently alienated in his own country, lives in a state of absolute depersonalisation.[67]

For Fanon, as Jean Khalfa has observed, such a state of affairs meant that it was no longer possible 'to want at any price to disalienate individuals' since the transition from psychiatric setting to everyday life depended on a distinction that did not apply.[68] It was not possible, as Fanon wrote to Lacoste, 'to put them back in their place in a country in which non-right, inequality and murder are erected into legislative principles, where the native, who is permanently alienated in his own country, lives in a state of absolute depersonalisation'.[69]

Fanon's letter to Lacoste draws together various thematic threads that have shaped this book. Writing with regards to a professional setting in which the act of listening was critical, Fanon details a wider Algerian context in which the refusal of rights is established as a legislative framework and where those to whom the framework is applied are permanently alienated from their environment, rendered, as Fanon describes it, depersonalized. What he details, in other words, is a hostile environment, a setting constructed by the absence of rights in which the lived experience is one of permanent alienation. The effect of Fanon's letter was that he was himself expelled, deported to Tunisia by the state whose practices he had confronted.

Grounded as such observations were in his work with people demonstrably damaged by colonial expulsion, it is in accounts such as Fanon presented to Lacoste that the power of his project endures. As Bashir Abu-Manneh puts it, in his assessment of Fanon's legacy, 'Fanon utilizes phenomenological language in order to highlight the generative connections between the individual and wider historical processes', the whole point of *The Wretched of the Earth* in particular being 'to connect social suffering to colonial relations and to identify ways to remedy it'.[70] Fanon's overarching remedy, as Abu-Manneh documents, was socialist revolution, where the underlying principle of opposition to colonialism was a commonality as inscribed in human rights. Fanon is a consistently subtle and probing thinker in this regard, constantly placing that driving aspiration to what he repeatedly called the new humanism—a model of humanism that drew deeply on the mid-century articulation of rights—in dialectical relation with the specifics of Algerian cultural reality that colonialism had dismantled and sought to render invalid. Abu-Manneh is right, therefore, to specify a plurality of remedies, or at least to signal that, for Fanon, the task of establishing what he called 'a new humanism' involved multiple modes of intervention since, as he puts it, for Fanon, 'a real and authentic decolonization would have to result in the emancipation of the individual'.[71] What Abu-Manneh points to here is an extraordinary quality of Fanon's work; that in his consideration both of the constant and daily damage done by the expulsions of colonialism and of the remedies necessary to resist and transform its effects, Fanon speaks if not to all of life (no writer speaks to all of life) then to an extraordinary richness and range of environments and relationalities. The 'new humanism' Fanon called for entailed a re-awakening of lived solidarities across all manner of cultural contexts, one crucial setting being what one might call the storytelling relation.

I use that awkward phase, the storytelling relation, because in so far as his accounts of political resistance and transformation turn to the phenomenon of story, as they do quite frequently, it was as much to the process of storytelling as the content of the stories told that Fanon wanted to draw the reader's attention. He provides a characteristic account of the situation he has in mind in the free-standing essay that concludes his discussion of 'National Culture' in *The Wretched of the Earth*—the passage in question, in its exemplary quality, being worth hearing at length.[72] Observing that 'Colonialism made no mistake when from 1955 on it proceeded to arrest these storytellers systematically', Fanon writes,

> Every time the storyteller relates a fresh episode to his public, he presides over a real invocation. The existence of a new type of man is revealed to the public. The presence is no longer turned in upon itself but spread out for all to see. The storyteller once more gives free rein to his imagination; he makes innovations and he creates a work of art [...] The storyteller replies to the expectant people by successive approximations, and makes his way, apparently alone but in fact helped on by his public, towards the seeking out of new patterns, that is to say national patterns. Comedy and farce disappear, or lose their attraction. As for dramatization, it is no longer placed on the plane of the troubled intellectual and his tormented conscience. By losing its characteristics of despair and revolt, the drama becomes part of the common lot of the people and forms part of an action in preparation or already in progress.[73]

SPEAKING 237

There is much to notice in Fanon's deliberate and detailed account of the politicization of the storytelling relation. The first thing to note is the historical fact that, from 1955 onwards, the colonial regime proceeded to arrest Algerian storytellers. Always when a regime looks to render a group of people non-persons, it will find a mechanism to expel the stories of the persons concerned. In the United Kingdom, in the present moment, as I have previously observed, asylum and immigration tribunals, in which people seeking asylum seek to make their case, are not courts of record.[74] In the midst of the many other mechanisms for the production of non-personhood that the contemporary UK regime has arrived at, it has sought to ensure that the stories of those expelled are not allowed to enter the record. The production of non-personhood requires the expulsion of the person's story. Colonialism made no mistake when it arrested the storytellers.

In so far, however, as Fanon proceeds to give an account of the function of the storyteller that might explain the regime's anxiety, it is towards the process rather than any particular content that his account points. What matters, above all, is the storyteller's relation to their public, where the relation enables—Fanon's word is 'invokes'—the acts of imagination that allow for new patterns of personhood and politics to emerge. The real danger, and therefore force, of storytelling as Fanon presents it, rests not in the affect generated by a given episode or series of experiences but in the fact that, in the situation in which a story is being told or shared, people encounter one another as people and are capable, in that encounter, of generating new patterns and possibilities. When he writes, therefore, that in the act of storytelling, 'The existence of a new type of man is revealed to the public', he means that the process itself is revelatory, that the humanization occurs in the act itself, where the act is constituted as much by those who listen as by the person who tells the story.

Arguably, it is in accounts such as this of the storytelling process, even as it borders on a fetishization of the act, that Fanon's understanding of the politics of culture become apparent. It is towards such accounts, I think, that Abu-Manneh points us when he asserts that for Fanon, 'What counts is a radical politics of culture—not cultural politics.'[75] The colonial regime arrests the storytellers because the storytelling relation is crucial to the process of re-humanization that the revolution both requires and makes possible; because in the participation it enables, it allows solidarities to form. At the same time, however, we need to notice that Fanon's account here of the storytelling process is, in its relative abstraction, a distillation. What really matters to him, in this respect, across the range of his writing are the material practices and settings in which expulsion is effected through the exclusion of stories and in which also, crucially, such exclusion is overcome. The great value of Fanon, in other words, lies in detailed accounts of actual settings in which the act of sharing stories is both thwarted and recovered. Two settings in particular allow him to demonstrate what is at stake: the domestic spaces in which stories told by the radio broadcast are received and interpreted and the psychiatric setting itself.

Writing in response to Fanon's essay, 'This is the Voice of Algeria' (published in *Studies in a Dying Colonialism*), Ian Baucom has helpfully observed that, for Fanon, as a professional listener, the act of listening was invariably accorded a central function in the text. As he puts it, spelling out the connection,

> As a practicing psychiatrist, Fanon spent much of his life as a professional listener. As a writer he produced texts that frequently function as transcripts of his diverse acts of listening.[76]

Think, for instance, of the extraordinary opening to *Black Skin, White Masks*, which comes at the reader simply as a voice in the ear, like the beginning of a novel, the narrator perhaps addressing another, or perhaps simply speaking to himself:

> The explosion will not happen today. It is too soon ... or too late.
> I do not come with timeless truths.
> My consciousness is not illuminated with ultimate radiances.
> Nevertheless, in complete composure, I think it would be good if certain things were said.
> These things I am going to say, not shout. For it is a long time since shouting has gone out of my life.[77]

Right there, at the beginning of his career as a writer, in the text he had hoped to submit as his PhD in psychiatry, Fanon's inaugural gesture is to call on the reader to listen, to hear the narrative voice speaking before the situation explodes.

Baucom is right, then, to focus attention on the act of listening in Fanon's writing and right also to observe that the text is often 'less "Fanon's" text than a compilation of those voices to which he has inclined his ear'.[78] One might add to this articulation of Fanon's modernism the fact that not infrequently his writing will, in a very deliberate sense, cite or stage a drama, the narrative voice exiting to leave persons in dialogue with one another. My concern, however, is less with the generalized emphasis on listening one finds in Fanon and more with the way he details the processes by which, in given material circumstances, the state thwarts the stories of those it has expelled and—because Fanon is always ultimately an optimist—the way those who have been expelled reconstruct the process of listening. 'This is the Voice of Algeria' is a key text in this respect.

As a brief history of the use of radio before and during the Algerian revolution, 'This is the Voice of Algeria' is, in one sense, a text book account of colonial cultural imposition. Fanon describes how the official state radio, Radio-Alger, was 'essentially the instrument of colonial society and its values'.[79] In its relentlessly metropolitan programming, 'Radio-Alger sustains the occupant's culture, marks it off from the non-culture, from the nature of the occupied.'[80] As in colonialism's urban planning, the point of its cultural programming is to draw a line, the racialized line that demarcates officially sanctioned personhood from non-personhood. As Fanon reports towards the end of the essay, writing from his professional practice, it was a demarcation that had demonstrable psychopathological effects. Thus,

> Before 1954, the monographs written on Algerians suffering from hallucinations constantly pointed out the presence in the so-called 'external action phase' of highly aggressive and hostile radio voices. These metallic, cutting, insulting, disagreeable voices all have for the Algerian an accusing, inquisitorial character.[81]

The voice of Radio-Alger was the voice of the hostile environment: cutting, insulting, accusing, inquisitorial.

Where the essay gets really interesting, however, is in its account of the way indigenous Algerians, led by the *Front de Libération Nationale*, having previously refused radio as the colonial imposition it was, set out to use its potential—and how the state, in response, set out to block such use. The word is 'jamming'. As Fanon puts it,

> Here we come upon a phenomenon that is sufficiently unusual to retain our attention. The highly trained French services, rich with experience acquired in modern wars, past masters in the practice of 'sound-wave warfare', were quick to detect the wave lengths of the broadcasting stations.

> The programs were then systematically jammed, and the *Voice of Fighting Algeria* soon became inaudible. A new form of struggle had come into being.[82]

The state practices Fanon describes here remain a phenomenon that should retain our attention. Systematic jamming is what state agencies do to the stories of those they expel because both the stories and the act of sharing those stories have intrinsic power; because to tell them and to listen to them is to facilitate transformation. The new struggle Fanon describes here is therefore the struggle to listen, where, in part, the task was simply to get the broadcast out since, during the course of a single broadcast, it would frequently be necessary to use a second station, 'broadcasting over a different wave-length'.[83]

The second aspect of the struggle, however, was the act of listening itself, given the multiple forms of interference generated by the state. Fanon describes the scene in detail and at length:

> The listener, enrolled in the battle of the waves, had to figure out the tactics of the enemy, and in an almost physical way circumvent the strategy of the adversary. Very often only the operator, his ear glued to the receiver, had the unhoped-for opportunity of hearing the *Voice*. The other Algerians present in the room would receive the echo of this voice through the privileged interpreter who, at the end of the broadcast, was literally besieged. Specific questions would then be asked of this incarnated voice [...] A real task of reconstruction would then begin. Everyone would participate, and the battles of yesterday and the day before be re-fought in accordance with the deep aspirations and unshakable faith of the group. The listener would compensate for the fragmentary nature of the news by an autonomous creation of information.[84]

What Fanon describes here, with due attention to the specifics of the situation, is the necessity and difficulty of the act of listening. Precisely what the state intrudes on, with its long experience of jamming, is the relation between the excluded storyteller, in this case *The Voice of Fighting Algeria*, and those who, in their listening, would make the story real. The attention to specifics of the situation is crucial since, as Fanon wants frequently to remind us, in situations of expulsion we have to find new ways to listen because, in an expulsive situation, listening is not a given act. There is no reason to assume, therefore, that the listening will always entail the act of autonomous creation Fanon describes in the reconstruction of the radio broadcast. There is no such practice of reconstruction, for example, in the account he gives of the storytelling relation in *The Wretched of the Earth*. Where the continuity lies, and what he wants constantly to insist on, is both the necessary labour of listening to the stories the state expels and the transformation such listening effects. And where he registers that necessity most clearly is in the context of psychiatry, a setting for Fanon in which all the difficulties of the storytelling relation were acutely present.

The use of psychiatry by the French state in occupied Algeria, its development as a form of racialized profiling and institutionalized expulsion, has been much discussed. Richard Keller provides a significant overview of that development in his cultural history of the 'theories, practices, and institutions of French psychiatry in colonial North Africa'.[85] Tracing the construction and treatment of mental illness in the Maghreb from the first French occupation of the city of Algiers in 1830, Keller focuses, in particular, on the practices of the 'Algiers School' that shaped colonial psychiatry from the 1930s to the moment of decolonization. In the hands of the School's practitioners, as Keller describes it, 'psychiatry'

> brought a new degree of sophistication to colonial racism. This was especially the case in Algeria, where a large settler population depended upon a rigid racial hierarchy as a means of defending its social and political status.[86]

The purpose of Keller's history is, in part, to contextualize Fanon, and, accordingly, he sets a reading of Fanon's critique of ethnopsychiatry alongside a range of contemporary responses to its institutional practices, notably in the emergent postcolonial theory of Albert Memmi and the fiction of Kateb Yacine.

What emerges, broadly speaking, is a twofold understanding. On the one hand, Keller documents the influence of psychiatry on mid-century colonial practice, the degree to which, 'the new discipline of ethnopsychiatry informed educational and professional discrimination against Muslims' and 'shaped discourse about immigration into France, and provided the essential background for the French army's psychological warfare programs during the Algerian struggle for independence'.[87] On the other hand, what Keller observes is how, in proportion to its influence, the psychiatric setting became itself a site of de-colonial resistance and struggle. Thus, just as

'French colonial institutions produced a colonized subject who lacked the essential qualities of humanity', so also they constituted 'the precise contexts in which the colonized contested the violence of these assumptions'.[88]

It was in that space—the clinical setting which 'served as [an] important initial site of confrontation between colonialists and indigenous populations'—that Fanon spent his professional life and where, on a daily basis, he sought to counter the expulsive processes of the colonial regime.[89] Until recently, the most comprehensive record of that ongoing act of professional resistance was provided in *The Wretched of the Earth* itself, with its concluding account, in the form of a taxonomy, of 'Colonial War and Mental Disorders'. Keller is right to set Fanon's studies of the causal relation between colonial power and psycho-affective illness alongside the responses of contemporary commentators, thereby both broadening and strengthening the force of his critique.[90] A further contextualization, however, is provided by the 'Psychiatric Writings' gathered by Jean Khalfa and Robert Young and published in *Alienation and Freedom* in 2018. What one finds in those writings is not just a document of the professional findings that supports the accounts of mental disorder that conclude Fanon's polemic against colonialism. What one finds also is a record of the constancy with which, in his daily practice, he intervened against the expulsive procedures of the state: from his critique and then condemnation of the ethnopsychiatric methodologies at Blida-Joinville to his development of group therapeutic settings both in Algeria and, latterly, at the Charles Nicolle Hospital in Tunisia. Constantly keyed in to his critique of the state, Fanon's psychiatric writings articulate an evolving imaginary, framed by the materialities of its colonial psychiatric setting but capable of effecting modes of solidarity by which the process of shared humanization might be modelled and sustained.

Two themes in particular shape Fanon's account of the colonial psychiatric setting. The first is a persistent determination to frame the realities of that setting in relation to mid-century practices of internment. As Jean Khalfa observes, in 'Fanon, Revolutionary Psychiatrist',

> In many cases, the hospital remained a simple place of internment, and patients whose problems were often minor at the start, would react to this environment, generating cycles of violence that in turn condemned them to perpetual confinement. After the Second World War, the memory of famine in French asylums and reports about concentration camps made the reality of the psychiatric hospital particularly intolerable.[91]

SPEAKING 243

Fanon, for whom the continuity with internment was observable on a daily basis, was more detailed. Witness his collaborative account, with Jacques Azoulay, of 'Social Therapy in a Ward of Muslim Men'. As Fanon and Azoulay report, shortly after Fanon's arrival at Blida-Joinville,

> Nurses were afraid of the patients, and the hairdresser demanded that the patients were tied up before being shaved. Out of fear of patients, or in order to punish them, the patients were left in secure units, sometimes shirtless, without mattresses, or without sheets on account of one's being a 'lacerator'. The eternal 'chronics' were often tied up with a belt even before acting out, as a preventative measure. As Paumelle showed so well, the same rhythm, the same vicious circle —agitation, restraint, agitation—always kept up a veritably concentration-camp mindset.[92]

The interest of such accounts, published as they were in psychiatric journals, lies in part in their factuality of tone and approach. What we have here is not the poetry of Fanon's more expansive critiques, the lyric articulations of embodiment that animate *Black Skin, White Masks* and *The Wretched of the Earth*, but an accumulation of the procedures whereby the resident of the colonial psychiatric hospital is held outside: the absence of clothing, of bed clothes, the use of a belt as mode of restraint; the incremental depersonalization of the individual patient. One might note, in this context, the reports of people who have experienced 'perpetual' (or indefinite) detention in the United Kingdom in the present moment, the fact that people picked up in the English channel arrive at removal centres after many hours of processing and transportation still wearing their dripping wet clothes; that once detained, the lights in their cells are left on for 23 hours a day.[93] This is to register that methodologies of expulsion continue, that people are dehumanized at the level of daily practice. It is also to observe that, for Fanon, his ongoing critique of ethnopsychiatric practice was inseparable from his ongoing critique of the expulsions of the colonial state. To work at Blida-Joinville was to witness mid-century internment at work and therefore the continued production, on a daily basis, of non-persons.[94]

But if, in his professional existence, Fanon observed the daily reproduction of non-personhood, the incremental brutalities that constituted the colonial psychiatric setting, so also, as he worked to reshape that setting, he established practices of engagement capable of re-humanization. Critical to such practices, both psychiatrically and politically, were precisely the complexities of the storytelling relation. The aim of state-sponsored practice was to jam, to prevent the stories being shared. The aim of Fanon's experiments, in socio-therapy in particular, was to establish contexts in which it was possible to listen.

Accounts of both the importance, and also the difficulty, of hearing stories run right through the psychiatric writings Khalfa and Young assemble in *Alienation and Freedom*. In 'Social Therapy in a Ward of Muslim Men: Methodological Details', written from Blida-Joinville in October 1954, Fanon and Azoulay report on their 'attempt to organise, from a social therapeutic perspective, a psychiatric ward of Muslim men'.[95] The purpose of the article (and also, as Khalfa suggests, of the experiment itself) was to document the difficulty of introducing a socio-therapeutic environment across the mixed demographic of Blida-Joinville. Thus, whereas the establishment of a 'framework of an increasingly enriched social life'—incorporating a whole range of activities from film nights to knitting clubs—soon came to benefit the rhythms and exchanges of European women, the atmosphere on the ward of Muslim men 'remained oppressive, stifling'.[96] The reason for this failure, as Fanon and Azoulay conclude, was that the basis of their approach was insufficiently structural. Given the double alienation experienced by Muslim men in a colonial regime, 'it was essential to go from the biological level to the institutional one, from natural existence to cultural existence', to register, rather than bracket off, 'geographical, historical, and cultural' frames.[97] The result was a material change of approach:

> The establishing of a Moorish café in the hospital, the regular celebration of traditional Muslim feasts, of periodical meetings around a professional 'storyteller', are already concrete facts. With each new event, the number of patients engaged in these activities increases. This social life is only in its beginnings, but already we believe that we have eliminated the methodological errors.[98]

The aim of the experiment was the production of a social life, an environment in which otherwise doubly alienated individuals felt able to speak. Critical to this process was the inclusion of a 'professional 'storyteller', where the working assumption was that stories enable, or even perhaps beget stories; the sharing of stories was modelled at the level of professional practice.

It is important to be clear what is being documented here. At the heart of his psychiatric practice, in the midst of the struggle to decolonize, Fanon and Azoulay institute a resistance to structural alienation by (among other things) the incorporation, in the expulsive environment, of the storytelling act. It is not a naïve gesture. More carefully than Arendt, because he is rooting his discourse in materially expulsive conditions, Fanon (in conjunction with various psychiatric colleagues) details the complications of the storytelling relation. What results is a meticulously observed account of a transformative speech act where the speech is the story (broadly understood) of the person who has been expelled and where the act is enabled by the continuous preparation of the conditions of listening.

For Fanon and Azoulay, in the commentary on the introduction of socio-therapy into a ward of Muslim men, what the requirement of listening entails, in part, is an extended consideration of 'interpretation'. Thus because, '[i]n normal circumstances, a patient may have encountered the image of the interpreter in his relations with the administration or the justice system', so 'the same need for an interpreter spontaneously triggers a distrust that makes all "communication" difficult'.[99] It is for this reason of institutionalized mistrust that Fanon and Azoulay draw on the storyteller because, as they describe it, 'in the douars', it is the itinerant storyteller who performs, and thereby facilitates, communication. What matters here, as in Fanon's account of the function of the radio, is the micro-attention he pays to the listening act. The story has been officially jammed. It is necessary to provide a context in which it can be heard. Fanon is exhaustive in his attention to the preparations necessary.

One could track this attention across his whole body of work as, among the many forms of vigilance he considers critical to the decolonial struggle, Fanon returns repeatedly to the necessity of enabling the story to be properly heard. One last situation, however, signals clearly what is at stake: the phenomenon of the denied or retracted confession. Writing with Raymond Lacaton, Fanon addresses this complex and revealing, but not uncommon, rhetorical situation in two short essays from 1955, 'Conducts of Confession in North Africa (1) & (2)'. The circumstance is that of the person who, having confessed to a crime when addressed by 'initial investigators', then 'from a certain moment on (in principle, after one or two months of detention) [. . .] goes back on his declarations, he denies them utterly (in the majority of cases, he claims that he confessed under coercion)'.[100] In this particular inquiry, Fanon and Lacaton are not concerned with the question of coercion, of forced confession, as much as that was an instrument of the French colonial regime. Their interest, rather, is in the implications of the retraction itself and of the processes of legitimization refused by the denial. What is at issue, as they argue, is the totality of the colonial speech act situation:

> Let us indeed recall that the criminal's reintegration via the confession of his act depends upon the recognition of the group by the individual. In short, there can be no reintegration if there has been no integration [...] The criminal's subjective assent, which founds the sanction and gives it its value, will not be granted in these conditions. Elementary adherence presupposes a coherent group, collective attitudes, an ethical universe.[101]

The underlying claim of Fanon's collaborative consideration of 'Conducts of Confession' is not legal, or moral, but rhetorical. His observation is that conditions do not exist in which the speech act of the confession can be made or heard; the whole environment of expulsion militates against the exchange. The criminal, who might have been inclined to speak, declines speech because to speak to is endorse a regime which produces their de-personalization.

This is the sense in which there is nothing naïve about Fanon's insistence on listening, his insistence, from his earliest published pronouncements, that the voice of the person expelled must be in the reader's ear. Undemanding as this can sound, what it actually demands is a structural transformation of the most profound order, a recalibration of the total environment that makes de-personalization possible. Fanon set out the stakes in a letter to his friend Maurice Despinoy, when Despinoy inquired whether Fanon might return to practice in the Antilles. As he put it by way of response,

> I assure you, Despinoy, that I am currently unable to make the least promise. There are more than 10 million people to treat here. Colonialist psychiatry as whole has to be disalienated.[102]

There is hardly a more simple or more human demand than that a person should be heard. And, as Fanon knew, hardly a more far-reaching requirement.

Conclusion

Let's try to put this in absolute terms. A violation of human rights is a violation of the human voice. It is a sweeping claim, one that could be tested and examined in all manner of different ways, but, in practice, in our understanding of such situations, where a violation of human rights occurs, we also witness an abuse of voice: whether the voices in question are stopped or silenced or whether the words spoken in the context of violation are uttered under duress. It is a connection that could be construed as causal, where the violation of voice is a consequence of the violation of human rights, because those committing the violation don't want the story to be shared. For certain human rights theorists, however, the connection is more intimate, the voice being the marker, one might almost say the bearer of rights. This, or something close to it, is the position taken by Joseph Slaughter.

Slaughter is especially interesting in this context because in his earliest articulation of the relation between human rights and the human voice, he focused his attention on the Algerian War of Independence. In that conflict, as Slaughter explains, and as Fanon, in his daily practice plainly understood, the mid-century question of rights, in its multiple implications, was brutally exposed. Whereas France, drawing on the legacy of its own revolutionary declaration, had been a significant contributor to the drafting of the Universal Declaration of Human Rights, in the context of its colonial occupation it refused the implications of the Declaration's text. The refusal was only possible, as Slaughter details, because of a systematic programme of racist de-personalization to which ethnopsychiatry was a significant contributing discourse. The ultimate expression of that process was torture, a practice to which, as Fanon knew and as Slaughter details, the occupying regime increasingly turned. As Slaughter puts it, 'During the Algerian War, the French-Algerian police and the French military began systematically employing torture in their attempt to retain the Algerian colony.'[103] Specifically, in 1957, 'during the battle of Algiers, the military abducted and tortured two French journalists, Maurice Audin and Henri Alleg (Audin was killed while "attempting to escape" and Alleg was later released).'[104] Among the most notorious instances of this practice was that of the 22-year-old Algerian woman, Djamila Boupacha, who was tortured in the French military prison El Biar and whose case *Le Monde* reported. Slaughter paraphrases the *Le Monde* report when he observes how, 'Continuing the questions, a few of the men attached electrical wires to her nipples, her anus, and her vagina.

They shouted that they would make her talk.'¹⁰⁵ It is there, in the fact that the men in question made Djamila Boupacha talk, that Slaughter identifies the intimacy of human rights and the human voice. As he argues, drawing on Ñacuñán Sáez's argument in *Torture: A Discourse on Practice*, 'the expressive language of the torture victim "comes from a body which is still (or already) controlled by the laws of language [...] [I]t produces the subject as already (or still) absent."'¹⁰⁶ 'Torture', Slaughter concludes, building on Sáez's discussion, 'fashions a nonentity out of the tortured's subjectivity'.¹⁰⁷

Although the Universal Declaration is, of course, emphatic on the question of torture (stating clearly, in Article 5, that 'No one shall be subjected to torture or to cruel, inhuman or degrading treatment or punishment'), it is a little less explicit on the integrity of voice to the concept of human rights. For Slaughter, however, it is precisely this connection that frames the document as a whole, written, as it is, into the Declaration's 'Preamble'. As the second paragraph of the Preamble puts it,

> Whereas disregard and contempt for human rights have resulted in barbarous acts which have outraged the conscience of mankind, and the advent of a world in which human beings shall enjoy freedom of speech and belief and freedom from fear and want has been proclaimed as the highest aspiration of the common people.¹⁰⁸

The question is if, as Slaughter suggests, there is an intrinsic link between human rights and the human voice (an intimacy, at the level of the conception and articulation of rights), what follows by way of implication?

One implication, always present, which the Universal Declaration is constantly alive to and which, by its assembled commitments, it aims to avoid, is expressed in the paragraph of the Preamble that follows: 'Whereas it is essential, if man is not to be compelled to have recourse, as a last resort, to rebellion against tyranny and oppression, that human rights should be protected by the rule of law.'¹⁰⁹ In an unpublished paper presented to the British Academy 'Hostile Environments' project, the Canadian poet and academic Stephen Collis reported on the repeated hunger strikes in the Canadian detention estate (hunger strikes being replicated at the time of writing by undocumented residents of Belgium). As Collis observed, left with nothing else to leverage, the people detained indefinitely under Canadian immigration rules leveraged their bodies, turning the violence of the system outwards by turning it on themselves.¹¹⁰ What the authors of the Declaration understood was that where the voice is denied leverage, it is the body and its actions that will very likely come to the fore, precisely to avoid which 'human rights should be protected'.

A second implication of the intrinsic relation between human rights and the human voice, as Slaughter himself proposes at the end of his article, is to explore the development of voice itself so that frameworks intended to secure rights comprehend better what they exist to enhance and protect. As he puts it, 'When the torturer destroys the voice and then forces the voice to acknowledge its own destruction, the torturer is, perhaps unwittingly, attesting to the importance of narration.'[111] For Slaughter, what the intimacy of rights and voice entailed was a comparative study of the intersection of narrative and subjectivity in the *Bildungsroman*, the novel form which charts the development of voice and which, as he sought to demonstrate, was influential on the articulation of personality inscribed in the Universal Declaration.

A further way to pursue the implications of the intimacy of rights and voice, however, as this chapter has argued, is to explore the work of writers motivated by the question of expulsion in the mid-century moment, when the production of non-personhood was vivid as historical fact. What one finds in Arendt, writing out of her lived experience as a refugee, Olson, as second-generation immigrant, and Fanon, whose confrontation with the state caused him to be displaced, is a determination—among other determinations—to imagine what it would mean to frame a space in which stories, and therefore voices, might be adequately heard. As each was writing in relation to the material fact of mid-century expulsion, so each pressed deep into the question of what it meant to leverage the voice. For Arendt, the act of narration was tied to the fact of arrival, with the figure of the newcomer, and all they had to tell, focusing the connection between personhood and voice. For Olson, the task was not only to produce a cultural space (which he modelled as open field poetics) in which stories could be assembled in relation to one another but also one in which, crucially, the stories of those the culture had expelled had to be told and heard. It was for Fanon, however, writing in the midst of colonial violence—where violence was the condition of his professional life—that the need to create spaces in which voices were enabled was most pressing. What one finds across his work, therefore, is the closest attention to the practice of listening, to the daily work of constructing spaces in which listening was possible. In one sense, it wasn't much, but in another sense, it was everything: critical as a mode of solidarity through which the new humanism could occur. The transformation required was total, at the level of institutional and economic relations and, at the same time, as Fanon demonstrated in his practice, a matter of constant and daily work. The racism of colonial capitalism depended, at some level, on voices being stopped. The silencing that underwrites expulsion has to be unjammed.

Notes

1. Hannah Arendt, 'We Refugees', in Jerome Kohn and Ron H. Feldman (eds), *The Jewish Writings* (New York: Schocken Books, 2007), p. 264.
2. Arendt, 'We Refugees', p. 264.
3. To occupy such a condition is to be denied a setting, as Ayten Gündoğdu observes, 'that could render [a person's] actions and speech relevant', where relevance would mean the minimal condition that, by either their actions or by their speech, their situation could, in theory, be materially changed (Ayten Gündoğdu, *Rightlessness in an Age of Rights: Hannah Arendt and the Contemporary Struggles of Migrants* [Oxford: Oxford University Press, 2015], p. 3).
4. Arendt, 'We Refugees', p. 264.
5. Arendt, 'We Refugees', p. 266.
6. Arendt, 'We Refugees', p. 269.
7. Arendt, 'We Refugees', p. 265.
8. Arendt, 'We Refugees', p. 274.
9. Paul Gilroy, *The Black Atlantic: Modernity and Double Consciousness* (London and New York: Verso, 1999), p. 2.
10. See, e.g. 'The Western World and the Fascist Experience in France', in Frantz Fanon, *Alienation and Freedom*, ed. Jean Khalfa and Robert J.C. Young, tr. Steven Corcoran (London: Bloomsbury Academic, 2018), pp. 607–610.
11. Gilroy, *Black Atlantic*, p. 4.
12. Lyndsey Stonebridge, *Writing and Righting: Literature in the Age of Human Rights* (Oxford: Oxford University Press, 2020), pp. 41–42.
13. To set this out in broad terms, the common task the authors set themselves was to articulate from within an existing geopolitics, organized according to the principle of national sovereignty, a space that resisted the regulation of personhood entailed by the nation state. Such a space was not to be cast in terms of utopianism but rather as a series of arguments within political history, out of which different principles of association would become possible to describe.
14. Hannah Arendt, *The Origins of Totalitarianism*, 3rd edn (San Diego, CA, New York, and London: Harcourt Brace Janovitch Publishers), p. 277.
15. Etienne Balibar, 'On the Politics of Human Rights', *Constellations* 20:1, 24.
16. Balibar, 'On the Politics of Human Rights', 24.

17. Balibar, 'On the Politics of Human Rights', 24.
18. As Stonebridge puts it, '[Arendt] invented new genres of political and history writing [. . .] because, like many who have spent time in detention centres, migrant communities, or endless queues for paperwork [. . .] she understood what it was like to try to survive in somebody's banality' (Stonebridge, *Writing and Righting*, p. 17).
19. Aristotle, *The Politics*, tr. T.A. Sinclair, rev. Trevor J. Saunders (London: Penguin Books, 1992), p. 176.
20. Aristotle, *Politics*, p. 169.
21. As Aristotle puts it, in aiming to analyse the state to its basic element and function:
'For the present let this be our fundamental basis: the life that is best for men, both separately, as individuals, and in the mass as states, is the life which has virtue sufficiently supported by material resources to facilitate participation in the actions that virtue calls for' (Aristotle, *Politics*, p. 393).
22. Aristotle, *Politics*, pp. 197–198.
23. Hannah Arendt, *The Human Condition* (Chicago, IL and London: University of Chicago Press, 1998), p. 198.
24. Gündoğdu, *Rightlessness in an Age of Rights*, p.173.
25. Gündoğdu, *Rightlessness in an Age of Rights*, p.164.
26. Arendt, *Human Condition*, p. 199.
27. Balibar, 'On the Politics of Human Rights', 25.
28. Arendt, *Human Condition*, p. 95.
29. As the *Refugee Tales* project has documented across four volumes, and as I have detailed in the afterwords to those collections of tales, among various other tactics, the UK government has sustained its production of non-personhood by a systematic refusal to generate the transcripts, records, and archives by which the reality of asylum seeking might be seen, heard, and remembered. See David Herd and Anna Pincus (eds), *Refugee Tales I, II, III, IV* (Manchester: Comma Press, 2016, 2017, 2019, 2021).
30. Arendt, *Human Condition*, p. 97.
31. Gündoğdu, *Rightlessness in an Age of Rights*, p. 156.
32. Arendt, *Human Condition*, p. 9.
33. Arendt, *Human Condition*, pp. 176–177.
34. Arendt, *Human Condition*, p. 185.
35. Etienne Balibar, 'What We Owe to the Sans-Papiers', tr. Jason Francis McGimsey and Erika Doucette, in Len Guenther and Cornelius Heesters (eds), *Social Insecurity* (Toronto: Anansi, 2000), p. 42.
36. Etienne Balibar, 'What We Owe to the Sans-Papiers', p. 43.
37. Charles Olson, *Collected Prose*, ed. Donald Allen and Benjamin Friedlander (Berkeley and Los Angeles, CA: University of California Press, 1997), p. 247.

38. Charles Olson, *The Collected Poems of Charles Olson (Excluding the Maximus poems)*, ed. George Butterick (Berkeley, Los Angeles, CA and London: University of California Press, 1997), p. 89.
39. Ralph Maud, *Charles Olson's Reading: A Biography* (Carbondale and Edwardsville, IL: Southern Illinois Press, 1996), p. 13.
40. Lytton Smith, 'Projective Citizenship: The Reimagining of the Citizen in Post-War American Poetry', unpublished PhD thesis, Columbia University, 2012, p. 33.
41. Engin Isin, *Being Political: Genealogies of Citizenship* (Minneapolis, MN: University of Minnesota Press, 2002), p. 386, cited in Smith, 'Projective Citizenship', p. 2.
42. For an excellent discussion of Susan Howe's relation to Olsonian poetics, see Will Montgomery, '"The Pictorial Handwriting of His Dreams": Charles Olson, Susan Howe, Redell Olsen', in David Herd (ed.), *Contemporary Olson* (Manchester: Manchester University Press, 2015), pp. 163–177.
43. For Miriam Nichols's outstanding discussion of Olson's poetics of outside, see her chapter 'Charles Olson: Architect of Place' in Radical Affections: Essays on the Poetics of Outside (Tuscaloosa, AL: University of Alabama Press, 2010), pp. 19–64.
44. Aseel Abdul-Lateef Taha, 'Charles Olson's Historical Vision in "The Kingfishers"', *Al-Adab Journal* 111 (2015), 56, https://aladabj.uobaghdad.edu.iq/index.php/aladabjournal/article/view/1533 (accessed 11 July, 2022).
45. Taha's claim is not that 'The Kingfishers' was the first anti-imperialist poem but that it was the first such poem in the emerging de-colonial era. Even so, the more accurate claim would be that the poem was among the first, not least because, as Fanon documented, Césaire was articulating precisely such a contemporary poetic.
46. Taha, 'Olson's Historical Vision', pp. 49–50.
47. Taha, 'Olson's Historical Vision', p. 55.
48. Olson, *Collected Poems*, p. 91.
49. Taha, 'Olson's Historical Vision', p. 54.
50. Ralph Maud, *What Does Not Change: The Significance of Charles Olson's 'The Kingfishers'* (London: Fairleigh Dickinson University Press, 1998), p. 123, cited in Taha, 'Olson's Historical Vision', p. 55.
51. That Olson thought of his poetics as anti-imperial is apparent from an early letter to Corman in which he sets out his coordinates: '(I am not local: I am playing this record against a background of events already played out: the Americanization of the world, now, 1950: soda pop & arms for France to fight, not in Europe, but in Indo-China the lie of it)' (Charles Olson, *Letters for Origin: 1950–1956*, ed. Albert Glover [London: Cape Goliard Press, 1970], p. 9).
52. Olson, *Collected Poems*, p. 92.
53. Smith, 'Projective Citizenship', p. 64.

54. From the outset, Olson's involvement in Corman's magazine *Origin* was predicated on the importance of correspondence, Olson's interest in the project was piqued, as he stated in an early letter to Corman: 'the moment I learned [. . .] that you were prepared to push by me the IDEA of correspondence not as of a notable but as a THING in itself' (Olson, *Letters for Origin*, p. 2).
55. For a probing discussion of Olson's correspondence with Boldereff, see Robert Hampson, '"When the Attentions Change": Charles Olson and Frances Boldereff', in Herd, *Contemporary Olson*, pp. 149–162.
56. Smith, 'Projective Citizenship', p. 64.
57. Smith, 'Projective Citizenship', p. 52.
58. Charles Olson, *The Maximus Poems*, ed. George F. Butterick (Berkeley, CA and London: University of California Press, 1983), pp. 64, 65.
59. Olson, *Maximus*, p. 68.
60. Olson, *Maximus*, p. 67.
61. M. NourbeSe Philip, *Zong* (Middletown, CT: Wesleyan University Press, 2008).
62. George Butterick, *A Guide to the Maximus Poems of Charles Olson* (Berkeley, Los Angeles, CA and London: University of California Press, 1978), pp. 96–97.
63. Olson, *Maximus*, p. 67.
64. Olson, *Maximus*, p. 67; Butterick, *Guide to the Maximus Poems*, p. 96.
65. Olson, *Maximus*, pp. 69–70.
66. The most notorious occasion of all was Olson's 'Reading at Berkeley', when, despite repeated attempts by organizers and audience to bring it to a close, Olson read and lectured for three hours. For the transcript of the event, see: Charles Olson, *Muthologos: Lectures and Interviews*, ed. Ralph Maud (Vancouver: Talon Books, 2010), pp. 137–192. For the full recording, see https://media.sas.upenn.edu/pennsound/authors/Olson/Olson-Charles_Complete-Recording_Intro-Robert-Duncan_UC-Berkeley_7-23-65.mp3 (accessed 17 June 2021).
67. Fanon, *Alienation and Freedom*, p.515.
68. Fanon, *Alienation and Freedom*, p. 514.
69. Fanon, *Alienation and Freedom*, p. 514.
70. Bashir Abu-Manneh, 'Who Owns Frantz Fanon's Legacy?', *Catalyst* 5:1 (Spring 2021), 18, 19.
71. Abu-Manneh, 'Fanon's Legacy', p. 15.
72. The essay is entitled 'Reciprocal Bases of National Culture and the Fight for Freedom', the text of which was first delivered as a 'Statement made at the Second Congress of Black Artists and Writers, Rome, 1959'.
73. Frantz Fanon, *The Wretched of the Earth*, tr. Constance Farrington, preface Jean-Paul Sartre (London: Penguin, 2001), p. 194.
74. See David Herd, 'The View from Dover', Los Angeles Review of Books (3 March 2015), https://lareviewofbooks.org/article/view-dover (accessed 13 July 2022).
75. Abu Manneh, 'Fanon's Legacy', p.39.

76. Ian Baucom, 'Frantz Fanon's Radio: Solidarity, Diaspora, and the Tactics of Listening', *Contemporary Literature* 42:1 (Spring), 15.
77. Frantz Fanon, *Black Skin, White Masks*, tr. Charles Lam Markmann, intro. Paul Gilroy (London: Pluto Press, 2017), p. 1.
78. Baucom, 'Frantz's Fanon's Radio', 15.
79. Frantz Fanon, *Studies in a Dying Colonialism*, tr. Haakon Chevalier, intro. A.M. Babu (London: Earthscan Publications Ltd, 1989), p. 69.
80. Fanon, *Dying Colonialism*, p. 71.
81. Fanon, *Dying Colonialism*, p. 88.
82. Fanon, *Dying Colonialism*, p. 85.
83. Fanon, *Dying Colonialism*, p. 85.
84. Fanon, *Dying Colonialism*, pp. 85–86.
85. Richard Keller, *Colonial Madness: Psychiatry in French North Africa* (Chicago, IL: Chicago University Press, 2007), p. 3.
86. Keller, *Colonial Madness*, p. 5.
87. Keller, *Colonial Madness*, p. 7.
88. Keller, *Colonial Madness*, p. 8.
89. Keller, *Colonial Madness*, p. 11.
90. Fanon also speaks from and to his experience as a psychiatrist in *Toward the African Revolution*, which gathers essays largely published in *El Moudjahid*. Consider, in particular, his essay 'The North African Syndrome', which addresses the prejudices North Africans experienced at the hands of French doctors. See Frantz Fanon, *Toward the African Revolution*, tr. Haakon Chevalier (New York: Grove Press, 1994).
91. Jean Khalfa, 'Fanon, Revolutionary Psychiatrist', in Fanon, Alienation and Freedom, p. 187.
92. Fanon, *Alienation and Freedom*, p. 361.
93. For a detailed documentation of the conditions in which people are held when incarcerated in contemporary UK immigration removal centres, see the Refugee Tales, 'Walking Inquiry into Immigration Detention', https://www.refugeetales.org/walking-inquiry (accessed 13 July 2022).
94. Fanon's critique of internment, and its centrality to colonial state violence, is his own, but clearly it also intersects with biopolitical arguments proposed in Foucault and Agamben.
95. Fanon, *Alienation and Freedom*, p. 353.
96. Fanon, *Alienation and Freedom*, pp. 357, 361.
97. Fanon, *Alienation and Freedom*, pp. 363, 363.
98. Fanon, *Alienation and Freedom*, p. 371.
99. Fanon, *Alienation and Freedom*, p. 367.
100. Fanon, *Alienation and Freedom*, p. 411.
101. Fanon, *Alienation and Freedom*, p. 412.
102. Fanon, *Alienation and Freedom*, p. 417.

103. Joseph Slaughter, 'A Question of Narration: The Voice in International Human Rights Law', *Human Rights Quarterly* 19:2 (May 1997), 423.
104. Slaughter, 'A Question of Narration', 423.
105. Slaughter, 'A Question of Narration', 424.
106. Slaughter, 'A Question of Narration', 426.
107. Slaughter, 'A Question of Narration', 426.
108. United Nations, Universal Declaration of Human Rights (Paris: United Nations General Assembly, 1948), https://www.un.org/en/universal-declaration-human-rights (accessed 14 June 2022).
109. United Nations, Universal Declaration.
110. The British Academy workshop at which Collis spoke took place on 30 June and 1 July 2021. Entitled 'Hostile Environments: Policies, Stories, Responses', the purpose of the project was to undertake comparative studies of hostile asylum regimes in the United Kingdom, Italy, Canada, and the United States. In his consideration of political responses to such regimes, Collis cited the fact that 190 immigration detainees in Ontario had gone on extended mass hunger strike in 2013, giving rise to the End Immigration Detention Network (EIDN), the point in part being that, by leveraging their bodies, it became possible to leverage a collective voice.
111. Slaughter, 'A Question of Narration', 430.

Conclusion

The Hostile Environment

This book had its origins, it first started to take shape, in Barking, East London in the summer of 2014. During that summer, I was visiting a property in Creekmouth, a network of housing estates and industrial estates at the intersection of the River Roding and the River Thames. The property in question was owned by Ready Homes, a subsidiary of the Clearsprings group, 'an established provider of outsourced services to the public and private sector' and of 'accommodation services to the Home Office since 2000'.[1] From 2014 to 2015 the property was home to two men, both housed under Section 4 of the 1999 Asylum and Immigration Act, the terms of which provided accommodation for so-called 'failed asylum seekers'. All such immigration categories are questionable, as the trajectories of the two men would make clear, though it is worth noting that the terms of Section 4 of the 1999 Act have since been restricted by the Immigration Act of 2016. As things stand, unless they can demonstrate 'destitution plus', which is to say detriment to health and well-being beyond the detriment caused by destitution, people in the United Kingdom whose asylum cases are deemed to have failed— though, in practice, they will probably be pending and might well eventually succeed—will be rendered homeless. But this was before the new round of legislation and so both men still had an entitlement to be housed. Disturbingly, in the summer of 2014, the property in Barking was experiencing an infestation.

The first man, whom I will call B, was from Guinea, a country which, since the end of the French colonial period, has been governed by a series of authoritarian regimes. B is Fulah, or Fulani, the Fulah being a tribe that stretches across some 20 West African countries but which in Guinea is an ethnic minority and has been repeatedly vulnerable to the governing regime of the moment. In 2002, when he was in his late teens, B fled Guinea after his participation in a student demonstration. The purpose of the demonstration, as he has told the Refugee Tales project, was to demand 'the electrification of the city and the lowering of the price of petrol', the exorbitant cost of which had made it impossible for children to get to school.[2]

B was detained, and while he was detained he was tortured. Knowing himself to be at further risk, and with the assistance of a friend of his father, he escaped the hospital in which he was being guarded and sought asylum in the UK, presenting, as evidence, the warrant for his arrest. His asylum case was refused, during which process the Home Office claimed to have lost his arrest warrant, the document on the basis of which any future appeal might be made. It would only reappear over 12 years later, when a judge finally insisted it was critical to the case.

Eventually, in 2007, having lived the limbo of the so-called 'failed asylum seeker' for five years, that limbo in which everything—a person's whole life—is held in suspense, B was arrested for trying to leave the country using false documents. It is ironic (let's put it that way) that he was arrested for leaving the country, the country having made it clear it didn't want him to stay. Even so, because he tried to leave the UK he was sentenced to a year's imprisonment, following which period he was detained indefinitely under immigration rules. When I first met B, it was shortly after Moussa Dadis Camara had seized power in Guinea in a coup, following which he had ordered the massacre of 157 Fulani protesters demonstrating at a rally in a football stadium in the capital Conakry. B was eventually released from detention on bail and for several years was moved from one Section 4 property to another, arriving in the house in Barking, with its infestation of rats, in the summer of 2014.

The second man, whom I will call R, fled Iran in 1997. He escaped, along with his family, with the intention of reaching Germany, travelling through Europe in the back of a truck. At some point on the journey, he was separated from the other members of his family and so, while they made it to Germany as intended, R ended up in Northern England. Since he did not possess official travel documents, he had been unable to relocate to Germany in the 18 years up to the time I met him. Nor, however, as will be apparent, had he been deported, though, like B, he had been detained indefinitely pending deportation. Nor, as will also be apparent, had he been granted leave to remain. In Barking, he kept chickens and a family of cats in what looked like an effort to conjure a feeling of some kind of belonging. He had a son, born in the UK, who would visit him from time to time. There seemed no prospect, after 18 years, that his case would be resolved.

Their national differences aside, the two men shared a common set of circumstances. As people seeking asylum, they were not allowed to work, a condition that had applied for 11 years and 18 years, respectively. In the absence of permission to work, they received subsistence-level financial support: £35.39 per week, £5.05 per day. Just as significant as the amount, however, was the form in which the payment was made. Rather than receiving cash or a payment into their bank accounts (accounts it would become illegal for them to hold following the 2016 Immigration Act), the payment was made by weekly top-up to a form of voucher known as an Azure card. The card carried restrictions in that it could only be used to purchase designated items at designated outlets, with public transport not listed as an item on which the card could be spent. For the men in question, the nearest designated outlet was over two miles from their house and, since they were unable to use public transport, they had to walk that distance to obtain any provisions. In some cases, for some people, occasional access to public transport would be afforded: on those days that they were required to register their continued presence at a Home Office Reporting Centre. There is variation, however, case by case, with some people seeking asylum having to walk several miles in order to sign at their nearest centre.

Such reporting, which had become fortnightly for B (having been daily immediately following his release), and monthly for R, was a source of ongoing anxiety since it was when they reported that they were most likely to be re-detained. The person seeking asylum, this is to observe, is designated permanently detainable and so, without prior process or explanation, people frequently find themselves taken back into detention. The sense of precarity such detention and re-detention produces is acute and is only compounded by the fact that at any moment a person accommodated under Section 4 provision can be relocated. Relocation can be to anywhere in the country, the Home Office term for the process being 'dispersal'. We might recall Fanon's discussion of the effects of arbitrary detention on the Algerian family in his consideration of 'Algeria Dispersed'. The consequence of such contemporary dispersal (as Fanon also observed) is that any community a person might have been able to establish is abruptly broken up. The significance of this, in turn, is that such community sometimes constitutes the basis (under Article 8 of the European Convention of Human Rights) for an individual's claim to the right to remain.

My point is this: the house in Barking constituted, and represented, and was situated at the intersection of what must properly be understood as a systematically negated space; a space whose rules of engagement have the design, as this book has observed, of rendering those who occupy it non-persons. Writing about such a negative ordering of space in a colonial setting, Fanon observed that 'The colonial world is divided into compartments.'[3] Such a compartmentalized world, he went on to state, 'is inhabited by different species', where 'what parcels out the world is to begin with the fact of belonging to or not belonging to a given race'.[4] Certainly, for the two men in question, racialized as they were by the immigration system, a ruthlessly enforced compartmentalization informed their experience of space. Witness the fact that they were only allowed to shop at certain outlets and that when they did so, permitted as they were to purchase only specified items, they had to present a card which amounted to a badge that designated their status, re-announcing their exclusion every time they shopped. What one really needs to try to imagine, however, is how such compromised mobility felt, or was intended to feel; what it meant for the individuals concerned that their relation to space was so intrusively managed.

In the house and at the reporting centre, the principal poles of their existence, the intention clearly, given the intrinsic precariousness, was that they should experience a state of permanent and acute anxiety. Elsewhere, as they made their journeys, whether between the house and the reporting centre or from the house to the shops, the effect of being compelled to walk everywhere was both attritional and fundamentally divisive. In and of itself, this is to say, the walk to and from a designated outlet signified their separation, as did both the time it took and the time they might allow it to take, given the absence of any other purposeful activity. In every principal situation, in other words, but also in every transition between situations, at every step along the way, the relation to space was so purposefully and profoundly negative (experienced as it had been over many years) as to shape and invert the individual's personhood itself.

Standing behind these aggressively delineated everyday spaces in the UK, giving meaning and force to their negative architectonics, is the institutional fact and spatial reality of indefinite detention. Such detention is, in theory, an administrative provision, reserved for people whose deportation or removal to their country of origin is imminent or at least pending. In practice, it is a deeply arbitrary and a frequently protracted experience. Since 2007, one trigger for such detention has been sentencing.[5] In the event that a non-citizen commits a crime – whether they are seeking asylum, a person whose case for asylum is deemed to have failed (though frequently that decision will eventually be reversed) or a person with limited leave to remain – and where the crime attracts a sentence of 12 months or more, then they automatically become liable for deportation and are therefore detainable the moment their sentence ends. There are many ways one might contextualize this practice. One might observe, for instance, just as Hannah Arendt observed of the crisis of statelessness following the Second World War, that the sheer precarity of the asylum process tends to criminalize the individual, typical offences being illegal working or the use of false papers. Either way, for the non-citizen caught in this context, the sentence served for an offence is not the end of the matter but a trigger for further—and this time indefinite—incarceration.

Equally likely, however, as Teresa Hayter observed in *Open Borders: The Case against Immigration Controls*, 'People may be picked up in the street, on the underground or at work, or their houses may be raided in the early hours.'[6] Such procedures of detaining have been documented by the Refugee Tales project, with the various accounts confirming both the systemic nature of the practice, in that the patterns are clearly discernible, and also its arbitrariness, in that the individual is neither warned nor charged. At the point of detention, the person detained will frequently only be allowed to take the clothes they stand up in; not, for instance, any medication they might be using or any evidence that might help to secure their release. More fundamentally, given that immigration detention is indefinite, they will not know when they will be released. Periods of detention can be short, a matter of days, or perhaps weeks, but a person can be detained for months and years. The longest period the Refugee Tales project knows a person to have been detained is nine years; a Somali man abandoned to and by the system and found by Her Majesty's Chief Inspector in Lincoln Prison.[7]

That detention informs and stands behind the negative spaces that constitute the non-person's environment flows from the fact that at any point, the person seeking asylum can be re-detained. At any point, in other words, and in any setting, the individual might be returned to that defining space of non-recognition, where their vulnerability to the processes of the state is immediate and absolute. Arendt provides an account of such vulnerability when she observes that her concern is with 'the arbitrariness by which victims are chosen, and for this it is decisive that they are objectively innocent, that they are chosen regardless of what they may or may not have done.'[8] Which is not to argue that the United Kingdom is analogous to the regimes Arendt describes in *The Origins of Totalitarianism*. It is to argue that many people living here in the present period experience a kind and degree of anxiety that answers to Arendt's description. The term that has come to capture that experience in the United Kingdom in the past decade is 'hostile environment', as first proposed by the British Home Secretary in 2012.[9] Arendt had another word for it: she called it terror.

How the two men temporarily located together in Barking have emerged, in so far as it has been possible for them to emerge, from the systematically negated space of the UK's hostile environment is instructive to note. In B's case, there was a change of fortune. Having arrived in 2002, and having, at that point, been refused asylum, and having therefore lived for many years in the state of precarity described above, in 2016, he won his appeal against deportation that had hung over him for almost a decade. During that whole period, his case had not materially altered. The circumstances in Guinea, though in constant flux, had remained acutely dangerous to returning dissidents. Finally, following the intervention of a proactive judge, the Home Office managed to locate the arrest warrant that confirmed the threat to his person and B was granted definite leave to remain. He has since reapplied and his protection has been extended for a further three years. It is clear that the UK authorities don't intend for him actually to feel safe. He is currently working in London, where he is employed as a care-worker, with a developing specialism in the provision of care for adults with challenging behaviour.

R's situation has not altered. He is still living in Barking. He is still vulnerable in all the ways and in all the spaces described above. When I met him, he barely spoke, except to point things out around the house. This is not because he had not acquired competence in English but because, as far as one could interpret, he had lost the will to articulate. He was a relatively slight man who, though he had a kindly presence, projected little or no personality whatsoever. This part of the account is impressionistic, of course, but I would hazard the judgement that his personality had collapsed, that under the pressure of absolute lived spatial exclusion, his personhood itself had eventually given way.

Both B and R have been almost entirely failed by contemporary politics, where the measure of that failure is the profound negativity of their relation to lived space. Both men followed an imperilled journey across the planet with a request for asylum. Instead of refuge, what each encountered was a series of interlocking spaces in which their recognition as persons was continuously denied. Their movement through such spaces has been both deeply thwarted and intrusively managed. In every setting in which they have been compelled to operate, their relation to those around them has been cast into doubt. In the case of B, whose defining condition is colonial, it is manifestly a travesty that an individual whose case for asylum was eventually settled on its original grounds should have been rendered as profoundly vulnerable as he was. What his case makes visible is the arbitrariness of the asylum process, the degree to which, according to its procedures, a person's existence can be held in suspense. R's situation, on the other hand, recalls the psychiatric studies with which Fanon concludes *The Wretched of the Earth*. At some point in the process, R would appear to have internalized his spatial reality. He would appear to have become, as his circumstances required him to be, 'depersonalized'.

Against the New Politics of Expulsion

It is alarming to observe—if, after the mid-century warnings this book has documented, not surprising—that, at the time of writing, the current politics of expulsion are set to intensify. Under proposals outlined in the British government's Nationality and Borders Act, it will no longer be legal to seek asylum in the United Kingdom. It will be possible to request asylum from elsewhere, from a refugee camp in another part of the world, and, under the terms of the government's resettlement programme, a person might be fortunate enough to be granted protection. It will not be possible, however, to arrive in the UK, having fled a life-threatening situation, and, on arrival, to ask for refuge. To do so, under the two-tier asylum system enforced, will be to risk a prison sentence of up to four years. Even then, even if a person was to serve their sentence and not immediately be removed, the prospect of removal would be always with them. Since they will be deemed to have arrived illegally (as if fleeing could be done with legal approval, as if a person forcibly displaced could first get all their paperwork in order), they will be subject, for as long as they are in the UK, to the threat of deportation. Under the terms of the new act, they will never be safe.

It is difficult to overstate the significance of the new legislation, the degree to which it severs the United Kingdom's responsibilities to people forced to seek refuge, but it is worth registering the fact that as the new bill made its way through parliament in the summer of 2021, it coincided with the seventieth anniversary of the Refugee Convention. First signed on 28 July 1951, and subsequently adopted, along with its 1967 Protocol, by 142 countries around the world, the Convention Relating to the Status of the Refugee built on the obligations inscribed in the Universal Declaration of Human Rights. The Refugee Convention is a complex document, but two principles are absolutely clear: that a person's right to seek asylum cannot be denied because they enter a territory 'without authorisation' (because as they flee persecution, how else are they going to enter) and that the contracting states shall not 'expel' a refugee. The Nationality and Borders Act is in breach of both principles. Not only will a person face imprisonment for having come to the United Kingdom to ask for refuge, but also if the government can operationalize its plan to deport to Rwanda, the person seeking asylum will be detained offshore. It is chilling to say so, but at the time of writing, the UK government is looking to usher in a world in which the right to *seek* asylum no longer applies. As the former Secretary General of the United Nations, Ban Ki-moon put it, attempting to build opposition to the proposed legislation,

> The U.K.'s new Nationality and Borders Bill also provides for off-shoring of asylum-seekers, following the damaging path set by Australia. It further proposes a two-tier system which would discriminate against those who arrive through irregular routes, even if their asylum claim is successful, effectively condemning them to a life of limbo with reduced rights. If implemented, the proposals would set a dangerous precedent in Europe—one which other European states should firmly reject.
> Such measures, designed to avoid or shift responsibility, are contrary to the 1951 Convention, the Global Refugee Compact and core principles of global responsibility-sharing and solidarity.[10]

To grasp the degree to which, as Ban Ki-moon put it, the UK government's policy sets 'a dangerous precedent', it is necessary, a moment, to look into the abyss. In his conclusion to *L'Univers Concentrationnaire*, David Rousset stepped outside the immediacy of his account of his experience in order to address the future reader. As he put it, drawing on the underlying logic he had experienced,

> The existence of the camps is a warning [...] Germany interpreted, with an originality in keeping with her history, the crisis that led her to the concentrationary universe. But the existence and the mechanism of that crisis were inherent in the economic and social foundations of capitalism and imperialism. Under a new guise, similar effects may reappear tomorrow.[11]

Rousset's warning was carefully calibrated. His concern was not precisely that the specific apparatus of the camps would be replicated but that because their existence was inherent in the 'foundations of capitalism and imperialism', some such conditions might reappear. For Arendt, building on Rousset, the task was to register the signs. As she put it, in an observation that should haunt contemporary thought and which seems ever more prescient the deeper into the contemporary crisis of the production of geopolitical non-personhood we press, 'The insane mass manufacture of corpses is preceded by the historically and politically intelligible preparation of living corpses.'[12] The task for the future, as Arendt understood, was to prevent the preparation of the living corpse, an historical warning that, in the past two decades, regimes of all kinds have seemed determined not to heed. For Etienne Balibar, whose reading of Arendt is properly critical, it is, nonetheless, in the logic of the production of non-personhood that contemporary politics finds its most alarming form. As he puts it, 'The problematic of phenomena like elimination, radical exclusion and disposable humans is indeed crucial today more than ever.'[13]

If we look into the contemporary abyss, especially, but not exclusively, from a UK vantage point, we see the logic of disposability at work. Through the mechanisms of the hostile environment, the United Kingdom has generated the negative spatialities through which the figure Arendt describes as the living corpse has been produced. It is because of that process, because people who have been compelled to move here have been internally expelled – expelled to the segregated spaces of the asylum regime – that it is now possible to outline plans that seriously propose not only to render the active seeking of asylum illegal but also to institute mass detention in offshore settings. In other words, 70 years after the Refugee Convention named human expulsion as that which the international order must commit itself to guarding against, the United Kingdom, with its capacity to influence international practice, is entirely in earnest when it proposes that people seeking refuge should be expelled. In contemplating this prospect, we must recognize the logic it articulates. As the developing climate emergency combines with existing causes of forced migration to compel people to move on an unprecedented scale, the UK government, as Ban Ki-moon states, is setting a most dangerous precedent as it proposes the offshore warehousing of persons seeking refuge. The prospect is terrifying but real. The legislation is being enacted as we speak.[14] Despite all the warnings, the logic of non-personhood has continued to intensify.

The purpose of this book has been to help remind us what is at stake when we permit a politics that engages in the production of non-personhood. It is alarming even to think that such reminding is necessary, but if we needed it, the Nationality and Borders Act is proof that such recognition is required. To help recover that understanding, to help us be minded again of the meaning of non-personhood, the book has revisited elements of a discourse that emerged in the post-war period, a moment when the geopolitical non-person had come clearly into view. The aim, in revisiting that discourse, has not been to insist on the findings of a given writer or thinker; we might want it to be the case, but we also surely know that the task of preventing the politics of expulsion is not as simple as that. The aim, instead, has been to present a multidisciplinary discourse shaped against the reality of mid-century expulsion and whose coordinating historical framework was the Declaration of Human Rights. In presenting that multidisciplinary discourse, I have looked to do two things. In the first place, because we must always be able to recognize it, I have looked to articulate the negative spatiality through which non-personhood is produced. In the second place, I have considered a set of shared thematics the writers in question arrived at as they have looked to articulate a non-expulsive space: the themes of moving, making, and speaking. It is such human practices that regimes actively deny when they frame the hostile environments that produce non-personhood. It is in such actions, accordingly, that human rights obtain, and in which the demands of those looking to claim or defend such rights take shape.

Which is not to argue, as this book has not at any point argued, that the Universal Declaration of Human Rights could ever be a sufficient political guarantee. Every writer considered here was right to document the manifest political fact that no such guarantee obtained. It is to argue, however, that there is much to learn from a moment when the principles of the Declaration were actively at issue. What those principles helped to shape were political imaginaries that looked to resist the expulsions of the sovereign and colonial state. They enable the articulation of a space we must constantly think through and towards; a space Jacques Rancière—'thinking', as Balibar would put it, 'with Arendt beyond Arendt'—calls the dissensus; a space Fanon, drawing on the universality of rights in the face of institutionalized racism, calls the new humanism. What a constantly active engagement with the principles of human rights permits, in other words, is the constantly active imagining of a non-national space, as Olson sought as he looked to model an anti-fascist poetic in the form of the poetry of the open field. But what an active engagement with the politics of rights also permits, as the more radical authors of the Universal Declaration explicitly intended, is the solidarity of the specific demand. In the face of an alarming acceleration of the global production of non-personhood, certain specific demands retain the potential to be transformative in any given environment: the right to move, the right to work, the right to speak and be heard, the right not to be detained. Such demands cut across the affiliations of national belonging and make possible the solidarity of human engagement.

In the contemporary moment, the task of imagining the nation state is not made difficult. It is in such imaginaries that the divisions and expulsions upon which capital, in its global exploitation, depend. How much harder, in the present moment, to imagine a non-expulsive international space, a space in which solidarities of human encounter and participation obtain. Even so, what we are witnessing in the UK, in ways that threaten to establish further dangerous precedents, is the necessity of always doing that imaginative work. Human rights are not given, they are articulated and claimed, and in being articulated and claimed they have radical political potential and force. It is an articulating we can all too easily forget to do since such rights would seem always to apply to somebody else. Except that one day you wake up and those rights are being withdrawn. Now, more than ever, we have to imagine and argue for a non-expulsive international space, and, to help us understand the stakes, we have to know that such arguments have been made before.

Notes

1. See https://www.propertymanagementco.co.uk/business/clearsprings-management and http://www.ready-homes.co.uk (accessed 26 July 2022). It is interesting to note that, whereas the parent company, Clearsprings, previously had a publicly accessible website, the link (www.clearsprings.co.uk) is now broken and the site no longer exists. In other words, it is difficult to trace the practices of Ready Homes to its financial source. There are, however, numerous reports detailing the living conditions to which people seeking asylum and living in Ready Homes and Clearsprings accommodation are subject and also the levels of profit the company makes. See, e.g. James Williams, 'Poor Asylum Seeker Housing Conditions Criticised', BBC News (4 December 2016), https://www.bbc.co.uk/news/uk-wales-politics-38196583; Rob Davies, 'Firm Running Asylum-Seeker Barracks in Kent Stands to Earn £1bn', The Guardian (3 February 2021), https://www.theguardian.com/uk-news/2021/feb/03/firm-running-asylum-seeker-barracks-in-kent-stands-to-make-1bn; CW6, 'Refugees Are Being Housed in Infested Hotels by the Home Office's Slum Landlords', Corporate Watch (27 January 2022), https://corporatewatch.org/refugees-are-being-housed-in-an-infested-hotel-while-the-home-offices-slum-landlords-are-raking-it-in (accessed 26 July 2022).

2. David Herd and Anna Pincus (eds), *Refugee Tales* III (Manchester: Comma Press, 2019), p. 99.
3. Frantz Fanon, *The Wretched of the Earth*, preface Jean-Paul Sartre, tr. Constance Farrington (Harmondsworth: Penguin, 2001), p. 29.
4. Fanon, *The Wretched of the Earth*, pp. 30–31.
5. See UK Borders Act 2007, Section 32, https://www.legislation.gov.uk/ukpga/2007/30/section/32 (accessed 26 July 2022).
6. Theresa Hayter, *Open Borders: The Case against Immigration Controls*, 2nd edn (London and Ann Arbor, MI: Pluto Press, 2004), p. xvii.
7. Frances Webber, 'Revealing the Impact of Immigration Detention', Institute of Race Relations (21 December 2012, https://irr.org.uk/article/revealing-the-impact-of-immigration-detention (accessed 26 July 2022).
8. Hannah Arendt, *The Origins of Totalitarianism*, 3rd edn (San Diego, CA, New York, and London: Harcourt Brace Janovitch Publishers), p. 6
9. See James Kirkup and Robert Winnett, 'Theresa May Interview: 'We're Going to Give Illegal Migrants a Really Hostile Reception', The Telegraph (25 May 2012), https://www.telegraph.co.uk/news/0/theresa-may-interview-going-give-illegal-migrants-really-hostile/ (accessed 26 July 2022).
10. Ban Ki-moon, '70 Years Ago, the World Made a Pact to Protect Refugees. Too Many of Our Leaders Are Failing to Uphold That Promise', Time (26 July 2021), https://time.com/6083151/1951-refugee-convention-anniversary/?utm_source=twitter&utm_medium=social&utm_campaign=social-share-article&utm_term=ideas_world-affairs (accessed 12 May 2022).
11. David Rousset, *The Other Kingdom*, tr. Ramon Guthrie (New York: Reynal and Hitchcock, 1947), pp. 171–172.
12. Arendt, *Origins*, p. 447.
13. Etienne Balibar, 'On the Politics of Human Rights', *Constellations* 20:1, 24.
14. As reported at the time of writing, a further reason for the United Kingdom's downgrading of human rights is trade. As *The Guardian* reported on 11 December 2022, following a speech by British foreign secretary James Cleverly, 'The UK will target a group of about two dozen middle-level countries for long-term diplomatic partnerships in what marks a downgrade of a commitment to human rights as a prerequisite for close relations with the UK' (Patrick Wintour, 'UK to Downgrade Commitment to Human Rights for Close Diplomatic Ties', The Guardian (11 December 2022), https://www.theguardian.com/politics/2022/dec/11/uk-to-downgrade-commitment-to-human-rights-for-close-diplomatic-ties (accessed 14 December 2022).

Acknowledgements

There are many people to thank. I am grateful to Sue Powell, Founder of Kent Refugee Help, and Anna Pincus, Director of Gatwick Detainees Welfare Group and Co-Founder of Refugee Tales, for all the insight they have shared over many years of co-working, collaborating, walking and talking. Both have built communities in which people who have experienced indefinite detention in the UK are made welcome. They are at the frontline of human rights work, and it has been a privilege to collaborate with them.

I am grateful for ongoing conversations with everybody at Kent Refugee Help, especially Alpha, Kate Adams, Jane Champion, Raga Gibreel, Pete Keenan, Bahriye Kemal, Hubert Moore, Chris Perks, and Lucy Williams. My thanks go to everybody who has walked with, and participated in, Refugee Tales since it started out in 2014. The walk is a collective and has been an education every step of the way. I am grateful to all those whose help make it happen but especially the organizers at Gatwick Detainees Welfare Group—Anna Pincus, Mary Barrett, Christina Fitzsimons, Ann Locke, and Jennifer Tindle —who invited me to help co-found the project, and to many people who have shared conversations along the way including, among many others, Pious, Kamsan, Seth, Osman, Ridy, Rashid, Mohammed, Ajay, Temi, Joe, Kasonga, John, Sal, Nicky, Andy, Barbara, Benjamin, Flick, George, Nelica, Ton, Josie, Marie, Frances, Aidan, and Hannah.

My huge gratitude goes to Steve Collis, who has helped at every stage of this book, from its conception through to its final draft, and whose conversations in all kinds of settings—at poetry events, in academic workshops, throughout Refugee Tales—have enabled me to understand what the book is trying to say. For me, as for many people, Steve is a guiding presence. The discussions that took place as part of the Hostile Environments project, many on zoom through the bleak days of lockdown, have been enriching at every point. I am grateful to the British Academy for funding the project and to everybody involved for their commitment and insight: Erol Balkan, Steve Collis, Erin Goheen, Claudia Gualtieri, Lidia De Michelis, Anna Pincus, Ayendri Riddell, Lytton Smith, Lyndsey Stonebridge, Maurizio Veglio, Matt Whittle, and Lucy Williams.

The book has benefited greatly from the opportunity to exchange ideas at a range of institutions, and I am glad to be able to thank colleagues for invitations to give keynote lectures, papers, and talks at: the Brussels School of International Studies, Duke University, Loughborough University, Simon Fraser University, SUNY Geneseo, the University of Kent, the University of Lodz, the University of Milan, the University of Oslo, the University of Strasbourg, and the University of Vienna. I am grateful to colleagues in the School of English at the University of Kent for enabling me to take study leave in 2017–2018 to begin work on the book proper and to Simon Fraser University and the Gloucester Writers' Center for fellowships which made parts of the writing possible. Thanks also to the editors and publishers of the following journals and essay collections in which early versions of parts of the book first appeared: *Contemporary Olson* (Manchester University Press), *European Journal of American Culture*, *From the European South*, *Los Angeles Review of Books*, *Narrating Flight and Asylum* (Wissenschaftlicher Verlag Trier), *Refugees on the Move: Crisis and Response in Turkey and Europe* (Berghahn Books), and the *Times Literary Supplement*.

In developing the arguments presented in *Writing Against Expulsion*, I have been grateful for conversations with many colleagues across the different fields the book addresses. In particular, I am glad to have the opportunity to thank: Bashir Abu-Manneh, Ammiel Alcalay, Rachel Blau DuPlessis, Oliver Brossard, Vincent Broqua, Stephen Fredman, Abdulrazak Gurnah, Robert Hampson, Ben Hickman, Angie Hobbs, Lyn Innes, Dan Katz, Simon Kirchin, Amanda Klekowski von Koppenfels, Margherita Laera, Abigail Lang, Peter Middleton, Vivek Narayanan, Miriam Nichols, Will Norman, Tom Parkinson, Sweta Rajan-Rankin, Denise Riley, Kamila Shamsie, Iain Sinclair, Ali Smith, Simon Smith, Miri Song, David Stirrup, Omid Tofighian, Ann Vickery, Marina Warner, and William Watkin. The book is much better than it would have been because of the numerous readers who have been generous enough to give it their time and attention, in particular as part of the Oxford University Press review process. I am deeply grateful to the editors of the OUP Mid-Century Studies series—Alan Hepburn, Adam Piette, and Lyndsey Stonebridge—for their time, support, guidance, and insight. My thanks also to the three anonymous reviewers whose comments were extremely helpful in enabling me to sharpen aspects of the argument. Works by Charles Olson published during his lifetime are copyright of the estate of Charles Olson; previously unpublished works are copyright of the University of Connecticut. Used with permission.

The people I can't ever thank enough are my family, Abi, Lily, and Eli. Walking and talking with you makes everything meaningful. Thank you for shaping our shared life.

Bibliography

Abu-Manneh, Bashir, 'Who Owns Frantz Fanon's Legacy?', *Catalyst* 5:1 (Spring 2021), 10–39.
Agamben, Giorgio, *Homo Sacer: Sovereign Power and Bare Life*, tr. Daniel Heller-Roazen (Redwood, CA: Stanford University Press, 1998).
Agamben, Giorgio, *State of Exception*, tr. Kevin Attell (Chicago, IL and London: University of Chicago Press, 2005).
Agamben, Giorgio, *What Is an Apparatus?*, tr. David Kishik and Stefan Pedatella (Stanford, CA: Stanford University Press, 2009).
Alcalay, Ammiel, *A Little History*, ed. Fred Dewey (Los Angeles, CA and New York: re:public/UpSet Press, 2013).
Alcalay, Ammiel and Tarlow, Kate, *Vincent Ferrini: Before Gloucester* (New York: CUNY Poetics Document Initiative: Lost and Found, 2014).
Allen, Donald (ed.), *The New American Poetry, 1945–1960* (Berkeley, CA: University of California Press, 1999).
Anderson, Bridget, *Us and Them? The Dangerous Politics of Immigration Control* (Oxford: Oxford University Press, 2013).
Anderson, Bridget, Gibney, Matthew J., and Paoletti, Emanuela (eds), *The Social, Political and Historical Contours of Deportation* (New York: Springer, 2013).
Arendt, Hannah, '"The Rights of Man": What Are They?', *Modern Review* 3.1 (1949), 4–37.
Arendt, Hannah, 'The Concentration Camps', in *The New Partisan Reader 1945–1953*, ed. William Phillips and Philip Rahv (New York: Harcourt, Brace, and Company, 1953), pp. 230–248.
Arendt, Hannah, *The Human Condition*, 2nd edn, intro. Margaret Canovan (Chicago, IL and London: University of Chicago Press, 1958).
Arendt, Hannah, *On Violence* (New York: Houghton Mifflin Harcourt Publishing, 1970).
Arendt, Hannah, *Crises of the Republic* (San Diego, CA, New York, and London: Harcourt Brace and Company, 1972).
Arendt, Hannah, *The Life of the Mind* (San Diego, CA: Harvest Harcourt Inc., 1978).
Arendt, Hannah, *The Origins of Totalitarianism*, 3rd edn (New York: Harcourt Brace Jovanovich Publishers, 1979).
Arendt, Hannah, *Men in Dark Times* (San Diego, CA: Harvest, Harcourt Brace & Co., 1983).
Arendt, Hannah, *Between Past and Future: Eight Exercises in Political Thought* (Harmondsworth: Penguin, 1993).
Arendt, Hannah, *Essays in Understanding, 1930–1954: Formation, Exile and Totalitarianism*, ed. Jerome Kohn (New York: Schocken Books, 1994).

Arendt, Hannah, *The Promise of Politics*, ed. Jerome Kohn (New York: Schocken Book, 2005).
Arendt, Hannah, *Eichmann in Jerusalem: A Report on the Banality of Evil* (London: Penguin, 2006).
Arendt, Hannah, *The Jewish Writings*, ed. Jerome Kohn and Ron H. Feldman (New York: Schocken Books, 2007).
Arendt, Hannah, *On Revolution* (London: Faber and Faber, 2013).
Aristotle, *The Politics*, tr. T.A. Sinclair, rev. Trevor J. Saunders (London: Penguin Books, 1992).
Augé, Marc, *Non-Places: Introduction to an Anthropology of Supermodernity*, tr. John Howe (London: Verso, 1995).
Balibar, Etienne, 'What We Owe to the Sans-Papiers', tr. Jason Francis McGimsey and Erika Doucette, in Len Guenther and Cornelius Heesters (eds), *Social Insecurity* (Toronto: Anansi, 2000), pp. 42–43.
Balibar, Etienne, *Masses, Classes, Ideas: Studies on Politics and Philosophy before and after Marx*, tr. James Swenson (London: Routledge, 2004).
Balibar, Etienne, 'On the Politics of Human Rights', *Constellations* 20:1 (2013), 18–26.
Baucom, Ian, 'Frantz Fanon's Radio: Solidarity, Diaspora, and the Tactics of Listening', *Contemporary Literature* 42:1 (2002), 15–49.
Benfey, Christopher and Harris, Mary Emma (eds), *Starting at Zero: Black Mountain College 1933–1937* (Bristol and Cambridge: Arnolfini and Kettle's Yard, 2005).
Benhabib, Seyla, *The Reluctant Modernism of Hannah Arendt* (Oxford: Rowman & Littlefield, 1996).
Benhabib, Seyla, *The Rights of Others: Aliens, Residents, and Citizens* (Cambridge: Cambridge University Press, 2004).
Bennoune, Mahfoud, *The Making of Contemporary Algeria, 1830–1987* (Cambridge: Cambridge University Press, 1988).
Bernstein, Charles, 'A Note on Charles Olson's "The Kingfishers"', in David Herd (ed.), *Cotemporary Olson* (Manchester: Manchester University Press, 2015), pp. 252–254.
Bernstein, Richard J., 'The Urgent Relevance of Hannah Arendt', *Philosopher's Magazine* 82:3 (2018), 24–31.
van den Beukel, Karlien, 'Why Olson Did Ballet: The Pedagogical Avant-Gardism of Massine', in David Herd (ed.), *Contemporary Olson* (Manchester: Manchester University Press, 2015), pp. 286–296.
Bhabha, Homi, 'Remembering Fanon: Self, Psyche and the Colonial Condition', in Patrick Williams and Laura Chrisman (eds), *Colonial Discourse and Post-Colonial Theory* (New York: Columbia University Press, 1994), pp. 112–123.
Billitteri, Carla, *Language and the Renewal of Society in Walt Whitman, Laura (Riding) Jackson, and Charles Olson: The American Cratylus* (New York: Palgrave Macmillan, 2009).
Birmingham, Peg, *Hannah Arendt and Human Rights: The Predicament of Common Responsibility* (Bloomington, IN: Indiana University Press, 2006).

Blau DuPlessis, Rachel, 'Olson and His *Maximus Poems*', in David Herd (ed.), *Contemporary Olson* (Manchester: Manchester University Press, 2015), pp. 135–148.

Blevins, Richard (ed.), *Charles Olson and Robert Creeley: The Complete Correspondence*, vol. 9 (Santa Barbara, CA: Black Sparrow Press, 1990).

Bloomfield, Mandy, *Archaeopoetics: Word, Image, History* (Tuscaloosa, AL: University of Alabama Press, 2016).

Boochani, Behrouz, *No Friend but the Mountains*, tr. Omid Tofighian (London: Picador, 2019).

Bosworth, Mary, *Inside Immigration Detention* (Oxford: Oxford University Press, 2014).

Burke, Roland, *Decolonization and the Evolution of International Human Rights* (Philadelphia, PA: University of Pennsylvania Press, 2010).

Butterick, George, *A Guide to the Maximus Poems of Charles Olson* (Berkeley, Los Angeles, CA and London: University of California Press, 1978).

Butterick, George (ed.), *Charles Olson and Robert Creeley: The Complete Correspondence*, vols 1–8 (Santa Barbara, CA: Black Sparrow Press, 1980–87).

Butterick, George, 'Charles Olson's "The Kingfishers" and the Poetics of Change', *American Poetry* 6 (Winter 1989), 2–69.

Byers, Mark, *Charles Olson and American Modernism: The Practice of the Self* (Oxford: Oxford University Press, 2018).

Byrd, Don, *Charles Olson's Maximus* (Urbana, IL: University of Illinois Press, 1980).

Cagli, Corrado. *From Cherbourg to Leipzig: Documents and Memories* (New York: Hugo Gallery, 1946).

Césaire, Aimé, *Discourse on Colonialism*, tr. Joan Pinkham, intro. Robin D.G. Kelly (New York: Monthly Review Press, 1972).

Césaire, Aimé, *The Complete Poetry of Aimé Césaire*, tr. A. James Arnold and Clayton Eshleman, intro. A. James Arnold (Middletown, CT: Wesleyan University Press, 2017).

Chaplain, Chloe and Ferguson, Emily, 'Inside the Rwanda Centre Which Will House Asylum Seekers and UK Channel Migrants', iNews, 14 April 2022, https://inews.co.uk/news/politics/inside-rwanda-centre-asylum-seekers-uk-channel-migrants-1575640 (accessed 22 April 2022).

Chari, Anita 'Exceeding Recognition', *Sartre Studies International* 10:2 (2004), 110–122.

Chibber, Vivek, 'Imperialism, Orientalism and Social Emancipation', lecture given at the University of Kent, 2 April 2019, https://www.youtube.com/watch?v=1n0STknbrIk (accessed 20 November, 2019).

Chomsky, Noam, 'The United States and the "Challenge of Relativity"', in Tony Evans (ed.), *Human Rights Fifty Years On: A Reappraisal* (Manchester: Manchester University Press, 1998), pp. 24–56.

Christensen, Paul, *Charles Olson: Call him Ishmael* (Austin, TX: University of Texas Press, 1979).

Clare, Stephanie, 'Geopower: The Politics of Life and Land in Frantz Fanon's Writing', *Diacritics* 41:4 (2013), 60–80.

Clark, Tom, *Charles Olson: The Allegory of a Poet's Life* (Berkeley, CA: North Atlantic Books, 2000).
Cohen, Gerard Daniel, *In War's Wake: Europe's Displaced Persons in the Postwar Order* (Oxford: Oxford University Press, 2011).
Cohen, Josh, *Not Working: Why We Have to Stop* (London: Granta, 2018).
Copeland, Roger, *Merce Cunningham: The Modernizing of Modern Dance* (New York and London: Routledge, 2004).
Cornelisse, Galina, *Immigration Detention and Human Rights: Rethinking Territorial Sovereignty* (Leiden and Boston, MA: Martinus Nijhoff Publishers, 2010).
Council of Europe, European Convention on Human Rights—Convention for Protection of Human Rights and Fundamental Freedoms (Strasbourg: Directorate of Information, 1952), https://www.echr.coe.int/documents/convention_eng.pdf (accessed 6 May 2022).
Creeley, Robert, 'Preface' to Charles Olson, *Selected Poems*, ed. Robert Creeley (Berkeley, Los Angeles, CA and London: University of California Press, 1997), p. xviii.
CW6, 'Refugees Are Being Housed in Infested Hotels by the Home Office's Slum Landlords', Corporate Watch, 27 January 2022, https://corporatewatch.org/refugees-are-being-housed-in-an-infested-hotel-while-the-home-offices-slum-landlords-are-raking-it-in (accessed 26 July 2022).
Davenport, Guy, 'Scholia and Conjectures for Olson's "The Kingfishers"', *Boundary 2* 2.1/2 (1973–1974), 250–262.
Davidson, Ian, *Ideas of Space in Contemporary Poetry* (Basingstoke: Palgrave Macmillan, 2007).
Davies, Rob, 'Firm Running Asylum-Seeker Barracks in Kent Stands to Earn £1bn', The Guardian, 3 February 2021, https://www.theguardian.com/uk-news/2021/feb/03/firm-running-asylum-seeker-barracks-in-kent-stands-to-make-1bn (accessed 26 July 2022).
Dembour, Marie-Benedicte, *When Humans Become Migrants: Study of the European Court of Human Rights with an Inter-American Counterpoint* (Oxford: Oxford University Press, 2015).
Derrida, Jacques, 'On Cosmopolitanism', in Stephen Cairns (ed.), *Drifting: Architecture and Migrancy* (London: Routledge, 2003), pp. 49–62.
Dewey, Anne Day, *Beyond Maximus: The Construction of Public Voice in Black Mountain Poetry* (Stanford, CA: Stanford University Press, 2007).
Dewey, Fred, *The School of Public Life* (Dijon: Les Presses du Réel, 2014).
Dorn, Edward, *What I See in the Maximus Poems* (Ventura, CA: Migrant Press, 1960).
DuPlessis, Rachel Blau, *Blue Studios: Poetry and Its Cultural Work* (Tuscaloosa, AL: University of Alabama Press, 2006).
DuPlessis, Rachel Blau, 'Olson and His *Maximus Poems*', in David Herd (ed.), *Contemporary Olson* (Manchester: Manchester University Press, 2015), pp. 135–148.
Dursun, Ayse and Sauer, Birgit, 'The Asylum–Child Welfare Paradox: Unaccompanied Minors in Austria', Humanities and Social Sciences Communications 8:1

(September 2021), https://doi.org/10.1057/s41599-021-00886-8 (accessed 6 June 2022).

Einarsen, Terje, 'Drafting History of the 1951 Convention and the 1967 Protocol', in Andreas Zimmerman (ed.), *The 1951 Convention Relating to the Status of Refugees and Its 1967 Protocol* (Oxford: Oxford University Press, 2011), pp. 37–74.

Evans, Martin, *Algeria: France's Undeclared War* (Oxford: Oxford University Press, 2012).

Fanon, Frantz, *Studies in a Dying Colonialism*, tr. Haakon Chevalier, intro. A.M. Babu (London: Earthscan Publications Ltd, 1989).

Fanon, Frantz, *Toward the African Revolution*, tr. Haakon Chevalier (New York: Grove Press, 1994).

Fanon, Frantz, *The Wretched of the Earth*, tr. Constance Farrington, preface John-Paul Sartre (London: Penguin Books, 2001).

Fanon, Frantz, *Black Skin, White Masks*, tr. Charles Lam Markmann, intro. Paul Gilroy (London: Pluto Press, 2017).

Fanon, Frantz, *Alienation and Freedom*, ed. Jean Khalfa and Robert J.C. Young, tr. Steven Corcoran (London: Bloomsbury Academic, 2018).

Faulkner, Doug, 'Channel Migrants: PM Calls on France to Take Back People Who Make Crossing', 26 November 2021, https://www.bbc.co.uk/news/uk-59423245 (accessed 12 May 2022).

Feller, Erika, 'Foreword' to Andreas Zimmerman (ed.), *The 1951 Convention Relating to the Status of Refugees and Its 1967 Protocol: A Commentary* (Oxford: Oxford University Press, 2011), pp. vii–viii.

Fraser, Nancy, 'Rethinking Recognition', *New Left Review* 3 (May–June, 2000), 107–120.

Fredman, Stephen, *The Grounding of American Poetry: Charles Olson and the Emersonian Tradition* (Cambridge: Cambridge University Press, 1993).

Gattrell, Peter, *The Unsettling of Europe: The Great Migration, 1945 to the Present* (London: Allen Lane, 2019).

Gentleman, Amelia, *The Windrush Betrayal: Exposing the Hostile Environment* (London: Guardian Faber Publishing, 2019).

Gibson, Nigel C., *Fanon: The Postcolonial Imagination* (Cambridge: Polity, 2003).

Gilroy, Paul, *The Black Atlantic: Modernity and Double Consciousness* (London and New York: Verso, 1999).

Gilroy, Paul, 'Introduction' to Frantz Fanon, *Black Skin, White Masks*, tr. Charles Lam Markmann (London: Pluto Press, 2017), pp.vi–xix.

Gizzi, Peter, 'Thinking about Kevin: In Memoriam Kevin Killian (1952–2019)', Chicago Review, 21 June 2019, https://www.chicagoreview.org/thinking-about-kevin-in-memoriam-kevin-killian-1952-2019 (accessed 27 June 2022).

Glendon, Mary Ann, *A World Made New: Eleanor Roosevelt and the Universal Declaration of Human Rights* (New York: Random House, 2011).

Glissant, Édouard, *Poetics of Relation*, tr. Betsy Wing (Ann Arbor, MI: University of Michigan Press, 1997).

Global Detention Project, 'Detention Centres: Map View', https://www.globaldetentionproject.org/detention-centres/map-view (accessed 26 April 2022).
Global Detention Project, 'United States', https://www.globaldetentionproject.org/countries/americas/united-states (accessed 22 April 2022).
Goodfellow, Maya, *Hostile Environment: How Immigrants Became Scapegoats* (London and New York: Verso, 2019).
Goodhart, David, *The Road to Somewhere: The Populist Revolt and the Future of Politics* (London: Hurst and Company, 2017).
Greif, Mark, *The Age of the Crisis of Man: Thought and Fiction in America, 1933–1973* (Princeton, NJ and Oxford: Princeton University Press, 2015).
Gündoğdu, Ayten, *Rightlessness in an Age of Rights: Hannah Arendt and the Contemporary Struggles of Migrants* (Oxford: Oxford University Press, 2015).
Gurnah, Abdulrazak, *By the Sea* (London: Bloomsbury, 2001).
Hailey, Charlie, *Camps: A Guide to 21st Century Space* (Cambridge, MA: MIT Press, 2009).
von Hallberg, Robert *Charles Olson: The Scholar's Art* (Cambridge, MA and London: Harvard University Press, 1978).
Hampson, Robert, '"When the Attentions Change": Charles Olson and Frances Boldereff', in David Herd (ed.), *Contemporary Olson* (Manchester: Manchester University Press, 2015), pp.149–62.
Harris, Mary Emma, *The Arts at Black Mountain College* (Cambridge, MA and London: MIT Press, 1992).
Hathaway, James C., *The Rights of Refugees under International Law* (Cambridge: Cambridge University Press, 2005).
Hayter, Theresa, *Open Borders: The Case against Immigration Controls*, 2nd edn (London and Ann Arbor, MI: Pluto Press, 2004).
Hegel, GWF, *Phenomenology of Spirit*, tr. A.V. Miller, intro. J.N. Findlay (Oxford: Oxford University Press, 1977).
Heidegger, Martin, *Basic Writings: Martin Heidegger*, ed. David Krell (London: Routledge, 1999).
Herd, David, '"From Him Only Will the Old State-Secret Come"': What Charles Olson Imagined', *English* 59:227 (Winter 2010), 375–395.
Herd, David (ed.), *Contemporary Olson* (Manchester: Manchester University Press, 2015).
Herd, David, 'The View from Dover', Los Angeles Review of Books, 3 March 2015, https://lareviewofbooks.org/article/view-dover (accessed 13 July 2022).
Herd, David and Collis, Stephen, 'Making Space for the Human: Rights, the Anthropocene and Recognition', *European Journal of American Culture* 39:1 (2020), 13–27.
Herd, David and Pincus, Anna (eds), *Refugee Tales I, II, III, IV* (Manchester: Comma Press, 2016, 2017, 2019, 2021).
Hickman, Ben, *Crisis and the US Avant-Garde: Poetry and Real Politics* (Edinburgh: Edinburgh University Press, 2015).

Home Office, 'Immigration Statistics, Year Ending 2019', updated 3 March 2022, https://www.gov.uk/government/statistics/immigration-statistics-year-ending-december-2021/how-many-people-are-detained-or-returned (accessed 22 April 2022).

Honneth, Axel, *The Struggle for Recognition*, tr. Joel Anderson (Cambridge, MA: MIT Press, 1996).

Howe, Susan, *The Birth-Mark: Unsettling the Wilderness in American Literary History* (Middletown, CT: Wesleyan University Press, 1993).

Hudis, Peter, 'The Revolutionary Humanism of Frantz Fanon', Jacobin, 26 December 2020, https://jacobin.com/2020/12/humanism-frantz-fanon-philosophy-revolutionary-algeria (accessed 20 July 2022).

Ingram, James D., 'What Is a "Right to Have Rights"? Three Images of the Politics of Human Rights', *American Political Science Review* 102:4 (November 2008), 401–416.

Isin, Engin, *Being Political: Genealogies of Citizenship* (Minneapolis, MN: University of Minnesota Press, 2002).

Jensen, Steven L.B., *The Making of International Human Rights: The 1960s, Decolonization, and the Reconstruction of Global Values* (Cambridge: Cambridge University Press, 2016).

Katz, Daniel, 'From Olson's Breath to Spicer's Gait: Spacing, Pacing, Phonemes', in David Herd (ed.), *Contemporary Olson* (Manchester: Manchester University Press, 2015), pp. 77–88.

Keller, Richard, *Colonial Madness: Psychiatry in French North Africa* (Chicago, IL: Chicago University Press, 2007).

Khalfa, Jean, 'Fanon, Revolutionary Psychiatrist', in Frantz Fanon, *Alienation and Freedom*, ed. Jean Khalfa and Robert J.C. Young, tr. Steven Corcoran (London: Bloomsbury Academic, 2018), pp. 167–202.

Ki-moon, Ban, '70 Years Ago, the World Made a Pact to Protect Refugees. Too Many of Our Leaders Are Failing to Uphold That Promise', Time, 26 July 2021, https://time.com/6083151/1951-refugee-convention-anniversary/?utm_source=twitter&utm_medium=social&utm_campaign=social-share-article&utm_term=ideas_world-affairs (accessed 12 May 2022).

Kindellan, Michael, 'Poetic Instruction', in David Herd (ed.), *Contemporary Olson* (Manchester: Manchester University Press, 2015), pp. 89–102.

King, J.C. and King, R.G., *Manifesto for Individual Secession into World Community* (Paris: Crosby Continental Editions, 1948).

Kinsella, John, *Legibility: An Antifascist Poetics* (New York: Palgrave Macmillan, 2022).

Kipfer, Stefan, 'Fanon and Space: Colonization, Urbanization, and Liberation from the Colonial to the Global City', *Environment and Planning D: Society and Space* 25 (2007), 701–726.

Kirkup, James and Winnett, Robert, 'Theresa May Interview: "We're Going to Give Illegal Migrants a Really Hostile Reception"', The Telegraph, 25 May 2012, https://www.telegraph.co.uk/news/0/theresa-may-interview-going-give-illegal-migrants-really-hostile (accessed 26 July 2022).

Klein, Axel and Williams, Lucy, 'Immigration Detention in the Community: Research on the Experiences of Migrants Released from Detention Centres in the UK', *Space and Place* 18:6 (2012), 741–753.
Kohlenberger, Judith, *Das Flucht Paradox: Über unseren widersprüchlichen Umgang mit Vertreibung und Vertriebenen* (Vienna: Kremayr & Scheriau, 2022).
Del Lago, Alessandro, *Non-Persons: The Exclusion of Migrants in a Global Society*, tr. Marie Orton (Rome: Italian Paths of Culture, 2009).
Lauterpacht, Hersch, 'The Declaration of Human Rights', *British Yearbook of International Law* 25 (1948), 354–381.
Lefebvre, Henri, *Critique of Everyday Life: Volume 1*, tr. John Moore (London, New York: Verso, 1991).
Lefebvre, Henri, *The Production of Space*, tr. Donald Nicholson-Smith (Oxford: Blackwell Publishing, 1991).
Macey, David, *Frantz Fanon: A Biography* (New York: Picador, 2000).
Magna Carta, with a new commentary by David Carpenter (London: Penguin Books Ltd, 2015).
Maritain, Jacques, *Creative Intuition in Art and Poetry* (New York: Noonday Press, 1953).
Maritain, Jacques, *Christianity and Democracy and the Rights of Man and Natural Law*, tr. Doris C. Anson (San Francisco, CA: Ignatius Press, 2011).
Marshall, Alan, 'Charles Olson Changes Objects: A Reinterpretation of "Projective Verse"', *Textual Practice* 33:7 (2018), 1–24.
Marx, Karl, 'Economic and Philosophical Manuscripts', in Karl Marx, *Early Writings* (London: Penguin, 1975), pp. 332–330.
Mason, Paul, *Clear Bright Future: A Radical Defence of the Human Being* (London: Allen Lane, 2019).
Maud, Ralph, *Charles Olson's Reading: A Biography* (Carbondale and Edwardsville, IL: Southern Illinois University Press, 1996)
Maud, Ralph, *What Does Not Change: The Significance of Charles Olson's "The Kingfishers"* (London: Fairleigh Dickinson University Press, 1998).
Maud, Ralph (ed.), *A Charles Olson Reader* (Manchester: Carcanet, 2005).
Mellors, Anthony, *Late Modernist Poetics: From Pound to Prynne* (Manchester: Manchester University Press, 2005).
Melville, Herman, *Moby Dick*, ed. David Herd (Ware: Wordsworth Editions, 2004).
Mezzadra, Sandro and Neilson, Brett, *Border as Method, Or, The Multiplication of Labour* (Durham, NC and London: Duke University Press, 2013).
Middleton, Peter, 'Discoverable Unknowns: Olson's Lifelong Preoccupation with the Sciences', in David Herd (ed.), *Contemporary Olson* (Manchester: Manchester University Press, 2015), pp. 38–51.
Miller, Phil, 'Dungavel Detention Centre in Slave Labour Shame as Asylum Seekers Paid Just £1 an Hour for Work', Daily Record, 15 January 2018, https://www.dailyrecord.co.uk/news/scottish-news/dungavel-detention-centre-slave-labour-11851052 (accessed 5 May 2022).

Minter, Peter, 'Transcultural Projectivism in Charles Olson's "The Kingfishers" and Clifford Possum Tjapaltjarri's *Warlugulong*', in David Herd (ed.), *Contemporary Olson* (Manchester: Manchester University Press, 2015), pp. 257–271.

Montgomery, Will, '"The Pictorial Handwriting of His Dreams": Charles Olson, Susan Howe, Redell Olsen', in David Herd (ed.), *Contemporary Olson* (Manchester: Manchester University Press, 2015), pp. 163–177.

Morsink, Johannes, *The Universal Declaration of Human Rights: Origins, Drafting, and Intent* (Philadelphia, PA: University of Pennsylvania Press, 1999).

Moyn, Samuel, *The Last Utopia: Human Rights in History* (Cambridge, MA: Harvard University Press, 2012).

Murray, Molly, 'Choreographics: Dance in Post-War American Poetry', unpublished PhD thesis, University of Sheffield, 2022.

Nail, Thomas, *The Figure of the Migrant* (Stanford, CA: Stanford University Press, 2015).

Nail, Thomas, *Theory of the Border* (Oxford: Oxford University Press, 2016).

National Constitution Center, The Constitution of the United States, https://constitutioncenter.org/media/files/constitution.pdf (accessed 3 May 2022).

Nichols, Miriam, *Radical Affections: Essays on the Poetics of Outside* (Tuscaloosa, AL: University of Alabama Press, 2010).

Nichols, Miriam, 'Myth and Document in Charles Olson's Maximus Poems', in David Herd (ed.), *Contemporary Olson* (Manchester: Manchester University Press, 2015), pp. 25–37.

O'Hara, Frank, *Standing Still and Walking In New York*, ed. Donald Allen (Bolinas, CA: Grey Fox Press, 1975).

Olson, Charles, 'People v. The Fascist, U.S. (1944)', Survey Graphic (August 1944), 356–357, 368.

Olson, Charles, *Call Me Ishmael* (New York: Reynal and Hitchcock, 1947).

Olson, Charles, *Selected Writings*, ed. Robert Creeley (New York: New Directions, 1966).

Olson, Charles, *Letters for Origin: 1950–1956*, ed. Albert Glover (London: Cape Goliard Press, 1970).

Olson, Charles, *The Special View of History*, ed. Ann Charters (Berkeley: Oyez, 1970).

Olson, Charles, *The Maximum Poems*, ed. George Butterick (Berkeley, Los Angeles, CA and London: University of California Press, 1983).

Olson, Charles, *The Collected Poems of Charles Olson (Excluding the Maximus Poems)*, ed. George Butterick (Berkeley, Los Angeles, CA and London: University of California Press, 1987).

Olson, Charles, *Collected Prose*, ed. Donald Allen and Benjamin Friedlander, intro. Robert Creeley (Berkeley, Los Angeles, CA and London: University of California Press, 1997).

Olson, Charles, *Selected Poems*, ed. Robert Creeley (Berkeley, Los Angeles, CA, and London: University of California Press, 1997).

Olson, Charles, *Selected Letters*, ed. Ralph Maud (Berkeley, CA and London: University of California Press, 2000).

Olson, Charles, *Muthologos: Lectures and Interviews*, ed. Ralph Maud (Vancouver: Talon Books, 2010).
Olson, Charles and Boldereff, Frances, *Charles Olson and Frances Boldereff: A Modern Correspondence*, ed. Ralph Maud and Sharon Thesen (Middletown, CT: Wesleyan University Press, 1999).
Olson, Charles and Creeley, Robert, *Charles Olson and Robert Creeley: The Complete Correspondence, Volumes 1–10*, ed. George Butterick (1–8), Richard Blevins (9–10) (Santa Barbara, CA: Black Sparrow Press, 1980–1996).
Olson, Charles and Prynne, Jeremy, *The Collected Letters of Charles Olson and J.H. Prynne*, ed. Ryan Dobran (Albuquerque, NM: University of New Mexico Press, 2017).
Parekh, Serena, *Hannah Arendt and the Challenge of Modernity: A Phenomenology of Human Rights* (London: Routledge, 2008).
Pedwell, Carolyn, *Affective Relations: The Transnational Politics of Empathy* (London: Palgrave Macmillan, 2014).
Philip, M. Nourbese, *Zong* (Middletown, CT: Wesleyan University Press, 2008).
Piore, Michael J., *Birds of Passage: Migrant Labour and Industrial Societies* (Cambridge: Cambridge University Press, 1979).
Pollock, Griselda and Silverman, Max, *Concentrationary Memories: Totalitarian Terror and Cultural Resistance* (London: Bloomsbury, 2015).
Pollock, Griselda and Silverman, Max, *Concentrationary Imaginaries: Tracing Totalitarian Violence in Popular Culture* (London: Bloomsbury, 2020).
Potter, Kevin, 'Centrifugal Force and the Mouth of a Shark: Toward a Movement-Oriented Poetics', *Ariel: A Review of International English Literature* 50:4 (October 2019), 51–78.
Potter, Kevin, 'Poetics of the Migrant', unpublished PhD thesis, University of Vienna, 2019.
Prost, Antoine and Winter, Jay, *René Cassin and Human Rights: From the Great War to the Universal Declaration* (Cambridge: Cambridge University, 2013).
Proudfoot, Malcolm, *European Refugees: 1939–1952* (London: Faber and Faber, 1957).
Prynne, Jeremy, 'Lecture on Maximus IV, V, VI', Simon Fraser University, 27 July 1971, transcribed by Tom McGauley, Iron (October 1971); reprinted in *Minutes of the Charles Olson Society* 28 (April 1999), http://charlesolson.org/Files/Prynnelecture1.htm and http://charlesolson.org/Files/Prynnelecture2.htm (accessed 31 May 2022).
Rancière, Jacques, 'Politics, Identification, and Subjectivization', *October* 61 (Summer 1992), 58–64.
Rancière, Jacques, 'Who Is the Subject of the Rights of Man?', *South Atlantic Quarterly* 103 (Spring/Summer 2004),.297–310.
Refugee Council, 'Latest Data on Ukrainian Arrivals—Refugee Council Response', 8 April 2022, https://www.refugeecouncil.org.uk/latest/news/latest-data-on-ukrainian-arrivals-refugee-council-response (accessed 24 May 2022).
Refugee Tales, 'Walking Inquiry into Immigration Detention', https://www.refugeetales.org/walking-inquiry (accessed 13 July, 2022).

Ross, Andrew, *The Failure of Modernism: Symptoms of American Poetry* (New York: Columbia University Press, 1986).

Rousset, David, *L'Univers concentrationnaire* (Paris: Éditions du Pavois, 1946).

Rousset, David, *The Other Kingdom*, tr. Ramon Guthrie (New York: Reynal and Hitchcock, 1947).

Ruhs, Martin and Anderson, Bridget, *Who Needs Migrant Workers?* (Oxford: Oxford University Press, 2010).

Safe Passage, 'Our Story', https://www.safepassage.org.uk/our-story (accessed 31 May 2022).

Sands, Philippe, *East West Street: On the Origins of 'Genocide' and 'Crimes against Humanity'* (London: Vintage Books, 2017).

Sands, Philippe, *The Last Colony* (London: Weidenfeld & Nicholson, 2022).

Sayers, Sean, 'Why Work? Marx and Human Nature', *Science & Society* 69:4 (October 2005), 606–616.

Schmitt, Carl, *Political Theology: Four Chapters on the Concept of Sovereignty*, tr. George Schwab, foreword Tracy B. Strong (Chicago, IL and London: University of Chicago Press, 2005).

Schmitt, Carl, *The Concept of the Political* (expanded edn), tr. George Schwab, foreword Tracy B. Strong (Chicago, IL: University of Chicago Press, 2007).

Sekyi-Otu, Ato, *Fanon's Dialectic of Experience* (Cambridge, MA: Harvard University Press, 1996).

Sharma, Sarah, 'Baring Life and Lifestyle in the Non-Place', *Cultural Studies* 23:1 (2009), 129–148.

Shaw, Lytle, *Fieldworks: From Place to Site in Postwar Poetics* (Tuscaloosa, AL: University of Alabama Press, 2013).

Simpson, John Hope, 'Foreword' to Malcolm Proudfoot, *European Refugees: 1939–1952* (London: Faber and Faber, 1957), pp. 17–18.

Sinclair, Iain, *American Smoke: Journeys to the End of the Light* (London: Penguin, 2014).

Slaughter, Joseph, 'A Question of Narration: The Voice in International Human Rights Law', *Human Rights Quarterly* 19:2 (May 1997), 406–430.

Slaughter, Joseph, *Human Rights, Inc.: The World Novel, Narrative Form, and International Law* (New York: Fordham University Press, 2007).

Smith, Ali, 'A Welcome from Our Patron', https://www.refugeetales.org/about (accessed 5 May 2022).

Smith, Lytton, 'Projective Citizenship: The Reimagining of the Citizen in Post-War American Poetry', unpublished PhD thesis, Columbia University, 2012.

Stonebridge, Lyndsey, *The Judicial Imagination: Writing after Nuremberg* (Edinburgh: Edinburgh University Press, 2011).

Stonebridge, Lyndsey, *Placeless People: Writing, Rights, and Refugees* (Oxford: Oxford University Press, 2018).

Stonebridge, Lyndsey, *Writing and Righting: Literature in the Age of Human Rights* (Oxford: Oxford University Press, 2021).

Sujo, Glen, *Legacies of Silence: The Visual Arts and Holocaust Memory* (London: Philip Wilson Publishers, 2001).

Taha, Aseel Abdul-Lateef, 'Charles Olson's Historical Vision in "The Kingfishers"', *Al-Adab Journal* 11 (2015), 45–62 https://aladabj.uobaghdad.edu.iq/index.php/aladabjournal/article/view/1533 (accessed 11 July 2022).

Taylor, Charles, 'The Politics of Recognition', in Amy Gutmann (ed.), *Multiculturalism: Examining the Politics of Recognition* (Princeton, NJ: Princeton University Press, 1994).

Taylor, Diane, 'Judge Rules £1/Hr Wages for Immigration Detainees Are Lawful', The Guardian, 27 March, 2019, https://www.theguardian.com/uk-news/2019/mar/27/judge-rules-1hr-wages-lawful-for-immigration-centre-detainees (accessed 6 May 2022).

UK Borders Act 2007, Section 32, https://www.legislation.gov.uk/ukpga/2007/30/section/32 (accessed 26 July 2022).

UNHCR (United Nations High Commissioner for Refugees), Convention and Protocol Relating to the Status of Refugees (Geneva: UNHCR, 2011), https://www.unhcr.org/uk/3b66c2aa10 (accessed 12 May 2022).

UNHCR, Global Trends: Forced Displacement in 2015, https://www.unhcr.org/576408cd7.pdf (accessed 29 April 2022).

UNHCR, Global Trends: Forced Displacement in 2020, https://www.unrefugees.org.uk/wp-content/uploads/Global-Trends-2020.pdf (accessed 22 April 2022).

UNHCR, Uganda: Refugee Policy Review Framework Country Summary as at 30 June, https://reporting.unhcr.org/document/1907 (accessed 22 April 2022).

United Nations, Universal Declaration of Human Rights (Paris: United Nations General Assembly, 1948), https://www.un.org/en/about-us/universal-declaration-of-human-rights (accessed 3 May 2022).

Vernant, Jacques, *The Refugee in the Postwar World* (London: George Allen and Unwin Ltd, 1953).

de Waal, Edmund, 'Black Mountain College and the Crafts', in Christopher Benfey and Mary Emma Harris (eds), *Starting at Zero: Black Mountain College 1933–1957* (Bristol: Arnolfini Gallery, 2005), https://www.edmunddewaal.com/essays/black-mountain-college-and-the-crafts (accessed 27 June 2022).

Walton, Jo and Luker, Ed (eds), *Poetry and Work: Work in Modern and Contemporary Anglophone Poetry* (New York: Palgrave, 2019).

Watkin, William, *Bioviolence: How the Powers That Be Make Us Do What They Want* (London: Routledge, 2021).

Webber, Frances, 'Revealing the Impact of Immigration Detention', Institute of Race Relations, 21 December 2012, https://irr.org.uk/article/revealing-the-impact-of-immigration-detention (accessed 26 July 2022).

Weiss, Paul, *The Refugee Convention, 1951: The Travaux Preparatoires Analysed with a Commentary by Dr Paul Weiss* (Cambridge: Cambridge University Press, 1995).

White, Hayden, *The Content of the Form: Narrative Discourse and Historical Representation* (Baltimore, MD: John Hopkins University, 1987).

Williams, James, 'Poor Asylum Seeker Housing Conditions Criticised', BBC News, 4 December 2016, https://www.bbc.co.uk/news/uk-wales-politics-38196583 (accessed 26 July 2022).

Wilsher, Daniel, *Immigration Detention: Law, History, Politics* (Cambridge: Cambridge University Press, 2012).
Wintour, Patrick, 'UK to Downgrade Commitment to Human Rights for Close Diplomatic Ties', The Guardian, 11 December 2022, https://www.theguardian.com/politics/2022/dec/11/uk-to-downgrade-commitment-to-human-rights-for-close-diplomatic-ties (accessed 14 December 2022).
Woodham, Tymek, 'Writing Agency: The Material Imaginations of Charles Olson, Langston Hughes, and Frank O'Hara', unpublished PhD thesis, University College London, 2021.
Woods, Tim, *The Poetics of the Limit: Ethics and Politics in Modern and Contemporary American Poetry* (New York: Palgrave Macmillan, 2002).
Woods, Tim, '"Moving among My Particulars": The "Negative Dialectics" of *The Maximus Poems*', in David Herd (ed.), *Contemporary Olson* (Manchester: Manchester University Press, 2015), pp. 233–251.
Yepez, Heriberto, *The Empire of Neomemory*, tr. Jen Hofer, Christian Nagler, and Brian Whitener (Oakland: Chainlinks, 2013).
Young-Bruehl, Elizabeth, *Hannah Arendt: For the Love of the World* (New Haven, CT: Yale University Press, 1982).

Index

For the benefit of digital users, indexed terms that span two pages (e.g., 52–53) may, on occasion, appear on only one of those pages.

1951 Convention Relating to the Status of Refugees, 5, 34–36, 64, 85–88, 95–97, 105, 127–128, 134, 173, 175, 262–264
Abu-Manneh, Bashir, 235–238
Agamben, Giorgio, 3–6, 22, 46–47, 82n61, 184–185
Albers, Anni, 159, 189–190
Albers, Josef, 157–159
Alcalay, Ammiel, 61
Algeria, 19, 68–69, 71–72, 74, 134–138, 140–141, 199–200, 211, 234–236, 238, 239–242, 258
Algerian War of Independence, 19, 117–118, 131–132, 211–214, 239, 247–248
Allen, Donald, 23, 98, 99
Anti-Semitism, 11–12, 14, 54, 61, 179
Arendt, Hannah, 6, 21, 25–26, 31–36, 43, 45, 48, 55–56, 59, 62–66, 70–77, 84–87, 89–90, 94–95, 102, 103–104, 109, 116, 118–120, 131–132, 148–149, 154, 174–175, 178–182, 211–214, 222–226, 234, 245, 249–250, 259–260, 263–266
  Eichmann in Jerusalem: A Report on the Banality of Evil, 78n15
  Newcomer, 149–152, 209, 221–223, 249
  The Human Condition, 17–19, 108–109, 149–153, 178, 181–185, 205n20, 214–222
  The Origins of Totalitarianism, 5–8, 11–15, 17–18, 27, 35, 55–56, 105–107, 154, 178, 181–182, 184–185, 194–195, 214–215
  Space of Appearance, 19, 73–74, 108
  On Violence, 23–25
  'We Refugees', 71–72, 209–211
Aristotle, 150, 216–219
Asylum, 1–3, 6, 10, 12–13, 16, 34–36, 48–49, 57–58, 74, 86–88, 95–97, 102, 132–133, 135, 139–140, 145–148, 151–153, 155, 177, 179, 180, 198, 203, 207n74, 210, 220, 237, 256–264
Augé, Marc, 45–48, 60
Azoulay, Jacques, 243–245

Balibar, Étienne, 25–26, 108, 215, 218, 220, 222–224, 263–266
Baraka, Amiri, 160–162, 226–227
Baucom, Ian, 238–239
Bauhaus, 20–21, 23, 97–98, 157–159, 189–190
Benhabib, Seyla, 31, 175–176, 181–182
Bildungsroman, 87–89, 112–113, 249
Black Mountain College, 23, 97–98, 157–160, 189–190, 193, 230
Blida-Joinville, 71–72, 75, 134, 199–200, 234
Boldereff, Frances, 97–98, 230–231
Boochani, Behrouz, 1–2
Border, 8–11, 85–86, 132–133, 137–140, 167n45, 145–147, 151–152, 156, 161–162, 173, 262–265
Boupacha, Djamila, 247–248
Buchenwald, 16–18, 43–45, 52, 55–56, 58, 70, 97–98
Burke, Roland, 122n22

Butler, Judith, 90
Butterick, George, 62, 160–161, 232, 233

Cagli, Corrado, 18, 43–45, 52–55, 58–60, 97–98
Césaire, Aimé, 31, 70, 111–112, 200–201
Chari, Anita, 90, 112–113, 119
Chiasmus, 115, 229, 231
Chibber, Vivek, 169n60
Clare, Stephanie, 133–134, 138, 199–201
Clark, Tom, 53–54, 157, 159
Cohen, Gerard Daniel, 5, 64, 88
Cohen, Josh, 178–179
Cold War, 34–35, 85–86, 88, 93, 165n17, 177
Collis, Stephen, 124n53, 125n79, 248–249
Colonialism, 12–13, 24–25, 44–45, 56, 66–71, 84–86, 133–136, 139, 199–201, 211–212, 235–237, 239, 242, 261–262
Communism, 61, 91–92
Copeland, Roger, 159
Corman, Cid, 230, 252n51
Council of Europe, 65–67, 127–128
Creeley, Robert, 97–98, 101–102, 185–188, 194, 230
Crosby, Caresse, 153–154
Cunningham, Merce, 158–159

Decolonization, 6, 19, 44, 199, 200, 228235–236, 241
Dembour, Marie-Benedicte, 66–67, 92
Derrida, Jacques, 102, 218
Detention, 1–4, 9–10, 22, 29, 57–58, 135, 136, 145–146, 220, 239, 243, 245–246, 248–249, 254n93, 255n110, 257–260, 264
Displaced Persons, 16, 44–45, 63–65, 88, 130, 143–146, 152, 165n17, 172–173
Dorn, Ed, 32–34

Dover Immigration Removal Centre, 1–2
Due Process, 51, 72
DuPlessis, Rachel Blau, 26–27

Einarsen, Terje, 95–96
Ekstein, Modris, 129
European Convention on Human Rights, 34–35, 66, 70–71, 92, 258
European Office for Refugees, 127–128
Expulsion, 1–266 *passim*

Fanon, Frantz, 20, 23–24, 26–27, 31–32, 36, 43–45, 56, 72–77, 84–85, 90, 92, 118–120, 131–142, 145–146, 160, 163–165, 178, 183, 202, 203, 211–214, 234–239, 241, 247–250, 258–259, 261–262, 265–266
Alienation and Freedom, 199–202, 242–246
Black Skin, White Masks, 17–18, 110–116, 133, 138, 238
Studies in a Dying Colonialism, 17–18, 71–72, 74, 132–133, 135, 238–241
The Wretched of the Earth, 17–19, 44, 68–72, 75, 76–77, 111, 117–118, 132–134, 136–142, 199, 236–237, 242
Fascism, 20–22, 24–25, 27, 51, 54–56, 60, 61, 66, 68–70, 93, 112, 116, 194, 211–212
Ferrini, Vincent, 58, 61–62
Fetterman, William, 159
First World War, 12–13, 154
Fraser, Nancy, 82n68, 119, 198–199
Fredman, Stephen, 81n47
Front de Libération Nationale, 71–72, 134, 234, 239

Gatrell, Peter, 4, 129, 134
Genocide, 44–45, 53, 60, 63–64, 85–86, 204n4
Gentleman, Amelia, 37n16

INDEX 285

Geopolitical non-personhood, 1–266 *passim*
Gilroy, Paul, 27–28, 111, 112–113, 116, 134, 200–201, 211–212
Gizzi, Peter, 187–188
Glissant, Édouard, 31–32
Global Detention Project, 2, 34–35
Goodfellow, Maya, 6
Goodhart, David, 47–48
Greif, Mark, 17–18, 87, 89–90, 105
Guantanamo, 1–4, 46–47
Gündoğdu, Ayten, 25–26, 106, 107, 178, 197–198, 217
Gurnah, Abdulrazak, 83n93
Gurs, 11–12, 71–72

Habeas Corpus, 11
Hayter, Teresa, 260
Hegel, G.W.F., 114–115
Heidegger, Martin, 199
Helmstedt, 55–56
Holocaust, 7, 210
Hostile Environment, 6, 145, 151–152, 164–165, 178, 203, 210, 235, 239, 248–249, 260–261, 264–265
Howe, Susan, 62, 226–227
Human Rights, 20, 22, 26–28, 31, 63–64, 68–71, 85–91, 122n22, 105, 107, 108–110, 114–117, 151, 164–165, 179–181, 184–185, 194–195, 213–214, 217, 218, 229–230, 235–236, 247–250, 267n14, 264–266
Humphrey, John P., 49–51, 94–95

Ingram, James, 90–91, 107, 119
International Labour Organization (ILO), 175–176
International Refugee Organization (IRO), 65, 143, 147–148, 165n17, 174, 204n10
Internment, 63–64, 72, 132, 200, 210, 230–231, 242–244
Isin, Engin, 226–227

Juridical Non-Personhood, 6, 8–9, 11–13, 34–35, 49–51, 72–73, 75–76, 136, 137–139, 141, 154–155, 163, 180–181, 197–198, 222

Kafka, Franz, 121n11
Keller, Richard, 241–242
Khalfa, Jean, 235, 242, 244
Ki-Moon, Ban, 86–87, 262–264
King, J.C and R.G, 53–54, 145, 146, 153–156
Kipfer, Stefan, 75

Lacaton, Raymond, 245–246
Lefebvre, Henri, 23–24, 27, 28–29, 45, 60–61, 71–72, 77, 84–85, 178, 183, 203
  Critique of Everyday Life Volume One, 21, 27–28, 201–202
  The Production of Space, 20–21
Lenin, Vladimir, 91
Lived Experience, 21, 27–28, 30, 70–72, 75–76, 90–91, 133, 136, 139, 174–175, 203, 235, 249–250

Magna Carta, 10–C0.23, 51
Malcolm X, 160–162
Maritain, Jacques, 87–88
Marx, Karl, 104, 182–183, 199, 201–202
Marxism, 19, 108–109, 178, 199–200
Mason, Paul, 26
Maud, Ralph, 52, 54, 79n26, 225, 228–230
Melville, 97–99, 171n102
Mezzadra, Sandro, 145
Morsink, Johannes, 49–50, 78n16, 91–92, 94–95, 146, 148
Moyn, Samuel, 17–18, 41n67, 85–86, 122n22

Nail, Thomas, 9, 104, 108–109, 131–132, 139–140, 146–147, 156
Nakba, 34–35

Nazism, 11–12, 23, 62–63, 65, 66, 71–72, 85–86, 112, 133–134, 179, 180, 211–212
Neilson, Brett, 145
Nichols, Miriam, 226–227
Non-place, 43–77,
  passim, 84–86, 102, 117, 130

Office of War Information, 18, 53–54.
O'Hara, Frank, 187
Olson, Charles, 18, 23, 26–27, 31–34, 43, 52–62, 90, 116, 118–120, 131–132, 145, 153–157, 159–160, 164–165, 178, 179, 185–186, 194, 195–196, 198–199, 203–204, 212–214, 224–227, 252n51, 230–231, 234, 249–250, 265–266
  Call Me Ishmael, 97–98, 157
  'Human Universe', 186–188
  'The Kingfishers', 97–98, 224–225, 227–231
  'La Préface', 15–18, 43–44, 70, 143–144
  The Maximus Poems, 16–18, 156–157, 160–163, 189–193, 225–226, 231–234
  Open Field Poetics, 19, 29–30, 97–102
  'People v. The Fascist, U.S. (1944)', 54, 60, 162–163, 194
  'The Post Office', 161, 187–188
  'Projective Verse', 17–18, 32, 97–103, 156–157, 188–189, 224
  'Proprioception', 159
  'The Resistance', 55, 58–62
  'The Special View of History', 193
Olusoga, David, 6

Philip, M. NoubeSe, 232
Polis, 162, 182, 213–218, 220, 221, 224–226, 230–231
Pollock, Griselda, 79n33
Proudfoot, Malcolm, 17–18, 33, 72, 126–131, 165n17, 180–181
Prynne, Jeremy, 162–163, 230–231

Rancière, Jacques, 25, 29, 85–86, 90–91, 106–107, 109–110, 142, 169n60, 178, 194–197, 203–204, 215, 223–224, 265–266
Recognition, 8–10, 12, 18–19, 48–49, 51, 60–61, 65–66, 82n68, 68–69, 84–120, 132–133, 138, 141, 147, 155–157, 159, 164–165, 178, 180–181, 183, 188–189, 196–201, 213–214, 223, 229–231, 245–246, 261–262
Refugee, 3, 5, 46, 64, 65–66, 71–72, 86–88, 95–97, 109, 126–130, 165n17, 134, 143–144, 172, 173–175, 180–181, 195, 197–200, 209–211, 221, 249–250
Refugee Tales, 77n1, 251n29, 254n93, 256–257, 260
Riesman, David, 54
Right to Work, 174–182, 184–185, 196–199, 203–204
Roosevelt, Eleanor, 147–148
Roosevelt, Franklin D., 18, 53–54, 97–98
Rousset, David, 21, 44–45, 51–60, 62–64, 68–69, 76, 84–86, 263–264
Rwanda, 2–3, 34–35, 262–263

Salem, Lilia Ben, 199–200
Sands, Philippe, 82n72, 168n59, 204n4
Sans-papiers, 222–224
Schmitt, Carl, 4, 10–11, 13
Second World War, 14, 16, 18, 44–45, 47, 63, 70–71, 84, 85–86, 88, 93, 97, 106, 111, 116, 126, 185, 259–260
Sekyi-Otu, Ato, 19, 31, 75, 133–134
Silverman, Max, 79n33
Simpson, John Hope, 33, 36, 72, 126, 127
Slaughter, Joseph, 17–18, 31, 58, 87–89, 213–214, 247–249
Smith, Ali, 77n1
Smith, Lytton, 62, 226–227, 230–231
Solomon, Enver, 168n48

INDEX 287

Sovereignty, 10–11, 29, 92–93, 105–107, 117–118, 211, 213–214, 250n13, 265–266
State, 13, 85–86, 95, 117, 128–130, 132–134, 136, 139, 145–147, 153, 154–155, 161, 175–177, 181, 211–217, 219, 220, 223–224, 227–235, 238–244, 249–250 n13, 260, 262–263, 265–266
State of Exception, 4, 130, 147–148
Statelessness, 63, 72–73, 86–87, 107, 108, 197–198, 214–216, 259–260
Stonebridge, Lyndsey, 17–18, 39n45, 31, 81n60, 121n11, 213, 216
Sujo, Glen, 53
Supreme Headquarters Allied Expeditionary Force (SHAEF), 127–128, 142–143

Taha, Aseel Abdul-Lateef, 227–229

United Nations, 18, 53–54, 64, 68–69, 127, 145, 147, 148, 165n17
United Nations High Commissioner for Refugees (UNHCR), 3–4, 127–128, 165n17, 172

UNHCR Global Trends report, 5, 14
Universal Declaration of Human Rights, 17–19, 26–27, 29, 32, 36, 44, 48–52, 59, 64, 66–67, 70–71, 76, 84–89, 121n11, 90–96, 122n22, 101, 105, 108–110, 116, 117–120, 131–132, 142, 145–148, 175–181, 184–185, 194–199, 212–214, 229–230, 247–249, 262–266
United Nations Relief and Rehabilitation Administration (UNRRA), 65, 127–128, 165n17, 142–144

Vernant, Jacques, 17–18, 120n3, 127, 129, 130, 165n17, 172–175, 178–179

Waal, Edmund de, 189–190
Watkin, William, 37n10, 78n8
White, Hayden, 87–88
Wilsher, Daniel, 9–10
Windrush, 6, 34–35
World Federation of Trade Unions (WFTU), 175–176